T0187364

# The Corpus Phonology of English

# The Corpus Phonology of English
**Multifocal Analyses of Variation**

## Edited by Anne Przewozny, Cécile Viollain and Sylvain Navarro

EDINBURGH
University Press

Edinburgh University Press is one of the leading university presses in the UK. We publish academic books and journals in our selected subject areas across the humanities and social sciences, combining cutting-edge scholarship with high editorial and production values to produce academic works of lasting importance. For more information visit our website: edinburghuniversitypress.com

© editorial matter and organisation Anne Przewozny, Cécile Viollain and Sylvain Navarro, 2020
© the chapters their several authors, 2020

Edinburgh University Press Ltd
The Tun – Holyrood Road, 12(2f) Jackson's Entry, Edinburgh EH8 8PJ

Typeset in 11/13pt Times New Roman by
Servis Filmsetting Ltd, Stockport, Cheshire
and printed and bound by CPI Group (UK) Ltd, Croydon, CR0 4YY

A CIP record for this book is available from the British Library

ISBN 978 1 4744 6699 8 (hardback)
ISBN 978 1 4744 6701 8 (webready PDF)
ISBN 978 1 4744 6702 5 (epub)

Published with the support of the CLLE Laboratory, University of Toulouse, France.

The right of Anne Przewozny, Cécile Viollain and Sylvain Navarro to be identified as the editors of this work has been asserted in accordance with the Copyright, Designs and Patents Act 1988, and the Copyright and Related Rights Regulations 2003 (SI No. 2498).

# Contents

# List of Figures

# List of Tables

# List of Contributors

**Hugo Chatellier** is associate professor in English linguistics at Université Paris Nanterre, France. He has a PhD (2016) in English linguistics from Université Toulouse Jean Jaurès which was conducted within the French PAC research programme on the sociolinguistic, phonological and phonetic characteristics of Mancunian English and its place among northern English varieties as regards regional dialect levelling. He has launched a transdisciplinary research project named 'The Norths in the English-speaking world' within the CREA research laboratory at Université Paris Nanterre which looks at the representation of northern identities and of the north/south divide in a variety of artistic productions.

**Jacques Durand** is emeritus professor at Université Toulouse Jean Jaurès and an honorary senior member of the Institut Universitaire de France. Formerly he was professor of linguistics at the University of Salford in England. He has held posts in Aberdeen, Essex, Paris and Aix-en-Provence. His publications are in linguistics (French, English, general) and in machine translation. As a specialist of phonology, he is the co-founder of three research programmes: PFC (Phonologie du Français Contemporain: usages, variétés et structure), PAC (Phonologie de l'anglais contemporain: usages, variétés et structure) and LVTI (Langue Ville Travail Identité). He has recently co-edited and contributed to *The Oxford Handbook of Corpus Phonology* (2014, Oxford University Press), *La prononciation de l'anglais contemporain dans le monde* (2015, Presses Universitaires du Midi) and *Varieties of Spoken French* (2016, Oxford University Press). He is the founder and co-editor of the Oxford University Press series: 'Phonology of the World's Languages'.

**Emmanuel Ferragne** is associate professor in the Department of English Studies at Université Paris Diderot, France. In his PhD (2008), he proposed a number of acoustic models to account for phonetic variation in thirteen English accents. Since then, his research interests have developed to include other topics such as L2 acquisition or forensic voice comparison, as well as other techniques for data acquisition (EEG, ultrasound tongue imaging, and so on) and data analysis (deep learning).

**Olivier Glain** is an associate professor of English linguistics at Université Jean Monnet de Saint-Étienne, France. He specialises in linguistic variation and change in English and French. His research focuses on the modelling of change, particularly consonant change.

**Bente Hannisdal** is associate professor of English linguistics in the Department of Foreign Languages at the University of Bergen, Norway.

**Daniel Huber** is senior lecturer at Université Toulouse Jean Jaurès, France, where he teaches English linguistics and phonology as well as specialisation courses on issues in Canadian linguistics. His research interests include English and theoretical phonology, English, Germanic and general historical phonology and dialectology. He is a member of the CNRS CLLE (UMR 5263) research laboratory.

**Mariko Kondo** is professor of linguistics and phonetics in the School of International Liberal Studies and the Graduate School of International Culture and Communication Studies at Waseda University in Tokyo, Japan. She is currently the director of Waseda University's Institute of Language and Speech Science, and since April 2019 has served as the chief editor of the Japan Phonetic Society journal. She specialises in speech communication and second language phonological acquisition. She has also been working to build a speech corpus of Japanese speakers' English.

**Małgorzata Kul** is a senior lecturer in the Faculty of English, Adam Mickiewicz University. An important part of her research effort has focused on the exploration of connected speech processes, and of reduction in particular. Another aspect of this research reflects her interest in the role of speech rate in connected speech processes. Another important strand in her research publications is the teaching and learning of advanced phonetics by learners of foreign languages, in which she incorporates the findings from her research into connected speech. Yet another area of her research activity is corpus phonology.

**Sylvain Navarro** is associate professor of English linguistics at Université Paris Diderot and co-director of the PAC programme. He specialises in the study of variation and sound change with a particular focus on phenomena relating to rhotics.

**Anne Przewozny** is associate professor in English linguistics at Université Toulouse Jean Jaurès, France. She is co-director of two scientific programmes in corpus-based phonology: PAC (The Phonology of Contemporary English: Usage, Varieties and Structure, since 2004) and LVTI (Language, Urban Life, Work and Identity, since 2011). She specialises in such issues as language contact, identity and representation, demolinguistics and its use in the definition of English varieties (mainly Australian English and its ethnolectal varieties), as well as applied research in the teaching and learning of English as ESL/EFL.

**James M. Scobbie** is Director of the CASL (Clinical Audiology, Speech and Language) Research Centre at Queen Margaret University, Edinburgh.

**Patrycja Strycharczuk** is lecturer in linguistics and quantitative methods at the University of Manchester.

**Madeline Travelet** completed her master's degrees, in English Linguistics and French as a Second Language respectively, at Université Paris Diderot in 2017. Her main research focuses on sociolinguistics and vowel shifts in the USA, and more specifically in Michigan where she conducted a survey with the PAC protocol. She now teaches English to young children in a private school in Belgium.

**Cécile Viollain** is associate professor in English linguistics at Université Paris Nanterre, France. She has a PhD (2014) in English linguistics from Université Toulouse Jean Jaurès which was conducted within the French PAC research programme which she now co-directs. She specialises in the Southern Hemisphere and Australasian varieties of English, and is especially interested in the sociolinguistic, phonological and phonetic characteristics of New Zealand English and the dynamics of vowel systems around the English-speaking world. Her most recent work has focused on the sociolinguistic representation of Northern identities and of the North/South divide in various productions, and notably in the popular TV series *Game of Thrones*.

**Franck Zumstein** is lecturer in the English Department at Université Paris Diderot and a member of the CLILLAC-ARP (E.A. 3967) research lab. His research domains are English phonetics and phonology, historical lexicography and corpus linguistics. He has studied English word-stress variations in standard British English with the help of a dictionary corpus in his doctoral work. His current research includes a further study of pronunciation variants that take into account authentic audio material from media outlets of various English-speaking countries and analyses of pronunciation data included in dictionaries of the eighteenth, nineteenth and twentieth centuries.

**Paulina Zydorowicz** is assistant professor at Adam Mickiewicz University in Poznań, Poland. Her research interests comprise phonetics and phonology with a special focus on phonotactics, casual speech processes, first and second language acquisition as well as corpus linguistics. She has published on the phonotactics of Polish and English in written corpora, the acquisition of L1 and L2 phonotactics, as well as sociophonetic variation in Polish. She has also participated in research projects focusing on the phonotactics of Polish and English, diachronic evolution of clusters in English and building a corpus of spoken Polish.

# Abbreviations

| | |
|---|---|
| AAA | Articulate Assistant Advanced |
| AAVE | African American Vernacular English |
| AESOP | Asian English Speech cOrpus Project |
| ANAE | Atlas of Northern American English |
| ANOVA | ANalysis Of VAriance |
| AusE | Australian English |
| C | consonant |
| DCT | Discrete Cosine Transform |
| DP | Dependency Phonology |
| DPC | Derived Phonological Contrast |
| F1 | the first formant |
| F2 | the second formant |
| F3 | the third formant |
| GA | General American |
| GPH | Gradient Phonemicity Hypothesis |
| GVS | Great Vowel Shift |
| H&H theory | Hypo and Hyper Speech theory |
| IDEA | International Dialects of English Archive |
| IPA | International Phonetic Alphabet |
| J-AESOP | Asian English Speech cOrpus Project (Japanese speakers' corpus) |
| JND | Just Noticeable Difference |
| L2 | second language |
| LVTI | Langue, Ville, Travail, Identité (Language, Urban Life, Work, Identity) |
| M | mean |
| ms | milliseconds |
| NCVS | Northern Cities Vowel Shift |
| NHK | Nippon Hoso Kyokai (Japan Broadcasting Corporation) |

| | |
|---|---|
| NM | Northern Michigan |
| NORM | a vowel normalisation and plotting suite |
| NZE | New Zealand English |
| ONZE | Origins of New Zealand English project |
| PAC | Phonologie de l'Anglais Contemporain (Phonology of Contemporary English) |
| PFC | Phonologie du Français Contemporain (Phonology of Contemporary French) |
| PSOLA | Pitch-Synchronous Overlap and Add |
| PU | Paradigm Uniformity |
| R | a language and environment for statistical computing |
| RP | Received Pronunciation |
| SD | Standard Deviation |
| SFVS | Short Front Vowel Shift |
| SLM | Speech Learning Model |
| SPE | *The Sound Pattern of English* (Chomsky and Halle 1968) |
| spont eng | spontaneous English |
| spont pl | spontaneous Polish |
| SPPAS | a package for automatic annotation and analyses of speech |
| sps | syllables per second |
| SSBE | Standard Southern British English |
| TT | Tongue Tip |
| UP | Upper Peninsula |
| V | vowel |

# Introduction

*Anne Przewozny, Cécile Viollain and Sylvain Navarro*

This volume materialises the many exchanges that took place during the PAC (Phonologie de l'Anglais Contemporain/Phonology of Contemporary English)[1] international conference entitled 'Variation, Change and Spoken Corpora: Advances in the Phonology and Phonetics of Contemporary English' at Université Toulouse Jean Jaurès, France, in 2015. The chapters in this volume are not replicas of the talks that were given at the conference, as these are not proceedings. Rather, this volume is evidence to the open-ended nature of the research endeavour and to the beneficial role of the exchanges between researchers in fashioning and furthering the debate on many different issues.

Since 2004, what started as Jacques Durand's idea for a local team project in Toulouse has developed into a research programme with a national and international scientific community, regular international conferences, and senior and junior researchers as well as PhD students. It has done so by setting collaborative goals for the creation of a large database on contemporary oral English, coming from a wide variety of linguistic areas in the English-speaking world (such as Great Britain, the Republic of Ireland, Canada, Australia, New Zealand, India and the USA), and by acknowledging the need for a larger methodological and theoretical debate on the scientific legitimacy and relevance of corpus phonology as one of the many fields of linguistic research.

The phonological foundation for the PAC programme is best summarised as follows (Durand 2017[2]):

> Corpus Phonology, as indicated by the name, is an approach to phonology which places spoken corpora at the centre of phonological research. As a sub-branch of corpus linguistics it comes in two forms: a strong version that states that the study of spoken corpora should be the aim of phonology; a weaker version which stresses that corpora should occupy pride of place within the set of techniques available (for example, intuitions, psycholinguistic and neurolinguistic experimentation, laboratory

1

phonology, the study of the acquisition of phonology or of language pathology, etc.). Whether one defends a strong or a weak version, corpora are part and parcel of the modern research environment and their construction and exploitation has been modified by the multidisciplinary advances made within various fields.

It is a fact that the development of high-quality spoken corpora has allowed for back-and-forths between descriptive phonology and theoretical phonology, at both the lexical and post-lexical levels. Other requirements, such as bigger bundles of data and representativeness of spoken data, together with ethical standards in recording protocols and advances in data and metadata processing (see Durand et al. 2014[3]), have reinforced a much-needed sociophonological perspective. One could argue that, along with technological progress and new quantitative options of measurement (Brezina 2018[4]), it is sociolinguistics that came to inspire corpus phonology.

Indeed, corpus phonology is generally driven by the ambition to make sense of the observed linguistic heterogeneity and variation within speech communities (be they native or non-native communities of speakers) through the analysis of common or distinct traits and behaviours. Yet corpus phonology remains – in our view, should remain, along with laboratory phonology and experimental phonology – a fundamental step in the study of the phonological structure of languages and varieties of languages, as well as in the theoretical exploration of the different models accounting for the observed variation (be they usage-based frameworks or accounts inspired by Optimality Theory, Government Phonology or studies in computational phonology, see section 4 of Durand 2017).

The PAC programme's ambitions are therefore to focus on phonology, sociophonetic variation, prosody, oral syntax, lexical variation, interphonology, language change, sociolinguistic and dialectological issues as well as pragmatic and interactionist concerns. Each survey in the PAC corpus database can therefore be understood as the result of a synthesis between the linguistic requirements of each specific variety of English under study and common principles that guide our protocols of enquiry, data treatment and interpretation. In a nutshell, these principles are concerned with (1) robust comparability of the data, both from internal (linguistic) and external (notably sociological and psychological) perspectives; (2) direct processing of the data through a variety of tools for the analysis of annotated speech corpora (notably Praat,[5] SPPAS,[6] Dolmen,[7] Phonometrica[8]); (3) transparent access to metalinguistic information about the survey and speakers; and (4) sustainability of the corpus.

Over the last few years, the PAC programme has developed into a variety of thematic research groups with dedicated research interests, such as LVTI (Langue, Ville, Travail, Identité – Language, Urban life, Work, Identity), which focuses on the sociolinguistic description of language in urban contexts and is featured in the present volume.

The present volume reflects the PAC collaborators' many scientific interests and the various echoes that can be found in the research carried out within the community and outside of it as far as the phonological, phonetic and sociolinguistic characteristics and modern evolutions of the varieties of English spoken worldwide are concerned. Seven contributions rely on data collected within the PAC programme (specifically the PAC Lancashire, Boston, Manchester, Michigan and Dunedin corpora) while five chapters resort to other types of corpora (such as the IDEA corpus or the Greater Poland Speech Corpus) and mostly exploit their own (specifically designed) corpora, but all demonstrate how various theoretical and experimental questions can be explored in the light of authentic oral data. This volume consequently presents advances in the study of contemporary spoken English which tackle variation with a multiplicity of methodological and theoretical approaches and focus on a wide range of phenomena. As editors, we consequently felt that entitling the volume *The Corpus Phonology of English: Multifocal Analyses of Variation* best matched the ambitions and principles shared by both the PAC programme and the contributors.

Given the intertwined and complementary perspectives provided on similar issues by the different contributions, organising this volume so as to offer the reader a wide-ranging yet structured journey into what phonologists, phoneticians and sociolinguists do with their corpora proved to be a challenging task. We were conscious that organising the volume along geographical or regional lines would not have reflected the diversity and depth of our exchanges with the contributors. In the same way, designing the volume along methodological lines would only have redundantly underlined the fact that all contributions aim at confronting the often variable reality of authentic oral data with the often constraining dimension of theoretical modelling. We consequently opted for a linear yet panoramic progression bridging traditionally separate fields such as experimental phonetics, theoretical phonology, language acquisition and sociolinguistics.

We start at the phonetic end with a chapter entitled 'Gestural delay and gestural reduction: Articulatory variation in /l/-vocalisation in Southern British English', in which Patrycja Strycharczuk and James M. Scobbie investigate /l/-vocalisation in a corpus of Southern British English recordings. They offer an ultrasound analysis of tongue tip gestures (complemented by acoustic inspection) and set out to determine whether gestural reduction and gestural delay are correlated or constitute two different strategies to achieve /l/-vocalisation. Their work builds on previous research into /r/-weakening which revealed covert articulations; that is, articulatory gestures that are not audible because they are significantly delayed. They observe considerable variation in the timing and magnitude of their informants' tongue tip gestures and conclude that while reduced gestures are usually delayed, the reverse is not true.

We then explore the interface between phonetics and phonology, as well as the continuum between allophony and phonemicity, with chapters that question the phonemic status of different phonetic categories. First, Emmanuel Ferragne, in 'The production and perception of derived phonological contrasts in selected varieties of English', proposes to test what he calls the Gradient Phonemicity Hypothesis on the basis of acoustic, articulatory and perceptual data from three corpora of audio recordings from Hull, Glasgow and Enniskillen (Ulster). His goal is to examine how vowel duration correlates with the speakers' labelling of a sound as allophonic or phonemic in order to shed light on the status of derived phonological contrasts, also called quasi-phonemic, compared to typical and documented phonemic distinctions. The author likens the theoretical and empirical background for his study to the framework of Exemplar Theory as he attempts to uncover how token (and/or type) frequency shapes mental/cognitive categories.

With similar concerns, Olivier Glain's chapter, 'The phonological fuzziness of palatalisation in contemporary English: A case of near-phonemes?', delves into the ambiguous status of the palato-alveolar fricatives that emerge in cases of contemporary palatalisation. It builds on previous research into the phonemic versus allophonic relationships between related segments. The author discusses the results of two experiments involving both production and perception as they reveal that palatalisation is not merely allophonic but seems to possess some cognitive reality. He further investigates the cognitive status of the palato-alveolar segments and discusses the theoretical issues pertaining to the interface between phonetics and phonology.

To complete this three-part survey, Mariko Kondo's chapter, 'Asymmetric acquisition of English liquid consonants by Japanese speakers', focuses on the interphonology of English and Japanese /l/ and /r/ on the basis of oral recordings with nine undergraduate L2 Japanese learners. The theoretical and empirical background for the author's study is the Speech Learning Model, according to which speakers for whom two sounds are not contrastive in their L1 (typically [l] and [ɾ] in Japanese) can acquire a phonemic opposition in an L2 (typically /l/ and /r/ in English) if one of the allophones in this L2 (the typical English [ɹ]) is clearly different from one of the allophones in their L1 (typically [ɾ]) because it forms a new phonetic category for that L2. Mariko Kondo therefore sets out to determine whether Japanese L2 learners acquire the English liquids /l/ and /r/ symmetrically or asymmetrically and, in the latter case, whether a new phonetic category for the liquid consonant is formed and how to use this finding at the didactic level for effective pronunciation teaching.

In keeping with the concepts that have been called forth in the previous chapters, we then move onto the next series of contributions articulated around both phonetic observations and phonological treatments, around both quantitative and qualitative analyses. They do not question phonetic and phonological categories as much as they embody the articulation between the two levels. If the following chapters mostly revolve around the study of PAC corpora, and consequently offer insight into PAC's core methodological principles as they provide details on the protocol used to obtain the relevant data in each survey location, they also focus on different varieties of English and adopt different approaches, be they comparative, sociolinguistic or variationist.

In order to introduce the reader to the founding principles of the PAC programme, which are consistent with those of its mother research programme, namely PFC (*Phonologie du Français Contemporain*/Phonology of Contemporary French), and to illustrate the results that they can yield, we start with a chapter entitled 'R-sandhi in English and liaison in French: Two phenomenologies in the light of the PAC and PFC data'. Cécile Viollain, Sylvain Navarro and Jacques Durand, who have already published theoretical discussions as well as quantitative and qualitative analyses on the occurrence of linking and intrusive 'r's in authentic oral data, offer a comparative approach to r-sandhi in English and liaison in French which have often been equated to one another. They investigate the theoretical implications and limitations of accounting for both phenomena from a strictly phonological point of view and use data from several corpora to shed light on the different factors conditioning and influencing the realisation or absence of r-sandhi and liaison respectively. By doing so, the authors' aim is to go beyond the tempting but also extremely approximate equation between the two phenomena that is still put forward, especially with L2 learners of English and French.

At the crossroads of interphonology and comparative linguistics, Małgorzata Kul and Paulina Zydorowicz, in 'A corpora-based study of vowel reduction in two speech styles: A comparison between English and Polish', set out to explore the process of phonetic vowel reduction in two different speech styles (read versus spontaneous) in two typologically unrelated languages (English and Polish) so as to establish whether this process is universal and whether it is conditioned by speech style and speech rate. On the basis of two authentic oral corpora (the PAC Lancashire corpus and the Greater Poland Speech Corpus which was inspired by the PAC methodology), the authors propose a thorough comparative approach to phonetic vowel reduction which leads to new research perspectives on the potential correlation between vowel and consonant reduction as compensating one another with regards to loss of phonetic information and intelligibility.

In an echo to the issue of reduction, Daniel Huber's chapter 'On "because": Phonological variants and their pragmatic functions in a corpus of Bolton (Lancashire) English' examines the different forms of the word 'because' found in the PAC Lancashire corpus and their pragmatic uses. This chapter illustrates how the PAC corpora can lend themselves not only to phonetic and phonological studies but also to morphological and pragmatic analyses. His findings reveal that the distribution of the variants (one of which is not listed in reference pronunciation dictionaries) in this variety of English follows a time-apparent pattern but that the use of monosyllabic versus polysyllabic forms does not correlate with speech rate or style. Age also seems to be a relevant factor in the pragmatic analysis of the phonological variants of 'because', whereby some discourse functions prove to be absent from older speakers' speech while common in younger and middle-aged speakers' speech and vice versa.

Logically, this leads us into the issue of variation and change from a phonetic and phonological standpoint. In 'On the New Zealand Short Front Vowel Shift', Cécile Viollain and Jacques Durand offer their perspective on this well-known chain shift, notably affecting the short front vowels KIT, DRESS and TRAP, by articulating the results of a phonetic-acoustic study conducted within the PAC programme (PAC Dunedin corpus 2010), Trudgill's new-dialect formation model and phonological theory. A push-chain shift hypothesis has been put forward in major publications and has mostly been modelled within the framework of Exemplar Theory. The authors provide an account of this phenomenon based on authentic oral data and inspired by the framework of Dependency Phonology and attempt to represent the evolution of the vowel system of New Zealand English through the historical competition between different systems that is characteristic of colonial environments.

Another well-known chain shift is discussed in the following chapter, 'The Northern Cities Vowel Shift in Northern Michigan', by Madeline Travelet and Franck Zumstein. They ask two straightforward questions: has the NCVS, originally discovered and described by Fasold and Labov in the 1970s in the Great Lakes region of the USA, spread towards Northern Michigan and its upper peninsula, that is north of the original isoglottic line? And if so, should this phenomenon still be known as the 'Northern "Cities" Shift' given that Northern Michigan is mostly a rural area? In order to answer both questions, the authors rely on three oral corpora: one dating back to the end of the 1960s (1966–1970), one collected fairly recently (2005–2016), and the PAC Michigan corpus (2016). Their study of variation in the contemporary evolution of the vowel system in Northern Michigan contributes to the debate on the mechanisms as well as the internal and external factors conditioning language change.

To complete this three-part examination of the vowel system of English and its contemporary evolution in different varieties of English, Hugo Chatellier, in 'Levelling in a northern English variety: the case of FACE and GOAT in Greater Manchester', investigates the specific case of Manchester in relation to the phenomenon of levelling and more precisely the fairly recent expansion of a supralocal northern variety in the north of England. On the basis of recent authentic and extensive oral data from the PAC-LVTI Manchester corpus (2016), the author presents a detailed description of the phonological and phonetic characteristics of the variety of English spoken in Greater Manchester, which shows that it is indeed a northern variety of English but that it is not levelling towards a pan-northern variety as far as the vowels of the FACE and GOAT lexical sets are concerned. Other vowels such as GOOSE and NURSE are subject to a more global case of levelling, as attested in other varieties of English spoken worldwide. His study therefore contributes to shedding light on the complex system dynamics of vowels and the role played by sociolinguistic evaluations in their diffusion or not.

To flesh out the picture drawn of the vowel system of English by the previous chapters, we conclude by exploring some aspects of its consonantal system. 'A study of rhoticity in Boston: Results from a PAC survey', presents a quantitative analysis of rhoticity in the PAC Boston corpus. Sylvain Navarro breaks down the coding system developed within the PAC programme to account for the distribution of /r/ in variably rhotic varieties. The results are in line with previous findings and show that the realisation of coda-/r/ is conditioned by phonological factors such as quality of the pre-/r/ vowel, degree of stress of the syllable and phonological environment, but also stylistic factors, as evidenced by significantly different frequencies of coda-/r/ realisation in various tasks of the PAC protocol. The author notes that the presence of r-intrusion in the speech of variably rhotic speakers suggests an ongoing restructuring of the Bostonian phonological system and argues that the inclusion of a detailed sociolinguistic profile of the informants is essential to the analysis of apparently atypical phonological behaviours.

Finally, in 'A corpus-based study of /t/ flapping in American English broadcast speech', Bente Hannisdal explores aspects of the extensive variation in the use of /t/ flapping in American English. Her aim is to provide quantitative data in order to shed light on the specific conditioning of this phenomenon, for which there is still no consensus among specialists. Although many phonological accounts have been put forward in the literature, less attention has been given to variation in actual use and how to account for the presence or lack of flapping in variable contexts. By relying on a large corpus of speech collected from American news broadcasts, and by proposing to focus on three environments in which /t/ flapping may or may not occur (post-nasally, post-laterally and between unstressed syllables), the author contributes to clarifying the complex internal and external factors conditioning and influencing /t/ flapping in American English.

There exists a necessary constraint of linearity for the purposes of a volume such as this one, but we would like to remind the reader that it does not have to be read right side up, but can be read backwards or based on each single reader's interests and perspectives. We feel that the current volume provides an insight into how researchers interested in the actual use of spoken English in different parts of the world and different contexts of interaction build and make the most of corpus data.

## Acknowledgements

This volume would not have been possible without the enthusiasm and commitment of the authors, from the genesis of this project that began with the PAC 2015 conference, to their hard work and patient cooperation throughout the process of editing the volume. We are very much indebted to them. We would especially like to thank Jacques Durand for his advice, his support and the vision he provided for the PAC programme and its future endeavours. Finally, this book is also the result of Heinz Giegerich's and Laura Williamson's support and guidance. We are very grateful to them and to all the editorial staff at Edinburgh University Press, especially Richard Strachan.

## Notes

1. See our website www.pacprogramme.net for a full presentation of the research programme.
2. Durand, J. (2017), 'Corpus Phonology', in M. Aronoff, *Oxford Research Encyclopedia of Linguistics*, Oxford: Oxford University Press, pp. 1–20. See also https://oxfordre.com/linguistics
3. Durand, J., U. Gut and G. Kristoffersen (2014), *The Oxford Handbook of Corpus Phonology*, Oxford: Oxford University Press. Especially part 1.
4. Brezina, V. (2018), *Statistics in Corpus Linguistics*, Cambridge: Cambridge University Press.
5. Boersma, P. and D. Weenink (2019), 'Praat: Doing Phonetics by Computer [Computer Program]', Version 6.0.56, http://www.praat.org/
6. Bigi, B. (2015), 'SPPAS – Multi-lingual Approaches to the Automatic Annotation of Speech', *The Phonetician – International Society of Phonetic Sciences*, 111–112, 54–69.

7. Eychenne, J. and R. Paternostro (2016), 'Analyzing Transcribed Speech with Dolmen', in S. Detey, J. Durand, B. Laks and C. Lyche (eds), *Varieties of Spoken French*, Oxford: Oxford University Press, D35–D52.
8. Eychenne, J. and L. Courdès-Murphy (2019), 'Phonometrica: An Open-source Platform for Phonometrics [Computer Program]', Version 0.4.1, http://www.phonometrica-ling.org

# 1

# Gestural Delay and Gestural Reduction: Articulatory Variation in /l/-vocalisation in Southern British English

*Patrycja Strycharczuk and James M. Scobbie*

## Overview

The vocalisation of /l/, as currently observed in Southern British English (SBE), involves weakening of the consonantal tongue tip (TT) gesture. Such weakening can be conceptualised in terms of spatial reduction, where the magnitude of the TT gesture is decreased, or in terms of temporal delay, where the TT gesture occurs relatively late, sometimes becoming masked. In this chapter, we use a corpus of articulatory (ultrasound) data to tease apart the relative contribution of delay and reduction in ongoing /l/-vocalisation in SBE. The most extreme case of vocalisation we observe involves deletion of the TT gesture. More frequently, we find gradient reduction in gestural magnitude, which may be accompanied by gestural delay. For one of our speakers, the TT gesture is delayed to the point of becoming covert. However, the considerable delay observed in this case is proportional to the advanced degree of gestural reduction. We argue for an interpretation where /l/-vocalisation is primarily a spatial phenomenon, and delay is mostly a secondary manifestation of weakening. We consider the significance of our findings to more abstractionist approaches, and their view of /l/-vocalisation as a categorical phenomenon.

## Introduction

The vocalisation of /l/ in Southern British English (SBE) is an example of a weakening change, in which the consonantal tongue tip (TT) occlusion is lost. Such loss is assumed to be phonetically gradual, and can be straightforwardly modelled in spatial terms as an incremental reduction of the degree of constriction. However, the loss of constriction can also be modelled in terms of articulatory delay, where the TT gesture is present, but it occurs relatively late, such that acoustic consequences of TT contact are not realised. The role of gestural delay in conditioning /l/-vocalisation is acknowledged by previous studies (e.g. Browman and Goldstein 1992; Gick 1999; Tollfree 1999), but it is not fully understood. We do not know whether gestural delay is an independent mechanism in /l/-vocalisation, or whether it is strictly tied to specific degrees of gestural reduction. We address this issue in the present chapter, looking at the relative contribution of delay and reduction in advanced and incipient /l/-vocalisation in SBE, using ultrasound data from a previously collected corpus (Strycharczuk and Scobbie 2015, 2016).

The corpus we use here was not compiled with /l/-vocalisation in mind, but it is a suitable resource for a study of this phenomenon, since it contains articulatory data on /l/ in systematically-controlled segmental and prosodic position, including word-final pre-consonantal/pre-pausal /l/, i.e. the potential context for vocalisation. The motivation for the present study comes from our earlier casual observation that some speakers in the corpus clearly vocalise their word-final /l/, but they achieve vocalisation in different ways. On the one hand, we see varying degrees of gestural reduction in TT raising, from complete alveolar contact to no raising at all. On the other hand, we also find instances where speakers raise the tongue tip when pronouncing a word-final /l/, but the gesture is delayed beyond the offset of voicing, and consequently, the gesture is not fully audible. This type of covert articulation has previously been observed in studies of word-final /r/-weakening in Standard Dutch (Sebregts 2015) and Glasgow English (Lawson et al. 2018), and it is also mentioned as an articulatory strategy involved in the production of /l/-vocalisation in a single speaker of American English (Recasens and Farnetani 1994). In this context, further documentation of such extreme delay in /l/-vocalisation is one of the goals of the present chapter. Another, related, goal is to illuminate the relative contribution of gestural reduction and gestural delay in incipient /l/-vocalisation. In addition to categorical vocalisers in our corpus, we also find speakers who clearly produce a TT gesture in word-final /l/, although the magnitude and timing of the gesture may vary. We analyse data from these speakers in order to verify whether gestural magnitude and timing are gradiently reduced, and, if so, how such reduction relates to the more categorical patterns we find in advanced vocalisers.

## /l/-vocalisation in Southern British English

/l/-vocalisation has been noted in Southern British English for at least three decades. The first reports of /l/-vocalisation identify it as a feature of London English (Gimson 1980: 202–203). Wells (1982) also observes that /l/-vocalisation is variable, and thus it should be considered a change in progress. Subsequent reports show that /l/-vocalisation spread to other regions of the UK, including Cambridge (Wright 1987, 1988), Essex and the Fens (Johnson and Britain 2007), and it is also found in Scottish English (Scobbie et al. 2007; Scobbie and Pouplier 2010; Stuart-Smith et al. 2013). The studies find a degree of variation, conditioned by phonological environment (Wells 1982; Wright 1987; Hardcastle and Barry 1989), style (Wright 1988) and socio-linguistic factors, including social practices (Stuart-Smith et al. 2013). Notably, numerous authors also comment on the variation concerning the degree of TT weakening in /l/-vocalisation. Two early electropalatography (EPG) studies on /l/-vocalisation, Wright (1987) and Hardcastle and Barry (1989), note instances of partial loss of alveolar contact in coda /l/, where there is some contact between the tongue tip and the alveolar ridge. These cases exist alongside apparently more categorical variants, in which the TT contact is lost altogether. Hardcastle and Barry (1989) acknowledge this as a methodological challenge that concerns classifying individual tokens of /l/ as vocalised or not. They go on to argue that instances of partial alveolar contact support the interpretation of /l/-vocalisation as an inherently gradient phenomenon. The hypothesis here is that suppression of alveolar contact is not a primary factor in vocalisation. Instead, the gesture is weakened, which leads to segmental variation: there may be no alveolar contact whatsoever before dorsals (e.g. 'milk'), whereas central alveolar contact is retained before other alveolar targets (e.g. 'built'), due to coarticulation. Scobbie and Pouplier (2010) also find both gradient and complete reduction of alveolar contact, which is mainly speaker dependent. Different speakers (five speakers of SBE and five speakers of Scottish English) produce varying degrees of alveolar contact in coda /l/ in the same segmental context (immediately before word-initial /b/ or /h/ in the following word). Some speakers have no alveolar contact in this context. However, even within speakers who do make the contact, the degree of contact varies. This behaviour appears to be the continuation of the change described by Hardcastle and Barry (1989): gradient reduction in the degree of alveolar contact is conditioned by gradient reduction in the magnitude of the apical gesture, and the gesture continues to reduce even after the contact is lost.

The speakers who have no alveolar contact appear to be, in some sense, categorically distinct from speakers who make alveolar contact, even if it is weakened. However, the absence of alveolar contact does not entail the absence of a TT gesture in /l/-vocalisers. Indeed, we know of cases where there is gradient variation affecting the TT position in /l/ in speakers who are vocalisers (i.e. they do not make alveolar contact in coda /l/). Some such cases are described by Wrench and Scobbie (2003), who analyse /l/-vocalisation using electromagnetic articulography (EMA) data and ultrasound. One of the measures they use is the distance of the TT sensor from the palate. This distance tends to vary gradiently: it is greater for pre-pausal /l/ compared to pre-labial. For pre-vocalic /l/, the distance is smaller yet, although it is still different from non-vocalised word-initial /l/s, where the sensor makes contact with the palate, so that average distance is zero. A similar gradient pattern of TT reduction can be seen in ultrasound data from an Essex speaker presented in Turton (2014). Turton compares averaged tongue tracings in /l/ in a variety of contexts stratified according to prosodic and morphological factors. She finds patterns of /l/-vocalisation in one speaker from Essex and two speakers from London. Data from these three speakers confirm that the tongue tip is consistently down for all word-final contexts. However, for the Essex speaker, the degree of TT raising appears to form a continuum from word-final 'heal' (where the tongue tip is relatively lowest) to word-medial 'healing' (where the tongue tip is raised, and there is no audible vocalisation). In contrast, there are more robust differences between 'heal', 'heal it' and 'healing' in the tongue root and tongue dorsum. The two London speakers in Turton's study show more of a categorical break in the degree of TT raising between vocalised word-final /l/s and non-vocalised word-medial and word-initial ones.

Turton (2014) discusses /l/-vocalisation in the context of another change affecting /l/, namely /l/-darkening. In many English dialects coda /l/s are dark, which can be manifested by dorsal retraction or velarisation. Thus, the vocalic gesture that forms a part of /l/ becomes augmented. The TT raising is sometimes talked about as the consonantal /l/-gesture (e.g. Gick (1999), see also the section 'Temporal factors in /l/-vocalisation' below). Weakening of this consonantal gesture could be viewed as an extension to increased dorsalisation, though the articulatory mechanisms for this are poorly understood. The enhancement of vocalic features and suppression of consonantal ones lead to /l/ being more vowel-like (see the section 'Discussion' below for more discussion on the relationship between /l/-darkening and /l/-vocalisation).

*Temporal Factors in /l/-vocalisation*

The individual studies surveyed in the section '/l/-vocalisation in Southern British English' are relatively small in scope and they use a variety of test items and methods, but, nevertheless, a coherent picture of gradient spatial reduction emerges when the various pieces of evidence are put together. We find instances of gradient reduction of the degree of apical contact in some speakers with incipient /l/-vocalisation, whereas in speakers with more advanced vocalisation, we may find gradient reduction pattern of the magnitude of the TT gesture. These two can be seen as subsequent steps of a single reduction pathway: initial less advanced reduction of the TT gesture may, under certain circumstances, result in partial alveolar contact. Once the reduction progresses, alveolar contact is no longer found, but we still see ongoing reduction in TT magnitude, depending on the phonological environment. However, such a picture is not complete, because it does not take into account temporal aspects of /l/-articulation and /l/-reduction.

To an extent, the opposition between dark and vocalised /l/ can be modelled just in terms of gestural magnitude: /l/-darkening involves increased dorsal retraction. However, going back to the seminal paper by Sproat and Fujimura (1993), timing has also been considered a key component in modelling the articulation of /l/. Sproat and Fujimura (1993) identify two distinct gestures which make an /l/: a dorsal gesture (retraction and/or raising of the back part of the tongue), and an apical gesture (raising of the tongue tip).[1] In an X-ray microbeam study of American English, Sproat and Fujimura (1993) find that both dark and light /l/ contain a dorsal and an apical gesture. However, the detail of the sequence of these two gestures can vary. In dark /l/, the apical gesture is delayed relative to the dorsal one. Furthermore, the tip delay increases gradiently depending on the strength of the levels of morphosyntactic boundary following /l/. There is increasing tip delay, comparing 'Mr Beelik', 'beal-ing', 'Beel equates' and 'Beel'. This observation by Sproat and Fujimura represents a major shift from an earlier, static, conceptualisation of /l/-positional variation (e.g. Giles and Moll 1975), and it shows that it is crucial to consider dynamic aspects of /l/-articulation in a description of darkening. In fact, Sproat and Fujimura argue that gestural magnitude is a consequence of position-specific gestural timing. Specifically, the dorsal gesture's magnitude can only be realised fully in word-final rimes, which are typically longer. In the relatively shorter word-initial and word-medial positions, on the other hand, the dorsal gesture is subject to articulatory undershoot.

This dynamic model also opens up the possibility that tip delay is one of the mechanisms involved in the actuation of /l/-vocalisation. If /l/-darkening involves a relatively late TT gesture, we can also imagine a situation where the TT gesture overlaps with the subsequent gesture (e.g. with the labial closure in 'feel me' across words or more commonly within such monomorphemic words as 'album', 'elbow' or 'alpha', or complex ones like 'almost' and 'always'). In such case, the TT gesture may be present, but is articulatorily masked and so may be inaudible, giving the percept of /l/-vocalisation. This hypothesis is formulated by Tollfree (1999), based on the models by Sproat and Fujimura (1993) and by Browman and Goldstein (1992), though only for pre-consonantal /l/. According to Tollfree, in word-final pre-pausal /l/, the tip gesture should always be audible. However, we can imagine a different scenario, in which gestural delay becomes phonologised, and increasing levels of such delay cause vocalisation even pre-pausally. A potentially attractive aspect of the delay driven view of /l/-vocalisation is that /l/ vocalisation is a straightforward extension of tip delay, a phenomenon independently observed in /l/-darkening.

Another possible way to think about gestural delay is that delay is one of the components in a more holistic process of weakening. This account seems consistent with a model put forward by Gick (1999) for final vocalisation of liquids. Gick proposes that vocalisation of final /r/ and /l/ inherently consist in the weakening of the consonantal gesture in coda, which is 'both reduced in magnitude (final reduction) and temporally delayed'. In this account, gestural delay is not so much a driving force for vocalisation, as one of its two closely correlated manifestations, along with spatial reduction.

*This Study*

In some of our own recent work, we analysed the timing of the apical gesture relative to the dorsal one for /l/ in SBE (Strycharczuk and Scobbie 2015). For word-final /l/, as produced by six native speakers of SBE, we analysed the temporal relationship between the dorsal and the apical gesture, and concluded that the apical gesture was indeed delayed relative to the dorsal one. According to our measure, the delay was ca. 120 ms. Furthermore, there was an apparent time effect, whereby younger speakers had greater tip delay than older speakers. The apparent time effect was as much as 75 ms in its most prominent context, namely when word-final /l/ was preceded by /uː/. Nevertheless, the TT maximum still occurred before the offset of voicing for all of the six speakers included in our 2015 study.

Here we extend our previous work to also investigate how the observed delay of the TT gesture relates to gestural magnitude. We provide such an analysis for eleven speakers, using a modified measure of magnitude as developed by Lin et al. (2014). We are also concerned with the acoustic consequences of the previously observed tip delay. We assess this in two ways. First, we measure the time lag between the apical gesture and the offset of voicing in final /l/ as a measure of the extent to which TT gesture is audible. We then investigate the acoustic effect of TT gestures depending on how late they are, relative to the voicing offset. The spectral measure we focus on is F2–F1 distance, an important correlate of /l/-darkening/vocalisation (Sproat and Fujimura 1993; Lin et al. 2014; Turton 2014).

## Materials and Methods

### Materials

The speech materials we analyse come from the corpus on segmental and morphological effects on SBE /uː/ and /ʊ/-fronting (Strycharczuk and Scobbie 2016, 2017). For the present study, we selected 864 tokens of /l/ in three contexts, where we expect varying degrees of /l/-darkening or /l/-vocalisation: (1) word-final pre-consonantal (pre-C, 'fool#five'); (2) word-final pre-vocalic (pre-V, 'fool#it'); and (3) word-medial ('fooling'). The preceding vowels were always /uː/ or /ʊ/. The word-final pre-consonantal context ('fool#five') is the potential environment for vocalisation, whereas the word-medial context ('fooling') is a baseline in which no vocalisation is expected. In the word-final pre-vocalic context, we expect some gradient weakening, but less so than in the word-final pre-consonantal context.

### Speakers

For the purpose of the present study we analysed data from eleven speakers, six younger (under twenty-five) and five older (forty-five+). All the speakers came from and grew up in the south of England, although they all spent some time in Scotland prior to the experiment. All speakers were female, except for one older male. Six of the speakers had been included in our previous study on tip delay (Strycharczuk and Scobbie 2015). The additional five speakers were selected from the corpus based on the quality of their ultrasound image. We chose all speakers for whom we could consistently track the tongue contour in the anterior part of the tongue.

### Acoustic Analysis

For the acoustic analysis, we manually annotated the duration of the vowel and the following /l/, and we measured the first three formants at 10 per cent intervals throughout the vowel+/l/ sequence, using a Praat script modified from Remijsen (2004). In this study, we use the formant measurement towards the end of the /Vl/ sequence (90 per cent into its duration), since we are interested in the acoustic consequences of articulatory events in the later part of the sequence where the phonetic reflexes of /l/ are most evident.

### Articulatory Analysis

The crucial aspect of our articulatory analysis is identifying the TT gesture and quantifying it in terms of magnitude and timing. The first step in this process was tracking tongue contour in the ultrasound data for the entire /Vl/ sequence, as well as throughout the preceding and following segment (defined acoustically). The contour tracking was performed semi-automatically by the Articulate Assistant Advanced software (AAA2.16 Articulate Instruments Ltd 2014), supervised by the first author. Manual corrections were performed where necessary.

The tongue contour tracks were then used to identify the TT gesture. We did this based on maximum displacement along a specific fan line chosen to best represent the approximation of the tongue to the alveolar ridge as a linear variable, analysed as it changed in normalised magnitude (see below). The fan lines are forty-two equidistant radials, with a maximal angle of ±67° relative to the centre of the ultrasound probe. Together they make up a reference frame (a fan) in which tongue shape and location can be plotted and changes in these parameters extracted for regions of interest in the vocal tract.

These speaker-dependent regions of interest were determined based on the pattern and extent of tongue surface movement through the region, with an eye to the specific radial vector on which the changing constriction would be measured. There is no a priori linear dimension (such as 'vertical') which is a preferred one for quantifying the approximation of one 3D tongue body to another. This issue persists for the 2D surface tracings we use. Therefore, for each speaker, we inspected ten example tokens by exporting all the tongue tracks from each token into a single coordinate frame. We then identified an anterior fan line along which the relatively greatest tongue displacement occurred, as illustrated in Figure 1.1. This was done by visual inspection, combined with examination of means and standard deviations of displacement values throughout a token for each fan line (Strycharczuk and Scobbie 2015; Heyde et al. 2016). We picked fan lines for which the standard deviation was relatively highest (indicating the most movement), but also paying attention to confidence values, since tongue contour tracking in the TT area is not always reliable.

We then analysed the displacement of the tongue contour tracing along the selected fan line and picked the contour with maximum displacement as representative of the TT maximum. For all TT maxima, we measured the distance between tongue contour and the hard palate along the selected fan line (see Figure 1.1). This approach is inspired by Lin et al. (2014), who also measured the distance between tongue tip and the hard palate tracing, although the distance was defined with respect to the image's vertical orientation. We relate to the distance measure as 'aperture'. We z-score normalised the aperture measure within speaker, since for some speakers the tongue tip and the hard palate are imaged better than for others. Normalisation addresses this issue to a certain extent, since we included a within-speaker baseline, i.e. the morpheme-final context ('fool-ing'), where we expect full TT contact.

We also recorded the time point at which the maximum occurred, and measured the time lag between this point and the acoustic offset of voicing in /l/ (for the 'fool#five' context only). The greater the time lag from TT maximum to the offset of voicing, the bigger the relative delay and the greater likelihood of a percept of vocalisation, all things being equal. A relatively earlier TT maximum (less delay)

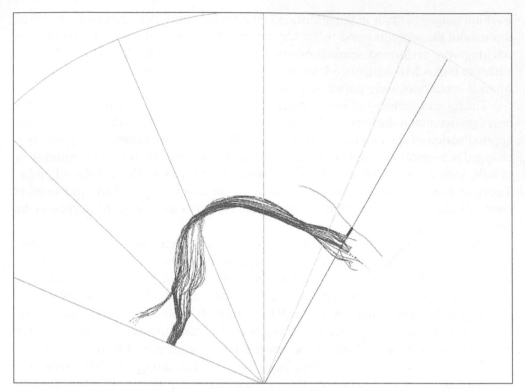

Figure 1.1 Example measurement of aperture for a selected token. The individual splines represent tongue contour tracings throughout the latter portion of the vowel and throughout the /l/. The hard palate contour is traced in light grey. Tongue tip is on the right. The aperture measurement (thickened part of the fan line, between the hard palate and individual splines) is the distance along the fan line with relative greatest variation in tongue displacement in the alveolar region. Aperture is measured between the spline representing maximum displacement and the hard palate

will appear less vocalised. We also wanted to know whether there is a continuum of relative timing between TT raising and the offset of voicing.

For one of the speakers who is an extreme vocaliser, YF6, there was hardly any TT displacement in the word-final pre-consonantal context ('fool#five'), and in consequence the TT gesture was not identifiable (note that Scobbie and Pouplier 2010 report a similar issue). For this speaker, we took the final ultrasound frame in the region corresponding to the acoustic duration of /Vl/ as representative of the maximum. In the section 'Relationship between magnitude and delay in the vocalisation context' below, we show data from this speaker as an illustration of extreme reduction. Time lag was not measurable for this speaker.

We complement the analysis of aperture and lag with analysis of averaged tongue contours (per speaker and per vowel) at the TT maximum. We used Smoothing Spline Analysis of Variance (SS-ANOVA) to obtain the averaged smooths (Davidson 2006;

Gu 2013, 2014). We ran the SS-ANOVA in Cartesian coordinates, as opposed to polar, since we find that the analysis using polar transformation, as it was operation-alised, sometimes distorted the tongue tip.

## Statistical Analysis and Results

### TT Aperture as a Function of Context

As the first step in our analysis, we investigated how aperture depends on the context, and how this changes depending on speaker age. We fitted a linear mixed-effects regression model with aperture as the dependent variable, and with context and age as main effects. We then added a random slope for context within speaker and found that the fit of the model improved significantly ($\chi^2 = 57.00$, df=5, p < 0.001). This suggests considerable individual variation with respect to aperture. In contrast, there was no significant main effect of age, as removing this predictor did not significantly affect the model fit ($\chi^2 = 0.03$, df=1, p=0.86). There was no significant interaction between age and context, as established by adding the interaction and comparing the model to the one with main effects only ($\chi^2 = 1.27$, df=2, p=0.53). The final model we present in Table 1.1 has age and context as main predictors, random intercepts for speaker and item, and a random slope for context within speaker. The p-values in this and subsequent model summaries were obtained using the stargazer package (Hlavac 2018), which also served as the model for formatting the model summaries in this chapter.

As shown in Table 1.1, the average aperture is significantly greater in the word-final pre-consonantal condition ('fool#five'), but there is no significant difference in average aperture between the intercept (word-medial pre-vocalic) and the word-final pre-vocalic condition. The effect of age is not significant.

Table 1.1 Summary of fixed effects from a linear model predicting the degree of normalised aperture depending on context and speaker age

|  | Dependent variable: Aperture (normalised) |
| --- | --- |
| Age: younger | −0.013 |
|  | (0.066) |
| Context: word-final pre-C | 0.739*** |
|  | (0.23) |
| Context: word-final pre-V | 0.177 |
|  | (0.173) |
| Intercept | −0.309** |
|  | (0.13) |

*Notes:*
*p <0.5; **p <0.01; ***p <0.001.
The intercept corresponds to a word medial /l/ pronounced by an older speaker.
Positive values indicate increased aperture (less tongue tip raising).

The results of the modelling confirm a degree of /l/-vocalisation in the word-final pre-consonantal position, but not in the word-final pre-vocalic context. Impressionistically, there were instances of word-final pre-vocalic vocalisation, but they were rare, and there was no significant difference in the gradient reduction in aperture in this context. We do not observe any significant apparent time effects and no interactions, which suggests that younger speakers do not have more vocalisation in the context where it is most expected, i.e. word-finally before a consonant. However, the absence of a significant main effect seems to be due to inter-speaker variability, as would be expected in a situation of variation and change. This is confirmed by the analysis of by-speaker coefficients showing the effect of context within participant illustrated in Figure 1.2.

As shown in Figure 1.2, there seems to be an overall increase in aperture in the word-final pre-vocalic context compared to word-medial, but speakers vary in how much increase in aperture they show. The word-final pre-consonantal context involves the most inter-speaker variation. The most extreme vocalisers, YF6, YF4 and YF5, are in the younger speaker group. At the same time, other younger speakers,

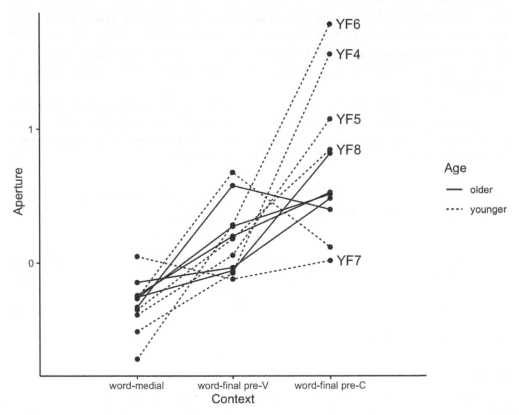

Figure 1.2 Average aperture depending on context and speaker. Younger speakers are in dotted lines, older speakers are in solid lines. Data from the labelled speakers are analysed in more detail in the section 'Degrees of /l/-vocalisation'

speakers YF1 and YF7, show no relative increase in aperture (no /l/-vocalisation). Older speakers seem to be relatively more consistent. Another noteworthy observation is that average aperture values in the word-final pre-consonantal condition are fairly continuous: from speaker YF7 (who has no /l/-vocalisation) to speaker YF6 (who is an extreme vocaliser with no residue of the TT gesture), all intermediate degrees of aperture are attested. In the section 'Degrees of /l/-vocalisation' below, we analyse average tongue contours from selected speakers, those labelled in Figure 1.2, to provide a more holistic illustration of entire tongue contours in vocalising and non-vocalising contexts.

*Degrees of /l/-vocalisation*

Figure 1.3 shows averaged tongue contour tracings for selected speakers, arranged from most extreme vocaliser, YF6, to YF7. YF6 had no TT gesture in the word-final pre-consonantal position, such that we could not measure it (for this speaker, tongue contours were extracted at the acoustic offset of /l/). The averaged smooths clearly show that the tongue tip is down for this speaker in the word-final pre-consonantal position, whereas there is TT raising in the word-medial context, as well as in the word-final pre-vocalic context. Also note that this speaker seems to show some gradient reduction in the TT contact for the word-final pre-vocalic context when the preceding vowel is /ʊ/.

Another extreme vocaliser is speaker YF4. Unlike YF6, YF4 did produce some TT raising in the word-final pre-consonantal condition, but we judge that there was never any TT contact in this context. What is particularly striking about this speaker is that word-finally before a consonant, the TT maximum occurred very late indeed. On average, the TT maximum was reached 50 ms after the voicing offset. We show an example token where such delay occurred in Figure 1.4. The tongue dorsum was not very well imaged for the speaker, but we can see the anterior part of the tongue relatively clearly. Comparing the two frames, the tongue blade continues moving upwards following the offset of voicing, and reaches its maximum after the voicing had ceased. Thus, although the TT gesture is present for this speaker, its severe reduction in magnitude and its considerable delay both contribute to an extreme acoustic reduction, typical of the type that renders any alveolar gesture of the /l/ acoustically untraceable, or covert.

Speaker YF5 is also a vocaliser who appears to have no TT contact in the word-final pre-consonantal context when the preceding vowel is /uː/, although there seems to be contact word-finally before a consonant when the preceding vowel is /ʊ/. Unlike YF6, however, YF5 shows some TT raising, and the TT gesture is not delayed beyond acoustic offset (as it happens for YF4). Thus, YF5's vocalisation seems more gradient, compared to either YF6 or YF4.

Another gradient vocaliser is speaker YF8, and, once again, the gradience is more apparent in the /uː/ context. Here we see that the tongue tip is raised in the word-final pre-consonantal context (as it is in the baseline context), but there seems to be a trend towards gradient reduction in the degree of TT contact.

/uː/ /ʊ/

YF6

YF4

YF5

YF8

YF7

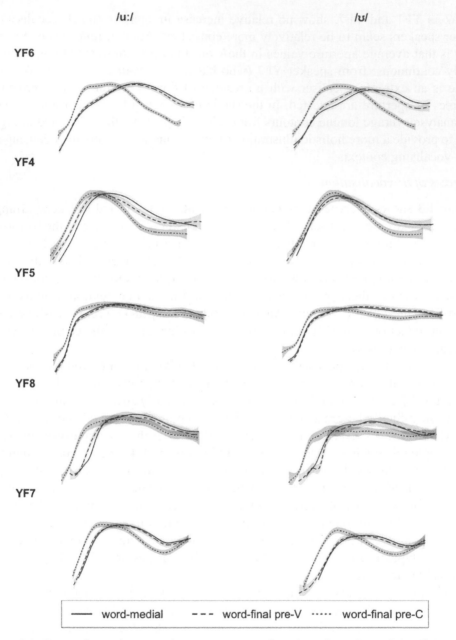

——— word-medial   - - - word-final pre-V   ⋯⋯ word-final pre-C

Figure 1.3 Comparison of averaged tongue contours for selected speakers, depending on context and the vowel preceding /l/

At the other end of the spectrum, we find speakers like YF7, who has the same degree of TT contact across all three contexts.

In summary, comparison of averaged tongue contours (for selected speakers) on an individual basis is compatible with the results of mixed-effects modelling of

Voicing offset                  TT maximum

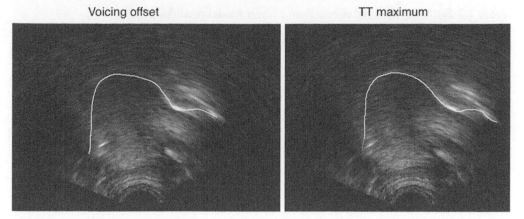

Figure 1.4 Example of gestural delay by speaker YF4. The left panel shows the image of the tongue at the offset of acoustic voicing. The right panel shows the image of the tongue when it reaches maximum TT displacement, ca. 50 ms after the offset of voicing

aperture reported in the section 'TT aperture as a function of context' above. For all speakers we find TT raising in the word-medial context, and typically also in the word-final pre-vocalic context. It is in the word-final pre-consonantal context, on the other hand, where we see the biggest potential for structured variation and change, given the wide range of productions observed. Our results quantify the wide range observed, covering all degrees of intermediate TT raising from no raising at all in speaker YF6 to full contact in speaker YF7. In addition, we have observed that speaker YF4 (but no other speaker) delays the maximum TT raising beyond the offset of voicing, such that the TT gesture is potentially inaudible (or its acoustic consequences are reduced). In the section 'Relationship between magnitude and delay in the vocalisation context' below, we turn to analysing the timing of the TT gesture for all speakers, to verify whether intermediate degrees of gradient TT reduction are correlated with degrees of gestural delay.

*Relationship Between Magnitude and Delay in the Vocalisation Context*

In order to analyse the relationship between aperture, timing and acoustics, we fitted a series of linear mixed models. These models were fitted to the data from word-final pre-consonantal items, since it is the environment in which between and within-speaker variation in the degree of vocalisation is potentially greatest. We excluded speaker YF6 from this part of the analysis because she had complete deletion of the TT gesture, which rendered acoustic delay not measurable.

We fitted a model predicting aperture based on gestural lag, vowel, speaker age and the F2–F1 difference. The F2–F1 difference was centred to improve model convergence. We then tested for all possible interactions and for random slopes, but found no significant improvements in model fit. The best-fitting model we present in Table 1.2 had only main effects, as well as random intercepts for speaker and item.

Table 1.2 Summary of fixed effects from a linear model predicting aperture

|  | Dependent variable: Aperture (normalised) |
| --- | --- |
| Gestural delay | 3.806** |
|  | (1.489) |
| Vowel: ʊ | 0.2 |
|  | (0.134) |
| Age: younger | 0.024 |
|  | (0.231) |
| F2–F1 distance (centred) | −0.119* |
|  | (0.062) |
| Intercept | 0.497** |
|  | (0.223) |

*Notes:*
*p <0.5; **p <0.01; ***p <0.001.
The intercept corresponds to /l/ preceded by /uː/ pronounced by an older speaker.
Positive values indicate greater aperture (more /l/-vocalisation).

Aperture increases significantly with gestural delay: delayed gestures are more likely to also be reduced. We also find, in line with previous reports, that decreased gestural magnitude is correlated with F1 and F2 coming together. There is no significant effect of preceding vowel, or speaker age. The effect of gestural delay on aperture is illustrated in Figure 1.5. The figure shows the raw data, and the line of best fit, according to the model. We can see that early TT gestures generally have small aperture values, i.e. they are fully realised, whereas considerably delayed gestures are invariably reduced. However, there is also a number of intermediate data points which correspond to gestures that are close to the acoustic offset of voicing, but where the maximum is reached before the voicing ceases. For this group, there is a general correlation between delay and increase in aperture, but we also find variation in this band: some gestures achieved ca. 50 ms before voicing offset is fully realised, whereas others may be reduced.

The next model we fitted predicted gestural delay based on vowel preceding /l/, speaker age, aperture and F2–F1 distance. We then tested for interactions and random slopes and found a significant model improvement after including an interaction between vowel and speaker age ($\chi^2 = 16.25$, df=1, p < 0.01). Furthermore, the model improved significantly when we also added an additional effect, that of combined vowel + /l/ duration ($\chi^2 = 73.04$, df=1, p < 0.01). The best-fitting model, whose fixed part is summarised in Table 1.3, had main effects of F2–F1 distance aperture, /Vl/ duration and an interaction between vowel and speaker age.

The only significant main effect is /Vl/ duration. There is a very strong negative correlation between duration and delay: in shorter segments, the TT gesture tends to occur relatively closer to the offset of voicing. In addition, we find that gestural delay is relatively greater for /uː/ than for /ʊ/ in older speakers, whereas in younger

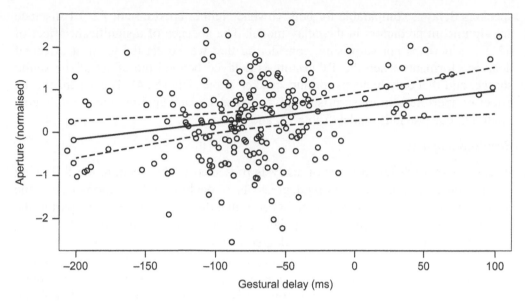

**Figure 1.5** The effect of gestural delay on aperture.

Table 1.3 Summary of fixed effects from a linear model predicting the degree of gestural delay

|  | Dependent variable: Gestural delay (ms) |
| --- | --- |
| Aperture (normalised) | −0.0004 |
|  | (0.002) |
| Vowel: ʊ | −0.05*** |
|  | (0.006) |
| Age: younger | 0.012 |
|  | (0.033) |
| F2−F1 distance (centred) | −0.001 |
|  | (0.002) |
| Duration (centred) | −0.039*** |
|  | (0.004) |
| Vowel ʊ: age younger | 0.034*** |
|  | (0.007) |
| Intercept | −0.062*** |
|  | (0.023) |

*Notes:*
*p <0.5; **p <0.01; ***p <0.001.
The intercept corresponds to /l/ preceded by /uː/ pronounced by an older speaker.
Positive values indicate greater delay.

speakers delay is comparable for both vowels. Neither aperture nor F2–F1 distance are significant predictors in the delay model. The absence of a significant effect of F2–F1 is perhaps not surprising, considering that we expect the greatest effect of delay on formants when the TT gesture is delayed beyond the offset of the sound source, and that only happens for one speaker in our data (YF4). The absence of an effect of aperture is more surprising, given that delay and aperture are strongly correlated in our previous model (Table 1.2 and Figure 1.5).

*Results Summary*

Putting together different types of analysis presented in this section, the following findings emerge. There are varying degrees of /l/-vocalisation (operationalised as the degree of aperture, a speaker-specific linear, radial distance between some part of the tongue surface and part of the hard palate in the alveolar region of interest). Along this dimension, a whole spectrum of degree of vocalisation is attested: from a full gesture resulting in contact between the tongue tip and the palate to complete deletion of the TT gesture. Individual speakers may occupy any space along this continuum, i.e. varying gradient degrees of reduction in TT magnitude are found. We do not find significant main speaker age effects, but analysis of individual variation shows that this is because younger speakers are extremely varied (from extreme vocalisation in some to none at all in others), whereas older speakers generally have TT contact (either full or partially reduced). Vocalisation is generally confined to word-final pre-consonantal context (out of the contexts we tested). We find very little of it in the word-final pre-vocalic context.

Regarding the relationship between increase in aperture and gestural delay, we find some correlation, but there are also caveats. Early TT gestures are always fully realised, while the extremely delayed ones (past the offset of voicing) are invariably reduced. However, somewhat late but still fully audible TT gestures may or may not be reduced: there is some correlation between aperture and delay in this group, but there is also significant variance. We also find that gradient gestural delay does not result in F2 and F1 coming together in the way gradient increase in aperture does. Finally, there is a very strong correlation between timing of the TT gesture and the duration of the /Vl/ sequence: the longer the sequence, the greater the delay of the TT maximum relative to the acoustic offset.

**Discussion**

In the section 'Introduction' above, we introduced two conceptualisations of /l/-vocalisation. According to one, /l/-vocalisation is primarily a gradual reduction in the magnitude of the TT gesture. The alternative proposal is that /l/-vocalisation is mainly driven by gestural 'timing' (specifically, a delay). If the TT gesture is frequently delayed, and consequently masked by the following gesture (or by the absence of sound source), this may lead to a perception-driven change, where listeners start weakening the consonantal gesture in their own speech. In principle, both scenarios of change may lead to the same result: considerable reduction accompanied by considerable delay (as seen in Speaker YF4 in our data), and, eventually, deletion of the TT gestures (as seen in speaker YF6). However, even if the end result is the same, discontinuities in the data and inter-speaker differences can give us clues about how transmission of vocalisation is achieved. If vocalisation is understood as gradual reduction of the magnitude of the TT gestures, this should be reflected in gradient variation of the TT aperture within speakers and across speakers. If, on the other hand, gestural reduction is a secondary diachronic consequence of delay, we may expect to see discontinuities in the degree of reduction and a more gradient distribution of the degree of delay.

Overall, our data appear more consistent with the idea that /l/-vocalisation is primarily about reduction in magnitude. The main argument for this comes from the observation that virtually all degrees of aperture are attested in our sample: from full contact, via intermediate degrees of increase in aperture, to full gestural reduction. While we find all possible degrees of reduction in TT magnitude, delay appears to be a secondary factor. All of our speakers who have any degree of vocalisation use TT reduction, but only one of them consistently uses gestural delay, and for this speaker, the degree of delay is proportional to the reduction in TT magnitude.

In contrast, we do not find instances where gestural delay occurs without gestural reduction. Such a possibility is predicted under the 'delay-first' scenario, where gestural reduction first appears due to perceptual reinterpretation of reduction as delay. Of course, the absence of such a pattern in our sample does not preclude its presence in a larger speaker population or different dialect. An additional consideration is that this type of delay is likely to be a property of casual speech that might be difficult to elicit under the conditions of instrumental research. Thus, while our current results seem more in line with the 'reduction-first' proposal, this interpretation would be considerably strengthened if we had evidence from other speakers who also make covert TT gestures in their final /l/. Data from such speakers could give us a better understanding of whether delay is always a factor involved in more advanced instances of vocalisation before the tongue tip gesture undergoes deletion.

In general, our findings invite more research into all speakers who appear to have /l/-vocalisation in English. Speakers who have lost the TT contact are by no means a monolithic group. On the contrary, there is variation among them which is strongly indicative of continuing sound change. We can generalise that gradient reduction of TT contact (as shown in earlier EPG studies, e.g. Hardcastle and Barry 1989) continues as a gradient reduction of the TT gesture. What has yet to be investigated is how reduction of the TT gesture propagates through speech communities once the TT contact has been lost.

Our results also challenge the view that /l/-vocalisation is a form of 'extreme darkening'. This kind of interpretation could be pursued if we take a strictly temporal interpretation of /l/-vocalisation, where /l/-darkening involves relative delay of the apical gesture beyond the dorsal one, and vocalisation is a step further, involving gestural delay that makes the apical gesture inaudible. Such a view is challenged by speakers who make a very strong use of spatial reduction in producing vocalised /l/, most notably Speaker YF6. We observed in the section 'Articulatory analysis' above, that we could not identify a distinct TT gesture for this speaker in word-final pre-consonantal /l/s, and so we were unable to measure gestural delay for this speaker. It is problematic to define vocalisation in terms of delay when such delay is not measurable, and so the vocalised variants appear to be, in some sense, categorically different from the tokens of dark /l/. By the same token, gestural deletion complicates measurements of aperture. Although we can still measure the distance between the tongue surface and the hard palate, we may not want to refer to it as a measure of gestural reduction, 'if there is no gesture'. The spatio-temporal consequences of gestural deletion preclude talking about it in terms defined for /l/-darkening.

While our data support the idea that there are prototypical and categorically distinct variants of light, dark and vocalised /l/, category boundaries are difficult to establish, which challenges attempts at categorising different variants of /l/ in terms of broadly-defined patterns. Such a categorisation is inherent to a phonemic or segmental analysis, which relies on categorically different allophonic variants of /l/ in formulating phonological generalisations. For instance, the clear /l/ vs. dark /l/ opposition is often analysed in terms of two segmental units whose distribution is conditioned by syllable structure: clear /l/ occurs in onsets, and dark /l/ occurs in codas. /l/-vocalisation seems to be sensitive to the interaction between segmental and prosodic factors: while vocalisation occurs word-finally, it is usually limited when a vowel follows in the next word. However, although such generalisations approximate observed patterns to some extent, they are difficult to reconcile with the demonstrably gradient and continuous nature of articulatory adjustments affecting /l/ in different contexts. The change from a clear /l/ to a dark one involves incremental increase to the dorsal gesture, coupled with relative delay of TT raising. /l/-vocalisation can be characterised as gradual loss of the TT contact, but we also know that the TT gesture may continue to undergo reduction in ostensibly vocalised cases. For those reasons, an allophonic split into three variants – clear, dark and vocalised /l/ – necessarily involves arbitrary cuts to an inherently gradient phenomenon, merely replicating categorical structural differences in a segmental domain.

The challenge to forcing different types of /l/ into broad categories even within the same structural position has been acknowledged from the methodological point of view by sociolinguists interested in quantifying the frequency of different /l/-variants in a speech community. The feasibility of identifying and labelling vocalised /l/ is discussed by Hall-Lew and Fix (2012), who note that auditory rating yields relatively consistent results, but confidence drops for more intermediate cases, which are often also the ones that are sociolinguistically interesting. Accumulating results of instrumental articulatory research into /l/-vocalisation suggest that labelling difficulties are not strictly due to the somewhat crude nature of auditory coding. Rather, these issues follow both from the continuous nature of variation between articulatory variants within one context and the difficulties of comparing similar articulatory variants across structurally distinct contexts. Even with much more detailed articulatory evidence at hand it is difficult to classify some intermediate cases.

Furthermore, different cases may be considered intermediate, depending on which phonetic dimension is being measured. If we focus on the degree of alveolar contact as the primary dimension, as is done in EPG studies, we might view partial contact cases as intermediate, and no contact cases as categorical /l/-vocalisation (e.g. Scobbie and Pouplier 2010). However, we know that the weakening of the TT gesture goes further than that, so we may also want to consider the cases where TT gesture is reduced as intermediate (or gradient), and cases where TT gesture is deleted as categorical. Therefore, some apparent categorical breaks may tell us more about the method we used to observe them than about the abstract organisation of the underlying system.

These considerations prompt us to recommend a mixture of different methodologies for further studies of /l/-vocalisation. The method we used, ultrasound tongue imaging, has the advantage of giving us a holistic view of the tongue posture and movement, unlike EPG, which cannot tell us about the tongue position where there is no contact with the palate. However, since the very tip of the tongue is typically not visible in the ultrasound image, this method necessarily involves inferring the TT position based on the data from the tongue blade. EMA can give us more precise measurements of TT displacement and velocity, but it is less well suited to studying the relationship between articulation and acoustics, since articulation is partially impeded in EMA studies by the presence of wires in the speaker's mouth, and coils need to be placed away from the precise location of contact. Furthermore, for practical reasons, like cost and portability, ultrasound is more appropriate for sociophonetic studies. A larger-scale carefully-sampled study of a single vocalising community would be the natural next step, and the best-case scenario would involve cross-comparisons of results from two methods (e.g. ultrasound and EMA) from a subset of the speakers, preferably incorporating within-speaker variation in style or register. Furthermore, for a more complete picture of /l/-vocalisation, labialisation also ought to be considered. For this reason, a fixed-ratio head-mounted video camera could be a useful additional tool in future instrumental studies of this phenomenon beyond the laboratory.

## Acknowledgements

We wish to thank the speakers for participating in our study, Steve Cowen for assistance with the recordings, and Alan Wrench for help with the ultrasound system. We thank an anonymous reviewer for their comments. The research reported in this paper was supported by a British Academy Postdoctoral Fellowship PDF/pf130029 to the first author.

## Note

1. Recasens (2016) argues that the two gestures are not identifiable in systems where dark /l/ is phonemic. In Southern British English, both gestures are measurable, at least in some vocalic contexts (Strycharczuk and Scobbie 2015).

# References

Articulate Instruments Ltd (2014), *Articulate Assistant Advanced Ultrasound Module User Manual, Revision 2.16*, Edinburgh, UK: Articulate Instruments Ltd.

Browman, Catherine P. and Louis Goldstein (1992), 'Articulatory phonology: an overview', *Phonetica* 49, 155–180.

Davidson, Lisa (2006), 'Comparing tongue shapes from ultrasound imaging using smoothing spline analysis of variance', *The Journal of the Acoustical Society of America* 120, 407–415.

Gick, Bryan (1999), 'A gesture-based account of intrusive consonants in English', *Phonology* 16, 29–54.

Giles, Stephen B. and Kenneth L. Moll (1975), 'Cinefluorographic study of selected allophones of English /l/', *Phonetica* 31, 206–227.

Gimson, A. C. (1980), *An Introduction to the Pronunciation of English by AC Gimson*, 3rd edn, London: Arnold.

Gu, Chong (2013). *Smoothing Spline ANOVA Models*, vol. 297, New York: Springer Science & Business Media.

Gu, Chong (2014), 'Smoothing spline ANOVA models: R Package gss', *Journal of Statistical Software* 58(5), 1–25, http://www.jstatsoft.org/v58/i05/

Hall-Lew, Lauren and Sonya Fix (2012), 'Perceptual coding reliability of (l)-vocalization in casual speech data', *Lingua* 122, 794–809.

Hardcastle, William and William Barry (1989), 'Articulatory and perceptual factors in /l/ vocalisations in English', *Journal of the International Phonetic Association* 15, 3–17.

Heyde, Cornelia, James M. Scobbie, Robin Lickley and Eleanor K. Drake (2016), 'How fluent is the fluent speech of people who stutter? A new approach to measuring kinematics with ultrasound', *Clinical Linguistics and Phonetics* 30(3–5), 292–312.

Hlavac, Marek (2018), *Stargazer: Well-formatted Regression and Summary Statistics Tables*, Bratislava, Slovakia: Central European Labour Studies Institute (CELSI), https://CRAN.R-project.org/package = stargazer

Johnson, Wyn and David Britain (2007), 'L-vocalisation as a natural phenomenon: explorations in sociophonology', *Language Sciences* 29, 294–315.

Lawson, Eleanor, Jane Stuart-Smith and James M. Scobbie (2018), 'The role of gesture delay to coda /r/ weakening: an articulatory, auditory and acoustic study', *Journal of the Acoustical Society of America* 143(3), 1646–1657.

Lin, Susan, Patrice Speeter Beddor and Andries W. Coetzee (2014), 'Gestural reduction, lexical frequency, and sound change: a study of post-vocalic /l/', *Laboratory Phonology* 5, 9–36.

Recasens, Daniel (2016), 'What is and what is not an articulatory gesture in speech production', *Gradus – Revista Brasileira de Fonologia de Laboratório* 1, 23–42, https://gradusjournal.com/index.php/gradus/article/view/2

Recasens, Daniel and Edda Farnetani (1994), 'Spatiotemporal properties of different allophones of /l/: phonological implications', in W. U. Dressler, M. Prinzhorn and J. R. Rennison (eds), *Phonologica 1992. Proceedings of the 7th International Phonology Meeting*, Turin: Rosenberg & Sellier, pp. 195–204.

Remijsen, Bert (2004), 'Script to measure and check formants', http://www.lel.ed.ac.uk/~bert/msr\&check$\_$f1f2$\_$indiv$\_$interv.psc

Scobbie, James M. and Marianne Pouplier (2010), 'The role of syllable structure in external sandhi: an EPG study of vocalisation and retraction in word-final English /l/', *Journal of Phonetics* 38, 240–259.

Scobbie, James M., Marianne Pouplier and Alan A Wrench (2007), 'Conditioning factors in external sandhi: an EPG study of English /l/ vocalisation', in *Proceedings of the 16th International Congress of Phonetic Sciences*, Saarbrücken: Universität des Saarlandes, pp. 441–444.

Sebregts, Koen (2015), *The Sociophonetics and Phonology of Dutch r*, vol. 379, Utrecht: LOT.

Sproat, Richard and Osamu Fujimura (1993), Allophonic variation in English /l/ and its implications for phonetic implementation', *Journal of Phonetics* 21, 291–311.

Strycharczuk, Patrycja and James M. Scobbie (2015), 'Velocity measures in ultrasound data. Gestural timing of post-vocalic /l/ in English', in *Proceedings of the 18th International Congress of Phonetic Sciences*, Paper 0309, https://www.internationalphoneticassociation.org/icphs-proceedings/ICPhS2015/proceedings.html

Strycharczuk, Patrycja and James M. Scobbie (2016), Gradual or abrupt? The phonetic path to morphologisation', *Journal of Phonetics* 59, 76–91.

Strycharczuk, Patrycja and James M. Scobbie (2017), 'Fronting of southern British English high-back vowels in articulation and acoustics', *The Journal of the Acoustical Society of America* 142, 322–331.

Stuart-Smith, Jane, Gwilym Pryce, Claire Timmins and Barrie Gunter (2013), 'Television can also be a factor in language change: evidence from an urban dialect', *Language* 89, 501–536.

Tollfree, Laura (1999), 'South East London English: discrete versus continuous modelling of consonantal reduction', in P. Foulkes and G. Docherty (eds), *Urban Voices: Accent Studies in the British Isles*, London: Arnold, pp. 163–184.

Turton, Danielle (2014), Variation in English /l/: synchronic reflections of the life cycle of phonological processes, University of Manchester PhD thesis.

Wells, John C. (1982), *Accents of English*, 3 vols, Cambridge: Cambridge University Press.

Wrench, Alan A. and James M. Scobbie (2003), 'Categorising vocalisation of English /l/ using EPG, EMA and ultrasound', in *Proceedings of the 6th International Seminar on Speech Production*, Manly, Sydney, pp. 314–319.

Wright, Susan (1987), 'The interaction of sociolinguistic and phonetically-conditioned CSPs in Cambridge English: auditory and electropalatographic evidence', *Cambridge Papers in Phonetics and Experimental Linguistics* 5, Department of Linguistics, University of Cambridge.

Wright, Susan (1988), 'The effects of style and speaking rate on /l/-vocalisation in local Cambridge English', *York Papers in Linguistics* 13, University of York, 355–365.

# 2

# The Production and Perception of Derived Phonological Contrasts in Selected Varieties of English

*Emmanuel Ferragne*

## Introduction

Derived phonological contrasts (DPCs) occur when the set of distinctions in poly-morphemic forms is greater than the set found in monomorphemic lexical items (Harris 1990). For instance, the past morpheme <ed> causes the vowel in the word 'brewed' to be appreciably longer than its counterpart in 'brood' in many speakers of Scottish English (Rathcke and Stuart-Smith 2016).

In structuralist phonological parlance, 'brood' and 'brewed' constitute a minimal pair; therefore, both vowels – were we to adopt this view – should qualify as fully-fledged phonemes. This option is probably not desirable because it misses at least two points. First, quite often, DPCs give rise to a very scarce functional load, which often correlates with unstable phonemicity. Second, many vowels involved in DPCs have a complementary distributional nature which would not be adequately captured if we allowed them to share the same status as vowel contrasts elicited with mono-morphemic items. Now, turning to the generativist paradigm, it should be noted that, in the SPE framework, DPCs are analysed in exactly the same way as allophones: a rule including information on morpheme boundaries generates two different surface realisations from a single underlying entity. This approach is not entirely satisfactory either. As Harris (1990) explains, the historical behaviour of DPCs has been shown to closely resemble that of genuine phonemic contrasts. Once DPCs have emerged, an additional lexical category is potentially available for inclusion in underived morphemes, and the contrast can eventually penetrate the phonemic inventory. In this chapter, I adopt an intermediate view, according to which DPCs have a status of their own, sometimes called quasi-phonemic (Scobbie and Stuart-Smith 2008; Hall 2013).

My goal is to examine acoustic and perceptual data from various locations in the British Isles – Enniskillen (Ulster), Glasgow and Hull – in order to better understand the production and perception of certain DPCs found in English. This research falls within a broader framework that I call the Gradient Phonemicity Hypothesis (GPH), according to which a whole range of cognitive statuses is assumed to exist between allophony and phonemicity, and a difference between two sounds can be described by some measure of how typically allophonic or phonemic their relation is. In addition to the well-known attributes of maximal phonemicity – e.g. phonological unpredictability, high functional load/type frequency, etc. – it is my contention that a more thorough understanding of gradient phonemicity can be gained by analysing acoustic, articulatory and perceptual data.

The testability of GPH therefore presupposes a very direct link between objectively measurable quantities and the way speech sounds are represented in the brain. The approach in this chapter draws on usage-based grammars and exemplar theory (Pierrehumbert 2001) in that it equates the formation of speech categories with statistical learning and does not presuppose a limited memory space that would prevent the storing of fine, contextual and redundant phonetic details. The recognition of a speech sound is then very similar to a classification task performed by some supervised machine learning algorithm. Many of the background concepts underlying the present work can be found in Feldman et al. (2009) and Kronrod et al. (2016).

This study focuses on two contrasts that rely most heavily – if not exclusively – on duration. Measurements of various spectral cues and duration will be performed on vowels belonging to the lexical sets TRAP and START in Hull, and on vowels belonging to the GOOSE and BREWED lexical sets in Glasgow. Similar measurements will also be performed with production data from Ulster. Then a perceptual task, involving the labelling of stimuli whose duration varied on a continuum between the short and the long vowel in each variety of English, will be run. The data from Hull will serve as a baseline – illustrating the acoustic and perceptual correlates of a typical phonemic distinction – against which data involving the DPC attested in Glasgow will be compared.

## Brief Phonological Background

### Hull

The Hull accent is a typical northern British accent, and it also exhibits pronunciation features of its own (Williams and Kerswill 1999). Among the latter, of particular interest to the current chapter, is the possibility that the distinction between the vowels of the TRAP and START lexical sets can be conveyed by duration only. In the words 'had' and 'hard', for instance, duration can be the only cue that conveys the phonemic opposition (note that the accent is non-rhotic). In Ferragne and Pellegrino (2010) we found that this was the case for some speakers while others maintained a perceptible – though sometimes subtle – difference in vowel quality.

### Glasgow

The patterns of vowel duration in the varieties of Scottish English are very different from those observed in most other accents of English (Wells 1982; Scobbie et al. 1999; Rathcke and Stuart-Smith 2016). These patterns are governed by the Scottish

Vowel Length Rule, and do not mirror the well-known phonemic length oppositions found elsewhere. Vowel duration in Glasgow is both phonologically and morphologically conditioned. The latter will be studied here because this type of conditioning generates what one would be tempted to call 'minimal pairs'; and these pairs perfectly exemplify the phonological problems briefly discussed in the Introduction. Among the three vowels which have been unanimously identified as good candidates for morphologically-conditioned lengthening – yielding DPC pairs like 'greed'-'agreed', 'brood'-'brewed', 'tide'-'tied' – the focus of this chapter is placed on the second one. Minimal pairs of the first type are very few; and the third type involves both duration and vowel quality changes. As a convention, I chose the keyword GOOSE to stand for the short member in pairs of the 'brood'-'brewed' type, and the word BREWED was chosen to denote the long items.

*Enniskillen*

The original motivation for collecting data from Ulster was that a number of the derived contrasts mentioned in Harris (1990) were attested there. There is also (scant) evidence that a contrast of the GOOSE-BREWED type might exist in this variety: Wells (1982) explicitly mentions this possibility, as well as a number of phenomena suggesting that vowel duration in Ulster follows patterns that are very similar to those found in Scotland. The data in Ferragne and Pellegrino (2010) suggested that some speakers had a difference in duration between the keywords 'hood' and 'who'd', while little to no spectral difference could be elicited.

**Audio Data**

*Hull*

Recordings from eighteen participants (aged 16–35) were collected in Hull in 2011. They were asked to read a list of ten words – i.e. five minimal pairs involving the TRAP vs. START contrast – and twelve distractors. Each word appeared at the end of the carrier sentence 'He said the word …' and each item (sentence + target word) was presented twelve times. In this chapter, for the sake of comparability with the Glasgow data, only three (out of the original twelve) tokens were randomly picked automatically to be included in the analysis. The dataset therefore contains 540 vowels: eighteen speakers × ten items × three repetitions. The target words were: 'back'-'bark', 'cad'-'card', 'cap'-'carp', 'match'-'march', 'pat'-'part'. Unless otherwise specified, the values for the three repetitions were averaged, so that most of the analyses further below were actually performed with 180 vowels. The recordings were carried out with ROCme! software (Ferragne et al. 2013) and an Audio Technica AT2020 USB microphone. The audio signal was digitised with a 16-bit resolution and a 44.1 kHz sampling rate in PCM mono format.

## Glasgow

The audio data is actually comprised of two subsets, GLA1 and GLA2, which served different purposes. The recordings took place in 2009 and 2010. GLA1 contains speech data from fifteen students from the University of Glasgow. The participants were asked to read a list of twelve potential minimal pairs embedded in the carrier sentence 'He said the word … and I didn't know how to spell it.' The list also included six distractors. Each sentence was read three times; the items were presented randomly, and the order varied from one participant to the next. The recordings were carried out thanks to a computer program we had written in the Tcl/Tk language: the participants managed the whole procedure in an autonomous, self-paced way. The audio signal was digitised with a 16-bit resolution and a 44.1 kHz sampling rate in PCM mono format. Since the goal of GLA1 was to provide descriptive acoustic data illustrating typical cases where the Scottish Vowel Length Rule applies, the participants whose data showed no sign of perceptible differences between the two members of a pair for at least six pairs were discarded. Participants 02, 09 and 15 were therefore removed from the analysis. So 792 vowels (twelve speakers × twenty-two items × three repetitions) were analysed; and since this chapter is only concerned with the GOOSE-BREWED derived contrast, this leaves us with 432 vowels (twelve speakers × twelve items × three repetitions) which, unless otherwise stated, will actually be reduced to 144 after computing averages over the three repetitions of each item.

The GLA2 subset includes a short reading task by twenty students before they took a perceptual experiment. They were prompted to read a short text that had been specially designed to elicit the derived contrasts under scrutiny. This task was meant to serve as a quick check that the participants had the contrast in their phonology. Since the perceptual experiment was particularly long, the text was kept as short as possible while we tried to maximise the number of occurrences of potential derived minimal pairs. As a consequence (and also given the low functional load associated with such pairs) the text sounds a little unnatural, and some of the words are rather rare. In the following text, the target items have been highlighted (in this chapter, only the 'crude'-'crewed' pair will be analysed):

> Captain Duncan **crewed** on two ships, one of which remained permanently **tied** to a pier in Ayrshire. It was said that he **wooed** fame and success; but few people knew that he actually **sighed** for early retirement, and had great **need** of rest. When the **tide** was high, the ship **would** sway from **side** to **side**, and Duncan **would** sit quietly, listening to the endless creak of the **wood**. One day, a fellow mariner made a very **crude** joke and Duncan **kneed** the poor lad overboard.

The recordings were made with a Zoom H4n digital recorder and stored as PCM mono files with a 16-bit resolution and a 44.1 kHz sampling rate. The subset of the corpus that will be analysed in this chapter contains forty items (twenty speakers × two words).

*Ulster (Enniskillen)*

Twenty-four speakers – eight staff members and sixteen students – from Portora Royal School in Enniskillen were recorded. The speech material was composed of twelve minimal pairs embedded in meaningful carrier sentences. Different sentences were indeed needed because some of the words in the original study (which had a broader scope) were homographs. For this chapter we will focus on two minimal pairs: 'brood'-'brewed' and 'crude'-'crewed'. The target words appeared in the following sentences:

A synonym for 'offspring' is '**brood**'.
Coffee is tastier when freshly **brewed**.
I can't believe she painted the nursery in magenta. This colour is so **crude**.
The captain was ready to cast off. His vessel was well-equipped and **crewed**.

The sentences were displayed and recorded with ROCme! software and an Audio Technica AT2020 USB microphone. The audio signal was digitised with a 16-bit resolution and a 44.1 kHz sampling rate in PCM mono format. The dataset analysed here contains 96 vowels (twenty-four speakers × four items).

**Acoustic Analysis**

The vowels were segmented and submitted to formant analysis using Praat scripts written by the author.[1] For each vowel, the parameters of the algorithm were manually adjusted until an optimal visual match between formant estimates and the underlying spectrogram was reached. Then formant tracks were saved with a fixed time interval of 5 ms. Matlab and R software were used for the analysis.

Frequency values for F1 and F2 were analysed as static as well as dynamic parameters. In the first case, the values were measured at the temporal midpoint of the vowel, and, as will be made explicit in the relevant sections, objective measurements in Hertz were often converted to the Bark scale and z-scored. In the second case, cubic spline interpolation was performed over whole formant trajectories, and the resulting contours were truncated so as to leave out portions corresponding to 20 per cent of the duration at the beginning and at the end of the contours. Discrete cosine transforms (DCT) were applied to the remaining points. In accordance with previous studies where a similar procedure was used – see e.g. Elvin et al. (2016) for more information on the underlying rationale – DCT coefficients 1 and 2 (i.e. excluding coefficient 0, which reflects the DC offset) were analysed. Instead of raw coefficients, the values in the present study were scaled so that the resulting coefficients represented the fraction of energy contained in the corresponding cosine basis function. Coefficient 1 reflects the magnitude of the formant slope and coefficient 2 corresponds to the degree of curvature. This part of the analysis remains exploratory since the a priori likelihood that the long and short vowels in this study should differ with respect to the shape of their formant contours is very low.

*Duration Modelling*

As a first descriptive step, Figure 2.1 displays kernel density estimates for duration; the black dashed curve shows the putatively short member of the pair while the grey dotted curve shows the long one. The grey area marks the amount of overlap between the two classes and the vertical line represents our best estimate of category boundary. Table 2.1 reports the mean duration and the range of duration values for each category as well as the threshold value (boundary) reflecting maximal uncertainty as to whether an item with this duration should be classified as short or long. As a quick measure for separability between the two classes, a logistic classifier was trained, and the correct classification rate is reported in the last column. The data from Ulster in Figure 2.1 fails to support the hypothesis that duration could serve as a reliable cue to distinguish between GOOSE and BREWED in this variety (hence it is not mentioned in Table 2.1).

The data from Hull, in the first panel, shows good – though not perfect – separability between TRAP and START words. A similar behaviour can be observed for GOOSE and BREWED in the GLA1 and GLA2 datasets. Two facts are of particular interest here. First, the temporal boundary between short and long differs between datasets; among other things, potential differences in speech rate should be checked since it is well known that speech rate has a decisive influence on boundary location and category shape (Miller and Volaitis 1989). Second, as is clear from Table 2.1 – and from the relative peakedness of the left density in each of the first three panels in Figure 2.1, especially the second one – there is a tendency for mean duration values to positively correlate with the corresponding range values. This could perhaps indicate that perceived duration is a decelerating function of objective duration (I return to this in the General Discussion).

There is a number of potential reasons why perfect separability was not achieved with the raw duration measurements in Figure 2.1: at least four factors were deliberately (temporarily) left out in this preliminary analysis: (1) speech rate is known to impact segment duration, especially vowels (Gay 1978), (2) some phonological environments may have shortening/lengthening effects (Klatt 1976), (3) secondary (spectral) cues can be used to enhance the distinction or compensate for weak separability in the time dimension, and (4) of course, depending on the speaker, the effect of these factors may vary, not to mention that some speakers may actually not produce a distinction, hence the need to perform individual analyses at some point.

In an attempt to assess the potential impact of speech rate, the duration of the first part of the carrier sentences for the Hull and GLA1 datasets – 'He said the word' – was measured. No such analysis was carried out with the other two datasets given that the conditions were quite different. Then linear regression was performed in order to examine to what extent carrier duration predicted vowel duration, after vowels had been split according to their expected phonological length. The results are shown in the first two panels of Figure 2.2 where the plain lines represent the least-squares fits and the dotted lines show 95 per cent confidence bounds. In each panel the black lines

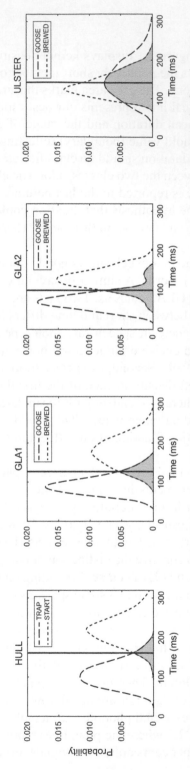

Figure 2.1 Kernel density estimates for the duration of short (black dashed line) and long (grey dotted line) vowels in the four datasets

Table 2.1 Mean and range of duration values (in ms) for the short and long vowels in Hull and Glasgow

| Dataset | Short item | | Long item | | | Classification |
| | mean | range | mean | range | Boundary | rate |
| --- | --- | --- | --- | --- | --- | --- |
| Hull TRAP-START | 109 | 133 | 221 | 199 | 161 | 95 |
| GLA1 GOOSE-BREWED | 96 | 102 | 179 | 151 | 129 | 91 |
| GLA2 GOOSE-BREWED | 74 | 93 | 129 | 99 | 100 | 93 |

*Notes:* The location of the boundary between the two categories is also given (in ms), as well as the percentage of correctly classified tokens obtained by training a logistic classifier with tenfold cross-validation. All values are rounded to the nearest integer.

and markers stand for the short vowel, and the grey lines and markers represent the long vowel. All four regressions showed significant effects (at least at the $p < 0.01$ level); adjusted $R^2$ values – reported in the figure – show the goodness of fit for each model. Worthy of note is the relatively high predictive power for BREWED in GLA1 (note the steeper slope reflecting stronger association between the two variables), and the relatively low predictive power for START in Hull, while the short vowels in both graphs display comparable $R^2$ values. The third panel displays kernel density estimates for the duration of the carrier sentence in Hull (black) and GLA1 (grey), showing that the duration of the carrier was on average longer in Hull and slightly more homogeneous. To sum up briefly, speech rate influences vowel duration in the target word – the longer the carrier sentence, the longer the vowel – but given the low to medium $R^2$ values, the predictive power of these models is limited: other factors might come into play, which calls for more advanced modelling.

So in order to further our understanding of the factors that affect vowel duration a linear mixed-effects regression model was fitted to the Hull data, with phonological

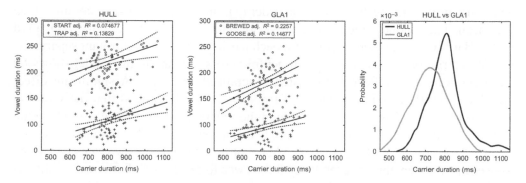

Figure 2.2 The first two panels show scatterplots of carrier sentence duration against vowel duration with ordinary least-squares regression lines and 95 per cent confidence bounds for short (dark lines and crosses) and long (grey lines and circles) vowels in the Hull and GLA1 datasets. The third panel shows kernel density estimates of carrier sentence duration for both datasets

length (TRAP vs. START), lengthening environment (yes vs. no)[2] and carrier sentence duration as fixed effects, and speaker as random effect. As expected, phonological length had the greatest effect ($F_{(1,176)} = 1415.6$, $p < 0.001$), then the next biggest effect was found for the lengthening environment ($F_{(1,176)} = 96.9$, $p < 0.001$). Oddly enough, carrier sentence duration did not reach statistical significance ($F_{(1,176)} = 0.10125$, $p = 0.75$), suggesting that once speaker-specific variations in vowel duration, phonological length and the lengthening environment have been taken into account, speech rate might not contribute to determining vowel duration. The adjusted $R^2$ value shows that the whole model accounts for 91 per cent of the variance in the dependent variable (vowel duration). After adjusting for all other terms in the regression, the model predicts that moving from TRAP to START causes the vowel to lengthen by 112 ms, and that a voiced environment lengthens the preceding vowel by 37 ms.

The same model without the lengthening environment factor – since all words ended in a voiced stop – was run with the GLA1 data. Phonological length had a large significant effect ($F_{(1,141)} = 603.5$, $p < 0.001$), and carrier sentence duration showed a small significant effect ($F_{(1,141)} = 5.4$, $p = 0.02$). The adjusted $R^2$ suggests that the model accounts for 85 per cent of the variance. Once the effect of other factors has been included in the model, moving from GOOSE to BREWED changes vowel duration by 84 ms. The net effect of carrier duration causes vowels to lengthen by 0.118 ms for every additional 1 ms in carrier duration.

*Formant Frequencies and Vowel Duration*

As a first approximation to checking whether formants are involved in the vowel length distinction, F1 and F2 frequencies measured at temporal midpoint were used as predictors in a logistic regression model, with vowel length (e.g. GOOSE vs. BREWED) as the response variable.

Since formant values are known to be highly speaker specific, proper ways to deal with them would be to include speakers as random effects in the model, and/or to explicitly transform the data a priori in order to minimise between-speaker unwanted variation. The second option was chosen: formant frequencies were first converted to the Bark scale, and then z-scored for each participant and each formant separately.

When run on the GLA1 data with tenfold cross-validation, the model shows 69 per cent correct classification (adjusted generalised $R^2$: 0.27). A significant effect of F1 ($p < 0.001$) could be found: as F1 decreases, the likelihood that the vowel is BREWED increases. This is clearly visible in the second panel of Figure 2.3, where the density estimate for BREWED (grey shape) is located slightly higher than that of GOOSE (dark shape) in the F1/F2 plane. In other words, although the two densities show substantial overlap, there is a tendency for BREWED to exhibit a higher vowel quality. It is also interesting to note that the area corresponding to the long vowel in the second panel of Figure 2.3 – 14.50 square standardised units – is smaller than that of the short vowel (18.56). A tentative explanation for this phenomenon could be that the additional time available to reach a (long) vowel target guarantees that the target will be reached more consistently.

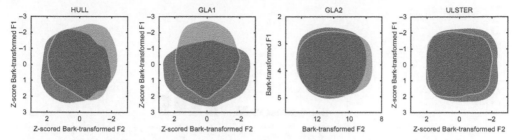

Figure 2.3 Bivariate density estimates showing the spread of the short (dark shape) and long (light grey shape with white contour) vowel for each of the four datasets in the F1–F2 plane after frequencies at vowel temporal midpoint were converted to Bark and z-scored for each speaker and formant separately. The shapes contain 99 per cent of the estimated density. The axes were reversed so the plots read like ordinary vowel spaces zoomed in on the particular region of interest. The GLA2 data was not z-scored owing to the fact that only two vowels were produced by each speaker

The same model was run on the Hull dataset, yielding a correct classification rate of 73 per cent (adjusted generalised $R^2$: 0.30). This time only F2 had a significant effect ($p < 0.001$), with estimated parameters indicating that as F2 increases, so does the likelihood that the vowel is TRAP. This is visible in the first panel of Figure 2.3. Contrary to what was found for GLA1, the areas enclosed within the $p = 0.01$ threshold of the densities do not show important differences (16.59 vs. 16.25 square standardised units for short vs. long).

And again the same model was run on the Ulster dataset, with a correct classification rate of 58 per cent (adjusted generalised $R^2$: 0.08). A mild effect ($p < 0.05$) could be found, with F2 being a poor – though statistically significant – predictor of class membership. A quick inspection of the fourth panel in Figure 2.3 (and the fourth panel in Figure 2.1 showing duration data for Ulster) leads to the conclusion that the DPC studied in this article could not be elicited in the Ulster dataset. These data will therefore not be analysed any further.

For the sake of completeness, logistic classification was also performed with the GLA2 data although the result is not directly comparable with that of the other three datasets on account of the lack of standardisation. The correct classification rate reached 65 per cent (adjusted generalised $R^2$: 0.17). A low, statistically significant effect was found for F2 ($p < 0.05$).

The models for the GLA1 and Hull datasets suggest that formant frequencies can predict, albeit to a small extent, phonological length. These frequencies are therefore potentially available for listeners as secondary cues. However two aspects should be checked. First, it may be that some speakers make a quality distinction while others do not. Second, bearing in mind that small spectral distinctions may simply be favoured by more time to reach an articulatory target, these distinctions may be too small to constitute reliable cues.

As a first step to answering these questions, mean silhouette values in the z-scored

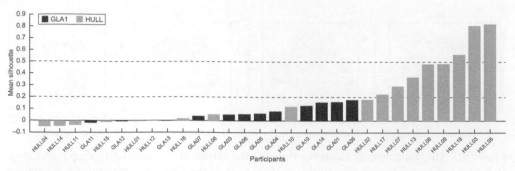

Figure 2.4 Mean silhouette values showing the separability of the long versus short vowel based on the Euclidean distances computed from z-scored Bark-transformed F1 and F2

Bark-transformed F1/F2 space were computed for each speaker in both datasets – note here that all repetitions of an item were included in the computation, not just the mean per items as in the rest of the analysis. A silhouette score measures how similar a vowel token is to tokens in its own class compared to tokens in the other class. The mean silhouette value therefore reflects the quality of a partition, which is used here as an index of separability between short and long vowels based on formants only. As a rule of thumb, mean values below 0.2 denote a lack of class structure while mean values above 0.5 reflect good separability (Everitt et al. 2011). Following these guidelines, Figure 2.4 shows that twenty-two speakers – all twelve speakers from GLA1 and ten of eighteen speakers from Hull – fall below the 0.2 threshold. Three speakers from Hull exhibit mean silhouettes higher than 0.5, which suggests that a consistent and reliable difference in vowel quality exists between TRAP and START for them. Five speakers from Hull have productions lying between these two values. These findings confirm the need to shift the focus from accent groups to individual cases at this stage of the analysis.

The productions of the five speakers from Hull displaying intermediate silhouette values between 0.2 and 0.5 were auditorily inspected. As it turned out, all displayed, at least to the author's ears, an audible – though sometimes very subtle – spectral difference. Oddly enough, speaker HULL17 produced a spectral distinction that was perceptually more salient than the three speakers whose silhouette values lie immediately to his right in Figure 2.4. That is, three speakers with higher acoustic separability between TRAP and START in the F1/F2 dimensions seem to display lower auditory discriminability. It so happens that, contrary to HULL17, these three speakers are women, which points to at least three possible explanations for this discrepancy between silhouette values in Figure 2.4 and the auditory analysis. It may well be that the author's perception is biased towards finer granularity for male voices. Or, the warping of the acoustic space (Bark transform and z-score) may have led to erase more perceptually-relevant information in men than in women. Yet another possibility is that the formant values measured at temporal midpoint fail to capture important spectral information.

Given the variability in mean silhouette values in Figure 2.4, especially in the Hull dataset, it is interesting to ask whether speakers adopt different cue-weighting strategies in production whereby poor separability in the spectral dimension would be compensated by enhanced separability based on duration and vice versa. Such a hypothesis would be supported by a negative correlation between the mean silhouette values in Figure 2.4 and the corresponding mean silhouette values for duration. As it turned out, a low – and non-significant – correlation ($r=0.06$, $p=0.74$) shows no evidence to back this hypothesis. Mean silhouette values for duration range from 0.53 to 0.94, with a mean of 0.82, with no statistical difference between GLA1 and Hull according to an independent-samples t-test ($t_{(28)}=1.2246$, $p=0.23$). All this suggests that all speakers exhibit good to excellent separability between long and short vowels based solely on duration, and even when duration is remarkably robust to convey the contrast, some Hull speakers produce an additional reliable distinction in the spectral dimension.

An additional method to assess whether the small spectral distinction found in some GLA1 speakers could serve as a secondary cue is to verify that this distinction is large enough for the resolving power of the auditory system to detect it. So the mean F1 distance between short and long items was computed for each speaker. Then, a decision rule following estimates of just-noticeable differences (JNDs) by Kewley-Port and Watson (1994) was applied. Their findings suggest that under optimal listening conditions a constant absolute JND of 14 Hz is expected. The mean F1 difference for the twelve GLA1 speakers was 20 Hz, with values ranging from − 12 Hz to 45 Hz. The one single value going in the 'wrong' direction (-12 Hz) – meaning that for this speaker the short vowel had a smaller F1 than the long one – is below the 14 Hz threshold. Out of the remaining eleven speakers, four exhibited differences below threshold, one had a difference of 15 Hz – which probably cannot be used for communication purposes – and the remaining six speakers had differences ranging from 21 Hz to 45 Hz. How many JNDs are necessary to convey reliable spectral information as secondary cue remains an open question; but I suggest that the five speakers who display values above 2 JNDs (GLA01, 04, 06, 08 and 14) produce a distinction that may be accessible to the listener.

Coming back to the potential relevance of information contained in the dynamics of formant trajectories, the scaled DCT coefficients 1 and 2 computed on the Hull dataset were used as predictors in a logistic classifier with vowel length as the response variable. The 52 per cent correct classification score fails to support the potential usefulness of dynamic information. The same analysis run with the GLA1 dataset yields exactly the same classification rate, leading to the same conclusion. That this method correctly characterises formant movements is unquestionable: when used to distinguish between GOOSE-BREWED words and the PRICE words that are available in the GLA1 dataset, the logistic classifier returns 99 per cent correct classification. And when used to distinguish between the members of pairs like 'tide-tied'[3] in the GLA1 dataset, 89 per cent correct classification is achieved. To sum up, formant trajectories do not seem to predict whether the vowel is a short or a long one in either dataset.[4]

*Perceptual Experiment*

In Glasgow, a labelling task involving stimuli varying in duration on a continuum ranging from typical values for 'brood' to values for 'brewed' was run. In Hull, a similar task with stimuli ranging from 'cap' to 'carp' was also carried out. A standard output in such experiments is the well-known S-shaped psychometric function. My own version of the GPH states that the steepness of the slope of such functions is an indicator of the degree of phonemicity associated with the contrast under study. Unfolding the whole reasoning on why this should be the case is beyond the scope of this chapter. However, a few comments are in order.

The slopes of sigmoid identification functions have been routinely used in studies concerned with categorical perception. Steep slopes – and the extent to which they predict peaks in discrimination functions – have been taken as evidence for categorical perception, or, at least, categorical precision (Bogliotti et al. 2008). It should be made clear that this chapter is not about categorical perception in the restricted, strong historical sense. My basic claim is that the processing of speech involves some form of categorisation whereby a given acoustic input is assigned to a phonemic category, and identification functions can be informative regarding the underlying process. More specifically, I assume that good phonemicity can be equated with good categoriality; the latter being in turn equated with good separability. I therefore embrace the view that if two adjacent categories in some perceptual space exhibit little overlap and minimal within-class variance, they should – as predicted by the model in Kronrod et al. (2016) – correlate with sharp identification slopes. And I take a relatively[5] sharp identification slope as evidence that the contrast under study meets the criteria for a high degree of phonemicity. The link between phonemicity and steep identification functions is supported by studies in the acquisition of phonology and related deficits (dyslexia) showing that as phonemic categories are acquired, identification functions become steeper, and that children with dyslexia, who show poor between- and relatively good within-category discrimination, exhibit shallow identification functions (Bogliotti et al. 2008).

*Material and Procedure*

In Glasgow, one occurrence of the word 'brewed' spoken by a male participant was chosen to construct the stimuli. The steady-state portion of the vowel was identified, and it was time compressed or expanded using the PSOLA method in Praat, yielding a set of twelve stimuli whose vowel duration ranged from 40 to 205 ms in 15 ms steps.

In Hull, one occurrence of the word 'carp' spoken by a male participant was selected to generate all the stimuli using the same procedure as in Glasgow, yielding again twelve stimuli with vowel durations ranging from 40 to 205 ms in 15 ms steps.

The twenty participants from Glasgow were the students whose production data is available in the GLA2 dataset. Ten of the eighteen participants from Hull were the speakers whose production was analysed in the previous sections.

In both locations, participants were seated in a quiet room, in front of a computer screen, and wore headsets equipped with TDH-39 earphones and Peltor noise-attenuating cups. The audio stimuli all appeared at the end of the carrier sentence: 'He said the word …'. The experiment was written in Matlab and run as a stand-alone executable; response times were collected but their reliability is doubtful because the technology used is inadequate for accurate timing. Trials were presented in random order, varying from one participant to the next. Each trial was played forty times in Glasgow and twenty times in Hull.[6] After hearing a 150-ms beep followed by 500 ms of silence, the stimulus (carrier sentence and target word) was played. Then the participants were prompted to decide as quickly as possible whether the word they had heard was 'brood' or 'brewed' (in Glasgow) or 'cap' or 'carp' (in Hull), and to press the corresponding key on a computer keyboard.

For each participant, the percentage of words identified as 'brewed' (Glasgow) or 'carp' (Hull) was computed for each of the twelve stimulus levels. Logistic curves were then fitted to individual datasets with the Palamedes Matlab toolbox (Kingdom and Prins 2010). The two parameters reflecting the underlying sensory mechanism we are interested in are the threshold – $\alpha$, corresponding to the duration value where the percentage of 'brewed' (or 'carp') responses reaches 50 per cent – and the slope, $\beta$, which reflects the steepness of the identification function. Individual curves are shown in the first two panels of Figure 2.5. The curves drawn with dashed lines appear – visually at least – to be outliers. The two dashed curves in the first panel have 50 per cent threshold values that do not seem to be consistent with the other curves, while the dashed curves in the second panel exhibit comparatively shallow slopes.[7]

In order to check whether the curves from the two datasets (Hull vs. Glasgow) were statistically different, two independent-samples t-tests were conducted, one with the $\alpha$ values, and the other with the $\beta$ values. The four 'outlying' curves were excluded from this analysis. The test for the $\alpha$ parameters fails to show a significant difference ($t_{(32)}=1.2424$, $p=0.22$). However, $\beta$ values were significantly different between the two groups ($t_{(32)}=2.3792$, $p<0.05$), with Hull exhibiting higher values (mean: 0.1405) than Glasgow (mean: 0.1173). Psychometric functions therefore had

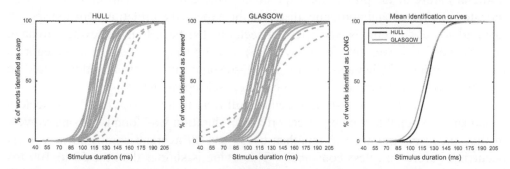

Figure 2.5 Individual identification functions showing the relationship between stimulus duration and the percentage of words identified as 'carp' – in Hull – or 'brewed' – in Glasgow. Mean curves are shown in the third panel

steeper slopes in the Hull data as expected. The mean $\alpha$ values are 122 ms and 119 ms for Hull and Glasgow, which are both very close to the centre of the continuum.

One of the two 'outlying' curves in the Hull experiment shows the performance of a participant whose production is also available: HULL15. According to Figure 2.4, she clearly does not use spectral cues to distinguish TRAP and START. Her mean silhouette value for duration is 0.92, i.e. among the highest. There is unfortunately nothing in her duration data that could let us infer why her threshold value in identification should be slightly higher than the rest of the group. As regards the two participants from Glasgow whose curves exhibit outlying $\beta$ values, nothing in their production seems to predict such values.

## General Discussion

Before turning to the question of potential acoustic or perceptual differences between a typically phonemic contrast and a derived contrast, a number of findings should be briefly reviewed.

Neither vowel duration nor formant values support the possibility that a DPC of the GOOSE VS. BREWED type exists in Enniskillen (Ulster). It must be said that the prior probability that such a contrast existed there was quite low.

Vowel duration exhibits a comparable discriminant power in the Hull – TRAP vs. START – and in the GLA1 and GLA2 – GOOSE VS. BREWED – datasets. When automatic classification was performed with duration as a predictor for length class membership (short vs. long), correct classification rates were all above 90 per cent, suggesting that raw vowel duration is a reliable cue to convey this distinction.

It was found that vowel duration was partially determined by speech rate (Figure 2.2), but only to a small (and sometimes negligible) extent. Closer inspection of Figure 2.2 shows that the assumed ordinary least-squares linear regression model is perhaps unsuitable given a certain amount of heteroscedasticity.[8] The minor size of the effect of speech rate on vowel duration is confirmed by the other analyses performed in connection with Figure 2.2. It is however doubtful that the duration of the carrier sentence should be taken as a good estimate of speech rate. The very artificial nature of the production experiment, where the same carrier sentence was repeated again and again probably distorted the expected correlation between speech rate and vowel duration. Nevertheless, speech rate has been found elsewhere to have an influence on vowel duration (Gay 1978) and the shape of perceptual categories based on duration (Miller and Volaitis 1989), so some sort of normalisation should be used to convert raw durations to a more perceptual representation.

The vowels in the set of stimuli used in Hull were followed by voiced or voiceless consonants. A reliable voicing effect on vowel duration was found, causing vowels in the voiced environment to lengthen by 37 ms on average compared to vowels occurring before voiceless consonants. This value is shorter than the 50 to 100 ms lengthening reported for vowels occurring in phrase-final syllables (Klatt 1976). With hindsight, for maximal comparability with the Glasgow data, the target words in Hull should have all ended in a voiced stop. This is one of the obvious shortcomings that the present study shares with a number of quasi-experimental studies comparing natural languages: confounding factors are not easily avoided. While, of course, the voicing issue could have been controlled better, the phonetic spectral difference between the vowels used in Hull and Glasgow – with perhaps intrinsic peculiarities leading to different behaviours – may constitute a bias here.

An interesting finding emerges from panels two and three in Figure 2.3 and the corresponding analyses: in the GLA1 dataset, where target words are pronounced rather clearly within the same carrier sentences, and where participants probably soon realised that extra care of articulation should be devoted to these targets, a faint difference in F1 occurs. The role of F1 in discriminating between GOOSE and BREWED is then confirmed by logistic regression, and its availability as a secondary cue tends to be supported in the production of five speakers whose F1 difference between GOOSE and BREWED spans at least two JNDs (Kewley-Port and Watson 1994). This difference is absent from the GLA2 dataset, where target words were embedded in a small text and were probably not identified as target words.[9] Previous reports on the GOOSE-BREWED distinction in Scotland – especially in Glasgow (Scobbie et al. 1999; Rathcke and Stuart-Smith 2016) – seem to exclude the possibility that the contrast could rely on vowel quality. The GLA1 dataset in the present study indicates that a lower F1 – which, I tentatively suggest, arises as a by-product of the additional time to reach the articulatory target made possible by the experimental conditions, is accessible as secondary cue signalling vowel length in this hyper-articulated context. But since duration on its own allows excellent separability between the two members of the pair (and is therefore presumably very effective as a perceptual cue), the small spectral distinction is redundant, and no effort is made by the speakers to maintain it in more 'natural' speaking styles. The individual analyses based on mean silhouette values assessing separability in terms of vowel quality (Figure 2.4) show that spectral differences alone are not enough to distinguish GOOSE and BREWED in any of the participants.

Turning to the differences in psychometric curves between Glasgow and Hull, I would like to sketch out a very tentative scenario. Building on the assumption that the shape of these curves reflects the shapes of the underlying mental categories (Kronrod et al. 2016), a better understanding of the mapping between acoustic and cognitive space is essential. This comes down to examining (for example) whether the first two panels in Figure 2.1 could faithfully reflect the way the TRAP-START and GOOSE-BREWED contrasts are stored in the brain, assuming that only duration is relevant. Figure 2.1 and the corresponding analyses show that duration is as good a cue in both cases. The obvious difference between the two datasets lies in the location of the boundary – which is probably due to differences in speech rate, as Figure 2.2 suggests. There is also a notable difference in the variances of these four densities in Figure 2.1: the two duration densities corresponding to HULL have similar shapes whereas those of the GLA1 dataset exhibit dissimilar shapes, with the second one displaying higher variance. A hasty interpretation could be that the steepness of the identification curve in our experiment echoes the steepness of the left tail of the density for the long member of the pair. But this interpretation would miss a number of important aspects; the production data pictured in Figure 2.1 is a very imperfect representation of the storage of phonological categories for the following reasons. First, the auditory and neural mechanisms involved have limited temporal resolution; in other words, the raw duration data must be binned, quantised – or granularised as Pierrehumbert (2001) puts it. A plausible binning algorithm would store tokens whose duration does not differ by more than one just-noticeable difference (JND) in the same bin. If the JND follows a constant Weber ratio,[10] i.e. if the absolute JND increases as stimulus duration increases, it follows that bin width should be larger for higher durations. In other words, vowel duration is very likely (log-) transformed[11] before being stored, in which case the higher variance for the BREWED density in GLA1 in Figure 2.1 could be perceptually irrelevant. If the GLA1 duration data were log-transformed, it would display a much more homogeneous variance across the two densities. Since there is good evidence that the duration of speech sounds is perceived logarithmically, and granted that logarithmic mapping between external stimuli and internal representations is ubiquitous – and probably reflects a strategy shaped by evolution that guarantees optimal storage and error reduction (Varshney and Sun 2013) – it would be good practice to transform durational data (just as we do formant or $F_0$ data) to achieve better perceptual relevance.

Now, the second and probably most misleading aspect of Figure 2.1 is that it ignores a key parameter in statistical models of categorisation, namely, frequency (Nosofsky 1988; Pierrehumbert 2001; Feldman et al. 2009). The area under each curve in Figure 2.1 is normalised to one, giving the illusion that each type of stimulus (TRAP, START, GOOSE and BREWED words) had occurred with the same token frequency. But presumably, the TRAP-START distinction has a greater functional load than GOOSE-BREWED; and perhaps BREWED words are not as frequent as GOOSE words. For the representations in Figure 2.1 to convey these crucial differences and their well-known impact on category learning and categorisation, 'histograms' reflecting actual counts (optionally recency-weighted) – rather than normalised probabilities – should have been plotted, had frequency data been available.

Imagine that the GOOSE category was shaped by a high number of tokens of experience while the BREWED category was fashioned by a relatively small number. The model in Feldman et al. (2009) predicts that this would result in a shift in boundary (the equivalent of the $\alpha$ parameter in our psychometric functions) towards the category with the lowest prior probability. In our imaginary case, the curve would be shifted towards BREWED, so that a larger region of the duration space would contain stimuli identified as GOOSE. No difference in the $\alpha$ parameter was found between Hull and Glasgow participants in the experiment, suggesting that no such imbalance existed.[12] However a difference was found in the slope of the identification curve, i.e. in the $\beta$ parameter of the logistic function. Variation in the steepness of such slopes is predicted, according to the model in Feldman et al. (2009), by within-category variability: categories with high variability result in shallower identification slopes (lower $\beta$). This would be consistent with the highest variability displayed by the BREWED data in Figure 2.1, panel 2; but the conclusion does not hold if duration is expressed as a

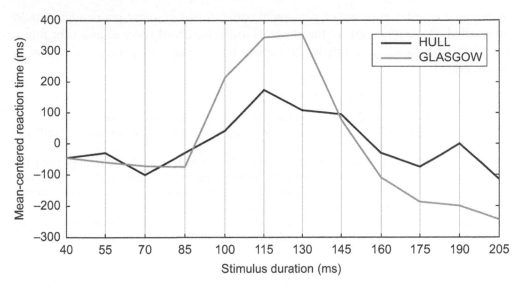

Figure 2.6 Mean reaction times (in ms) for the experiments in Hull (dark line) and Glasgow (grey line) as a function of stimulus duration (in ms). The data were centred to compensate for the potential different intrinsic latencies of the different systems used for the two experiments

logarithm. Mean reaction times for the two experiments – however unreliable they may be – tend to show higher values around category boundary for the Glasgow data (Figure 2.6). This potentially indicates that the participants in Glasgow experienced more difficulty with the three stimuli whose duration ranged from 100 ms to 130 ms, and it points to the possibility that higher reaction times around category boundary correlate with the steepness of identification curves. Incidentally, starting with the 160 ms stimulus, reaction times look much faster for Glasgow than for Hull which is perhaps an indication that even for long stimuli some Hull participants may have 'expected' an additional spectral distinction to make a quicker decision while, in Glasgow, the exclusive role of duration in the contrast generates faster decisions.

**Conclusion**

This study has explored two vowel contrasts conveyed by duration, one of them having full phonemic status (TRAP-START in Hull), the other one being morphologically conditioned, and therefore, not prototypically phonemic in that it is predictable (GOOSE-BREWED in Glasgow). Durational and spectral cues were examined in an exploratory attempt to highlight acoustic differences between the two types of contrasts. A perceptual experiment was run and led to the conclusion that the boundary between TRAP and START is somewhat better defined than that between GOOSE and BREWED. A tentative explanation for this discrepancy is the role of token (and/or type) frequency in shaping mental categories. That phonemicity is a gradient has been amply demonstrated elsewhere (e.g. Hall 2013); the current study modestly sought to examine whether acoustic or perceptual correlates of gradient phonemicity could be isolated. Hopefully some of the elements tested here will serve as bases for future studies, where the obvious missing ingredient here – usage frequency – will have to be integrated.

**Notes**

1. Available for download at https://github.com/emmanuelferragne/CminR-Praatik
2. Lengthening environment refers to words ending with a voiced consonant, i.e. 'cad' and 'card'.
3. This is another well-known derived contrast in Scottish English, stemming from the same process as the contrast studied in the current chapter, but whose realisation involves both duration and vowel quality (Scobbie et al. 1999). Here I only used these data as a benchmark to validate the whole DCT procedure.
4. It should be pointed out that, out of curiosity, all automatic classification tasks in this chapter were systematically tried with the different flavours of discriminant analyses, support vector machines, decision trees, $k$-nearest neighbour (etc.) available in Matlab. None of them outperformed the simple logistic classifier, suggesting that the latter provides a good enough solution for the simple boundaries to be drawn in the parameter spaces studied here.
5. All else being equal: stop consonants – with their sharp categorical effect – should obviously not be compared with vowels.
6. Chronologically, the first experiment took place in Glasgow; it lasted more than fifty minutes, and we realised it was extremely tedious for the participants. So we chose to reduce the number of trials for the Hull experiment.
7. Note that all $\alpha$ and $\beta$ values in each dataset were submitted to a formal test aimed at detecting outliers (an outlier being a value lying more than three scaled median absolute deviations away from the median), and according to this method only one curve – the flatter in the Glasgow dataset – would count as an outlier.
8. This is particularly visible in the BREWED vowels of GLA1 in Figure 2.2: as carrier duration increases, so does the variability in vowel duration.
9. As a matter of fact, an informal survey after the reading task confirmed that the participants had no idea what the linguistic phenomenon of interest was.
10. This seems to be the case according to Rossi (1972): a Weber ratio of 22.5 per cent was found for standard vowel stimuli ranging from 130 to 290 ms. Shorter vowels exhibit a constant absolute JND of about 30 ms.
11. When the GLA1 duration data was log-transformed, the densities were much more similar in shape.
12. Though the experiment probably caused substantial ad hoc reorganisation of the categories.

**References**

Bogliotti, C., W. Serniclaes, S. Messaoud-Galusi and L. Sprenger-Charolles (2008), 'Discrimination of speech sounds by children with dyslexia: comparisons with chronological age and reading level controls', *Journal of Experimental Child Psychology* 101(2), 137–155.

Elvin, J., D. Williams and P. Escudero (2016), 'Dynamic acoustic properties of monophthongs and diphthongs in Western Sydney Australian English', *The Journal of the Acoustical Society of America* 140(1), 576–581.

Everitt, B., S. Landau, M. Leese and D. Stahl (2011), *Cluster Analysis*, Chichester: Wiley.

Feldman, N. H., T. L. Griffiths and J. L. Morgan (2009), The influence of categories on perception: explaining the perceptual magnet effect as optimal statistical inference', *Psychological Review* 116(4), 752–782.

Ferragne, E., and F. Pellegrino (2010), 'Formant frequencies of vowels in 13 accents of the British Isles', *Journal of the International Phonetic Association* 40(01), 1–34.

Ferragne, E., S. Flavier and C. Fressard (2013), 'ROCme! Software for the recording and management of speech corpora', *Interspeech*, Lyon.

Gay, T. (1978), 'Effect of speaking rate on vowel formant movements', *The Journal of the Acoustical Society of America* 63(1), 223–230.

Hall, K. C. (2013), 'A typology of intermediate phonological relationships', *The Linguistic Review* 30(2), 215–275.

Harris, J. (1990), 'Derived phonological contrasts', in S. Ramsaran (ed.), *Studies in the Pronunciation of English: A Commemorative Volume in Honour of A. C. Gimson*, London: Routledge, pp. 87–105.

Kewley-Port, D. and C. S. Watson (1994), 'Formant-frequency discrimination for isolated English vowels', *Journal of the Acoustical Society of America* 95(1), 485–496.

Kingdom, F. A. A. and N. Prins (2010), *Psychophysics: A Practical Introduction*, Amsterdam: Elsevier.

Klatt, D. H. (1976), 'Linguistic uses of segmental duration in English: acoustic and perceptual evidence', *The Journal of the Acoustical Society of America* 59(5), 1208–1221.

Kronrod, Y., E. Coppess and N. H. Feldman (2016), 'A unified account of categorical effects in phonetic perception', *Psychonomic Bulletin & Review* 23(6), 1681–1712.

Miller, J. L. and L. E. Volaitis (1989), 'Effect of speaking rate on the perceptual structure of a phonetic category', *Perception & Psychophysics* 46(6), 505–512.

Nosofsky, R. M. (1988), 'Similarity, frequency, and category representations', *Journal of Experimental Psychology: Learning, Memory, and Cognition* 14(1), 54–65.

Pierrehumbert, J. B. (2001), 'Exemplar dynamics: word frequency, lenition and contrast', in J. L. Bybee and P. J. Hopper (eds), *Typological Studies in Language*, Amsterdam: Benjamins, pp. 137–157.

Rathcke, T. V. and J. H. Stuart-Smith (2016), 'On the tail of the Scottish vowel length rule in Glasgow', *Language and Speech* 59(3), 404–430.

Rossi, M. (1972), 'Le seuil différentiel de durée', in A. Valdman (ed.), *Papers in Linguistics and Phonetics to the Memory of Pierre Delattre*, Berlin: De Gruyter, pp. 435–450.

Scobbie, J. M. and J. Stuart-Smith (2008), 'Quasi-phonemic contrast and the fuzzy inventory: examples from Scottish English', in P. Avery, B. E. Dresher and K. Rice (eds), *Phonology and Phonetics*, Berlin: Mouton, pp. 87–113.

Scobbie, J. M., N. Hewlett and A. Turk (1999), 'Standard English in Edinburgh and Glasgow: the Scottish vowel length rule revealed', in P. Foulkes and G. Docherty (eds), *Urban Voices: Accent Studies in the British Isles*, London: Arnold, pp. 230–245.

Varshney, L. R. and J. Z. Sun (2013), 'Why do we perceive logarithmically?' *Significance* 10(1), 28–31.

Wells, J. C. (1982), *Accents of English. The British Isles*, Cambridge: Cambridge University Press.

Williams, A. and P. Kerswill (1999), 'Dialect levelling: change and continuity in Milton Keynes, Reading and Hull', in P. Foulkes and G. Docherty (eds), *Urban Voices: Accent Studies in the British Isles*, London: Arnold, pp. 141–162.

# 3

# The Phonological Fuzziness of Palatalisation in Contemporary English: A Case of Near-phonemes?

*Olivier Glain*

## Introduction

This chapter builds upon a number of studies that have focused on various processes of palatalisation in several varieties of contemporary English and equated them with changes in progress (for example, Wells 1997, 2008; Harrison 1999; Altendorf 2003; Durian 2004; Hannisdal 2006; Bass 2009; Rutter 2011; Glain 2013). What the various processes have in common is that they all yield palato-alveolars. In addition, these palatalised variants started to become prominent in the second part of the twentieth century and they are mostly associated with younger speakers. Therefore, I have used the label 'contemporary palatalisation' (as opposed to 'historical pala-talisation') as an umbrella term to refer to them collectively. From a phonological point of view, contemporary palatalisation expresses product-oriented, rather than source-oriented generalisations (cf. Bybee 2001: 126) as the various processes under study systematically yield palato-alveolars. After defining contemporary palatalisa-tion and summarising previous research on the topic, this chapter will address the ambiguous question of its linguistic status. Is it phonetic or phonemic? To go beyond the -emic/-etic opposition, I will concentrate on the cognitive status of the resulting palato-alveolar forms, by reporting on two experiments carried out with seventy-eight British and American speakers. In a significant number of cases, the results indicate that the palato-alveolars are more than mere connected speech phenomena and that they seem to have 'some' sort of cognitive reality for the informants. The results lead to a discussion of certain theoretical implications, as well as propositions formulated within the framework of cognitive linguistics: events happening at the interface of phonetics and phonology can account for speakers' gradual reanalyses of previous occurrences of phonemes as different units (cf. Ohala 1989), which fos-silises palatalised forms through time. In addition, an interaction between linguistic and non-linguistic factors of change seems to be necessary for the actuation of the sound change, that is, its diffusion into the community.

## Contemporary Palatalisation: Summary of Previous Work

While some instances of word palatalisation are considered to be standard in a great many varieties of English (for example, 'issue', 'nature'), the status of others, mostly associated with the latter part of the twentieth century and the beginning of the twenty-first century, has been more controversial from a prescriptive point of view. I have labelled such phenomena instances of 'contemporary palatalisation', so as to distinguish them from previous processes in the history of the English language. By contrast, I refer to the latter collectively as 'historical palatalisation'. Contemporary palatalisation occurs in four environments:

1. The (tju, dju) variables: yod coalescence after /t, d/ in stressed syllables (for example, 'tune' ['tʃuːn], 'dune' ['dʒuːn]).[1]
2. The (sju, zju) variables: yod coalescence after /s, z/ in stressed syllables (for example, 'assume' [ə'ʃuːm], 'presume' [prɪ'ʒuːm]).
3. The (stj, str) variables: palatalisation of /stj, str/ clusters and, to a lesser extent, the (st, sk) variables : palatalisation of /st, sk/ clusters (for example, 'student' ['ʃtjuːdənt], 'street' ['ʃtriːt], 'stop' ['ʃtɒp], 'score' ['ʃkɔː]).
4. The (sr) variables: palatalisation of /s/ by /r/ (for example, 'anniversary' [ˌænɪ'vɜːʃ(ə)ri], 'grocery' ['grəʊʃ(ə)ri], 'restaurant' ['reʃt(ə)rɒnt], 'classroom' ['klɑːʃruːm]).

The production of [ʃ, ʒ, tʃ, dʒ] through various processes of palatalisation is a very productive pattern in English. From a diachronic point of view, contemporary palatalisation seems to be the continuation of a historic process whereby palato-alveolar fricatives and affricates have gradually diffused into English. They have repeatedly been created as allophones of pre-existing phonemes. Throughout the history of English, the phonetic innovations thus produced have eventually been fossilised (phonologised). Stévanovitch (2008: 24) describes the following assimilation processes, cases of historical palatalisation:

5. In Old English, [k] → [tʃ] in certain environments (for example, Old English 'Cinn' [k] → Contemporary English 'chin' [tʃ]; Old English 'tæcan' [k] → Contemporary English 'teach' [tʃ]).
6. In Middle English, then Modern English (fifteenth century: rare; sixteenth and seventeenth centuries: more common), [sj] → [ʃ] (for example, 'nation' [nasjõ] → [neɪʃən]; 'sure' [syr] → [sjuːr] → [ʃʊə]).
7. In the seventeenth century [zj] → [ʒ] (for example, 'measure' [məzyr] → [mezjuːr] → [meʒə]).
8. In the seventeenth century [tj] → [tʃ] (for example, 'nature' [natyr] → [naːtjuːr] → [neɪtʃə]; 'fortune' [fortyn] → [fortjuːn] → [fɔːtʃən]).
9. In the seventeenth century [dj] → [dʒ] (for example, 'soldier' [soʊldjər] → [səʊldʒə]).

Wells (1997: 22) notes that yod coalescence ([tj] → [tʃ] and [dj] → [dʒ]) 'widened its scope' in the mid-twentieth century as it spread to new words (for example, 'actual', 'perpetual', 'gradual', 'graduate'). In the second part of the twentieth century, it then reached the (tju, dju, sju, zju) variables in stressed syllables, as in (1) and (2).

On account of certain articles,[2] contemporary palatalisation has perhaps mistakenly been associated with the south-east of England and/or with Estuary English. However, as soon as one starts paying attention to the pronunciation of native speakers from the whole of the English-speaking world, it becomes obvious that it is a much more widespread phenomenon. It has been observed in the British Isles, North America and Southern Hemisphere varieties of English (summary in Glain 2013: 142–149). Of course, palatalised variants do not occur in the first two environments described above in varieties that display /j/ elision.

In order to conduct a study in apparent time for my PhD thesis (Glain 2013), I used Paul Meier's IDEA[3] online public corpus and worked on 531 recordings of English, Scottish, American, Canadian, Australian and New Zealand speakers, comparing age groups. Scripted speech (based on reading) and unscripted speech (based on a more spontaneous kind of interaction) were both studied. The analyses were strictly auditory. However, acoustic measurements were used for the experiment with the text 'Friendship' and the list of words (cf. the section 'The text "Friendship" and the list of words'). The results for Australia and New Zealand are rather inconclusive. However, the British and North American parts of the corpus point to rather clear changes in progress (Glain 2013, 2014). The dichotomy traditional forms/palatalised forms remained a matter of relatively stable variation until the latter part of the twentieth century. Starting with the speakers born after the Second World War, occurrences of palatalisation have become more and more common, decade after decade (in both scripted and unscripted speech). What is more, an acceleration of the change is clearly observable with the speakers born in the late 1960s or the early 1970s, both in Britain and in the USA. This is illustrated in Figure 3.1.

Figure 3.1 is a good example of the results of the IDEA study. It focuses on the percentage of speakers who display variable contemporary palatalisation[4] of the (str) variable. The overall pattern is quite clear and the change gathers momentum with the speakers born in the 1970s. We will see later how the date can be accounted for. In both British and American varieties, high-frequency items are more likely to exhibit palatalisation and to be affected first. This is very much in keeping with Labov's (1994: 543) typology of sound change, whereby consonant changes in place of articulation follow a principle of lexical diffusion (high-frequency items are affected first) and do not fit with the neogrammarian model of regular sound change, which posits that change is phonetically gradual but lexically regular, which means that all words are affected simultaneously.

From a sociolinguistic point of view, the degree of palatalisation is higher for men. Indeed, 84 per cent of British men and 64 per cent of American men display variable contemporary palatalisation. The figures are 74 per cent for British women and 45 per cent for American women. Within Britain, it is higher in Scotland (93

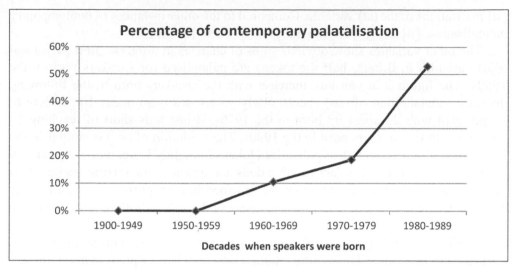

Figure 3.1 Palatalisation of the (str) variable, England and Scotland, unscripted speech.
*Source:* Glain (2013: 313).

per cent of the Scottish informants) than in England (75 per cent). The only place that is virtually 'contemporary palatalisation-free' is the north-east of England, more precisely the geographical area that constituted the heart of the Danelaw. This is the region where the historic influence of the Scandinavians has remained the greatest. It may not be a coincidence, as Scandinavian languages have historically shown resistance to processes of palatalisation, such as the palatalisation of velars described in (5), which did not occur in Old Norse and Scandinavian languages as it did in Old English.

Within the USA, the highest degree of palatalisation is to be found with southern speakers (63 per cent) and speakers of African American Vernacular English (82 per cent). The national average is 53 per cent.

Let us turn to the distribution of contemporary palatalisation.[5]

Palatalisation of (sk) is non-existent in the IDEA corpus. The (st) variable is never palatalised in scripted speech and very rarely in unscripted speech. Out of a total number of 450 occurrences in the recordings based on unscripted speech, /st/ is palatalised only twelve times. The speakers are a Scottish woman born in 1978 in Dundee, a man from Kansas born in the 1930s, a man from Virginia born in the 1940s, a man from Illinois born in 1953, two men from North Carolina born in 1959 and 1960, a man from Oklahoma born in 1972, a man from Ohio born in 1975, a man from Michigan born in 1976, a woman from Kentucky born in 1982, and a man from Texas born in 1990. The items that undergo palatalisation are 'under_stand', 'stick' (twice, same speaker), 'started' (four times, four different speakers), 'still' (twice, two different speakers), 'state', 'festival'. With the possible exception of 'festival', these words are all high-frequency items. None of the eleven speakers who display this kind of palatalisation does it exclusively. They all have more frequent

[st] realisations of the (st) variable. Compared to the other instances of contemporary palatalisation, [ʃt] and [ʃk] remain marginal in the IDEA corpus.

The other variables show obvious signs of changes in progress. In the (tju) and (dju) variables in Britain, half the tokens are palatalised for speakers born in the 1950s. The figure is in constant increase with the speakers born in the following decades. Palatalisation of (str) spectacularly progresses from under 10 per cent to 35 per cent with the speakers born in the 1970s. It just falls short of reaching 50 per cent with the speakers born in the 1980s. The evolution of (str) is similar in the USA, even if the overall rate of palatalised tokens is slightly lower with the youngest speakers (40 per cent). The (sr) variable does not appear in the recordings based on scripted speech. In those based on unscripted speech, it progresses in a similar way and reaches 50 per cent with the speakers born in the 1980s, both in Britain and the USA. However, the number of tokens is too limited and this can be no more than a mere indication of its gradual diffusion in apparent time. The (sju) and (zju) variables are too rare in the IDEA corpus (both scripted and unscripted) to allow for any kinds of conclusions.

**Phonemic or Phonetic?**

The phonetic grounding of all cases of contemporary palatalisation is quite clear:

(1) is a type of assimilation where the approximant [j] fuses, or coalesces, with preceding [t, d], resulting in affricates [tʃ, dʒ]; the [j] is the assimilator.
In (2), the assimilator is [j], which retracts the articulation of both [s] and [z], resulting in coalesced forms [ʃ, ʒ].
(3): in (str), the [r] retracts the articulation of the alveolar fricative and makes it palato-alveolar; in (stj), [j] is the assimilator that triggers the retraction to [ʃ].[6]
In (4), the [r] triggers the assimilation process by retracting the articulation of [s] to [ʃ].

Given that instances of contemporary palatalisation originate in connected speech phenomena, a few theoretical questions arise when 'true' palato-alveolars, that can be categorically measured as such, are produced. Are they still mere surface phenomena? If not, to what extent can we say that those palato-alveolars are part of the speakers' phonological representations?

Let us consider what characterises deep processes versus surface processes, as described in such different works as Giegerich (1992: 218) and Montreuil (2001: 120–121). In summary, deep processes affect the words in isolation, they are opaque, have exceptions and are morphologically conditioned. On the other hand, surface processes also affect the word in the sentence, they are transparent and might vary for different accents and/or speakers.

Similar processes of palatalisation may occur within words (for example, 'assume' and 'strong' with [ʃ]) or across word boundaries (for example, 'I miss you' with [ʃ] between 'miss' and 'you'; 'this train' with [ʃ] between 'this' and 'train'), which seems to indicate that contemporary palatalisation has no underlying reality. However, instances of contemporary palatalisation being frequency-driven variants, they have – by definition – exceptions, which appears to tip the scales in favour of an underlying/phonemic status. As regards opacity, 'a phonological process is said to be opaque if its original phonetic grounding is no longer apparent' (Carr 2008: 115). This is not really the case for the processes at stake in contemporary palatalisation, as they are phonetically grounded in the tendency towards ease of articulation that is typical of assimilations. However, it is worth noting that most palatalisation processes that have led to the production of palato-alveolars in the history of English (particularly (5), (6), (7), (8), opacity not being so obvious for (9)), have become opaque to the vast majority of laypeople. Could this be happening with contemporary processes? Contemporary palatalisation is undoubtedly morphologically conditioned, as it manifests itself exactly in the same way in morphologically related items such as 'tune' and 'tuneless'. This short analysis reveals that contemporary palatalisation is ambiguous, as it shares features with both surface and deep processes.

From a theoretical point of view, categorical palato-alveolars would be classified as phonemes by structuralists, as /ʃ, ʒ, tʃ, dʒ/ belong to the phonemic inventory of English and as no phoneme can be derived from another phoneme in traditional phonology. In addition, a certain degree of assimilation is clearly regarded as allophonic in structural phonology. Therefore, the production of a palatal fricative like [ç] (or of any other allophones) in a word like 'tune', for instance, would be considered as allophonic within that framework. In generative phonology, the conclusions are polar opposites. Generativists tend to regard [ʃ, ʒ, tʃ, dʒ] in (1), (2), (3), (4) as surface forms of underlying /tj, dj, sj, zj, s/.

In his typology of assimilation, Pavlík (2009) makes a difference between phonological and phonetic assimilations. He explains that phonological assimilations are mentally planned before articulation:

> [Phonological assimilations are] based on the assumption that there is a look-ahead mechanism which causes all segments unspecified for a particular feature to have that feature spread from some later (or earlier) segment [...] On the other hand, coarticulations are often seen as coproduction, which means that sounds (elements) or individual articulatory gestures are coproduced naturally, and no look-ahead mechanism is necessary. Put differently, the changes in the properties of sounds in connected speech are due to low-level, non-phonological, biomechanical interaction of articulators. (Pavlík 2009: 3)

In other words, phonological assimilations are more than coarticulations. They are what Ohala (1993: 167) calls 'fossilised coarticulations', which points to an interface between phonetics and phonology. It is usually considered that the relationship between two sounds is either contrastive or allophonic. However, some linguists have expressed scepticism about the strictly categorical opposition between phonemic and allophonic. A number of studies (for example, Scobbie and Stuart-Smith 2008; Currie-Hall 2009; Ferragne et al. 2011) have shown that there can be intermediate phonological relationships between two phones. Currie-Hall remarks that 'intermediate relationships abound', that they 'change over time', and that 'frequency affects phonological processing, change and acquisition' (Currie-Hall 2009: 25). She agrees with Bybee (2001) and Shockey (2003) that high-frequency items often undergo some sort of reduction, a principle which contemporary palatalisation is in keeping with. Let us therefore try to go beyond the categorical opposition phonemic *vs.* allophonic with two experiments aimed at finding out what sort of cognitive reality contemporary palatalisation might have for individual speakers.

## The Cognitive Status of Palatalisation

### *The Text 'Friendship' and the List of Words*

In a preliminary experiment of a cognitive nature (detailed in Glain 2013: 320–336), fifteen English and fifteen American informants[7] were asked to read a text that contained a number of potential examples of contemporary palatalisation. Then they had to read a list of words very slowly, syllable by syllable. Some words could be found both in the text and in the list. The point of the experiment was to try and determine the cognitive status of the palato-alveolars when such palatalised variants were effectively produced. The text, entitled 'Friendship', was specifically produced for the experiment. It is reproduced below.

The text

Friendship

Christian **Stoddart** and his friend **Stuart** were big fans of **Steven** Spielberg's. On Sundays, they usually went to the **grocery** store, bought some food and rented a DVD. The local groceries were fantastic and they never got tired of watching movies by their favourite director.
'This is the best you can have in life,' **Steward** often said to his friend.

Christian eventually fell in love with a young **student** named Cathy and they moved into a small **studio** together, not too far from **Stuart's** apartment. It only took **Stuart** 15 minutes to get there by **tube** when there was no queue at the ticket office.
**Stuart** somehow **assumed** that he and Christian would **still** be best friends. He thought they would **resume** their habits once novelty had worn off. But Christian's attitude wasn't what it once used to be.

'God! Sexual hormones can really mess up your brain,' **Stuart** complained to his father, a former soldier to whom the very mention of sex was controversial.
'I **presume** you expect me to agree with you,' the **strong** soldier casually remarked.
'I'll be off now. I'm **due** at the barracks at four to celebrate the Jones's 40th **anniversary**.'
He put on a fleece jacket and left his son alone.

'The old fart pictures himself fighting in the desert again, with **dunes** all around him. He's lost it.' **Stuart** thought to himself. 'Nothing new but I won't **endure** this any more. Who does he think he is? My teacher? This house feels like a **classroom**, or **worse**, a **nursery**.'
He decided to **reduce** the number of weekly visits to his father's.

**Stuart** now felt **miserable**. He decided to go and see <u>Christian</u> and his **student** of a girlfriend.
'The whole thing **stinks**. But I'm an <u>educated</u> person and we'll just have a **straight-forward**, <u>factual</u> conversation.'
He left his father's apartment and went **straight** to <u>Christian's</u>, singing an old **tune** to himself as he walked up the main **street**. '**Presumably**, they'll be very happy to see me,' he thought **during** the twenty-minute walk.
<u>Actually</u>, <u>Christian</u> was angry to be disturbed while wearing a **Superman** <u>costume</u>, barely holding with **straps**, and he nearly had a <u>seizure</u>.
'You look fantastic … **super**,' **Stuart** said emphatically. 'Has your girlfriend talked you into this?'
'What do you want?' <u>Christian</u> curtly asked.
'In <u>case you</u>'ve forgotten, I'm your friend. That's why I came.'
'Will you just leave me alone?'
'Is that <u>what you</u> want? <u>Do you</u> want me to just walk out of your life?'
'That's what I'm saying, yeah. <u>Immediately</u>, please. This is getting <u>tedious</u>. Thank you.'
'I'm leaving.'

**Steward** picked up a toy arm that lay discarded on the floor and handed it to <u>Christian</u>. This was not to be <u>negotiated</u>. **Stuart** walked out and went **straight** to the <u>gymnasium</u>, sighing all the way. Dreaming was all he had left now. As he was working out, he decided he would like to go on a <u>Parisian</u> holiday – or better – an <u>Indian</u> or <u>Indonesian</u> holiday. Everything would work out just fine.

The potential instances of contemporary palatalisation of the text are in bold in the extract above. They display the following patterns:

- palatalisation of (stj): 'Stuart', 'student', 'studio' for speakers who do not exhibit yod dropping;
- palatalisation of (sr): 'grocery', 'groceries', 'anniversary', 'classroom', 'nursery', 'miserable';
- yod coalescence in (tju, dju) in stressed position: 'tube', 'due', 'dunes', 'endure', 'reduce', 'tune', 'during'; and also 'student', 'Stuart', 'studio' for speakers who exhibit yod dropping;
- yod coalescence in (sju, zju) in stressed position: 'assumed', 'resume', 'presume', 'presumably', 'Superman', 'super' for speakers who do not exhibit yod dropping;

- palatalisation of (str): 'strong', 'straightforward', 'straight' (two occurrences), 'street', 'straps'.

The words underlined in the text above are indicative of possible palatalisation of a non-contemporary type, both within words and across word boundaries. They were selected to determine how effective realisations of palatalised variants in such environments correlated with the speaker's attitude towards contemporary palatalisation. For instance, it was assumed that a speaker who would not have a palatalised variant in (tju) in unstressed position (for example, in 'atti<u>tu</u>de') would be very unlikely to palatalise stressed occurrences of the same variable (for example, 'tune'), given that palatalisation historically reached unstressed syllables first. However, the analysis of the pronunciation of these words did not prove conclusive in relation to contemporary palatalisation. Therefore, the result tables below only focus on contemporary palatalisation within words, not on other instances of palatalisation, and not on palatalisation across word boundaries.

When the specific nature of the variants produced was challenging to identify with an auditory analysis, I relied on spectrograms to categorise the data. For example, it was sometimes difficult to judge whether the variant was an intermediate allophonic form (such as an intermediate realisation between [s] and [ʃ]) or a true palato-alveolar. Durian (2007: 70) explains that clusters that display a high concentration of spectral energy at or below 2500 Hz can be coded as [ʃtr] (with a categorical palato-alveolar). By contrast, [str] clusters have a concentration of energy at or above 4000 Hz, while clusters with energy between 3000 and 3500 Hz can be considered intermediate forms. The following spectrogram[8] of the word 'grocery' as read by a young American male shows the typical strong amplitude of [ʃ], which is circled. Intermediate realisations have not been counted as instances of contemporary palatalisation in the figures given below.

Unsurprisingly, not a single informant palatalises the items 'Superman' and

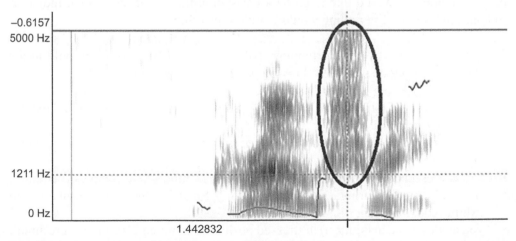

Figure 3.2 Spectrogram of 'grocery' [ˈɡroʊʃri]

Table 3.1 Effective contemporary palatalisation, English speakers, text

|                   | (stj) % | (sr) % | (tju, dju) % | (sju, zju) % | (str) % |
|-------------------|---------|--------|--------------|--------------|---------|
| No. 1             | 21.4    | 0      | 42.9         | 0            | 33.3    |
| No. 2             | 0       | 33.3   | 57.1         | 0            | 10      |
| No. 3             | 0       | 16.7   | 57.1         | 25           | 0       |
| No. 4             | 85.7    | 33.3   | 42.9         | 0            | 16.7    |
| No. 5             | 78.6    | 16.7   | 71.4         | 0            | 16.7    |
| No. 6             | 55.6    | 8.3    | 0            | 50           | 16.7    |
| No. 7             | 7.1     | 0      | 57.1         | 0            | 0       |
| No. 8             | 35.7    | 33.3   | 25.6         | 100          | 0       |
| No. 9             | 7.1     | 33.3   | 42.8         | 75           | 0       |
| No. 10            | 0       | 0      | 28.6         | 0            | 0       |
| No. 11            | 7.1     | 16.7   | 57.1         | 75           | 0       |
| No. 12            | 14.3    | 16.7   | 57.1         | 100          | 16.7    |
| No. 13            | 64.3    | 83.3   | 42.9         | 100          | 66.7    |
| No. 14            | 0       | 0      | 42.9         | 0            | 0       |
| No. 15            | 0       | 0      | 42.9         | 25           | 0       |
| **Speakers' average** | **25.1%** | **19.4%** | **44.6%** | **36.7%** | **11.8%** |

*Note:* The figures indicate the percentage of palatalised forms in relation to traditional ones for a given variable.

'super'. Yod elision is virtually universal in these words for the age group under study. It has even prevailed in careful Received Pronunciation (Hannisdal 2006: 211). This is the reason why the items 'super' and 'Superman' have finally not been included in the results given in Table 3.1 and Table 3.2. Neither have the items corresponding to the (st) variable, which is never palatalised by our informants. Apart from speaker 22, an American woman born in 1969 and the second oldest of our speakers, all the informants exhibit at least some degree of contemporary palatalisation. Such was not the case with the speakers of the IDEA corpus, a greater percentage of whom displayed zero contemporary palatalisation. A logical explanation is that the IDEA corpus has informants of all ages and that its average speaker is much older. Of course, Americans do not palatalise in (tju, dju, sju, zju) because of almost systematic yod elision in these environments. This is the reason why these variables have been removed from Table 3.2.

If we consider the distribution of palatalised variants, yod coalescence in (tju, dju) in stressed position is the most common instance of contemporary palatalisation for English speakers (approximately 45 per cent of palatalised forms). It is followed by (sju, zju) in stressed position (approximately 37 per cent), (stj) (approximately 25 per cent), (sr) (approximately 19 per cent) and (str) (approximately 12 per cent). In the latest edition of the *Longman Pronunciation Dictionary* (2008), Wells writes that 'assume' is palatalised by 5 per cent and 'presume' by 8 per cent of British English speakers (Wells 2008: 50, 638). This experiment indicates that palatalisation of (sju,

Table 3.2 Effective contemporary palatalisation, American speakers, text

|  | (sr) % | (str) % |
|---|---|---|
| No. 16 | 33.3 | 0 |
| No. 17 | 14.3 | 0 |
| No. 18 | 0 | 50 |
| No. 19 | 14.3 | 100 |
| No. 20 | 33.3 | 0 |
| No. 21 | 33.3 | 0 |
| No. 22 | 0 | 0 |
| No. 23 | 33.3 | 33.3 |
| No. 24 | 33.3 | 20 |
| No. 25 | 14.3 | 50 |
| No. 26 | 33.3 | 0 |
| No. 27 | 33.3 | 0 |
| No. 28 | 33.3 | 33.3 |
| No. 29 | 33.3 | 0 |
| No. 30 | 33.3 | 0 |
| **Speakers' average** | **25.1%** | **19.1%** |

*Note:* The figures indicate the percentage of palatalised forms in relation to traditional ones for a given variable.

zju) in stressed position is in fact much more common. Three speakers from different regions of England, all born in the 1990s, even display a 100 per cent palatalisation rate in (sju, zju) tokens.

In the USA, palatalisation of (sr) is the most common instance of contemporary palatalisation (approximately 25 per cent of palatalised forms). It is followed by (str) (approximately 19 per cent). One speaker, a young man born in San Francisco in 1996, palatalised 100 per cent of (str) tokens.

The item 'grocery' is palatalised by a minority of English speakers (13 out of 15 use a traditional variant in 'grocery store' and 'groceries'). On the other hand, it is the item most commonly palatalised by Americans (12 out of 15 use a palatalised variant). This seems to confirm Glain's supposition (2013) that the change to /ʃ/ is nearing completion in American English for that word. The exact opposite logic applies to the word 'miserable', which is palatalised by nine English speakers, but only one American.

The following remarks allow us to convey a more complete picture of contemporary palatalisation. Speakers 1, 4, 5, 6, 8 and 13 tend to display palatalisation of /stj/ clusters in 'Stuart' and 'student'. When they do, the initial /s/ is palatalised into [ʃ] but the yod remains a glide and does not become homorganic with the palato-alveolar created. This triggers ['ʃtjuːət, 'ʃtjuːdənt]. These speakers do not combine /s/ and /j/ palatalisation (['ʃtʃuːət, 'ʃtʃuːdənt]).

Apart from the three speakers who always palatalise (sju, zju) and the speaker who does the same with (str), palato-alveolar realisations of each variable are not systematic. They depend on how frequent the word or morpheme is used, as is the case with the IDEA corpus.

The wordlist

The informants were explicitly asked to read the words slowly, syllable by syllable. Here is the wordlist that was used:

| | |
|---|---|
| tube | (tju) in stressed position |
| astute | (tju) in stressed position |
| actual | |
| nature | |
| constitute | |
| prostitute | |
| dune | (dju) in stressed position |
| reduce | (dju) in stressed position |
| assume | (sju) in stressed position |
| presume | (zju) in stressed position |
| resume | (zju) in stressed position |
| student | (tju) in stressed position and (stj) or (st) for speakers who exhibit /j/ elision |
| street | (str) |
| stop | (st) |
| start | (st) |
| Australia | (str) |
| anniversary | (sr) |
| grocery | (sr) |
| classroom | (sr) |
| force | |
| pew | |
| huge | |
| secure | |
| peculiar | |

As was the case with the 'Friendship' text, the words that display no potential contemporary palatalisation were meant to help us compare the attitude of speakers in front of different other types of palatalisation. Unfortunately, it did not prove useful and it failed to form the basis of generalisations of a correlative type.

Some informants used palato-alveolars when they read the text, but not the list of words, which fits with speakers' usual behaviour with connected speech phenomena. Other speakers palatalised the same items both in the text and in the list of words. This seems to be an indication that, for those particular informants, the palato-alveolars might be more than mere coarticulations. The forms thus produced were undoubtedly close to the speakers' citation forms of these items. There might indeed be some sort of mental 'look-ahead mechanism' (Pavlík 2009: 3) at work. The informants' speech being slower and less variable when the words were read syllable by syllable, it was more likely to bring the speakers' true underlying representations to the fore. More surprisingly, other speakers occasionally palatalised an item when they read it syllabically, but not when it was part of the text. It does not seem absurd to suggest that the apparent variation in the citation forms of the items reflects in fact different cognitive realities within the group considered. The informants were almost all unaware that they exhibited palatalisation when asked about it (in a non-technical way) once the recordings had been made. Some were not even aware of the possible variation that characterises the words they read. This seems to be an indication that the processes have become opaque to some speakers. There appear to be 'variable phonological representations' of the items considered.

*The American Questionnaire*

The second experiment specifically targeted young American speakers. It relied on a questionnaire that was given to twenty-four Texas university students[9] and twenty-four Michigan middle-school students,[10] in two very distant regions of the USA. The questionnaire is reproduced below. Yod elision being the norm in US English, the questions concerning the (tju, dju, sju, zju) variables have not been reproduced below (the questionnaire is also meant to be administered to speakers of other varieties).

The questionnaire

**NAME (optional)**          **AGE:**          **SEX:**
**Place of birth:**

This is a short questionnaire that I'm using in order to carry out research in linguistics at the University of Saint-Étienne (France).
The results can be sent to Olivier Glain at the following address: olivierglain@univ-st-etienne.fr
You may also use that address if you have any questions.
Thank you very much for your help if you decide to fill in this questionnaire.

Please don't ask anyone what they think the answer should be. I'm only interested in what *you* think.

Question: what sound(s) do you personally associate with the following letters? (The letters that are in bold and that are underlined.)
Please underline or highlight your answer.

| | | |
|---|---|---|
| street | a/ the first sound in sore | b/ the first sound in Sean or shore |
| strong | a/ the first sound in sore | b/ the first sound in Sean or shore |

Australia     a/ the first sound in sore    b/ the first sound in Sean or shore
anniversary    a/ the first sound in sore    b/ the first sound in Sean or shore
grocery      a/ the first sound in sore    b/ the first sound in Sean or shore
nursery      a/ the first sound in sore    b/ the first sound in Sean or shore
classroom    a/ the first sound in sore    b/ the first sound in Sean or shore
restaurant    a/ the first sound in sore    b/ the first sound in Sean or shore

Thank you.

Because the attention of the informants was drawn to the written forms of the items, they could only be influenced by the spelling. These written forms point to traditional, non-palatalised variants (all things being equal, it makes more sense to associate a graphic <s> to /s/ rather than /ʃ/). Consequently, all the answers indicating palatalisation ('Sean or shore') must certainly be particularly relevant of the cognitive status of the palato-alveolars for the informants. Here are the results. The figures indicate the number of speakers who have opted for one or the other of the answers.

Students of the Van Hoosen Middle School in Rochester, MI

(str) variable
- street       a/ the first sound in sore: 14   b/ the first sound in Sean or shore: 10
- strong      a/ the first sound in sore: 13   b/ the first sound in Sean or shore: 11
- Australia    a/ the first sound in sore: 12   b/ the first sound in Sean or shore: 12

(sr) variable
- anniversary a/ the first sound in sore: 23   b/ the first sound in Sean or shore: 1
- grocery     a/ the first sound in sore: 4    b/ the first sound in Sean or shore: 20
- nursery     a/ the first sound in sore: 21   b/ the first sound in Sean or shore: 3
- classroom   a/ the first sound in sore: 24   b/ the first sound in Sean or shore: 0
- restaurant   a/ the first sound in sore: 11   b/ the first sound in Sean or shore: 13

Students of The University of Houston Clear Lake, TX
(str) variable

- street       a/ the first sound in sore: 17   b/ the first sound in Sean or shore: 7
- strong      a/ the first sound in sore: 18   b/ the first sound in Sean or shore: 6
- Australia    a/ the first sound in sore: 14   b/ the first sound in Sean or shore: 10

(sr) variable
- anniversary a/ the first sound in sore: 17   b/ the first sound in Sean or shore: 7
- grocery     a/ the first sound in sore: 5    b/ the first sound in Sean or shore: 19
- nursery     a/ the first sound in sore: 15   b/ the first sound in Sean or shore: 9
- classroom   a/ the first sound in sore: 21   b/ the first sound in Sean or shore: 3
- restaurant   a/ the first sound in sore: 16   b/ the first sound in Sean or shore: 8

Particularly striking is the fact that nearly half the Rochester students associate a palato-alveolar with the words of the (str) variable. The (sr) variable seems to be more lexically conditioned, 'grocery' being the word most often associated with a palatalised variant. This confirms the hypothesis that /ˈgroʊʃgri/ is becoming the norm in American English. Among the Michigan students, the rate of palatalisation is particularly high when the word 'restaurant' is concerned. As was the case with the first experiment, it does not seem far-fetched to posit that the palato-alveolars of some lexical words have a cognitive, underlying reality for the speakers who associate them with 'the first sound in "Sean" or "shore"'.

## Theoretical Implications: A Cognitive Framework

### Recategorisation of Occurrences of Phonemes

Of course, there is always considerable variation in phonetic realisations from one speaker to the next *and* for the same speaker. If we take into account the dispersion areas of phonemes and the coarticulatory nature of speech, it becomes obvious that contemporary palatalisation operates at the interface of phonetics and phonology. Daniel Jones's traditional definition of the phoneme was that of 'a family of related sounds' (Jones 1956: 172). A more recent definition is given by Valimaa-Blum, who works within the framework of cognitive linguistics. She argues that 'the phoneme is a prototype-centred, gradient class of phonetically similar sounds which all serve the same distinctive function' (Valimaa-Blum 2005: 57). Her definition is very useful as it allows us to reconcile the psychological and the functional views of the phoneme. Smith (2007: 19) also draws on Jones's image of the sound family and he gives it a cognitive orientation. The related sounds that constitute the phoneme are organised around a prototypical value, which can vary from one speaker to another, as illustrated in Figure 3.3.

Contemporary palatalisation operates as shown in Figure 3.4, at the interface of phonetics and phonology.

Certain realisations of phoneme A for speaker A overlap certain realisations of phoneme B for speaker B. Usually, variation in the signal is normalised through parsing. However, the signal may sometimes be misparsed. This is one of the main causes of sound change according to Ohala, who has long argued for an interface between phonetics and phonology. In that case, listeners may 'fail to recognise the variation as totally predictable from context, incorporate it into their own mental lexicon, and base their own pronunciation on the new norm' (Ohala 1993: 163). As a result, certain occurrences of phoneme B can be recategorised as phoneme A for speaker A. According to Ohala, 'many sound patterns in languages are cases of fossilised coarticulation' (Ohala 1993: 155). In other words, synchronic or phonetic contextual variation can lead to diachronic change. Blevins's model (2004) of Evolutionary Phonology is also based upon the phonetic variation inherent to language and the listening errors that continuous speech implies. Both theories link diachrony and synchrony, as they do phonetics and phonology, insofar as phonetic innovations are

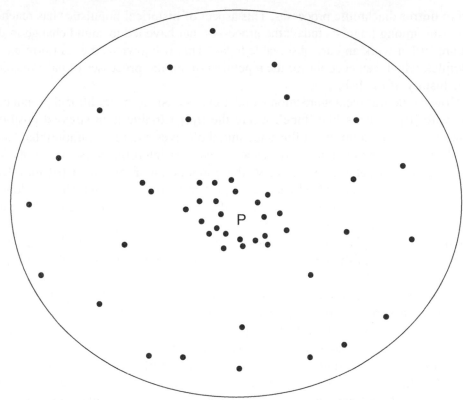

Figure 3.3 A family of sounds (. = actual realisations, P = prototypical realisation)
*Source:* Smith (2007: 20).

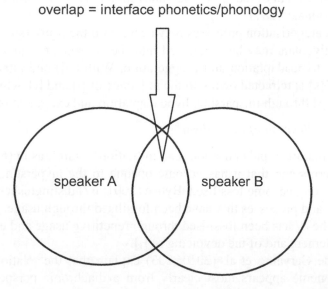

Figure 3.4 Overlap of the realisations of two different phonemes for two different speakers

seen to mirror diachronic processes. This aspect of historical linguistics has reached consensus among linguists today: the processes that have led to sound change in the past are still at work and are observable today. This is known as the 'uniformitarian principle', which can account for the repetition of similar processes of palatalisation in the history of English.

How would this recategorisation work? Let us consider the traditional pronunciations with [tj] of items like 'tune', where the (tju) variable is in stressed position. Owing to the affrication that follows the initial plosives and the aspiration that leads to a delay in the phonation of [j], listeners may misinterpret the sequence as /tʃ/, following several parsing errors. First, the phonetic environment of [tj] may lead to the production of the palatal fricative [ç] (as in German *ich*), which is no longer phonemic in English today but which is often phonetically produced and is very close to a devoiced [j] (Ashby 2005: 35). Then, the palatal [ç] can be perceived as the palato-alveolar [ʃ] as the two phones are phonetically and acoustically very close. The reason why English-speaking listeners are likely to perceive [ʃ] is that /ʃ/ is part of the phonological system of contemporary English, while [ç] is not. They would then analyse [ç] as phonological /ʃ/. Finally, when listeners become speakers, [ç] is exaggerated and produced as [ʃ], exaggeration being typical of misparsing (Ohala 1993). The presence of the affricate /tʃ/ in the consonant system of English may further prompt the production of [tʃ]. This is perfectly in keeping with Ohala's and Lindblom's model of sound change known as the H&H theory (Lindblom 1986, 1990). It relies on the listener's hypoadaptation and hyperadaption[11] to the speech signal. When hypoadaptation occurs, listeners may underarticulate to reproduce sounds that they have not properly perceived and thus 'miss the target' (Smith 2007: 18). This way, the realisation of a phoneme based on coarticulation may be perceived as an innovative variant of that unit. That innovation may well be generalised to other environments (Ohala 1981).

Similar recategorisation processes may occur with the (dju), (sju) and (zju) variables: palato-alveolars may be introduced into the consonant sequences as a result of misparsing, hypoadaptation and exaggeration. With (stj) and (str) variables, the articulation of [s] is retracted owing to the influence of [j] and [r], which leads to the production of [ʃ] through misparsing, hypoadaptation and exaggeration.

## Diachronic Fossilisation of Palatalisation

It is clear that historical palatalisation (e.g. in 'nation', 'sure', as in (6)) is clear only in historical terms and that it has become opaque to the layperson, as the palato-alveolars have long become fossilised. Bybee (2001: 67) distinguishes between variable processes and processes that have been fossilised through usage. In an item like 'confession', the /ʃ/ has been fossilised through repetitive usage and exaggeration of the fricative element and of the devoicing of [j].

Brandão de Carvalho et al. (2010: 233) explain that the relationship between word and phoneme appears most clearly from a diachronic perspective, through phonologisation/fossilisation. Let us consider the evolution of the following instance of yod coalescence in words like 'nature', as in (8), from phonetic into phonological and compare it with the palato-alveolar in words like *chance*.

| Phonemes | surface realisations |
|---|---|
| a. /tʃ/ (for example, 'chance') | [tʃ] |
| b. /t + j/ (for example, 'nature') | [tʃ] or [tj] |
| c. /t + j/ (for example, 'tuberculosis') | [tj] |

First, the allophonic variation certainly had no incidence on the speakers' phonological representations. Little by little, as the memory of realisations with [j] faded, even in conservative usage, the kind of surface [tʃ] that came from the palatalisation of /tj/ came to be identified with underlying /tʃ/ of items like 'chance'. As a result, an ever-increasing number of speakers analysed 'nature' with phonological /tʃ/. That phonological analysis became the norm and, eventually, the only relevant one. There was gradual fossilisation of [tj] into /tʃ/, except in low-frequency, sophisticated or 'technical' morphemes/words like 'tuberculosis' (Glain 2013: 267–279). According to the uniformitarian principle, it is more than likely that instances of palatalisation in the history of English (for example, (1), (2), (3), (4), (5), (6), (7), (9)) developed in the exact same way, with fossilisation of palatalised forms operating gradually at the level of morphemes. For a given morpheme, if the palatalised form eventually took over, the traditional form gradually became a relic of history as the process became opaque. Following the same principle, this may well be true of contemporary palatalisation. Therefore, I posit that similar processes of phonological reanalyses are under way today in the (tju), (dju), (sju) and (zju) variables in common morphemes, as lexical frequency implies that high-frequency morphemes are affected first. The same logic applies to (str) and (sr). The retracted [s] is reanalysed as the categorical palato-alveolar of words like 'shore'. The loss of the phonetic environment is that of /r/, which triggers s-retraction. This is in keeping with Bybee (2001: 56), who explains that there is a strong historical tendency for phonetically-conditioned variants to become contrastive and morphologically conditioned.

It follows from these theoretical considerations that the cognitive status of instances of contemporary palatalisation may be variable. Out of all the speakers who palatalise, some speakers have traditional, non-palatalised forms in their phonological representations, even if they sometimes produce surface palatalised forms. Other speakers have phonological representations with palatalised forms. The more common the item, the more likely it is to be stored with a categorical palato-alveolar by a great number of people, if we adopt a two-level model of phonology. Therefore, the consonant subsystem of speaker A may vary from that of speaker B, as follows:

SA (subsystem of speaker A)
/tʃ/     'chance', 'actually', 'fortune'
/dʒ/     'June', 'duality', 'durability'
/tj/     'tune', 'tutor'

/dj/     'dune', 'reduce'
/s/      'sore', 'cycle', 'super', 'street', 'strong', 'grocery', 'restaurant'
/ʃ/      'shore', 'shop', 'shoe', 'shirt'

SB (subsystem of speaker B)
/tʃ/    'chance', 'actually', 'fortune', 'tune', 'tutor'
/dʒ/   'June', 'duality', 'durability', 'dune', 'reduce'
/s/     'sore', 'cycle', 'super'
/ʃ/     'shore', 'shop', 'shoe', 'shirt', 'street', 'strong', 'grocery', 'restaurant'

As time passes, more and more speakers may shift under the influence of subsystems like SB. Whether the change to subsystems like SB will generalise to the entire community, as was the case with historical palatalisation, or whether it will remain at an intermediate stage (or even revert back to more subsystems such as SA) is still unclear at this stage.

*An Interaction of Non-linguistic and Linguistic Factors*

Smith's model (2007) draws on the theories of change based on the coarticulatory nature of speech (cf. section 'Phonemic or phonetic?' above). At the same time, Smith includes the social dimension of change in his cognitive model of sound change. Within a cognitive framework, there is no clear-cut boundary between the mental processes associated with human language and those related to the rest of human experience. The traditional dichotomy between internal and external change is not relevant as cognitivists 'posit an intimate, dialectic relationship between the structure and function of language on the one hand, and non-linguistic skills on the other' (Taylor 1996: ix). It follows that there has to be an interaction between extra- and intra-linguistic factors at a particular time in order for a particular change to occur and then to diffuse into the community (Smith 2007: 10). This raises the question of the actuation of change on a large scale (Weinreich et al. 1968). Why is a given change actuated at a particular time? Why not earlier? Why not later? Smith (2007) argues that the reason why some innovations catch on in the community is often related to social considerations. Early in the twentieth century, Meillet (1926: 17–18) had already argued that social change was the only element that could allow us to account for linguistic change. The evolution may even originate in major historical events or ideological changes (Labov 2010: 44).

    Social changes played a major part in the actuation of the palatalisation-driven changes (6) to (8). The items that were palatalised are borrowings from French that penetrated English following the Norman Conquest of England. However, it is interesting to note that the actual sound changes are dated to the fifteenth, sixteenth and seventeenth centuries, that is, after the period of linguistic domination exercised by the French language. It follows that, if the lexical items under consideration were borrowed as a result of the prestige of French, their pronunciation in contemporary English is due to their assimilation into the phonological system of the natives, once

English had again resumed its position as the more prestigious language in England. It is therefore the result of an interaction between speakers with different phonological systems.

Contemporary palatalisation is associated with the second part of the twentieth century and it gathered speed with the speakers born in the late 1960s/early 1970s. In Britain, the decades following the Second World War were characterised by major social changes. In order to fight pre-war social inequalities, the Labour government implemented social reforms. The 1944 Education Act made secondary education compulsory in England and Wales. In addition, Local Education Authorities had to provide free education to all children aged above eleven (Charlot 1997: 162–164). As a result, the number of universities doubled between 1944 and 1946 and positions of responsibility gradually became open to people from the lower social strata and speakers of non-standard varieties of English. In the following years, media interest in non-standard pronunciations grew. Regional accents appeared on the BBC and have been on the increase in all media ever since, sometimes at the expense of Received Pronunciation, the standard accent. That phenomenon has had tremendous psychological repercussions. Because of a long prescriptive tendency, many speakers experience a lack of linguistic confidence because they believe that the way they speak is inferior to the standard variety. That form of linguistic insecurity started to decline with the increase of exposure of non-standard varieties in the media. The democratisation of British society therefore went hand in hand with a certain linguistic democratisation in Britain, which triggered linguistic changes based on more casual forms. The rise of non-standard instances of contemporary palatalisation must be seen within that context of social change.

What about the USA? Labov et al. (2006: 46) observe that, after the Second World War, Standard American pronunciation shifted away from a sort of international English based on Received Pronunciation. McWhorter (2012: 109–111) notes that the second part of the twentieth century witnessed a gradual shift to a more informal kind of English. The shift was part of a more general change towards questioning the establishment, which culminated in the countercultural movements of the 1960s. By the 1980s, at which point the USA had become more conservative again, American language culture had changed, and 'even orators took pride in sounding like the common man' (McWhorter 2012: 111).

In both the USA and Britain, the 1945–1970 era witnessed a radical change in speaking standards as a result of social and ideological changes. In shifting to a more informal language culture, the period seems to have participated in an overall change favourable to processes of phonetic reductions and of assimilations based on coarticulation and hypoadaptation, such as contemporary palatalisation.

The reason why the change towards palatalised variants became even more prominent with the speakers born in the late 1960s/early 1970s is probably due to a phenomenon called 'incrementation'. Through successive generations, linguistic changes are taken to a higher level of evolution (Labov 1994, 2010). A first generation of speakers born after the Second World War probably started to diffuse palatalised forms into the community. Their children took the change to a higher level of evolution. We see that Smith's cognitive model of change can be applied entirely to contemporary palatalisation.

## Conclusion

The theoretical problem posed by the phonological fuzziness of contemporary palatalisation ceases to be one if we agree on an interface between phonetics and phonology and if we agree to link diachrony and synchrony. Contemporary palatalisation is therefore an example of a synchronic process that is in fact the manifestation of systematic, diachronic ones. Ohala (1994: 375) maintains that the coarticulation of phonemes in synchrony has the exact same effect as other co-occurrences, which have been identified at the diachronic level. Blevins (2004: 18) shares the same view, arguing that phonetic innovations often mirror diachronic processes. The ambiguity noted in this article is therefore a reflection of an intermediate stage in an evolutionary process of phonologisation. Whether that process will run its complete course remains to be seen. Contemporary palatalisation consists in a recategorisation of the occurrences of certain phonemes. In other words, it implies gradual fossilisations that operate at the level of morphemes or words (that is, units of first articulation). This brings about new phonological representations that can vary from one speaker to the next. Internal mechanisms of change (such as economy and analogy) are of course at work. However, it is only an interaction between internal and external factors of change that can account for the actuation of contemporary palatalisation and explain why it became really apparent with the speakers born in the late 1960s/early 1970s.

## Notes

1. In this article, transcriptions with / / refer to an unambiguous phonemic/deep status. Phonetic phenomena or actual pronunciations of words are noted with [ ]. If the linguistic status of the item considered is ambiguous as regards the phonemic/phonetic opposition, [ ] are used as the default notation.
2. For example, Coggle (1993: 51–52), Wells (1982: 331; 2008: xix), Altendorf (2003: 69), Altendorf and Watt (2008: 213), Cruttenden (2008: 87).
3. Many thanks to IDEA (International Dialects of English Archive), http://dialectsarchive. com
4. 'Variable' contemporary palatalisation means that the speakers exhibit some degree of contemporary palatalisation, as opposed to those who do not have it at all in their speech. No speaker exhibits exclusive contemporary palatalisation, to the exclusion of more traditional variants, in all the words that contain the variables under study.
5. As the number of tokens is extremely variable from one speaker to the next and one age group to the next in unscripted speech, the figures given in this section correspond to the recordings based on scripted speech, unless unscripted speech is specifically mentioned.
6. This is how it works for marginal cases. Where (sk) is concerned, [k] is the assimilator. In the case of (st) clusters, identification of a particular assimilator is much less obvious, as [s] and [t] are both alveolar. Such instances of palatalisation may well be the result of a paradigmatic type of assimilation, through analogy with other [s]-initial clusters.
7. Two of them were in their forties. All the others were under the age of thirty, with a majority aged 15–25, and with an equal number of speakers of either sex.

8. Spectrogram done with Praat, created by Boersma and Weenink, http://www.fon.hum. uva.nl/praat
9. Many thanks to Michele Kahn, from the University of Houston Clearlake, TX, for administering the questionnaire for me.
10. Many thanks to Amanda Brzezicki, from Van Hoosen Middle School in Rochester, MI, for administering the questionnaire for me.
11. Following Smith (2007), the terms 'hypo-' and 'hyperadaptation', as opposed to 'hypo-' and 'hypercorrection', will be used in this chapter so as to avoid confusion with sociolinguistic hypercorrection.

## References

Altendorf, Ulrike (2003), *Estuary English: Levelling at the Interface of RP and South-eastern British English*, Berlin: Gunter Narr Verlag Tübingen.
Altendorf, Ulrike and Dominic Watt (2008), 'The dialects in the south of England: phonology', in B. Kortmann and C. Upton (eds), *Varieties of English 1: The British Isles*, Berlin: Mouton de Gruyter, pp. 194–222.
Ashby, Patricia (2005), *Speech Sounds*, Abingdon: Routledge.
Bass, Michael (2009), 'Street or shtreet? Investigating (str-) palatalisation in Colchester English', *Essex Student Research Online* 1(1), 10–21.
Blevins, Juliette (2004), *Evolutionary Phonology*, Cambridge: Cambridge University Press.
Brandão De Carvalho Joaquim, Noël Nguyen and Sophie Wauquier (2010), *Comprendre la phonologie*, Paris: Presses Universitaires de France.
Bybee, Joan (2001), *Phonology and Language Use*, Cambridge: Cambridge University Press.
Carr, Philip (2008), *A Glossary of Phonology*, Edinburgh: Edinburgh University Press.
Charlot, Monica (1997), *British Civilians in the Second World War*, Paris: CNED – Didier Érudition.
Coggle, Paul (1993), *Do you Speak Estuary? The New Standard English*, London: Bloomsbury.
Cruttenden, Alan [1962] (2008), *Gimson's Pronunciation of English*, 7th edn, London: Hodder Education.
Currie-Hall, Kathleen (2009), A probabilistic model of phonological relationships from contrast to allophony, unpublished PhD thesis, Columbus, Ohio State University.
Durian, David (2004), 'The social stratification of word-initial (str) in Columbus, OH shopping malls', Columbus, OH: Ohio State University, http://www.ling.ohio-state.edu/~ddurian/ STR.htm
Durian, David (2007), 'Getting [s]tronger every day? Urbanization and the socio-geographic diffusion of (str) in Columbus, OH', *University of Pennsylvania Working Papers in Linguistics* 13(2), 65–79.
Ferragne, Emmanuel, Nathalie Bedoin, Véronique Boulenger and François Pellegrino (2011), 'The perception of a derived contrast in Scottish English', International Congress of Phonetic Sciences, August 2011, Hong Kong SAR China, ICPHS <hal-00613604>.
Giegerich, Heinz (1992), *English Phonology – An Introduction*, Cambridge: Cambridge University Press.
Glain, Olivier (2013), Les Cas de Palatalisation Contemporaine (CPC) dans le monde anglophone, unpublished PhD thesis, Lyon, Université Jean Moulin – Lyon 3.
Glain, Olivier (2014), 'Introducing contemporary palatalisation', *York Papers in Linguistics*, *PARLAY Proceedings Series* 1, 16–29.
Hannisdal, Bente (2006), Variability and change in Received Pronunciation, a study of six phonological variables in the speech of television newsreaders, unpublished PhD thesis, Bergen, University of Bergen.

Harrison, Shelly (1999), 'English /(s)tr/ clusters', *Linguist List*, 10(217), http://linguistlist.org/issues/10/10-217.html

Jones, Daniel (1956), *Pronunciation of English*, Cambridge: Cambridge University Press.

Labov, William (1994), *Principles of Linguistic Change, Volume 1: Internal Factors*, Chichester: Wiley-Blackwell.

Labov, William (2010), *Principles of Linguistic Change, Volume 3: Cognitive and Cultural Factors*, Chichester: Wiley-Blackwell.

Labov, William, Sharon Ash and Charles Boberg (2006), *Atlas of North American English: Phonetics, Phonology and Sound Change*, Berlin: Mouton de Gruyter.

Lindblom, Björn (1986), 'On the origin and purpose of discreteness and invariance in sound patterns', in J. Perkell and D. Klatt (eds), *Invariance and Variability in Speech Processes*, Hillsdale: Lawrence Erlbaum Associates, pp. 493–523.

Lindblom, Björn (1990), 'Explaining phonetic variation: a sketch of the H&H theory', in W. Hardcastle and A. Marchal (eds), *Speech Production and Speech Modelling*, Amsterdam: Kluver, pp. 403–439.

McWhorter, John (2012), *Myths, Lies and Half-Truths of Language Usage*, Chantilly, VA: The Great Courses.

Meillet, Antoine [1921] (1926), *Linguistique historique et linguistique générale*, 2nd edn, Paris: Librairie Ancienne Honoré Champion.

Montreuil, Jean-Pierre (2001), *La phonologie de l'anglais*, Rennes: Presses Universitaires de Rennes.

Ohala, John (1981), 'The listener as a source of sound change', *Papers from the Parasession on Language and Behavior*, Chicago: Chicago Linguistic Society, pp. 178–203.

Ohala, John (1989), 'Sound change is drawn from a pool of synchronic variation', in L. Breivik and E. Jahr. (eds), *Language Change: Contributions to the Study of its Causes*, Berlin: Mouton de Gruyter, pp. 173–198.

Ohala, John (1993), 'Coarticulation and phonology', *Language and Speech* 36, 155–170.

Ohala, John (1994), 'Hierarchies of environments for sound variation; plus implications for 'neutral' vowels in vowel harmony', *Acta Linguistica Hafniensia* 27, 371–382.

Pavlík, Radoslav (2009), 'A typology of assimilations', *SKASE Journal of Theoretical Linguistics* 6(1), 2–26.

Rutter, Ben (2011), 'Acoustic analysis of a sound change in progress: the consonant cluster /stɹ/ in English', *Journal of the International Phonetic Association* 41(01), 27–40.

Scobbie, James and Jane Stuart-Smith (2008), 'Quasi-phonemic contrast and the fuzzy inventory: examples from Scottish English', in P. Avery, E. Dresher and Keren Rice (eds), *Contrast in Phonology Theory, Perception, Acquisition*, Berlin: Mouton de Gruyter, pp. 87–114.

Shockey, Linda (2003), *Sound Patterns of Spoken English*, Oxford: Blackwell.

Smith, Jeremy (2007), *Sound Change and the History of English*, Oxford: Oxford University Press.

Stévanovitch, Colette [1997] (2008), *Manuel d'histoire de la langue anglaise des origines à nos jours*, 2nd edn, Paris: Ellipses.

Taylor, John (1996), *Linguistic Categorization*, Oxford: Oxford University Press.

Valimaa-Blum, Rita (2005), *Cognitive Phonology in Construction Grammar: Analytic Tools for Students of English*, Berlin: Mouton de Gruyter.

Weinreich, Uriel, William Labov and Marvin Herzog (1968), *Empirical Foundations for a Theory of Language Change*, Austin: University of Texas Press.

Wells, John (1982), *Accents of English 1, An Introduction*, Cambridge, Cambridge University Press.

Wells, John (1997), 'Whatever happened to Received Pronunciation?', in C. Medina and C. Soto (eds), *II Jornadas de Estudios Ingleses*, Jaén: Universidad de Jaén, pp. 19–28.
Wells, John [1990] (2008), *Longman Pronunciation Dictionary*, 3rd edn, London: Longman.

# 4

# Asymmetric Acquisition of English Liquid Consonants by Japanese Speakers

*Mariko Kondo*

## Overview

It is well known that Japanese speakers have difficulty in differentiating the liquid consonants /l/ and /r/. This is because /l/ and /r/ are not contrastive in Japanese, and allophonic variations of both /l/ and /r/ occur in Japanese speech. The most common realisation is alveolar tap [ɾ], but [l] also occurs in natural speech. However, these variants are phonemically all recognised as /r/ in Japanese. A study of Japanese speakers' English pronunciation errors using a large English learner corpus, J-AESOP, found that Japanese speakers produced more mistakes in /l/ than /r/. The Japanese speakers substituted /r/ for /l/ (418 examples out of 2,142 consonantal errors) much more often than they substituted /l/ for /r/ (124 examples out of 2,142 consonantal errors). Research is being conducted to examine the acquisition of English liquid consonants by Japanese speakers in relation to the concept of new phonetic categories proposed by the Speech Learning Model. Furthermore, it is important to assess how L2 learners use a new phonetic category when they face a new variant of a phoneme, produced in a different accent to that which they had already studied in the target language. Previous analysis of Japanese speakers' mimicry speech of (a) American English and (b) English-accented Japanese suggested that Japanese speakers were aware of acoustic and articulatory features of English approximant [ɹ] (Kondo 2016). The Japanese speakers overused approximant [ɹ] and r-coloured vowels in their mimicries of both (a) and (b). Further articulatory analysis of Japanese and English consonants showed that the English approximant [ɹ] is quite distinct from Japanese consonants, all of which lack lip rounding and tongue retraction. The results of these studies suggest that Japanese speakers may not be able to recognise English /l/ and /r/ as separate phonemes, but that they can hear the approximant [ɹ] as it forms a new phonetic category, i.e. /ɹ/. In contrast, they recognise English /l/ as a sound in the same category as Japanese /r/. Based on these earlier data, the current chapter assesses the effectiveness of pronunciation training for Japanese students. We discuss the abilities of ninety trained and ninety untrained Japanese speakers to form a new phonetic category of an approximant [ɹ]. The study also investigates if the trained group can use the new phonetic category when they face a different accent of English which has a different phonetic variant, such as [ɾ] in Scottish English. The chapter discusses the relative abilities of the two groups to form a new phonetic category [ɹ] and use this to discriminate [ɾ] from allophones of /l/ in the different English accent. These results help understand how language learners use a new phonetic category in L2, and whether they can extend it to analyse a new accent with a different sound structure.

## Introduction

It is well known that Japanese speakers have difficulty in differentiating the liquid consonants /l/ and /r/ (Miyawaki et al. 1975; Yamada and Tohkura 1992; Flege et al. 1996; Aoyama and Flege 2011, and many more). This has been one of the most well-researched topics in Japanese phonology and second language (L2) phonological acquisition by Japanese speakers for both production and perception. Various allophones of /l/ and /r/ actually occur in Japanese natural speech: for example, [l], [ɾ] and [r], with the most common realisation being alveolar tap [ɾ]. Various variants of /l/ also occur as variants of /r/ (Arai 1999). Trill [r] is also commonly heard, usually stigmatised as vulgar pronunciation. However, all these varieties of /l/ and /r/ are not contrastive in Japanese, and they are all recognised as the same phoneme by native Japanese speakers, which is usually represented as /r/ (Vance 2008; Labrune 2014). In Japanese orthography, there is no way to differentiate allophonic variations of the liquid consonant.

In Japanese phonology, /r/ is an unstable sound. It is a common sound in Japanese speech, but it is not common in the word-initial position, and it is less likely to take the lexical accent in loanwords (Labrune 2014). For example, the most common lexical accent position of the loanwords *tiramisu* 'tiramisu' and *Noruwei* 'Norway' are /'tiramisu/ and /noru'wee/ respectively (NHK Broadcasting Culture Research Center 2016), even though the default accent position of loanwords in Japanese is the third mora from the end, i.e. /ti-'ra-mi-su/ and /no-'ru-we-e/ (the accent is on the underlined mora and is also marked with an apostrophe, and here the hyphen indicates a mora boundary). In these two loanwords, the onset of the syllable in the default accent position is a liquid /r/, therefore the accent is shifted to an adjacent mora.

So, can Japanese speakers actually hear the difference between /l/ and /r/ in some conditions? Most studies have not shown any ability of Japanese speakers to distinguish /l/ and /r/, but some studies have reported that they could detect a difference under certain conditions. Studies such as Guion et al. (2000), Aoyama et al. (2004) and Hattori and Iverson (2009) all found that Japanese speakers of English were able to identify English /r/ better than /l/. These studies discussed their results in relation to new phonetic categories of the Speech Learning Model (SLM) (Flege 1995). They claim that English /r/ is very different from Japanese /r/ sound and it forms a new category in L2 English. Therefore, Japanese L2 learners of English can identify English /r/ better than /l/ as a sound different from other Japanese sounds. Similar results have been reported about the acquisition of English front vowel /æ/ by Japanese speakers. Japanese speakers are able to discriminate /æ/ from /ʌ/ better than they can discriminate /i/ from /ɪ/ because the vowel /æ/ does not share the same vowel space as any Japanese vowels (Nishi and Strange 2008; Matsumura 2014). So, the vowel /æ/ seems to form a new phonetic category for Japanese L2 learners of English.

In this study, I will examine Japanese speakers' production and perception of English liquid consonants and assess if they are acquired with equal difficulty or with differences. It is true that Japanese speakers have difficulty differentiating the English liquids, but Japanese speakers may be able to recognise the phonetic features of one of the liquids better than the other as being claimed. So, I will study Japanese speakers' sensitivity to English liquids by first analysing English loanwords into Japanese. Then I will present the results of four experiments: (1) mimicry of English pronunciation, (2) mimicry of English accented Japanese, both of which were performed by native Japanese speakers, (3) judgement of the mimicry performance (2) above, and (4) the effect of articulation training on the perception of /l/ and /r/.

The results will be discussed in relation to the SLM and how a new phonetic category for the liquid consonant is formed. Based on the results, if acquisition of the liquid consonants is not symmetrical, I will consider how to use their asymmetricity in the teaching of L2 phonemic contrast and how to apply it to effective pronunciation teaching.

## The Production of English Liquids by Japanese Speakers

It has been believed that Japanese speakers confuse /l/ and /r/ in English, and use /l/ and /r/ randomly when they speak English. However, a study of Japanese speakers' English pronunciation errors using a large English learner corpus, J-AESOP, found that Japanese speakers produced more errors in /l/ than /r/ (Kondo et al. 2014 and Kondo et al. 2015). The Japanese speakers wrongly substituted /r/ for /l/ (418 examples out of 2,142 consonantal errors) much more often than they substituted /l/ for /r/ (124 examples out of 2,142 consonantal errors). This result suggests that /l/–/r/ substitution does not occur randomly, but that there is a tendency in their errors. So, Japanese speakers may be able to hear some acoustic features of English /l/ and /r/ and differentiate them in some conditions and environments.

When examining loanword phonology from English to Japanese, there are certain segmental mapping rules from English consonants to Japanese. Japanese has fewer consonantal phonemes than English, so more than one English phoneme is mapped into a single Japanese consonant. As mentioned above, both English /l/ and /r/ are mapped to a single consonant /r/ in Japanese, as shown in Table 4.1.

However, in some phonological environments English /l/ and /r/ are realised differently in loanwords in Japanese orthography. Japanese has three writing systems,

Table 4.1 Phoneme mapping of consonants in English loanwords in Japanese

| English | b | v | s | θ | z | Ð | ʒ | dʒ | l | r |
|---|---|---|---|---|---|---|---|---|---|---|
| Japanese | | b | | s | | z([dz]~[dz̥]~[ɹz]~[z]) | | | r([ɾ]) | |

Table 4.2 Realisation of English /l/ and /r/ in English loanwords in Japanese

| Position in syllable | English | Japanese | | English words | Japanese realisation |
|---|---|---|---|---|---|
| Onset | /l/ | | [1] | lamp, light | /raNpu/, /raito/ |
| | | | [2] | slwice, cloak | /suraisu/, /kurooku/ |
| | /r/ | /r/ | [3] | rope, room | /roopu/, /ruumu/ |
| | | | [4] | cream, brunch | /kuriimu/, /buraNti/ |
| Coda | /l/ | | [5] | cool, tall | /kuuru/, /tooru/ |
| | | | [6] | cold, pulp | /koorudo/, /parupu/ |
| | /r/ | /V/ | [7] | idle, couple | /aidoru/, /kaQpuru/ |
| | | | [8] | car, door, tour | /kaa/, /doa/, /tuaa/ |
| | | | [9] | cart, pearl, port | /kaato/, /paaru/, /pooto/ |

*hiragana*, *katakana* and *kanji* (Chinese characters), with hiragana and katakana being moraic writing systems that reflect pronunciation. Each hiragana and katakana letter represents a mora, which comprises an optional consonant and a vowel (/(C)V/) with some exceptions of moraic consonants. Most loanwords, apart from loanwords from Chinese, are usually written with katakana. There are five katakana letters representing the phoneme /r/ each followed by one of the five Japanese vowels, /ra/, /ri/, /ru/, /re/ and /ro/, which cover both English /l/ and /r/. Examples of English loanwords in Japanese vocabulary are listed in Table 4.2.

In most cases English /l/ and /r/ in loanwords are realised as /r/ in Japanese, but sometimes /r/ is realised as a vowel (Lovins [1973] 1975). It appears that the realisation of /l/ and /r/ in their Japanese forms is determined by their position in a syllable. For example, when they occur in word-initial position, both /l/ and /r/ are realised as /r/ in Japanese (Table 4.2 [1] and [3]). Please note that the position of the liquid consonants in the Japanese realisation is based on the rules of loanword phonology in Japanese. The positions of the liquid consonants in a syllable may be different from those in English because they may be resyllabified to fit the Japanese syllable structure. When they occur syllable-finally and the following syllable starts with a vowel, they are resyllabified with the following vowel and become syllable-initial and realised as /r/ in Japanese as shown in (1) below. This is because most Japanese syllables are light syllables and have an open /CV/ structure, and cannot be closed by either /l/ or /r/. The same rule is applied to /l/ and /r/ in the non-initial syllable onset position, as shown in Table 4.2 [2] and [4], where the vowel is epenthesised to break up consonant clusters, and the liquid consonants become syllable initial /r/ in Japanese.

(1)    Word-internal English /l/ and /r/ followed by a vowel in loanword realisation in Japanese. Here a dot indicates syllable boundary.

English transcription            Japanese realisation
'calendar'    /kæl.ən.dər/       /ka.reN.daa/
'jelly'       /dʒel.i/           /ze.rii/
'America'     /ə.mer.ɪ.kə/       /a.me.ri.ka/
'syrup'       /sɪr.əp/           /si.roQ.pu/

However, when /r/ occurs in the syllable coda position, either word-internally followed by a consonant or in the word-final position, /l/ and /r/ are realised differently (Table 4.2 [5]–[9]). English /r/ in the syllable coda position is often perceived as a vowel by many language speakers as well as Japanese speakers (Cruttenden 2014) and coda /r/ is often perceived as approximant /w/ by French speakers (Hallé et al. 1999). With /l/, the vowel after /l/ is epenthesised and /l/ is resyllabified with the epenthesised vowel, becoming syllable-initial and realised as /r/ in the Japanese realisation (single underlined) as in [5]~[7]. On the other hand, when /r/ occurs in these positions it is realised as a vowel, either doubling the preceding vowel or realised as /a/ as in [8] and [9].

Resyllabification rules of /l/ and /r/ in the coda position are explained in (2) below, where realisation of English /l/ is shown with a single underlined Japanese /r/, and English /r/ is shown with a double underlined Japanese /r/.

(2)    English /l/ and /r/ in the coda position, either word-finally or followed by a consonant, in loanword realisation in Japanese. Here a dot indicates syllable boundary.

English transcription            Japanese realisation
'kilt'     /kɪlt/                /ki.ru.to/
'skirt'    /skɜːrt/              /su.kaa.to/
'call'     /kɔːl/                /koo.ru/
'share'    /ʃeər/                /sjea/
'circle'   /sɜːr.kᵊl/            /saa.ku.ru/

The loanword examples indicate that Japanese speakers discriminate English /l/ and /r/ in the coda position, although they do not seem to hear the difference between these liquids in other environments.

So, do Japanese speakers actually hear the difference between English /l/ and /r/ in some environments? The following sections present the results of four experiments about Japanese speakers' production and perception of English /l/ and /r/, and an assessment of what they hear and what they can discriminate.

## Mimicry of English Accent by Japanese Speakers

*Experiment 1: Mimicry of English Pronunciation*

In normal speech communication, speakers mimic other people's speech: for example, pronunciation, intonation, voice quality, vocabulary, speech style, gestures and facial features (McNeill 2015). Speakers copy what they hear and try to depict the characteristics of the person whose speech they try to mimic. By examining mimicry speech, it is possible to consider how speakers perceive and recognise speech and then try to reproduce it. Another reason for studying mimicry speech is that English teachers have noticed that students who are interested in learning pronunciation tend to overuse /r/ when they speak English (personal communication). This may be a kind of hypercorrection by the students. The English teachers also mention that the pronunciation of speakers who tend to overuse /r/ is often rated very high by their peer group learners. That indicates that average students actually can hear the /r/ sound and probably think it is a typical sound of English.

Subjects

In this experiment, nine native Japanese speakers, two male and seven female speakers, participated in the experiment. They were all undergraduate students of a university in Tokyo, aged between eighteen and twenty-four. Their native Japanese accent varied, but it should not have affected the result of the experiment because there are virtually no consonantal differences in accents of Japanese. Seven out of the nine subjects had spent some time outside of Japan in various countries: from one year to six years in Australia, Germany, Indonesia, Italy, Malaysia, the USA and the UK. At the time of the experiment, all of them studied at an English medium faculty where all courses are taught in English. Their English level was from lower intermediate to advanced level, better than the average for university students in Japan. I chose subjects of this English level because of the relative difficulty of the experimental tasks. Another reason is that earlier studies of Japanese speakers' English production errors found that even fairly advanced-level speakers made at least some pronunciation errors concerning /l/ and /r/, which are the phonemes assessed in this study (Kondo et al. 2014 and Kondo et al. 2015). Therefore, English fluency should not be a big issue in this experiment. All nine subjects self-assessed their English levels and said that they had some problems with differentiating /l/ and /r/ in both production and perception.

Method

Twenty English test phrases were created that included the liquids /l/ and /r/. Each phrase contained two target words with an /l/, and two target words with an /r/. All liquid consonants appeared either word-initially or -medially, both followed by a vowel. It has been reported that Japanese speakers have more difficulty differentiating English /l/ and /r/ in word-initial position than in final position (Flege et al. 1995). In ten of the test phrases, the two words with an /l/ appeared before the words with an

/r/, as in the examples shown in (3) below, and in the other ten phrases the words with an /r/ appeared before the words with an /l/ in (4) below.

(3)  I like listening to rock and reggae music.
     The salad includes lettuce, radish and raisins.
     I have a long list of Russian restaurants.
     The lemon soufflé was rich and creamy.
     I love climbing, reading and writing.
(4)  The foreign press liked the leader.
     I had raspberry, cherry, lime and chocolate cakes.
     I had crabs, shrimps, lobsters, and melon.
     We bought red rubies, and a blue necklace.
     She wrote a story about a black elephant.

The phrases comprised relatively easy words which appear in junior high school English textbooks (Kazijima and Seki et al. (2012), *New Horizon English Course* 1–3). Some of the target words – for example, 'reggae', 'rubies' and 'soufflé' – are not particularly high-frequency words, but they are used commonly as loanwords in Japanese vocabulary, and so the subjects were expected to know these words.

A male native speaker of American English recorded thirty phrases: the twenty test phrases and ten dummy phrases. The thirty recorded phrases were arranged in random order. Each subject sat in a soundproof studio with a headset on. Since the words used in the test phrases were relatively easy words, the phrases were not presented visually, and only their sound was broadcast through the headset. A phrase was broadcast each time a subject clicked that phrase number on the studio monitor. The subjects were allowed to listen to the phrases as often as they wished, until they could understand the meaning of the phrases and were confident about imitating them. The subjects were instructed to then mimic what they heard as accurately as possible. To minimise any effect of their existing knowledge of the test words and the words' spelling, the subjects were told that the speaker sometimes pronounced some words deliberately wrong, although in actual fact all the phrases were pronounced correctly. For example, the subjects were told that the word 'newspaper' /njuːzpeɪpər/ may be pronounced [njuːzḇeɪpər] and that 'garden' /gɑːɹdən/ may be pronounced [gɔːɹdən]. If they heard [njuːzḇeɪpər] for 'newspaper' or [gɔːɹdən] for 'garden', they were told to imitate what they heard, and not to imitate the pronunciation they might have expected to hear based on their prior knowledge of the words. They were also told that it was perfectly all right to reproduce ungrammatical or nonsense English phrases, so the subjects were told to listen to each pronunciation very carefully. They were allowed to re-record mimicry speech of each phrase several times until they were happy with their performance.

A native speaker of English then listened to their recorded performance and judged their liquid pronunciation as either [l] and its variants, [ɹ~ɻ] and its variants, or other realisations.

Results

A total of 360 samples of mimicry production of English /l/ (2 sample words x 20 phrases x 9 speakers) and 353 samples of English /r/ (2 sample words x 20 phrases x 9 speakers – 7 completely mispronounced or omitted samples) were recorded. Figure 4.1 shows the percentage ratio of mimicry of American English /l/ pronunciation realised as either [l], [ɹ~ɻ], or another realisation (other) by the nine Japanese speakers (A–I). /l/ was realised as [ɹ~ɻ] in 85 out of the 360 samples (23.61 per cent), with all subjects producing quite a few /r/-like sounds, i.e. [ɹ~ɻ], except for subject F who had a 100 per cent success rate for mimicry production of English /l/. Figure 4.2 shows the result of the mimicry production of English /r/ by the same subjects (A–I). The percentage ratio of /r/ realised as [l] was 15.58 per cent (55 out of 353 samples).

The rate of substituting /r/ for /l/ was higher than that of /l/ for /r/, which is the same finding as in the J-AESOP corpus study mentioned earlier (see section 'The production of English liquids by Japanese speakers' above, and Kondo et al. 2014 and Kondo et al. 2015). However, in the current study the number of errors of /r/ for /l/ was only approximately 1.5 times more than the number of errors of /l/ for /r/, whereas in the corpus study it was approximately 3.3 times. Samples in the 'other' category were [ɾ] or uvular fricative [ʁ] which were substituted for both /l/ and /r/. As mentioned earlier, [ɾ] is the most common realisation of the Japanese /r/ phoneme, which means that the subjects would have heard the correct phoneme /r/ but then failed to mimic the English /r/ ([ɹ~ɻ]) sound correctly. Subject F used [ʁ] instead of [ɹ~ɻ] for five instances of /r/, and his results were quite different from the other subjects. He did not make any errors for /l/ (Figure 4.1) and substituted [l] for /r/ in 85 per cent (34/40) of the samples (Figure 4.2). In contrast, the other eight speakers substituted [l] for /r/ in only 6.7 per cent of the samples (21/313). If the results of

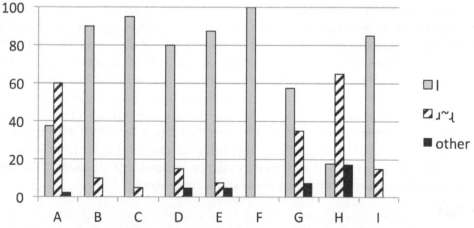

Figure 4.1  Realisation ratio (%) of [l], [ɹ~ɻ] and other sounds in nine Japanese speakers' (A–I) mimicry of American English /l/ pronunciation

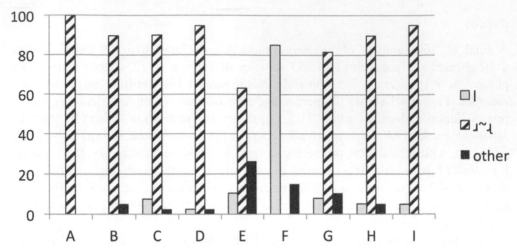

Figure 4.2 Realisation ratio (%) of [l], [ɹ~ɻ] and other sounds in nine Japanese speakers' (A–I) mimicry of American English /r/ pronunciation

subject F are eliminated, then the substitution of /r/ for /l/ was 26.56 per cent (85/320 samples). In that case, the substitution of /r/ for /l/ was nearly four times more than the substitution of /l/ for /r/ (26.56 per cent versus 6.7 per cent), which is much closer to the results of the earlier corpus-based study. The different pattern of subject F may be a result of his L2 language background. He speaks fluent German, and the most common realisation of German /l/ is clear [l], and that of German /r/ is uvular fricative [ʁ], both of which are quite different from English liquids. These allophonic variations of German liquids may have affected the results of subject F. The results of subject F will be discussed again in the sections 'Results' and 'Discussion'.

*Experiment 2: Mimicry of English-Accented Japanese Speech*

The next experiment is mimicry of English accented Japanese speech. The same subjects (A–I) were asked to perform the role of a native speaker of American English who speaks Japanese with a heavy American English accent. The aim of this experiment is to examine Japanese speakers' image of English accent. I limited the English accent to 'American' because (1) Japanese learners are used to the American accent due to it being used as the model pronunciation in school English teaching, (2) most Japanese have more opportunity to hear American English-accented Japanese speech on TV and in everyday life much more than Japanese speech with accents of other types of English, and (3) the quality of American English /r/ is an important issue in the study, which will be discussed fully in the section 'Discussion'. The main focus of pronunciation in this experiment is the consonant /r/.

Method

Fifteen Japanese phrases containing words with the /r/ ([ɾ]) phoneme were composed along with five dummy phrases. Examples of the test phrases are listed in (5) below.

In the test phrases, each /r/ is followed by one of the five Japanese vowels /i, e, a, o, u/. The fifteen phrases (ten test phrases and five dummy phrases) were randomised and presented on a monitor one phrase at a time. The subjects were asked to study each phrase and then try to pronounce it as if they were an American person speaking Japanese. They were allowed to redo their performance for each phrase as many times as they wished, until they were satisfied with their performance.

(5)

a. *Rusuchuu ni atarashii reizouko no haitatsu no renraku ga arimashita.*
'I was informed that a new fridge is going to be delivered next week.'
b. *Tera to shiro no mawari ni hori o megurasemasu.*
'A moat will be built around the temple and castle.'
c. *Raigetsu wa ressha de Hiroshima to Tottori ni ikimasu.*
'I'm going to Hiroshima and Tottori by train next month.'
d. *Hiruma wa haremasu ga yoru wa kumori desu.*
'It will be sunny during the day but cloudy in the evening.'

Results

The recorded performances of each subject were analysed by a native English speaker. The fifteen test phrases contained sixty-seven examples of /r/ which yielded a total of 603 examples of /r/ production for all speakers (67 examples x 9 speakers). The pronunciations of the Japanese /r/ phonemes in the utterances were categorised as [l], [ɹ~ɻ] or other by the native English speaker. The results of the analysis are presented in Figure 4.3.

In their mimicry of American English-accented Japanese /r/, five subjects (A, B, C, D and E) used mainly approximants [ɹ~ɻ], with very little use of [l]. Figure

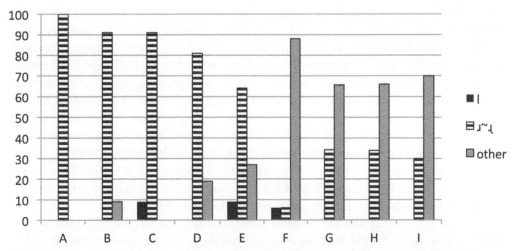

Figure 4.3 Realisation ratio (%) of [l], [ɹ~ɻ] and other sounds in nine Japanese speakers' (A–I) mimicry of American English-accented Japanese /r/ pronunciation

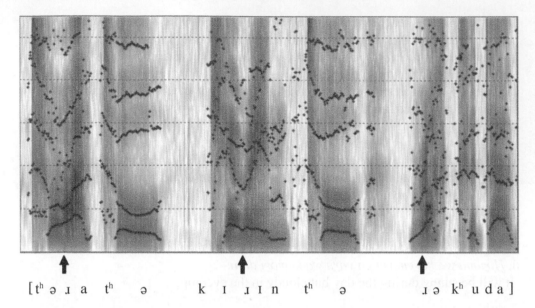

[tʰ ə ɹ a tʰ ə      k ɪ ɹ ɪ n tʰ ə      ɹ ə kʰ u d a]

Figure 4.4 Mimicry speech of English-accented Japanese of *tora to kirin to rakuda* ('tigers, giraffes and camels') by speaker A

4.4 shows an example of an utterance with approximant [ɹ]. Its spectrogram shows very low F3 during the production of the /r/ sound, which is a characteristic of [ɹ] (indicated by black upward arrows). Four of the speakers (F, G, H and I) mainly used 'other' sounds for the /r/. There were very few instances of [l] being used in the utterances (2.65 per cent, 16/603 examples). Approximately half of the time /r/ was pronounced as [ɹ~ɻ] (59.04 per cent, 356/603 examples), and 38.31 per cent (231/603 examples) was identified as 'other' sounds. The most common realisation of the 'other' sound was alveolar tap [ɾ] (172 examples), which was produced by six subjects. Figure 4.5 shows an example of an utterance with tap [ɾ] (indicated by white upward arrows) by subject I, whose utterance sounded like normal Japanese speech. It had a very brief tongue tip closure with the alveolar ridge of [ɾ] appearing almost like a very short voiced stop closure. Subject F, who produced the highest number of 'other' category sounds, did not produce the tap [ɾ], but instead produced mainly uvular fricative [ʁ] (88.05 per cent, 59/67 examples), with a very few examples of [l] and [ɹ~ɻ] (4/67 examples, 6 per cent for both). Once again his performance was quite different from the other speakers, as in the English mimicry experiment in section 'Experiment 1: Mimicry of English pronunciation' above, and it is possible that his L2 German phonology also affected his performance in this experiment. See the section 'Discussion' for a further exploration of German /r/.

The results suggest that the Japanese subjects often produced the English /r/ type sounds [ɹ] or [ɻ] to mimic English-accented Japanese. Three subjects (G, H and I) used [ɾ] more (65.67 per cent, 65.67 per cent and 70.15 per cent respectively) than approximants (34.33 per cent, 34.33 per cent and 29.85 per cent respectively), but

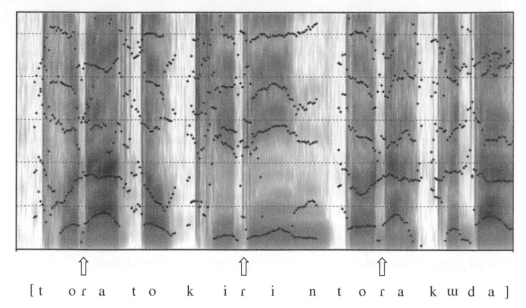

[t  oɾa  t o  k  iɾi  n  t oɾa  kɯd a ]

Figure 4.5  Japanese pronunciation of *tora to kirin to rakuda* with little foreign accent by speaker I

they also used approximants in about 30 per cent of all cases. Mimicry is not only about particular sounds; it affects many different sounds and various suprasegmental characteristics. However, as far as liquid consonant production is concerned, there were very few instances of the Japanese subjects using [l]. It has been reported that English speakers use approximants [ɹ] or [ɻ] for Japanese /r/ when they speak Japanese (Tsurutani 2008). This may be due to the alphabetised Japanese orthography in which the Japanese liquid consonant is written with 'r' and so English speakers substitute the English approximant allophone for the Japanese [ɾ]. Therefore, some of the Japanese subjects may have previously heard the English approximant [ɹ~ɻ] in English speakers' Japanese speech and thus reproduced it in their mimicry. Alternatively, some of the subjects may not have heard such speech by English speakers, and so just used [ɾ], the typical allophone of Japanese /r/, in their performance.

The mimicry performance of some of the subjects described in this section was not particularly good. The quality of performance varied a lot and some performances sounded like normal Japanese speech with very little foreign accent. It appears that the task was too difficult for many ordinary speakers to perform, and so a subsequent experiment was conducted.

*Experiment 3: Japanese Speakers' Judgement of English-Accented Japanese*

Method

The recorded performance of the second mimicry experiment of English-accented Japanese speech (see section 'Experiment 2: Mimicry of English-accented Japanese speech' above) was presented to twenty-seven native Japanese speakers who were university undergraduate students of a non-linguistic major at the time of the experiment. They were told that they had to guess the mother tongue of the speakers whose Japanese utterances they were going to hear. They were not informed that all the speakers were in fact native Japanese speakers. The twenty-seven students were provided with an answer sheet containing a list of possible first languages for each of the speakers: Chinese, English, French, German, Italian, Korean, Russian, Spanish and 'Don't know'. It is not easy to guess a speaker's accent or first language unless the subject knows the language or is familiar with the accent. So, the choices of languages were listed on the answer sheet to make the judgement easier, because these are the languages that the twenty-seven subjects were most likely to have studied or be studying at university or school and so they may also have had a chance to listen to Japanese produced by native speakers of these languages. Another reason was that the choice of language apart from 'English' was not important in this experiment. They were asked to write reasons for their language choice and any comments on the speakers' pronunciation.

Results

Table 4.3 lists the number of subjects who thought that each speaker's first language was English. Speakers A, B, C and D were considered to be native English speakers by quite a high number of subjects, but the other five speakers were almost never considered to be English speakers. The choice of 'English' is related to the high frequency use of approximants [ɹ~ɻ] by speakers A–D (Figure 4.5). All four of these speakers produced approximants for over 80 per cent of the positions of Japanese /r/ in their mimicry speech. In contrast, speakers G, H and I produced [ɾ] in over 65 per cent of examples, and they were almost never judged to be English speakers despite the fact that they did use approximants in about 30 per cent of Japanese /r/ examples. Speaker F, who used uvular fricative [ʁ] in the place of most Japanese /r/ positions, was not considered to be an English speaker by any of the subjects. In the subjects' comments about the pronunciation features of the speakers and the reasons for their decisions about the first language of the speakers, many of the subjects mentioned the quality of /r/, as a sign of being a native English speaker. The subjects did not specifically describe the /r/ as being approximant [ɹ~ɻ], but many of them mentioned that the speakers' /r/ pronunciation sounded like that of English speakers. However, even though speaker E also used the approximant [ɹ] in the majority of examples (64.18 per cent, 43/67), none of the subjects thought that she was an English speaker. It is likely that other segmental and suprasegmental features of her performance influenced the subjects' judgement.

Table 4.3 First language judgement of mimicked American English-accented Japanese speech (Experiment 2) by native Japanese speakers (n=27)

| Speaker | A | B | C | D | E | F | G | H | I |
|---|---|---|---|---|---|---|---|---|---|
| Judged as American | 18 | 25 | 10 | 12 | 0 | 0 | 2 | 2 | 0 |

Other phonological features suggested in the comments as reasons for deciding the native language of the speakers, apart from the pronunciation of the Japanese liquid consonant, were: (1) aspiration of voiceless plosives, in particular /t/, at the beginning of stressed syllable, (2) use of voiceless post-alveolar fricative [ʃ] for Japanese [ɕ] in /si/ and /sja, sju, sjo/, (3) vowel reduction in unaccented syllables, (4) wrong lexical accent position, either word-initial or on the penultimate syllable, and (5) intonation. These comments indicate that Japanese speakers detect these phonetic features when they hear English speech and feel that speech with these features is typically English.

The results of the three experiments indicated that Japanese speakers seem to be able to recognise the English approximant /r/ sound, or at least can detect some of its phonetic features as being different from Japanese sounds. Similar results have also been found in studies by Guion et al. (2000) and Aoyama et al. (2004). However, the subjects were not particularly sensitive to English /l/ sound, or did not pay special attention to it. As discussed above, if approximant [ɹ~ɻ] forms a new phonetic category in Japanese speakers' L2 English, and Japanese speakers develop sensitivity to recognise the sound as a new sound in English, then we can use it to train Japanese speakers to be able to differentiate English /l/ and /r/.

The next experiment tested if Japanese speakers become able to discriminate English /l/ and /r/ after learning about the articulatory features of /l/ and /r/, with a strong focus on the lip rounding of /r/.

## Experiment 4: Identification of English Liquids by Japanese Speakers

*Overview of the Study*

This study was conducted to test whether Japanese learners of English become sensitive to acoustic differences between English /l/ and /r/ through articulatory training and the development of sensitivity to articulatory and acoustic cues to discriminate the liquid consonants. English /l/ and /r/ are both described as alveolar, but Raphael et al. (2012) posit that the main difference is related to tongue tip configuration and position. The tongue tip for /l/ lightly touches the alveolar ridge, dividing the airflow into two streams that are emitted along the sides of the tongue. For /r/, the tongue tip does not touch the alveolar ridge, and also the tongue is grooved and, for many speakers, the raised tongue tip is often bent backwards to be retroflexed. Another important feature of /r/ articulation is that the lips are often rounded. Acoustically, vowels and sonorants produced with lip rounding have lower frequencies because lip rounding protrudes the lips and elongates the oral cavity. Similarly, tongue retraction for approximant [ɹ] and retroflex [ɻ] also has lower frequencies. Lip rounding lowers F3 and moves it towards F2, resulting in a lowering of all formants (Reetz and Jongman 2011).

In contrast, Japanese consonants generally lack lip rounding. Even the bilabial consonants [m] and [w] are not articulated with lip protrusion, but rather with compression (Vance 2008). That means that Japanese speakers are not used to the acoustic signals of lip rounding, and either do not notice it or recognise it as a new sound category.

*Method*

To test the effect of articulatory training on the discrimination of English liquid consonants, a study was carried out at a secondary school located near Tokyo. The school is a senior high school with all female students aged between 15 and 18 years old. The school is regarded as being of a very high level academically, one of the top schools in the region, and almost all students continue to study at university level.

Two English language teachers helped to conduct the study. Students in four first year classes (students aged 15–16 years old) taught by the two teachers participated in the study. The classes were divided into two groups: (1) classes with initial articulatory training after the first test (pre-test) (experimental group), and (2) classes that only received articulatory training after the second test (Test 1) (control group). Since the study was conducted as part of the school's general English language curriculum, it is not fair to provide pronunciation training to some classes only but not to others. Therefore, the maximum educational consideration was taken and the students in the control group also received training after the second test (Test 1) until just before the third test (Test 2). Each teacher taught one class with initial articulatory training and one class with training delayed for approximately ten weeks until after the first test. There were forty or forty-one students in each class, and all 162 students in the classes participated in the experiment. However, some of the students were brought up, or had spent a few years, in English-speaking countries or in a non-Japanese language education system after entering primary school. There were also some students who spoke different languages at home. These students' results were eliminated from the analysis (ten students). Further, some students missed one of the tests because they were absent from the class when the tests were conducted; all test results of these students were eliminated from the analysis (ten students). Therefore, the results of 142 students were analysed: seventy-three students in the experimental group and sixty-nine students in the control group.

The training was provided by the teachers in the normal English class. The first training was to show the experimental group a video of the mouth movements of a native American English speaker producing English words with /l/ and /r/. The video clearly showed the tongue tip contact with the alveolar ridge for [l] articulation and the lip rounding for [ɹ] articulation. During the training period, the teachers demonstrated the articulation of /l/ and /r/ when they taught new English words containing /l/ and /r/, with some extra pronunciation training focusing on lip rounding and tongue retraction of /r/ at the end of classes whenever they had time.

Three tests were conducted over about a sixteen-week-period, which included a two-week holiday period and two one-week school exam periods when no normal classes were conducted: (1) pre-test before any training for either group, (2) Test 1 after about ten weeks' training (including the exam and holiday periods) for the experimental group but no training for the control group, and (3) Test 2 after sixteen weeks' training for the experimental group and six weeks' training for the control group.

*Stimuli*

All the tests were single-stimulus, two-alternative, forced-choice identification tasks. The identification tasks consisted of minimal word pairs contrasting /l/ and /r/. The test format was made simple so that it could be easily conducted in normal school time with the available facilities. The students were given a test paper with a list of word pairs. For each word pair, they listened to a recording of one of the words and then had to select which word of the pair they thought they had heard. The sound stimuli for the tests were recorded in a soundproof studio by three native speakers of American English. A different speaker's voice was used in each test: female voice for the pre-test, male voice for Test 1, and a different female voice for Test 2. For all the tests, the test words were chosen mainly from junior high school-level English textbooks, but some senior high school-level words were added to construct the minimal pairs. Since the tests only required the students to select one of the words in each word pair that they heard, which are contrastive only by /l/ and /r/, using a previously unstudied word in some pairs should not have affected the difficulty of the task, as long as one of the words in the pair was familiar to the students. All the stimuli were recorded on CD with a five-second pause between each word. The students had to choose the word they heard during the pause. The tests were conducted by playing the CD in classes. This is a normal way to conduct listening or dictation tests at school.

The pre-test consisted of forty-four pairs of words containing either /l/ or /r/ in: (1) word-initial position, for example 'lock'-'rock', (2) word-medial position, for example 'alive'-'arrive', (3) word-final position, for example 'heal'-'hear', and (4) in consonant clusters, for example 'fly'-'fry'. There were twenty-two word stimuli with the /l/ sound and twenty-two word stimuli with the /r/ sound, which were presented randomly. Test 1 and Test 2 consisted of the same ninety-two word pairs, some of which were also used in the pre-test. There were forty-six word stimuli with /l/ and forty-six word stimuli with /r/. Each word appeared only once in the test, but in order to avoid any effect of the students perceiving the other word in another word pair the students were told that 'the same word may appear more than once'.

*Results*

Identification of /l/ and /r/ in the three tests

The identification accuracies of the three tests are presented in Figures 4.6 and 4.7. There were some questions which the students either did not answer or where both of the pair words were selected. Therefore, individual percentage ratios of correct answers were obtained for each speaker. Both groups correctly identified /r/ marginally better than /l/.

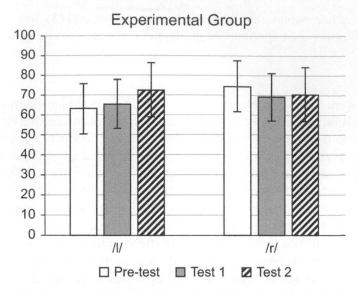

Figure 4.6  Identification accuracies (%) of /l/ and /r/ of pre-test, Test 1 and Test 2 by the experimental group (Error bars = 1 SD)

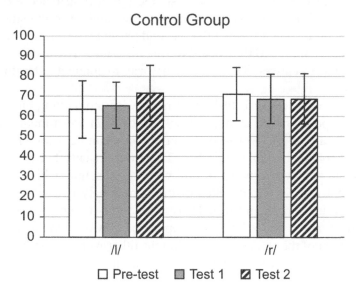

Figure 4.7  Identification accuracies (%) of /l/ and /r/ of pre-test, Test 1 and Test 2 by the control group (Error bars = 1 SD)

During the ten-week-period between the pre-test and Test 1, the experimental group had articulatory training with a strong focus on lip rounding for [ɹ], in order to enhance their discriminability of the /r/ sound, as well as tongue tip contact with the alveolar ridge and lateral release for /l/. Despite the fact that only the experimental group had received any training, the identification accuracies of /l/ improved slightly for both the experimental and control groups. However, the identification of /r/ did not improve for either group, and was actually lower than the pre-test for both groups.

Test 2 was conducted about six weeks after Test 1. In the period between these two tests, the students in the control group started to receive articulatory training during their normal English classes, while the students in the experimental group received continued training. As Figures 4.6 and 4.7 show, there was significant improvement in identification of /l/ for both groups, but not much improvement in /r/.

All the tests were forced choice tests, so the students had to choose one of the words in the pair as an answer even when they were not sure which word they had heard. Therefore, based on the signal detection theory (Macmillan and Creelman 2005), their d–prime scores were obtained to examine the effect of articulatory training on the discriminability of the liquid consonants by the training groups. These data were then submitted to a three-way repeated-measures ANOVA by training group (experimental and control groups), test (pre-test, Test 1, Test 2) and consonant type (/l/ and /r/). The results are shown in Figure 4.8. There were significant differences between training groups ([F(1, 840)=6.05, p<.05] and tests [F(2, 840)=12.09, p<.001). Further analysis by the Tukey HSD test found that there was a significant difference between Test 2 and the other two tests (the pre-test and Test 1). There was no significant difference between the consonants and no significant interactions between any of the factors.

In both the experimental and the control group, the discriminability of the /l/ and /r/ liquids was much higher in Test 2 than in previous tests, after both groups had received at least six weeks of articulatory training. Despite the fact that the

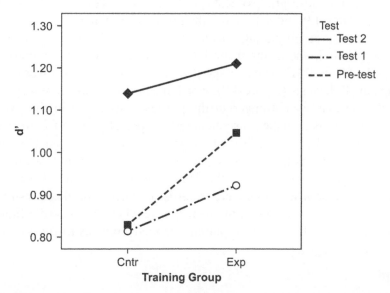

Figure 4.8 Detectability index (d–prime) of English liquid consonants in the three tests by Japanese speakers in two training groups

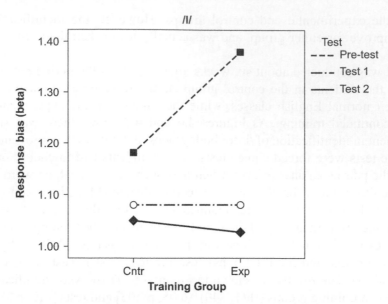

Figure 4.9 Response biases (β) towards /l/ in the three tests by two training groups, β>1 means response bias towards /l/

experimental group received training between the pre-test and Test 1, their discriminability of the liquids was actually lower in Test 1 compared with the pre-test.

In order to examine any response bias of the students, β values were calculated and submitted to a three-way repeated-measures ANOVA by training group (experimental and control groups), test (pre-test, Test 1, Test 2) and consonant type (/l/ and /r/). Figures 4.9 and 4.10 show the results of the analysis with β values. In this analysis there was only a significant difference for the consonant factor [F(1, 840)=22.58, p<.001], and a significant interaction between test and consonant type [F(2, 840)=18.55, p<.001]. The average β values of the /l/ stimuli were above 1 for both groups in all the tests (Figure 4.9), which means that there were response biases towards /r/. The bias was stronger in the pre-test, especially in the experimental group, but it was weaker in the subsequent tests, especially in Test 2. In contrast, the average β values of the /r/ stimuli for both groups were lower than 1 in the pre-test and Test 1, which means that the response biases of the /r/ stimuli were towards /r/ in those tests (Figure 4.10). In Test 2 the β values were higher than 1 for both groups which means the response biases were towards /l/. Therefore, these results indicate that the students initially favoured the /r/ response when they heard a liquid consonant, but after training their response pattern changed tendency towards /l/, especially for the experimental group.

## Discussion

The raw scores of correctly identified answers did not show significant differences between the training groups or consonant types. Both training groups improved their

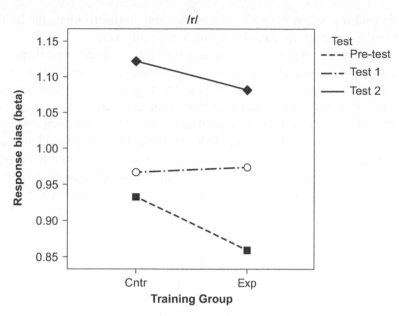

Figure 4.10 Response biases (β) towards /r/ in the three tests by two training groups, β>1 means response bias towards /r/

identification of /l/ in Test 2 compared to the earlier tests, but not for /r/. However, further analyses by the signal detection theory did find an effect of articulation training on the test scores of both groups. The d–prime scores showed that both groups improved their discriminability in Test 2 after receiving articulatory training. It is not surprising that the control group did not show any difference between the pre-test and Test 1 because they did not receive any training between these two tests. But, the experimental group also did not show any improvement between these two tests, despite the fact that they had received articulatory training. In fact, the discriminability shown by the experimental group in Test 1 was lower than in the pre-test. One possible reason for the lack of improvement by the experimental group is that even though the students received training between the tests, there was a two-week school holiday and an exam week before Test 1 when there were no normal classes and therefore no training. There was a clear improvement in the discriminability of both groups in Test 2: with continuing training for the experimental group and the start of training for the control group. The results from Test 2 suggest that the articulation training was effective in helping the students become able to discriminate /l/ and /r/ with more confidence.

The response bias (β value) analysis indicated that both groups changed their response patterns during the course of the study; from 'towards /r/' for /l/ stimuli at the pre-test to 'towards /l/' for /r/ stimuli at Test 2. As discussed in the section 'The production of English liquids by Japanese speakers' above, Japanese speakers generally seem to be more sensitive to English /r/ than /l/. Therefore, before receiving the articulatory training, when the students were not able to discriminate the liquids, they may have had a tendency to consider liquid consonants as /r/.

The change in the response bias β scores by Test 2 suggests that there was some beneficial effect of the articulatory training. A possible reason for the beneficial effect of the pronunciation training is the method of training for [ɹ] with a strong emphasis on lip rounding. Lip rounding has a distinct characteristic of lowering F3, which subsequently affects and lowers other formants. Since Japanese speakers can already sense acoustic cues for /r/, the training would have enhanced the students' ability to depict these features. But, if some recorded /r/ stimuli were not realised with obvious lip rounding, then sometimes the students may have thought that it was not /r/. Auditorily, most /r/ sounded like approximant [ɹ], but articulatorily some /r/ sounds lacked clear lip rounding and therefore acoustically their F3 stayed high. In that case, the students may have chosen /l/ by elimination of /r/. The Japanese speakers learned the articulation and acoustic features of /l/ and /r/, and either directly or indirectly used the phonetic information to identify the sounds.

A question arises about the status of tap in the perception of English /l/ and /r/ by Japanese speakers. As explained earlier, [ɾ] is the most common realisation of Japanese /r/, and it is also a variant of English /r/. It occurs as a common realisation of /r/ in some accents of spoken English, for example the Scottish accent and Philippine English. In the rest of this discussion, I will present new phonetic categories of English sounds for Japanese speakers between vertical lines, as '| |'. If Japanese speakers form a new phonetic category of |ɹ| and also develop sensitivity to identify [l] as |ɾ|, as described in Figure 4.11 (left), phonological mapping occurs between English /r/ and Japanese |ɹ|, and between English /l/ and Japanese /r/([ɾ]). Then how do they react to tap [ɾ]? For example, if Japanese speakers develop |ɹ| as a new phonetic category, and become able to differentiate English /l/ and /r/ as Japanese /r/([ɾ]) and |ɹ|, respectively, do they extend their knowledge to identify /l/ and /r/ in different English accents, as in Figure 4.11 (right), and in other languages, as in Figure 4.12 (left) and Figure 4.12 (right)?

One factor in support of a new category of |ɹ| is the results of subject F in the mimicry experiments described in the section 'Mimicry of English Accent by Japanese Speakers' above. His L2 German phonology enabled him to identify German /r/, which is uvular fricative [ʁ] or uvular trill [R], as a new category sound |ʁ|. Therefore, he used /l/ for English /r/ which is different from German /ʁ/. Another factor is that a subsequent study recently conducted supports this analysis. Japanese speakers have become able to identify English approximant [ɹ] after receiving intensive articulatory training of /r/ ([ɹ]) and /l/ with American English. After a five-week training period was completed, their /l/–/r/ identification was tested with American and Scottish English. The results showed that Japanese speakers improved /l/–/r/ identification by 11.05 per cent with an American accent but saw only 0.62 per cent improvement with a Scottish accent. They have learned to discriminate American /r/ ([ɹ]) and /l/, but not Scottish /r/ ([ɾ]) and /l/. These results imply that the Japanese speakers learned approximant [ɹ] which formed a new phonetic category |ɹ|, but they did not acquire

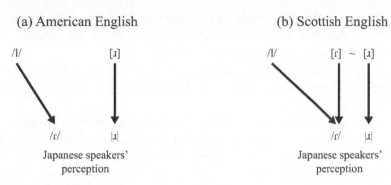

Figure 4.11 Japanese speakers' perception of liquid consonants of American English (left) and Scottish English (right). Here new category sounds in Japanese are presented between vertical lines (| |), and the symbols used are pseudo-phonemic

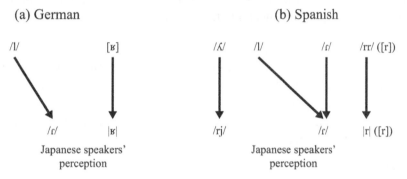

Figure 4.12 Japanese speakers' perception of liquid consonants of German (left) and Spanish (right). Here new category sounds in Japanese are presented between vertical lines (| |), and the symbols used are pseudo-phonemic

the English phoneme /r/ and its allophones (Kondo and Konishi 2018). Further investigation is needed to assess how Japanese speakers develop a new category of L2 sound, become able to use it as a new reference sound in L2 speech perception, and whether they can acquire new L2 phonemes.

## Conclusions

The results of the first two experiments on the mimicry of English and English-accented Japanese performed by Japanese speakers showed that Japanese speakers' production of English /l/ and /r/ is biased towards /r/. The Japanese speakers produced /r/ far more than /l/ when they spoke English. These results support previous conclusions from analyses of L2 English speech corpora.

The analysis of the identification tests of /l/ and /r/ (Experiment 4), based on the signal detection theory, showed the effect of articulatory training on discrimination of the liquid sounds: higher discriminability in Test 2 after articulatory training for both groups. Further analysis by response bias (β) found that before receiving any training there was a bias towards /r/ in words with /l/, but that after training the bias shifted in favour of /l/ in words with /r/. This shift may have been due to the subjects' improved sensitivity to lip rounding and tongue retraction for [ɹ].

Articulatory training of [ɹ] probably helped to form a new phonetic category of |ɹ|, which indirectly helped the students to discriminate /l/ and /r/ and increased the probability of identifying /l/.

Other languages also have various liquid sounds. For example, Spanish has four liquid consonants /ʎ/–/l/–/ɾ/–/rr/([r]), and Punjabi also has four liquid consonants /ɾ/–/ɽ/–/l/–/ɭ/. Shinohara et al. (2015) reported that Japanese speakers have difficulty differentiating the four liquid consonants of Panjabi. So, it will be very interesting to study how Japanese speakers form new categories of sounds in the L2 phonology in order to hear these liquid consonants and produce them.

Future studies are needed to investigate the effect of intensive training about /l/, in addition to /r/, and also to assess the production and perception of liquid consonants of different English accents and other languages.

## Acknowledgement

This study was supported by MEXT grant no. 15H02729. I would like to thank the two English teachers of the high school, as well as the school principal and vice principal, for allowing me to conduct experiments, and I also thank the students who participated in the training and underwent testing for about sixteen weeks, despite their very busy school schedule.

## References

Aoyama, K. and J. E. Flege (2011), 'Effects of L2 experience on perception of English /r/ and /l/ by native Japanese speakers', *Journal of the Phonetic Society of Japan*, 15(3), 5–13.

Aoyama, K., J. E. Flege, S. G. Guion, R. Akahane-Yamada and T. Yamada (2004), 'Perceived phonetic dissimilarity and L2 speech learning: the case of Japanese /r/ and English /l/ and /r/', *Journal of Phonetics* 32, 233–250.

Arai, T. (1999), 'A case study of spontaneous speech in Japanese', *Proceedings of the 14th International Congress of Phonetic Sciences*, San Francisco, pp. 615–618.

Cruttenden, A. (2014), *Gimson's Pronunciation of English*, 8th edn, Abingdon: Routledge.

Flege, J. E. (1995), 'Second language speech learning: theory, findings, and problems', in W. Strange (ed.), *Speech Perception and Linguistic Experience: Issues in Cross-language Research*, Timonium, MD: York Press, pp. 233–277.

Flege, J. E., N. Takagi and V. Mann (1995), 'Japanese adults can learn to produce English /r/ and /l/ accurately', *Language and Speech* 38, 25–55.

Flege, J. E., N. Takagi and V. Mann (1996), 'Lexical familiarity and English-language experience affect Japanese adults' perception of /r/ and /l/', *Journal of the Acoustical Society of America* 99, 1161–1173.

Guion, S. G., J. E. Flege, R. Akahane-Yamada and J. C. Pruitt (2000), 'An investigation of current models of second language speech perception: the case of Japanese adults' perception of English consonants', *Journal of the Acoustical Society of America* 107, 2711–2724.

Hallé, P., C. T. Best and A. Levitt (1999), 'Phonetic vs. phonological influences on French listeners' perception of American English approximants', *Journal of Phonetics* 27, 281–306.

Hattori, K. and P. Iverson (2009), 'English /r/–/l/ category assimilation by Japanese adults: individual differences and the link to identification accuracy', *Journal of the Acoustical Society of America* 125, 469–479.

Kazajima, J., N. Seki and 36 writers (2012), *New Horizon English Course*, 1, 2 & 3, Tokyo: Tokyo Shoseki Co. Ltd.

Kondo, M. and T. Konishi (2018), 'Acquiring L2 phonemes and recognition of their allophonic variances', in A. Botinis (ed.), *Proceedings of 9th Tutorial and Research Workshop on Experimental Linguistics*, 28–30 August 2018, Paris, France, pp. 69–72.

Kondo, M., H. Tsubaki and Y. Sagisaka (2015), 'Segmental variation of Japanese speakers' English: analysis of "the North Wind and the Sun" in AESOP corpus', *Journal of the Phonetic Society of Japan* 19(1), 3–17.

Kondo, M., H. Tsubaki, T. Konishi and Y. Sagisaka (2014), 'Building and analysis of Asian English speech corpus: Japanese speakers' phonemic recognition of English consonants', in S. Ishikawa (ed.), *Learner Corpus Studies in Asia and the World*, vol. 2, Kobe: Kobe University Press, pp. 103–114.

Labrune, L. (2014), *The Phonology of Japanese*, New York: Oxford University Press.

Lovins, J. B. (1975), *Loanwords and the Phonological Structure*, revised version of PhD thesis submitted to University of Chicago, USA in 1973, reproduced by the Indiana University Linguistics Club.

Macmillan, N. A. and C. D. Creelman (2005), *Detection Theory: A User's Guide*, 2nd edn, New York: Psychology Press.

McNeill, D. (2015), 'Speech-gesture mimicry in performance: An actor → audience, author → actor, audience → actor triangle', *Journal for Cultural Research* 19(1), 15–29.

Matsumura, K. (2014), Japanese listeners' perception of English vowel pairs: /i/–/ɪ/ and /æ/–/ʌ/, BA dissertation, School of International Liberal Studies, Waseda University, Japan.

Miyawaki, K., W. Strange, R. Verbrugge, A. M. Liberman, J. Jenkins and O. Fujimura (1975), 'An effect of linguistic experience: the discrimination of [r] and [l] by native speakers of Japanese and English', *Perception & Psychophysics* 18, 331–340.

NHK Broadcasting Culture Research Center (ed.) (2016), *NHK Japanese Pronunciation and Accent New Dictionary*, Tokyo: NHK Publishing.

Nishi, K. and W. Strange (2008), 'Acoustic and perceptual similarity of Japanese and American English vowels', *Journal of the Acoustical Society of America* 124(1), 576–588.

Raphael, L. J., G. J. Borden and K. S. Harris (2012), *Speech Science Primer: Physiology, Acoustics, and Perception of Speech*, 6th edn, Baltimore, MD: Lippincott Williams & Wilkins.

Reetz, H. and A. Jongman (2011), *Phonetics: Transcription, Production, Acoustics, and Perception*, Chichester: Wiley-Blackwell.

Shinohara, S., Q. Hussain and T. Ooigawa (2015), 'Does allophonic knowledge of L1 contribute to the correct discrimination of non-native Sounds?', *Proceedings of the 18th International Congress of Phonetic Sciences*, no. 0368, Glasgow, UK.

Tsurutani, C. (2008), *Daini Gengo toshiteno Nihongo no Hatsuon to Rizumu* [Pronunciation and Speech Rhythm of Japanese as a Second Language] (in Japanese), Hiroshima: Kisuisha.

Vance, T. J. (2008), *The Sounds of Japanese*, Cambridge: Cambridge University Press.

Yamada, R. A. and Y. Tohkura (1992), 'The effects of experimental variables on the perception of American English /r/ and /l/ by Japanese listeners', *Perception & Psychophysics* 52(4), 376–392.

# 5

# R-sandhi in English and Liaison in French: Two Phenomenologies in the Light of the PAC and PFC Data

*Cécile Viollain, Sylvain Navarro and Jacques Durand*

## Introduction

Internal and external sandhi phenomena have long been discussed by phonologists in the different languages of the world from a synchronic or a diachronic perspective, and often from both simultaneously. The emergence of these phonetic processes which occur at morpheme or word boundaries, as well as the scientific interest in these phenomena, are therefore far from new, as Laks (2018) accurately points out:

> Déjà en sanscrit et dans les langues indo-européennes archaïques, la syllabe finale d'unité constituait la position la plus faible de la chaîne. Amuïssement et chute de la consonne fermante étaient très courants devant consonne initiale. Devant initiale vocalique, la consonne fermante se maintenait souvent et se liait à cette voyelle si bien que dès l'indo-européen on a pu parler de liaison, même si le phénomène n'y a ni la régularité ni l'ampleur qu'il acquerra en français.
> [Already in Sanskrit and in archaic Indo-European languages, the final syllable of a unit constituted the weakest position in the chain. The weakening and deletion of the closing consonant were very frequent before an initial consonant. Before an initial vowel, the closing consonant often remained and linked with that vowel so much so that ever since Indo-European we were able to talk about linking, even though the phenomenon had neither the regularity nor the scope it would later acquire in French.][1]

However, the debate is still being fuelled by new corpus data and diverse theoretical analyses and models, notably as far as French liaison and English r-sandhi are concerned. Indeed, in both individual languages, these phenomena have been widely discussed, which does not mean that the issues relating to their relevant method of investigation or their suitable phonological modelling no longer lend themselves to controversial and conflicting interpretations. On the contrary, with the advent of corpus phonology, studies have extensively shown that both phenomena are variable in the different varieties of French (Detey et al. 2016) and English (Soum-Favaro et al. 2014; Durand et al. 2015; Navarro 2016) around the world. Consequently, providing a satisfactory definition for them, along with a comprehensive inventory of the contexts in which they arise and a phonological model able to account for their individual mechanics, has proved problematic.

Furthermore, the specific issues of French liaison and English r-sandhi have not often been tackled with a comparative approach, or, if they have, often quite superficially from a phonological point of view. Indeed, the parallel between French liaison and English r-sandhi has often easily been made, mostly for pedagogical reasons when addressing L2 learners of French or English, as both phenomena fall under the cover of external sandhi phenomena and show similarities from a strictly formal point of view. As we shall see, this apparently self-evident parallelism has had major theoretical implications as the phonological interpretation of how French liaison works has been transposed, so to speak, to English r-sandhi, regardless of the corpus data indicating that both phenomena are, in fact, constrained very differently at the syntactic, phonological, phonetic and sociolinguistic levels.

Besides, even when scholars recognise that French liaison and English r-sandhi should not be lumped together so lightly, they do not go into much detail as to the constraints that apply to these phenomena. For example, Deschamps et al. (2004: 24) offer the following introduction to their section on linking addressed to French L2 students of English:

> The French phonological system is well known for the phonetic phenomenon of
> *liaison* observed in *grand enfant* [gʁɑ̃ + ɑ̃fɑ̃ = gʁɑ̃tɑ̃fɑ̃] vs. *grand garçon* [gʁɑ̃ gaʁsɔ̃].
> The use of linking consonants in French is subject to syntactic restrictions and
> dependent on syntactic structure: linking will not occur in *enfant adroit* [ɑ̃fɑ̃ adʁwɑ].
> The situation is different in English, where the linking process appears to be more
> strictly phonetic, even to the extent that linking sometimes occurs between the end
> of a sentence and the beginning of another by the same speaker.

It is interesting to note that French liaison is defined as a phonetic process whereas English r-sandhi is presented as 'more strictly phonetic' (we shall try and explain what that means, see the section 'Conclusions' below), along with an example that suggests that the domains of application of English r-sandhi and French liaison are different (see the section 'Domain' below). Consequently, in this chapter[2] we offer to thoroughly explore the comparison between these two phenomena by relying on the results provided by the study of various corpora from the PAC (Lancashire, Boston and New Zealand corpora: Navarro 2013; Viollain 2010, 2014) and PFC (mainland France as well as Canada, Belgium, Switzerland, etc.: Durand and Lyche 2008; Durand et al. 2009) programmes, in order to shed light on what we consider to be two distinct phenomenologies.[3]

We shall first contextualise our research by providing definitions for the phenomena under scrutiny and summarising the theoretical issues surrounding their phonological modelling. Among the many factors reported to constrain liaison in French and r-sandhi in English, we will focus on whether these phenomena are sensitive to geographical (dialectal) variation and investigate the link between these phenomena and speakers' orthographic knowledge.

We shall then present the principles and methodology shared by the PAC and PFC programmes as far as corpus building and subsequent treatment of the data are concerned. For the obvious sake of brevity, we will not go into too much detail regarding the coding systems that have been designed to study both liaison and r-sandhi (Durand et al. 2014, 2015), and the tools used to extract information about these phenomena (such as Dolmen; Eychenne and Paternostro 2016). We will however point out the discrepancy between French and English in terms of frequency and therefore explain the strategies that have been put in place to study r-sandhi in English. This will also allow us to reconsider the methodological validity of reading tasks as the latter are often criticised in the literature for their lack of spontaneity (Gadet and Guérin 2012).

Finally, we shall provide our most recent results on liaison and r-sandhi and systematically compare the two phenomena with regards to register, morphosyntactic (syllabic make-up and grammatical nature) and prosodic (lexical stress in English and prosodic groups) structure, type of linking (is there 'enchaînement' or not?) and influence of speakers' orthographic knowledge. We will demonstrate that both liaison and r-sandhi are variable phenomena and subject to intra- as well as inter-speaker variability, which renders them challenging issues for phonological theory. We will then offer conclusions to reassert our position regarding the essential contribution of corpus data to the study of these phenomena as well as to the theoretical models that we find are best able to account for what we observe in the different varieties of French and English around the world.

**The Debate on R-sandhi and Liaison: Definitions and Theoretical Issues**

As we have mentioned in our introduction, the term 'sandhi' is borrowed from Sanskrit and refers to a variety of phonological and phonetic processes that occur at morpheme or word boundaries in the languages of the world. Indeed, many languages exhibit linking phenomena which bear different names, and among them French liaison and English r-sandhi. Providing relevant and comprehensive definitions for these phenomena is not an easy task when one wants to remain as neutral as possible from a theoretical point of view. Indeed, the scientific approach we want to follow here, and which is generally adopted within the PFC and PAC programmes, consists in remaining as theory-neutral as possible when studying a variety of phonological phenomena so as not to presuppose anything about their nature, their behaviour or their underlying mechanisms and causes.

*Defining French Liaison*

As far as French liaison is concerned, there is rather general consensus in saying that 'la liaison correspond à la prononciation entre deux mots d'une consonne qui n'apparaît dans aucun de ces mots prononcés dans d'autres contextes' (Côté 2005) [liaison corresponds to the pronunciation in between two words of a consonant which does not appear in any of these words in other contexts].[4]

Laks (2018) encourages his readers to consider the following parallel forms in French, in which realised liaisons are symbolised by [⌢] and non-realised liaisons are symbolised by [/].

(1a) des savants ⌢ anglais 
(2a) un pied ⌢ à terre 
(3a) de temps ⌢ en temps 
(4a) des dessinateurs ⌢ illustres 
(5a) nous irons ⌢ au parc 
(6a) trop ⌢ âgé 

(1b) des marchands de draps / anglais 
(2b) le pied / à l'étrier 
(3b) le temps / était chaud 
(4b) des dessinateurs / illustrent ce journal 
(5b) nous irons / au zoo 
(6b) vous ne ferez jamais un bon marin, vous êtes trop / homme de terre 

On the basis of these parallel forms, some elementary observations can be formulated, on which an accurate definition of the phenomenon will rely. First, the nature of the consonant is variable: it can be [z] as in (1a), (3a), (4a) and (5a), [n], [t] as in (2a), [p] as in (6a) and [r].[5] The variability of the nature of the consonant can be considered as the major formal difference between French liaison and r-sandhi, hence the name of the phenomenon in English.

What is more, we would like to quote Soum-Favaro et al. (2014: 1) here:

> Cette alternance phonologique du français se manifeste par l'apparition d'une con-sonne entre deux mots, souvent appelés mot-1 et mot-2 ou mot de gauche et mot de droite, après certains mots-1 seulement (*les*, *petit*, *est*, etc.) et uniquement lorsque le mot-2 commence par une voyelle, comme dans *petit* [t] *ami*.
> [This phonological alternation in French manifests itself through the emergence of a consonant in between two words, often named Word-1 and Word-2, or left word and right word, after certain Words-1 only (*les*, *petit*, *est*, etc.) and exclusively when Word-2 starts with a vowel, as in *petit* [t] *ami*.][6]

Indeed, linking consonants only appear when followed by a vowel, in specific morphosyntactic contexts. Compare:

petit écolier   [ptitekɔlje] 
petit copain   [ptikɔpɛ̃]   *[ptitkɔpɛ̃] 
il est petit   [ilɛpti]   *[ilɛptit] 

Besides, as Laks (2018) also explains, from the classical period onwards, grammarians have described an extremely variable phenomenology, which they have divided into three distinct categories (Durand and Lyche 2008), to which we will refer throughout this chapter:

• Categorical liaisons, which are systematically realised by the speakers across all registers, and whose non-realisation is considered as incorrect and potentially foreign.

- Unattested/forbidden liaisons, which are never realised by the speakers across all registers, and whose realisation is considered as incorrect and potentially foreign.
- Variable liaisons, which are variably realised by the speakers, and which are therefore dependent on register, type of interaction and social status.

These elements provide a basic typology of French liaison in which variability appears to be central, not only as far as the nature of the consonant is concerned, but also since frequencies of distribution of the consonants differ from one variety of French to another (see Côté 2012 for Laurentian French), and since stylistic, sociolinguistic, interactional and morphosyntactic parameters can influence the rate of realisation of this phenomenon.

*Defining R-sandhi*

We shall use the same theory-neutral approach here when defining r-sandhi. The phenomenon of rhoticity creates an essential distinction among the varieties of English spoken around the world as it divides them into two major families: non-rhotic vs. rhotic varieties. In rhotic varieties, as in the American standard accent (General American; Cruttenden 2014), /r/, whatever its position in the syllable, is always realised: 'red' [ɹɛd], 'carry' [kæɹi], 'bar' [bɑːɹ], 'barn' [bɑːɹn], 'Barney' [bɑːɹni].

Conversely, in non-rhotic varieties of English, as in the British standard accent (General British; Cruttenden 2014), /r/ is realised in onset position but never realised when in coda position: 'red' [ɹɛd], 'carry' [kæɹi] vs. 'bar' [bɑː], 'barn' [bɑːn], 'Barney' [bɑːni].

There is an exception to this rule, when /r/ is word- or morpheme-final and followed by a vowel-initial word or morpheme, namely linking-r: 'store[ø]' vs. 'sto[ɹ] ing', 'sto[ɹ]age', a 'ba[ɹ] in London', 'core[ɹ] of'.

An [ɹ] may also be pronounced where there is no <r> in the spelling in between a vowel-final word or morpheme (traditionally described as [- high], i.e. [ə, ɑː, ɔː]) and a vowel-initial word or morpheme, as in: 'idea[ɹ] of' [aɪdɪəɹəv], 'draw[ɹ] a picture', 'draw[ɹ]ing'.

This phenomenon is traditionally called intrusive-r. We, along with other phonologists (Sudbury and Hay 2002), consider these phenomena as relics of a major historical change, namely the de-rhoticisation of Southern British English. With the gradual weakening and subsequent deletion of final /r/, two phenomena emerged: linking-r when an etymological <r> is present and, by analogy, intrusive-r when no etymological <r> is present, creating formal alternations such as 'letter' [Ø] – 'letter' [ɹ] and 'vanilla' [Ø] – 'vanilla' [ɹ] as well as 'car' [Ø] – 'car' [ɹ] and 'spa' [Ø] – 'spa' [ɹ] (McMahon 2000; Navarro 2016). We shall wonder in the next section (see 'Theoretical issues') whether linking-r and intrusive-r should be treated as one single r-sandhi phenomenon, or as two distinct sub-phenomena.

Variability is also central to the typology that has been made of the varieties of English with regards to r-sandhi. However, unlike what happens in French, this variability does not affect the nature of the linking consonant, as it is always [ɹ] in

English, but whether the realisation of r-sandhi is categorical or not. Consequently, in the literature, four idealised[7] varieties of English have been established with regards to r-sandhi:

1. Type A, in which linking-r is categorical and intrusive-r is absent, as in Received Pronunciation (RP as described by Jones 1917 or Wells 2008).
2. Type B, in which linking-r is categorical but intrusive-r is variable, as in Derby (Foulkes 1997) and Lancashire (Navarro 2013).
3. Type C, in which both linking-r and intrusive-r are categorical, as in Boston (as described by McCarthy 1991, 1993) and according to Hughes et al. (2005: 65).
4. Type D, in which both linking-r and intrusive-r are variable, as in Newcastle (Foulkes 1997).

*Theoretical Issues*

On the basis of the elementary definitions and typologies developed above (see sections 'Defining French liaison' and 'Defining r-sandhi'), there appear to be some common features shared by French liaison and English r-sandhi. For instance, the alternation between two phonetic forms in different contexts is central to the mechanics of both phenomena, and is also the reason why they are so often and so easily compared and considered as equivalents in both languages.

The issue of prescriptivism is also relevant to the study of both phenomena as we have pointed out that the distinction between linking-r and intrusive-r relies exclusively on orthographic information and knowledge, which explains why intrusive-r is often stigmatised and considered as non-existent in the early descriptions of RP. In the same way, in French, spelling is the key dimension in distinguishing between motivated liaisons, which rely on orthographic cues (*trop* [p] *appuyé*), and faulty liaisons (*trop* [z] *appuyé*), which are not motivated by orthographic information but by analogy with other potential colocations (*pas* [z] *appuyé*, *très* [z] *appuyé*).

What is more, we have shown that, with the descriptions yielded by the observation of corpus data, from the PFC and PAC data notably, French liaison and English r-sandhi are variable.

Nonetheless, there also appear to be some major discrepancies between French liaison and r-sandhi, and first of all in the different ways that variability affects these phenomena. On the one hand, we have pointed out that the typology of French liaisons is conditioned by Word-1, in terms of nature of the linking consonant, and sensitive to morphosyntactic information. On the other, the typology of English r-sandhi is conditioned by orthographic information in terms of nature of the phenomenon (linking vs. intrusion) and imbalance between the two phenomena, as well as frequency of realisation.

Consequently, it is because French liaison and English r-sandhi are variable that they constitute interesting challenges for phonological theory. And it is also because they are apparently similar, but differently variable, that they should be treated differently at the theoretical level.

Classical generative phonology

However, that is not what happened as both phenomena have been modelled in very similar ways within different theoretical frameworks. Indeed, in classical generative phonology for instance, a rule of deletion of an underlying consonant, as well as a rule of insertion of a surface segment, have been put forward to account for both phenomena.

For French liaison, Schane's early work (1968) was developed and extended within variants of the standard SPE model (Chomsky and Halle 1968) by Schane himself and by specialists such as Dell, Milner, Selkirk, Vergnaud, etc. They all shared the assumption that the liaison consonant is a final latent consonant on a par with fixed consonants, and that accounting for liaison is actually accounting for non-liaison: i.e. liaison is the passive result of the presence of a final consonant whenever it is not deleted by a process of truncation.

For English r-sandhi, the idea that words and morphemes have an underlying form that recapitulates the historical development of the language and therefore includes an /r/ has had many champions (Durand 1990; Carr 1999). It can easily account for varieties in which linking is categorical but intrusion is absent (type A). The corresponding deletion rule can be represented as follows:

$$/r/ \rightarrow \emptyset \ / \ \underline{\qquad} \ \{(\#,+)C, \#\#\} \text{ (categorical)}$$

Another way of looking at the issues of French liaison and English r-sandhi is to consider that they are not processes of deletion or truncation of an underlying consonant before a consonant or a pause, but processes of epenthesis of a phonetic segment before a vowel. In other words, this theoretical hypothesis corresponds to the inversion of the rule that we have just presented, and can be represented as follows:

$$\emptyset \rightarrow C \ / \ V \ \# \ \underline{\qquad} \ \# \ V$$

For French liaison, it has been defended by Klausenburger (1974), Tranel (1974) or Morin and Kaye (1982), to name but a few. As far as English r-sandhi is concerned, such an insertion rule has also been put forward, notably to account for varieties of English in which both linking and intrusion are categorical (type C). It can be represented as follows:

$$\emptyset \rightarrow \textipa{\*r} \ / \ [V, \text{-high}] \ \underline{\qquad} \ \# \ V \text{ (categorical)}$$

For varieties of English in which linking is categorical but intrusion is variable, two classes of words have been distinguished, namely words with a final <r> on the one hand and words with a final V on the other, in order to account for the imbalance between the two phenomena. Consequently, in such cases, both the deletion rule and the insertion rule presented above are required. This scenario has not been put forward in the literature on French liaison, even though it could be argued that the insertion rule would then account for faulty liaisons of the *quatre* [z] *enfants* type.

Even though such rules are still defended by many authors in order to account for these phenomena in both languages, the deletion or truncation rule has been deemed more suitable to account for French liaison whereas the epenthesis rule seems more problematic in the sense that the linking consonant in French is variable. Conversely, the insertion rule seems best able to account for English r-sandhi inasmuch as the linking consonant is unique ([ɹ]) and only appears after three types of vowels ([ə, ɑː, ɔː]). This would provide an argument for considering that English r-sandhi is 'more phonetic' (see section 'Conclusions') than French liaison. However, for varieties of English in which an imbalance is observed between linking and intrusion, postulating two separate rules, and therefore a distinction which is strictly based on spelling, has been deemed irrelevant from a phonological point of view.

Multilinear phonology

Even though many models of French liaison and English r-sandhi have benefited from the classical SPE take on these issues, many phonologists have tried to account for these phenomena within alternative theoretical frameworks, such as multilinear phonology for instance. Instead of looking at these issues with a set of transformational rules which apply in specific environments, multilinear phonology takes the view that such phenomena should be dealt with at the level of the syllable.

In fact, in the 1980s a large number of researchers converged towards the idea that liaison consonants are in some sense special: they are either extra-metrical or floating. If there is a free onset to the right, which can act as a host for the extra-metrical or floating consonant, it is saved. Otherwise, it is deleted by general convention or simply not 'heard'. For French liaison, such a hypothesis has been defended by Clements and Keyser (1981), Booij (1983), Encrevé (1983, 1988), Durand (1986), de Jong (1994), Davis (2000), to name but a few. As for English r-sandhi, the 'floating-r' hypothesis has mostly been championed by Harris (1994) within the specific framework of Government Phonology (GP).

Within such a model, a sequence such as *trop âgé* in French ('too old') would receive the following representations for its initial structure and in the case of a linked forward liaison. In the top representation (see Figure 5.1), it appears that the floating consonant ([p] in this specific case) is not anchored to the skeleton, whereas in the bottom representation, this floating segment is anchored to the skeleton as the following free onset is filled.

In the same way, in English, we can compare the respective representations (see Figure 5.2) of the sequence 'fear the', in which an <r> is followed by a consonantal onset, and 'fear a', in which an <r> is followed by a free onset. It appears, in the top representation, that the floating segment ([ɹ] in this specific case) is anchored to the skeleton as the following free onset is filled, whereas in the bottom representation, the same segment remains unlicensed as there is no free onset to dock onto.

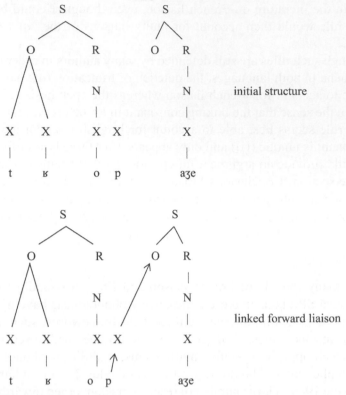

Figure 5.1 Floating segment interpretation of the sequence *trop âgé* in French

Multilinear phonology offers a common advantage to the treatment of both French liaison and English r-sandhi: the floating segment does not affect Word-1 but still provides a potential syllabic onset for such lexical processes as inflection, derivation and, of course, linking. In the case of English r-sandhi, the floating-r hypothesis provides a synchronic justification for the presence of centring diphthongs (NEAR, SQUARE and CURE; Wells 1982) in non-rhotic varieties of English. However, it has other limits, notably since it fails to account for the presence of a centring diphthong in words which do not alternate, such as *beard* for instance (see Durand et al. 2015; Navarro 2016: 109–114).

Optimality Theory

As there appear to be major arguments in favour of both previous accounts of French liaison and English r-sandhi, but also counter-arguments, phonologists have tried to model these phenomena by resorting to a set of constraints such as NO CODA, NO HIATUS, ONSET, FAITHFULNESS (MAX/DEP) and ALIGNMENT within the framework of Optimality Theory (OT) (Prince and Smolensky 1993). Within this framework, the selection of an optimal output form does not mean that it violates no constraint. The optimal output of a given input is the one which violates

*fear a*

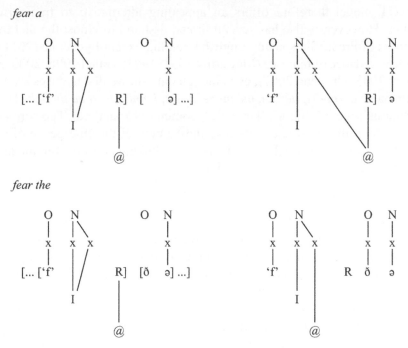

*fear the*

Figure 5.2 Floating-r representation of the sequence 'fear a' versus 'fear the' in English
*Source:* Harris (1994).

only the constraint(s) situated lower in a given hierarchy than the most penalising constraints.

For instance, when dealing with the sequence *petit anneau* in French ('small ring'), we would postulate that the first candidate (see Table 5.1) violates the Dep(L) constraint which states that one cannot add material to the input. And the second candidate violates the NO HIATUS constraint. As the latter constraint is ranked higher in the hierarchy than the Dep(L) constraint, the optimal candidate can therefore only be the first candidate, in which we observe a linked forward liaison.

As for English r-sandhi, McCarthy (1991, 1993) and Uffmann (2007) have put forward a similar treatment, notably based on the competition between two constraints: NO HIATUS, which requires a consonant or a glide in final position, and CODA COND which bans [ɹ] from post-nuclear position (see also Durand et al. 2015; Navarro 2016: 109–114).

Table 5.1  OT treatment of the sequence *petit anneau* in French

| /pəti {t} ano/ | *VV | Dep(L) |
|---|---|---|
| ☞ pœti t ano | | * |
| pœti ano | *! | |

*Source:* Tranel (2000: 52).

The OT model therefore offers an appealing alternative to transformational approaches. However, it also has several limits; first and foremost the fact that most OT accounts of French liaison and English r-sandhi, except Eychenne (2011), see as central the avoidance of hiatuses (McCarthy 1991, 1993; Tranel 1996, 2000; Steriade 1999; Féry 2003; Uffmann 2007), even though data shows that hiatuses are legion in both languages: *aéroport, aérien, méandre, oasis, Léon, Léa a eu un bébé* [Léa had a baby] / 'hiatus', 'go in', 'do it', 'key on', 'geometry', 'koala' etc. The core notion of the optimality of the anti-hiatus strategy, and namely of the emergence of a linking consonant, especially [ɹ] which is rarely used as a linking consonant in the languages of the world, can consequently be questioned.

Usage-based accounts

Finally, in our overview of the theoretical accounts that have been made of both liaison in French and r-sandhi in English, we would like to say a few words about usage-based accounts, which are the most recent models that have been put forward to deal with these phenomena, in the wake of the development of corpus phonology and data-mining tools. They rely on the close observation of variation and on the statistical frequency of use of the competing realisations of a form. They postulate that all the occurrences of a word, sound or colocation are stored within the speaker's memory along with fine phonetic and contextual details. Depending on the context/ situation, the speaker will use the most accurate, the most suitable, form.

For French liaison, this 'suppletion' scenario has been defended by Long (1977) and Gaatone (1978) for instance, who have hypothesised that speakers can have two or more forms in their lexicon: one that is used for liaison, and one or more for other contexts. Consequently, the form *gros* [big] would have three associated realisations: /groz/ (in a liaison context such as *gros ami* [big friend]), /gros/ (when associated with a feminine noun, as in *grosse entreprise* [big company]) and /gro/ (which would be the default realisation in all other contexts, such as *gros défaut* [big flaw]).

The same general mechanics can be postulated for English r-sandhi as well: Exemplar Theory (Bybee 2001; Pierrehumbert 2001, 2006) specifically claims that when a speaker interacts with another speaker, he/she produces the most accurate occurrence of the word or sound from what is called his/her cloud of exemplars, and that whenever a speaker hears a word, sound or colocation, his/her cloud of exemplars is updated. On the basis of this hypothesis, Sóskuthy (2009) has put forward a convincing account of r-sandhi which relies on the frequency of realisation of an [ɹ] before a vowel and on the memorisation of such colocations as 'better in', 'better at', 'better off' with a realised [ɹ] by speakers (see Table 5.2).

Discussion

We have shown that in dealing with French liaison and English r-sandhi simultaneously, in order to offer an in-depth comparison of both phenomena, we encounter many obstacles: namely, the two phenomenologies point to several directions that do not all seem compatible. Indeed, we have seen that defining these phenomena with a

Table 5.2 Cloud of exemplars for the word 'better' in a non-rhotic variety of English

| betə # ɹ # V | betə # C | betə ## |
|---|---|---|
| *better in* | *better parent* | *it's better.* |
| *better at* | *better teacher* | *You'd better.* |
| *better off* | *better care* | *Better. Faster.* |
| betə # ʔ # V | | |

*Source:* Sóskuthy (2009).

theory-neutral approach is not so simple given that formulations such as 'emergence' or 'realisation' of a segment can infer that such segment is present at the underlying level for instance. What is more, we have briefly indicated that both phenomena are variable, from a geographical point of view but also in terms of behaviour, context of appearance, etc., which makes them challenging for phonological theory. And, indeed, several competing accounts of how liaison and r-sandhi work have been put forward, all of which have advantages and limits. Moreover, the advantages and the limits are not necessarily the same depending on whether we are considering French liaison or English r-sandhi, which suggests that both phenomena are difficult to account for with the same theoretical approach, which again suggests that we are in fact dealing with two distinct phenomenologies. We hope to have pointed to several essential elements in recognising that both liaison and r-sandhi have formal, and not so formal, points in common, but also major discrepancies that make them differently compatible with the diverse theoretical hypotheses that have been put forward to account for them.

Before moving on to a thorough comparison of how both phenomena work on the basis of authentic oral data from the PAC and PFC programmes, we would like to say a few words about how these tricky issues have been tackled from a methodological point of view.

## Methodological Issues: The PAC and PFC Data on R-sandhi and Liaison

As we have already mentioned, starting with Schane (1968), most theoretical studies on French liaison and English r-sandhi have been using data inherited from the prescriptive tradition, and in particular manuals for teaching French and English to foreign learners (Grevisse, Fouché, etc.). The type of data used for the theoretical modelling of these phenomena has had a major impact on the corresponding terminology: for instance, obligatory and forbidden liaisons (see section 'Defining French liaison').

The PFC programme developed at the end of the 1990s in order to study such phonological phenomena as liaison on the basis of authentic and recent oral data collected from all the French-speaking regions of the world. A few years later, the PAC programme was born with the same goal: to build a large database of spoken English in its geographical, stylistic and social diversity.

The methodology adopted within the PAC programme is inspired by the classical work of Labov (e.g. 1966, 1972, 1994, 2001) and relies on the construction of corpora of recordings of spoken English throughout the world. This methodology is similar to that of the PFC programme (see Durand et al. 2003, 2009) and revolves around four registers. It includes reading tasks, and more specifically the reading aloud of two wordlists focusing on segmental phonology as well as the reading aloud of a text which gives researchers additional access to segmental aspects as well as aspects of post-lexical phonology (notably liaison and r-sandhi as far as we are concerned here). As orthographic knowledge along with prestige and stigma have proved to be relevant factors in the study of both French liaison and English r-sandhi, both the PFC and PAC programmes continue to include reading tasks in their core methodology, despite the criticism that goes along with the inclusion of the unnatural, non-ecological elicitation of speech by informants.

The PFC and PAC methodology, most importantly, includes conversational contexts, and more specifically a semi-guided conversation between the fieldworker and the informant as well as an informal conversation involving two or three speakers belonging to the same close network (friends or family members). This latter conversation ideally takes place outside of the presence of the fieldworker and is crucial as it offers access to the type of linguistic interaction that involves the least self-monitoring and hypercorrection. It brings the data closer to what can be drawn from surreptitious recordings, an unacceptable method on ethical grounds.

As for PAC more specifically, the two wordlists combined with the text and conversations notably help researchers determine whether the system under study is rhotic or non-rhotic and to explore the consequences of the presence or absence of /r/ on the vowel system. It contains several potential sites of r-sandhi (both linking and intrusion).

The protocol we describe here is systematically applied to each survey point, within PFC and PAC, which allows for comparisons between varieties of French and varieties of English respectively, but also between French liaison and English r-sandhi. Investigators are nonetheless free to add other elements if they wish, and for the study of r-sandhi, adding an extra reading task (short sentences in the New Zealand PAC corpus; Viollain 2014: 381–385) proved necessary as the natural contexts for the emergence of r-sandhi are rare.

Indeed, while the PFC programme has collected more than 50,000 codings for liaison based on recordings with close to 400 speakers from seventy-seven different corpora, the PAC programme has only been able to collect about 2,000 codings from three corpora (PAC Lancashire, Boston and New Zealand) with twenty-six speakers. We should nevertheless add that the study of liaison and r-sandhi within PFC and PAC respectively is ongoing and that the figures provided here are bound to evolve, especially as far as r-sandhi is concerned since the PAC-LVTI Manchester corpus (see Chatellier 2016 as well as this volume) is currently being coded for rhoticity and r-sandhi. Still, these figures eloquently illustrate the discrepancy between French liaison and English r-sandhi in terms of frequency, and we shall come back to this issue in the next section.

One conclusion that can quickly be drawn from studying the codings is that, on the basis of the PAC corpora for English r-sandhi, no case of 'liaison non-enchaînée' is attested in consistently non-rhotic speakers, whereas it is definitely present in the PFC corpora for French liaison. The codings revealed other major differences between the two phenomena that we shall systematically explore in the next section.

## Results: A Systematic Comparison of the PFC and PAC Data

In this section, we wish to proceed with our comparison of French liaison and English r-sandhi by discussing the results yielded by the PFC and PAC data and their implications for the theoretical modelling of these phenomena. We will consider some of the linguistic factors which condition the two processes, and notably: left context (number of syllables, lexical frequency and lexical category of Word-1), right context (number of syllables, frequency and lexical category of Word-2), W1–W2 relationship (syntactic and prosodic dependence, collocational frequency). As mentioned in the section 'Methodological issues: the PAC and PFC data on r-sandhi and liaison' above, the PFC and PAC methodologies include reading tasks and conversational contexts, and thus provide us with information about stylistic variation.

At this point, we would like to underline the fact that the category known as 'h-aspiré' in French (Gussman 2002: 69–72 for a brief review), which blocks liaison since W2 is analysed as underlyingly consonant-initial (e.g. *les*[Ø] *haricots*), has no equivalent in English. All things being equal, r-sandhi can be realised when the W2-initial /h/ is not realised phonetically. This happens mostly on reduced variants of grammatical words (e.g. 'for him' [fəɹɪm]), but also on lexical words in the specific case of /h/ dropping[8] (e.g. 'they're horrible' [ðeəɹˈɒɹɪbl̩]).

*Domain*

The domains of application of French liaison and that of r-sandhi have been proven to differ on the syntactic and prosodic levels. Some syntactic environments are indeed hostile to liaison. To give but one example at this point (we shall come back to morphosyntactic conditioning in the section 'Morphosyntactic conditioning'), liaison is not allowed between a noun phrase (NP) and a verb phrase (VP). For instance, the liaison after W1 *petit* is realised within the NP [le petit ami] while it is unattested in sequences such as [le petit] [arrive], where *petit* and *arrive* belong to two separate syntactic constituents. The PFC data confirm the weight of this constraint, since even in the most formal register (reading out loud of a text), no occurrence of realised liaison can be found in NP-VP constructions.

In the same way, liaison is blocked by sentence boundaries. French is however relatively flexible from a rhythmic standpoint as its sensitivity to pauses is somewhat limited. Forward linking after a pause or hesitation (e.g. *mes* [PH] … [z]*amis*) is attested and in fact quite frequent in the PFC data. The possibility in French to realise a liaison consonant without forward linking ('liaison non-enchaînée') also testifies to this low sensitivity to rhythm. Nevertheless, this type of liaison is usually limited to the speech of politicians, journalists, teachers, lawyers, etc., and often corresponds to scripted speech or to what Durand and Lyche (2008: 51) describe as 'contexts of marked linguistic tension'. Unlinked forward liaison represents only 0.35 per cent of realised liaison occurrences in the PFC database (Mallet 2008) and, when found in spontaneous speech, those cases generally involve marked hesitations. Cases of liaison across speakers are even attested as in the following example noted by Morin (in Durand 1990: 195):

Speaker 1: *Je cherchais des* [ʒəʃɛʁʃede] … [I was looking for …]
Speaker 2: … [z]*allumettes* [zalymɛt]? [matches?]

Such cases constitute a first argument supporting the fact that French liaison cannot be treated as a mere hiatus breaking strategy.

If we turn to the results from the PAC database, our first observation is that (as opposed to what happens in French) syntactic boundaries do not block r-sandhi. In the PAC Lancashire corpus alone, we have found six occurrences of realised r-sandhi cases between two independent clauses:

LB1: *Oh yeah, I do have a brother121, I, I haven't mentioned him.*
MO1: *I'm not sure111, it looks a bit peculiar.*
LC1: *Oh, I'm sure111, I'm sure.*
MO1: *I mean when he, when he was younger121, I mean he was in dramatics.*
ST1: *I did have a good career121, I worked hard to, to get on the airline.*
ST1: *Probably because of my drama121, I don't know.*

However, these occurrences are not sufficient to fully discard syntactic boundaries as being relevant to r-sandhi conditioning. Indeed, upon inspection of the cases of non-realised r-sandhi in the Lancashire corpus, we noted that out of the 148 cases of non-realised linking-r, 120 involve an <h> clue in coding field 4 (i.e. a pause or hesitation) and sixty-five of them are followed by a comma <,>. In the PAC (and PFC) orthographic transcription conventions, a comma is used to separate repeated items, signal a brief pause or mark tone-unit boundaries, the last generally coinciding with syntactic boundaries. Consequently, we argue that syntactic boundaries remain relevant insofar as they have a rhythmic interpretation in the form of pauses.

Unlike French, English does not allow linking across a pause or hesitation. Even though we left open the possibility of observing an English equivalent to French liaison non-enchaînée, the cases of <rh> coding are only marginal. Navarro (2013: 269) found four such occurrences in the Lancashire corpus (e.g. 'when you're111rh, in, in the er, in the States'), nine occurrences in the Boston corpus (e.g. 'I like soccer121rh and'), and Viollain's (2014: 437–438) analysis of the PAC New Zealand data yielded ten occurrences (e.g. 'there wasn't any talk of the poor111rh or the needy'). In most cases, these occurrences can be interpreted as residual traces of rhoticity, especially when they occur before a relatively long pause. However, when produced by speakers whose non-rhoticity is stable, they can be viewed as cases of an anticipated r-sandhi hampered by a rhythmic accident. Finally, as regards the unattested realisation of r-sandhi after a pause or hesitation, let alone across speakers, the PAC data confirms their absence. Therefore, we argue that U (utterance) is the relevant prosodic domain of r-sandhi, since the only condition for its realisation is a phonetic fluidity which excludes pauses.

### Influence of Stress

The influence of stress on the realisation of r-sandhi has been tested on the basis of the PAC corpora by enriching the basic coding system used in PAC (Navarro 2013: 239–240; Viollain 2014: 421–422). We added two coding fields to account for the degree of stress: S1 (Syllable 1, the last syllable of W1) and S2 (Syllable 2, the first syllable of W2). Given the general lack of agreement on the stress properties of English syllables in connected speech, we have established three non-controversial categories in order to remain as neutral as possible from a theoretical point of view:

1. corresponds to a nuclear or tonic syllable;
2. corresponds to a non-nuclear syllable (the distinction between primary and secondary (possibly tertiary) stresses, at the lexical level, is not taken into account);
3. corresponds to an unstressed syllable (whether its vowel is full or reduced).

The quantitative results of this analysis are summarised in Table 5.3.

Our coding of the PAC data reveals that the degree of stress of S1 seems to have slightly more impact on the realisation of r-sandhi than that of S2. R-sandhi is less frequent when S1 is the tonic syllable of the unit, with only 36 per cent of realisation when S2 is stressed, and 60 per cent when S2 is unstressed. In thirty-nine out of the forty cases of non-realisation after a nuclear S1, we find an <h> or <h,> clue in the coding indicating the presence of a pause or the resort to an alternative hiatus breaking strategy such as glottal stop or laryngealisation. We believe that in those cases, the absence of r-sandhi disrupts the flow of connected speech and therefore isolates Word-1, which contributes to the emphasis created by the nuclear stress. Even though it is not as significant, the adjacency of an unstressed S1 and a nuclear S2 produces relatively little r-sandhi in our data (in line with Foulkes 1997 and Hannisdal

Table 5.3 Frequency of realisation of r-sandhi as a function of stress level of S1 and S2 in the PAC Lancashire corpus

|  | Syllable 2 nuclear stress % | Syllable 2 Stressed % | Syllable 2 Unstressed % |
|---|---|---|---|
| **Syllable 1 nuclear stress** |  | 36 | 60 |
| **Syllable 1 stressed** | 75 | 80 | 72 |
| **Syllable 1 unstressed** | 67 | 72 | 72 |

*Source:* Navarro (2013: 252).

2006). Occurrences found in the PAC Lancashire corpus such as 'in their schoolbag for013112h hours' or 'The sky was never013122h empty of planes' (where the bold alphanumeric symbols indicate the degrees of stress), in which S2 has a glottalised onset, suggest that the stressed vowel requires extra articulatory effort which makes it more likely to be preceded by a glottal stop, which in turn prevents r-sandhi.

Such an analysis of the influence of stress on liaison has not been carried out in PFC. One obvious reason for that is that French is a syllable-timed language and has no lexical stress, but as is the case for English, specialists tend to disagree on the stress properties of French utterances. However, it has been pointed out by Coustenoble and Armstrong (1934: 142–143) that one of the motivations for liaison non-enchaînée was the introduction of an emphatic stress on S2. They comment on the following example: *Je suis enchanté de vous voir*. According to them, a vowel-initial word can receive an 'intensive stress' on the first of its syllables beginning with a consonant (i.e. *Je suis*[z] *en''chanté de vous voir*), but when that emphatic stress is placed on the first syllable, '[t]he liaison consonant is pronounced but it does not function as a liaison consonant, the speaker inserting the glottal plosive which starts the emphasised syllable in its stead: ʒ sɥiz ''ʔɑ̃ʃɑ̃te d vu 'vwaʁ [...]'. If a significant proportion of the occurrences of liaison non-enchaînée found in the PFC data were characterised by a nuclear S2, we could support the hypothesis of an influence of stress on liaison. But as we have mentioned above (see section 'Domain'), most cases of liaison non-enchaînée in the PFC corpora involve hesitation rather than emphasis on S2.

*Sensitivity to Register*

The PFC and PAC protocols allow for the comparison of liaison and r-sandhi in three connected speech tasks – namely, the reading out loud of a text, a semi-guided interview and an informal conversation – providing access to three types of register decreasing in formality. Recent investigations of the PFC database have revealed that the difference in frequency of realisation between formal (43.13 per cent) and informal (44.52 per cent) conversations is not statistically significant (Durand et al. 2011: 126). This limited disparity could be due to a lack of differentiation between the two types of conversations (although they have been shown to differ in terms of their phonological properties (Boula de Mareüil et al. 2007)), and significant differences may only be found through a more fine-grained analysis of the various variable contexts (Eychenne 2011) rather than in overall frequencies.

At any rate, we have observed the same tendency in the frequencies of realised r-sandhi in the PAC data. In the Lancashire corpus (Navarro 2013), the formal conversations produce 79 per cent of realised sandhi and the informal conversations yield 73 per cent overall (individually, a higher rate may be observed in the informal conversation) and Viollain's (2014) analysis of the PAC New Zealand data indicates comparable results, with means of 62 per cent realised r-sandhi in the semi-guided interview and 64 per cent in the informal conversation. These results show that the formality of the conversation does not impact r-sandhi realisation and, as suggested by Durand et al. (2011) for liaison, a much more formal style such as public speaking may be necessary to observe macroscopic differences.

While both liaison and r-sandhi seem to behave in a statistically similar manner in the spontaneous speech tasks, a remarkable difference emerges from the analysis of the text. Indeed, the PFC data show a significant increase in overall liaison realisation between the conversations (43.4 per cent) and the text (59.4 per cent). In the latter task, the speakers seem to make use of the available orthographic information to produce liaison more frequently in the variable contexts. This influence of orthographic knowledge (or of the availability of orthographic information) on phonology is known as the Buben effect (after Buben 1935, see Laks 2005 and the references therein).

Interestingly, the situation in English is the opposite since the reading task in our corpora systematically yields lower rates of realised r-sandhi than the conversations. As an example, the text produces only 71 per cent of realised r-sandhi, and the two conversational styles combined average 75 per cent in the Lancashire corpus. Even though they are comparable, these scores seem to indicate that the orthographic information is of no help in the realisation of r-sandhi. We believe that the lower rate of realised r-sandhi in the text reading task can be explained by a slower rhythm and more frequent pauses and hesitations that generally disfavour connected speech processes. However, we must remain cautious and explore the relationship between speech tempo and r-sandhi realisation in more detail since individual scores range from 50 per cent to 100 per cent, and the speaker who scores 100 per cent does not necessarily seem to read twice as fast as the speaker who scores 50 per cent. Unexpectedly, we found that the score for non-etymological r-sandhi (intrusive-r) in the text (39 per cent) was comparable to that of the conversations (31 per cent). Given the limited number of occurrences of intrusion in the corpus, we are not able to assess the statistic imbalance between the two tasks. However, it is important to notice that intrusion is not blocked by the available orthographic information. Bearing in mind the stigmatisation which is usually attached to it, we had predicted that our informants would take advantage of the orthographic information to avoid intrusions.

*Number of Syllables of W1 and W2*

The syllabic make-up of Word-1 and Word-2 constitutes a possible point of convergence between French liaison and r-sandhi. Statistical work on the PFC database by Mallet (2008) has shown that realised liaison is significantly more frequent after a monosyllabic W1 (66 per cent) than after a polysyllabic W1 (7 per cent). Although not as dramatic, we do observe a similar discrepancy in the three PAC corpora we have investigated (Viollain 2010, 2014; Navarro 2013). The length of W1 seems to be the determining factor, as can be seen in Table 5.4 based on the Lancashire, Boston and New Zealand surveys. A monosyllabic W1 is followed by a realised r-sandhi in 65.1 per cent of cases and this frequency drops to 54.1 per cent after a polysyllabic W1. The mono- or polysyllabicity of W2 only amounts to a difference of only 3.4 points. These results are also consistent with Hannisdal's (2006) analyses.

Table 5.4 Influence of the number of syllables of W1 and W2 on the frequency of realisation of r-sandhi in the PAC Lancashire, Boston and New Zealand corpora

|  | W2 monosyllabic % | W2 polysyllabic % | Total % |
|---|---|---|---|
| **W1 monosyllabic** | 62.7 | 72.5 | 65.1 |
| **W1 polysyllabic** | 56.3 | 45.1 | 54.1 |
| **Total** | 60.3 | 63.7 | 100 |

Compared to the overall results, Viollain's (2014) analysis of this factor in the PAC New Zealand corpus shows a higher difference between monosyllabic (53 per cent) and polysyllabic W2 (68.3 per cent) when W1 is monosyllabic. However, she explains that this discrepancy may be due to the fact that she considered the hesitation marks, conventionally transcribed as 'er' within PAC, as potential linking-r sites, most of which were not realised (2014: 442).

Considering these results from a strictly phonological point of view may be somewhat misleading as this discrepancy may in fact be due to syntactic and lexical factors. In both French and English, grammatical words tend to be mono-syllabic rather than polysyllabic, and the realisation of liaison and r-sandhi may in fact undergo the influence of the syntactic category of W1 and W2, to which we now turn.

*Morphosyntactic Conditioning*

As we have mentioned above, French liaison is very sensitive to morphosyntactic conditioning. The contexts in which liaison is traditionally described as categorical, variable or unattested are actually defined by the syntactic category of W1 and W2. Below are but a few examples.

Categorical liaison between:
- a determiner and an adjective or a noun (e.g. *un*[n] *heureux hasard, les*[z] *enfants*);
- a proclitic and another proclitic or a verb (e.g. *vous*[z] *en*[n] *avez, on*[n] *arrive*);
- a verb or enclitic and an enclitic (e.g. *dit*[t]-*il, allez*[z]-*y, allez-vous*[z]-*en*);
- compounds and fixed phrases (e.g. *accent*[t] *aigu, comment*[t] *allez-vous, tout*[t]-*à-fait*).

Variable liaison (Coquillon et al. 2010) between:
- an adjective and a noun (e.g. PFC text *grand*[t] *honneur* vs. *grand*[t/Ø] *émoi*);
- a preposition and another constituent (e.g. *en*[n/Ø] *une heure, chez*[z/Ø] *un copain*).

Unattested liaison between:
- a singular noun and an adjective (e.g. *un coup*[Ø] *imprévu*);
- a noun and a verb (e.g. *les enfants*[Ø] *arrivent*).

Recent PFC quantitative work has investigated a subcorpus of 16,873 occurrences of realised liaison to assess the productivity of the various morphosyntactic environments. The results show that a very limited number of environments can account for the vast majority of realised liaison occurrences. When reducing the various grammatical categories of W1 and W2 to twelve large categories, (noun, verb, adjective, adverb, preposition, etc.), Durand et al. (2011: 120–122) obtain 111 possible combinations. When ranked from the most frequent to the less frequent combination, it appears that the first twenty-one of these combinations account for more than 90 per cent of the realised liaison occurrences. They conclude: 'Ainsi, la maîtrise d'un très petit nombre de constructions extrêmement fréquentes et d'un lexique très limité suffit à rendre compte de l'usage réel de la liaison en français contemporain' (Durand et al. 2011: 121). [Thus, the mastering of a very small number of extremely frequent constructions and of a very limited lexicon is enough to account for the real usage of liaison in contemporary French.][9]

It is important to note that there is no equivalent to compulsory, variable and unattested contexts in the study of r-sandhi. To our knowledge, there is no single context in which r-sandhi can be considered compulsory, that is to say in which non-rhotic native speakers would deem an absence of r-sandhi incorrect. As a matter of fact, there seem to be no restrictions whatsoever on the syntactic category of W1 and W2, and the morphosyntactic environments described above as hostile to the realisation of French liaison can potentially host an r-sandhi site. Even a unit such as the hesitation marker 'er', whose lexical status is questionable, allows r-sandhi. It can be found frequently in W2 position in the PAC database (e.g. 'in their[ɹ] er', 'most of us are[ɹ] er') and is also attested in W1 position ('just … [əːɹ] a bit more' noted by Heselwood 2006). Such occurrences therefore reinforce the idea that r-sandhi is a rather low-level phenomenon which only requires a final non-high vowel and a following vowel to be rhythmically close to each other.

Although no single morphosyntactic context can be considered prohibitive in English, some authors have mentioned a greater tendency for r-sandhi to be realised after a grammatical word than after a lexical word. Viollain (2014) has calculated the proportion of grammatical (prepositions, pronouns, possessive adjectives, auxiliaries) and lexical (nouns, verbs, adjectives, adverbs) W1 words in cases of realised r-sandhi in the PAC New Zealand corpus. Her results are summarised in Table 5.5.

It appears in Table 5.5 that grammatical words favour r-sandhi more than lexical words, with respective proportions of 64 per cent and 36 per cent. Among those

Table 5.5 Proportion of grammatical and lexical words in cases of realised r-sandhi after a monosyllabic W1

| *for* | *here/there/ where* | *BE (were/are/'re)* | *your* | *or* | *her* | *our* | *their* | lexical words |
|---|---|---|---|---|---|---|---|---|
| 17,25% | 12.75% | 21% | 4.25% | 4.25% | 1.75% | 1.5% | 1.25% | 36% |

*Source:* Viollain (2014: 443).

grammatical words, the various <re>-final allomorphs of the BE auxiliary are well represented (21 per cent), as are the preposition 'for' (17.25 per cent), and the adverbs of place 'here' and 'there', and the adverb/conjunction/pronoun 'where' (amounting to 12.75 per cent). These results may explain why r-sandhi is proportionally less frequent after a polysyllabic W1. Indeed, most of these polysyllabic W1s are lexical words. Viollain (2014) goes on to show that the number of polysyllabic grammatical W1s is relatively limited and includes the prepositions 'over', 'after', 'before' and 'under', the adverbs 'never' and 'ever' (and the derived forms of 'ever'), the conjunctions 'either' and 'whether', as well as the derived forms of 'where' ('somewhere', 'anywhere', 'everywhere'). These grammatical words represent only 19.3 per cent of the words that trigger r-sandhi in her data, which means that 80.7 per cent of r-sandhi triggering polysyllabic W1s are lexical. The results confirm that in addition to the number of syllables of W1, its syntactic category (grammatical vs. lexical) is a relevant factor for r-sandhi variation.

*Lexical Frequency Aspects*

As we have shown in the previous section, PFC research has confirmed that a small core of categorical liaison environments account for the usage of liaison in contemporary French, whereas PAC's analyses of r-sandhi reveal no such limitation but, rather, indicate a higher rate of realised r-sandhi after a grammatical W1 than after a lexical W1.

Such contexts as <Adjective + Noun> and <Prep + X> have traditionally been treated as prime examples of categorical liaison environments in French (Delattre 1951, 1966). However, a narrower investigation of the PFC database shows that those contexts are in fact variable and reveals that the token frequency of W1 and W2 is a relevant factor in the conditioning of their variability.

The first significant observation is that <Adjective + Noun> sequences appear frequently in the PFC database but rarely in liaison contexts, and, when they do, liaison is not categorical. For instance, Durand and Lyche (2008: 45) record 139 prenominal occurrences of the adjective *gros* in the database and only eight of them occur in a liaison environment. Among those eight occurrences, liaison is realised in six plural forms (e.g. *gros*[z] *ouvrages*) and in the set phrase *gros*[z] *oeuvre*, but it is absent from the singular *gros*[Ø] *immeuble*. Other examples from PFC presented by Durand et al. (2011: 116) (*petits*[Ø] *entrepreneurs*, *petit*[Ø] *accent*, *longues*[Ø] *années*) suggest that the emblematic examples chosen by phonologists to illustrate categorical liaison are not as regular as originally thought and, most importantly, that speakers tend to avoid situations in which they will have to make a decision concerning the realisation vs. non-realisation of liaison.

Another meaningful observation is that the frequency of liaison after a prenominal adjective is significantly correlated with the frequency of co-occurrence of W1 and W2. Coquillon et al. (2010) illustrate this tendency by examining 256 readings of the PFC text where the sequences *grand émoi* and *grand honneur* can be found. The first of these two sequences is relatively uncommon (41,900 occurrences on Google) and only produces 208 liaisons in [t], along with forty-one non-realisations and seven erratic liaisons. The second expression, which is roughly twelve times more frequent (528,000 occurrences on Google[10]) yields 241 expected liaisons in [t], along with fourteen non-realisations and two erratic liaisons). These results indicate that the familiarity of speakers with a given sequence has an impact on the realisation of liaison.

Viollain (2014) has analysed the various potential sites for linking-r and intrusive-r in a task of short sentence reading which she added to the PAC protocol in order to elicit more r-sandhi contexts. Her results seem to indicate that the collocational frequency of W1 and W2 has an impact on both linking and intrusion. Indeed, frequent collocations such as 'for a while', 'far away' or 'law and order' produce nearly categorical r-sandhi, while less common collocations such as 'other option' or 'bra and' generate variable r-sandhi (Viollain 2014: 433–435). This suggests that speakers do not store only words but also phrases, and that along with those segments, r-sandhi is also stored.

This type of effect relating to token frequency may however be subject to inter-speaker variation since the usage of a given lexical item may vary from one speaker to the next. The PAC Lancashire data provide us with an illustration involving the word 'dyslexia'. While the latter cannot be described as a frequent word in everyday language use, one of the PAC Lancashire speakers, MD1, who is a PhD student in psychology doing research on that condition and to whom this word is very familiar, pronounces an intrusive-r in all three occurrences of the word ('dyslexia and' (x 2) and 'dyslexia it').

*Additional Elements*

To complete this comparison of French liaison and English r-sandhi, we wish to offer a few additional observations that emerged from the analysis of the PFC and PAC data.

As was mentioned in the section 'Methodological issues: the PAC and PFC data on r-sandhi and liaison', the overall incidences of the two phenomena are very different. Although r-sandhi is more frequently realised than French liaison, its average number of occurrences (potential sites) per speaker is more limited. The PAC Lancashire and Boston corpora yield an average of sixty occurrences per speaker and the New Zealand corpus, with its extra reading task, offers around ninety occurrences per speaker. In comparison, PFC data produce an average of 135 occurrences per speaker. Keeping in mind that the text and five minutes of each conversation are usually coded in PFC, whereas ten (or more) minutes of each conversation have generally been coded in PAC, one can assess the amount of data necessary to obtain statistically significant r-sandhi results. It is all the more difficult to collect solid intrusive-r data that the latter is even less frequent than linking-r (e.g. around seventeen occurrences per speaker in the PAC New Zealand corpus). However, we wish to point out that one of the most solid empirical studies on r-sandhi is that of Foulkes (1997) who worked with an average of thirty-one potential sites per speaker in his Derby study and thirty-seven potential sites per speaker in his Newcastle study.

Even though the incidence of intrusive-r is limited, we have gathered enough data to be able to evaluate the balance between linking and intrusion in our corpora. As was mentioned above, some phonologists (e.g. Harris 1994) deny the existence of what we have defined as type B varieties, in which there is an imbalance between linking and intrusion. Nevertheless, our coding scheme seems to confirm that the rate of realisation of linking-r is superior to that of intrusive-r. In the PAC Lancashire corpus for instance, the overall rate of linking-r realisation in conversational tasks is 75 per cent vs. 31 per cent for intrusive-r. Given that many cases of non-realisation of r-sandhi involve a pause, we have calculated those frequencies again, this time eliminating all cases which involve an <h,> coding. Thus, the cases of non-realisation we are left with are only true hiatuses. The frequencies we obtain are 84 per cent for linking-r vs. 46 per cent for intrusion. This shows that even when eliminating the main obstacle to r-sandhi (i.e. random pauses), linking is still more frequently realised than intrusion and probably so because of the stigmatisation of the latter in most varieties of English. This ratio is slightly different in the PAC New Zealand corpus where the conversational tasks produce 62 per cent of realised linking and 46 per cent of realised intrusion. The imbalance is thus still significant but somewhat reduced. The higher frequency of realised intrusion is reminiscent of what Foulkes (1997) found in his Newcastle data and which he attributed to the fact that intrusive-r is not stigmatised in Newcastle but, rather, treated as a prestigious or formal feature (1997: 83–84). However, this hypothesis does not seem to apply to the PAC New Zealand corpus since the frequency of realisation of intrusion drops to 18 per cent in the more formal reading task.

## Conclusions

In this chapter we have shown that French liaison and English r-sandhi may seem similar at first glance, in that they consist in an alternation between the presence or absence of a consonant at the boundary between W1 and W2. The two phenomena have therefore received similar theoretical treatments from specialists who often built their analyses on a limited number of randomly collected examples that do not necessarily account for real usage. In the PFC and PAC programmes, we are committed to a methodology that addresses the shortcomings of traditional approaches by investigating these two phenomena in a thorough and systematic manner. The analyses based on our coding results indicate that liaison and r-sandhi are in fact conditioned by constraints of a different nature.

As we have shown in the sections 'Domain' and 'Sensitivity to register' above, orthography has a much stronger impact on liaison than it does on r-sandhi. Even though it is extremely rare and restricted to scripted speech, unlinked forward liaison testifies to this impact in French and remains unattested in English, where the only aspect linked to orthography is the potential stigmatisation of non-etymological r-sandhi. Relatedly, analyses of the PFC and PAC corpora also attest to a greater sensitivity of French to stylistic variation, with a significant increase of realised liaison in reading tasks compared to conversations, while the opposite tendency is observed with r-sandhi, as the latter seems to be dependent mostly on rhythm. What is more, we have underlined that in cases of obligatory liaison (e.g. between an article and a noun), the absence of liaison is deemed incorrect by French native speakers whereas an absence of linking-r is generally not frowned upon. These observations suggest that French liaison is more socially stratified than English r-sandhi. We must however remain cautious on these questions. Indeed, while de Jong (1994) found a significant effect of gender on the realisation of liaison, Eychenne et al. (2014) do not confirm the influence of that variable based on PFC data. As far as English is concerned, the literature does not generally mention any effect of gender on r-sandhi, but Viollain (2014) found that female speakers in the PAC New Zealand corpus produced significantly less r-sandhi than men and had a greater tendency to exploit alternative hiatus breaking strategies such as laryngealisation.

It is essential to stress that French liaison as a whole is better described by the use of several concurrent mechanisms (Côté 2005). For instance, Durand and Lyche (2008) suggest that liaison involving plural forms (e.g. *les*[z] *amis*, *petits*[z] *immeubles*) seems well suited for a treatment by epenthesis. They demonstrate that the /z/ in *les*, *des*, *ces*, etc. cannot be argued to be underlying because their vowel would surface as [ɛ] (*[lɛzami], *[dɛzami]) rather than [e] in southern French varieties, violating the 'loi de position' (see Durand 1976). A treatment such as Morin's (2003) in which /z/ is posited as a special prefix of W2, on the grounds that it sometimes surfaces outside of liaison environments (e.g. *On prend quoi comme z-affaires, Je préfère la version z-années soixante*) is also problematic because erratic forms such as *Etudiants* [zetydjã] or *Avocats* [zavɔka] never seem to appear in utterance-initial position. Durand and Lyche comment: 'It should however be observed that when noun phrases consist of plural nouns in utterance-initial position which are not echo repetitions of some other utterance, it does not seem that one observes plural [z] markers' (2008: 55).

Nonetheless, in a number of cases, a truncation analysis seems better adapted to the data. For instance, Durand (1988) maintains that in southern French, the final nasal in such words as *mon, ton, bon* must be underlyingly present in coda (or nuclear) position in order to account for the mid-open vowel that surfaces in e.g. *mon ami* [mɔnami]. If the nasal segment were epenthetic, extrametrical or prefixal in W2, the expected surface form would be *[monami], which is not what is observed. In addition to these transformational mechanisms, suppletion analyses such as Steriade's (1999) seem particularly well-adapted to the modelling of liaison involving prenominal adjectives. In such cases, the hiatus can be resolved by resorting to the feminine allomorph of the adjective since it is often consonant-final, e.g. if $_{masc}$/bõ/ and $_{fem}$/bɔn/ are available, liaison between *bon* and *ami* will be achieved by selection of the feminine allomorph, hence /bɔnami/. In contrast, r-sandhi is more straightforward and seems to require one, possibly two, mechanisms to account for the [r]/Ø alternation, whether formulated in terms of rules, extrametrical segment or constraints.

Thus, the fundamental difference between liaison and r-sandhi lies in the fact that French liaison is a multidimensional process which involves stylistic, morphosyntactic and phonological information, while r-sandhi is a lower-level phonological process which is little influenced by factors other than rhythmic ones.

Beyond the classical phonological accounts which seek to provide models in which words are considered individually and combined through a variety of mechanisms, we have stressed the necessity of considering the possibility for holistic sequences to be stored along with their liaison consonant in both French and English. Combinatorial models can indeed be challenged by the notion of collocational frequency. As we have shown in the section 'Lexical frequency aspects' above, the word *grand* in the PFC text triggers the expected liaison in [t] much more frequently in the common phrase *grand honneur* than in the comparatively rarer phrase *grand émoi*. If the realisation of liaison relied exclusively on a well-oiled low-level (morpho) phonological rule or principle, we would expect the frequency of realised liaison to be similar, even if not categorical, in both sequences. In the same way, it seems that r-sandhi can be influenced by the frequency of co-occurrence of W1 and W2, as argued by Viollain (2014) who found categorical linking-r and intrusive-r realisation in the common phrases 'for[r] a while', 'far[r] away', 'stare[r] at', 'law[r] and order', while less frequent sequences triggered variable r-sandhi or no r-sandhi at all.

Relatedly, it seems difficult to account for the overall statistical imbalance we observe between linking-r and intrusive-r by resorting only to insertion and/or deletion mechanisms. Indeed, if linking-r and r-intrusion conform to the same rule, we must explain why it applies almost categorically after etymologically /r/-final words but variably after etymologically vowel-final words. This discrepancy may well be due to the fact that intrusion, which is a more recent development in non-rhotic varieties of English, involves the combination of isolated words more often than linking, which is inherited from potentially stored sequences in which the final /r/ of W1 has always been pronounced. Nevertheless, it must be noted that the memorisation of holistic sequences is more difficult to establish in English because r-sandhi involves a single consonant and is consequently less frequent than liaison. We must therefore continue to gather more corpus data if we want to offer a treatment of r-sandhi that takes significant variation into account and reflects the actual usage of speakers.

However, one should keep in mind that usage is prone to change. As we have seen with the case of prenominal adjectives, the boundary between categorical and variable liaison is not set in stone, and changes in French liaison usage seem to occur, as it were, one lexical item at a time. While intrusion has been shown to be on the rise (Hay and Sudbury 2005), the tendency seems to be more uniform across the English lexicon, suggesting that r-sandhi is a more general and strictly phonological phenomenon.

## Notes

1. Our translation.
2. The content of this chapter was originally presented on 18 November 2016 at the *Journées FLORaL – PFC 2016* international conference in Paris, http://projet-pfc.net/floral-2016. html

3. We will use this term, throughout our chapter, not in its philosophical sense but in its scientific sense, i.e. insofar as it refers to empirical observations as being the basis of subsequent theoretical analyses and interpretations.
4. Our translation.
5. We use [r] as a cover symbol to be interpreted as 'phonetic realisation of /r/', not necessarily an alveolar trill.
6. Our translation.
7. By 'idealised' varieties of English, we mean that they are descriptions found in pronunciation manuals which do not systematically rely on authentic oral corpus data but are mostly based on speakers' intuitions and therefore constitute conservative, traditional accounts of such varieties as Received Pronunciation, but also of unspecified varieties taken as theoretical objects. As an example, the literature on the subject has moved from Jones (1917), who claimed that he, along with a majority of RP speakers, never used intrusive-r, to Hughes et al. (2005: 65) who describe it as 'so automatic that if speakers with a southeastern-type English accent fail to use intrusive [r], especially after /ə/ or /ɪə/, they are probably non native speakers'. Corpus data seem to tell a different story inasmuch as the PAC corpora are closer to either type B or type D, in which either linking or intrusion, or both, are variable.
8. We use a broad definition of '/h/ dropping' which refers to a non-realised etymological /h/. The question of the lexical status of this initial /h/ will not be discussed here (see Wells 1982: 253–256).
9. Our translation.
10. Google searches performed on 3 May 2017.

## References

Booij, G. (1983), 'French c/0 alternations, extrasyllabicity and lexical phonology', *The Linguistic review* 3, 181–207.

Boula de Mareüil P., M. Adda-Decker and C. Woehrling (2007), 'Analysis of oral and nasal vowel realisation in northern and southern French varieties', *6th International Conference on Phonetic Sciences, Saarbrücken*, pp. 2221–2224, http://www.limsi.fr/Individu/mareuil/publi/1240.pdf

Buben, V. (1935), *Influence de l'orthographe sur la prononciation du français moderne*, Genève: Droz.

Bybee, J. L. (2001), *Phonology and Language Use*, Cambridge: Cambridge University Press.

Carr, P. (1999), *English Phonetics and Phonology*, Oxford: Blackwell.

Chatellier, H. (2016), Nivellement et contre-nivellement phonologique à Manchester : étude de corpus dans le cadre du projet PAC-LVTI, PhD thesis, Université Toulouse Jean Jaurès.

Chomsky, N. and M. Halle (1968), *The Sound Pattern of English*, New York: Harper & Row.

Clements, G. N. and S. J. Keyser (1981), 'A three-tiered theory of the syllable', *Occasional Paper* 19, The Center for Cognitive Science, MIT.

Coquillon, A., J. Durand, C. Lyche and J. Eychenne (2010), 'French liaison: from global results to local varieties', PHONLEX international conference, Université de Toulouse II–Le Mirail, 8–10 September 2010.

Côté, M.-H. (2005), 'Le statut lexical des consonnes de liaison', *Langages* 158, 66–78.

Côté, M.-H. (2012), 'Laurentian French (Québec): extra vowels, missing schwas and surprising liaison consonants', in R. Gess, C. Lyche and T. Meisenburg (eds), *Phonological Variation in French: Illustrations from Three Continents*, Amsterdam: John Benjamins, pp. 235–274.

Coustenoble, H. N. and L. E. Armstrong (1934), *Studies in French Intonation*, Cambridge: W. Heffer & Sons Ltd.

Cruttenden, A. (2014), *Gimson's Pronunciation of English*, New York: Routledge.

Davis, J. L. (2000), French liaison: a case study of the syntax-phonology interface, PhD thesis, University of Indiana, Bloomington.

de Jong, D. (1994), 'La sociophonologie de la liaison orléanaise', in C. Lyche (ed.), *French Generative Phonology: Restrospective and Perspectives*, Salford: AFLS/ESRI, pp. 95–130.

Delattre, P. (1951), *Principes de phonétique française à l'usage des étudiants anglo-américains*, Middlebury, VT: Middlebury College.

Delattre, P. (1966), *Studies in French and Comparative Phonetics*, The Hague: Mouton.

Deschamps, A., J. L. Duchet, J. M. Fournier and M. O'Neil (2004), *English Phonology and Graphophonemics*, Paris: Ophrys.

Detey, S., J. Durand, B. Laks and C. Lyche (2016), *Varieties of Spoken French*, Oxford: Oxford University Press.

Durand, J. (1976), 'Generative phonology, dependency phonology and southern French', *Lingua e Stile* 11, 3–23.

Durand, J. (1986), *Dependency and Non-Linear Phonology*, London: Croom Helm.

Durand, J. (1988), 'Phénomènes de nasalité en français du midi. Phonologie de dépendance et sous-spécification', *Recherches linguistiques* 17, 29–54.

Durand, J. (1990), *Generative and Non-Linear Phonology*, London: Longman.

Durand, J. and C. Lyche (2008), 'French liaison in the light of corpus data', *Journal of French Language Studies* 18(1), 33–66.

Durand, J., B. Laks and C. Lyche (2003), 'Le projet "phonologie du français contemporain"', *La tribune internationale des langues vivantes* 33, 3–10.

Durand, J., B. Laks and C. Lyche (2009), *Phonologie, variation et accents du français*, Paris: Hermès.

Durand, J., S. Navarro and C. Viollain (2014), 'Le "r" de sandhi en anglais : corpus et méthodologie', in C. Soum-Favaro, A. Coquillon and J.-P. Chevrot (eds), *La liaison : approches contemporaines*, Berne: Peter Lang, pp. 317–344.

Durand, J., S. Navarro and C. Viollain (2015), 'R-sandhi in English: how to constrain theoretical approaches', *Global Communication Studies*, vol. 2, *World Englishes*, Makuhari, Japan: Global Communication Institute, Kanda University of International Studies, pp. 103–132.

Durand, J., B. Laks, B. Calderone and A. Tchobanov (2011), 'Que savons-nous de la liaison aujourd'hui?', *Langue Française* 169, 103–135.

Encrevé, P. (1983), 'La liaison sans enchaînement', *Actes de la recherche en sciences sociales* 46, 39–66.

Encrevé, P. (1988), *La liaison avec et sans enchaînement*, Paris: Seuil.

Eychenne, J. (2011), 'La liaison en français et la théorie de l'optimalité', *Langue française* 169, 79–101.

Eychenne, J. and R. Paternostro (2016), 'Analyzing transcribed speech with Dolmen', in S. Detey, J. Durand, B. Laks and C. Lyche (eds), *Varieties of Spoken French*, Oxford: Oxford University Press.

Eychenne, J., C. Lyche, J. Durand and A. Coquillon (2014), 'Quelles données pour la liaison en Français : la question des corpus', in C. Soum-Favaro, A. Coquillon and .J-P. Chevrot (eds), *La liaison : approches contemporaines*, Berne: Peter Lang, pp. 33–60.

Féry, C. (2003), Liaison and syllable structure in French, manuscript, Potsdam.

Foulkes, P. (1997), 'English [r]-sandhi: a sociolinguistic perspective', *Histoire, Epistémologie, Langage* 19(I), 73–96.

Gaatone, D. (1978), 'Forme sous-jacente unique ou liste d'allomorphes (À propos des con-sonnes de liaison en français)', *Linguistics* 214, 33–54.

Gadet, F. and E. Guérin (2012), 'Des données pour étudier la variation: petits gestes méthodologiques, gros effets', *Cahiers de linguistique* 38(1), 41–65.

Gussmann, E. (2002), *Phonology: Analysis and Theory*, Cambridge: Cambridge University Press.

Hannisdal, B. R. (2006), Variability and change in Received Pronunciation. a study of six sociolinguistic variables in the speech of television newsreaders, PhD thesis, University of Bergen.

Harris, J. (1994), *English Sound Structure*, Oxford: Blackwell.

Hay, J. and A. Sudbury (2005), 'How rhoticity became /r/-sandhi', *Language* 81, 799–823.

Heselwood, B. (2006), 'Final schwa and r-sandhi in RP English', *Leeds Working Papers in Linguistics & Phonetics* 11, 78–95.

Hughes, A., P. Trudgill and D. Watt (2005), *English Accents and Dialects*, London: Edward Arnold.

Jones, D. (1917), *An English Pronouncing Dictionary*, 1st edn, London: Dent.

Klausenburger, J. (1974), 'Rule inversion, opacity, conspiracy: French liaison and elision', *Lingua* 34(2–3), 167–179.

Labov, W. (1966), *The Social Stratification of English in New York City*, Washington, DC: Center for Applied Linguistics.

Labov, W. (1972), *Sociolinguistic Patterns*, Philadelphia: University of Pennsylvania Press.

Labov, W. (1994), *Principles of Linguistic Change. Vol. 1. Internal Factors*, Oxford: Blackwell.

Labov, W. (2001), *Principles of Linguistic Change. Vol. 2. Social Factors*, Oxford: Blackwell.

Laks, B. (2005). 'La liaison et l'illusion', *Langages* 158, 101–125.

Laks, B. (2018), 'Diachronie de la liaison', in S. Prévost, C. Marchello-Nizia, B.Combettes and T. Scheer (eds), *Grande Grammaire Historique du Français*, Berlin: De Gruyter.

Long, M. (1977), 'On the role of selection rules in generative grammar', *Papers from the 13th Meeting of the Chicago Linguistic Society*, Chicago: Chicago Linguistic Society, pp. 339–351.

McCarthy, J. J. (1991), 'Synchronic rule inversion', in L. Sutton, C. Johnson and R. Shields (eds), *Proceedings of the Seventeenth Annual Meeting of the Berkeley Linguistics Society*, Berkeley: Berkeley Linguistics Society, pp. 192–207.

McCarthy, J. J. (1993), 'A case of surface constraint violation', *Canadian Journal of Linguistics* 38, 169–195.

McMahon, A. (2000), *Lexical Phonology and the History of English*, Cambridge: Cambridge University Press.

Mallet, G. (2008), La liaison en français : descriptions et analyses dans le corpus PFC, Thèse de doctorat, Université Paris Ouest Nanterre.

Morin, Y. C. (2003), 'Remarks on prenominal liaison consonants in French', in S. Ploch (ed.), *Living on the Edge – 28 Papers in Honour of Jonathan Kaye*, Berlin and New York: Mouton de Gruyter, pp. 385–400.

Morin, Y. C. and J. Kaye (1982), 'The syntactic bases for French Liaison', *Journal of Linguistics* 18, 291–330.

Navarro, S. (2013), Rhoticité et 'r' de sandhi en anglais : du Lancashire à Boston, PhD thesis, Université de Toulouse 2.

Navarro, S. (2016), *Le /r/ en anglais : histoire, phonologie et variation*, Dijon: Editions Universitaires de Dijon.

Pierrehumbert, J. (2001), 'Stochastic phonology', *Glot International* 5, 195–207.

Pierrehumbert, J. (2006), 'The next toolkit', *Journal of Phonetics* 34, 516–530.

Schane S. A. (1968), *French Phonology and Morphology*, Cambridge, MA: The MIT Press.

Sóskuthy, M. (2009), Why R? An alternative look at intrusive-R in English, Mémoire de Master, Université Eotvos Lorand.

Soum-Favaro, C., A. Coquillon and J. P. Chevrot (eds) (2014), *La liaison : approches contemporaines*, Berne: Peter Lang.

Steriade, D. (1999), 'Lexical conservatism in French adjectival liaison', in B. Bullock, M. Authier and L. Reed (eds), *Formal Perspectives in Romance Linguistics*, Amsterdam: John Benjamins, pp. 243–270.

Sudbury, A. and J. Hay (2002), 'The fall and rise of /r/: rhoticity and /r/-sandhi in early New Zealand English', *University of Pennsylvania Working Papers in Linguistics* 8(3), article 21 (available at https://repository.upenn.edu/pwpl/vol8/iss3/21).

Tranel, B. (1974), The phonology of nasal vowels in modern French, PhD thesis, University of California, San Diego.

Tranel, B. (1996), 'French Liaison and elision revisited: a unified account within Optimality Theory', in C. Parodi, C. Quicoli, M. Saltarelli and M. L. Zubizarreta (eds), *Romance Linguistics in Los Angeles*, Washington, DC: Georgetown University Press.

Tranel, B. (2000), 'Aspects de la phonologie du français et la théorie de l'optimalité', *Langue française* 126, 39–72.

Uffman, C. (2007), 'Intrusive [r] and optimal epenthetic consonants', *Language Sciences* 29, 451–476.

Viollain, C. (2010), Sociophonologie de l'anglais à Boston : une étude de la rhoticité et de la liaison, Master's thesis, Université de Toulouse 2.

Viollain, C. (2014), Sociophonologie de l'anglais contemporain en Nouvelle-Zélande : corpus et dynamique des systèmes, PhD thesis, Université Toulouse Jean Jaurès.

Wells, J. C. (1982), *Accents of English*, Cambridge: Cambridge University Press.

Wells, J. C. (2008), *Longman Pronunciation Dictionary*, Harlow: Longman.

# 6

# A Corpora-based Study of Vowel Reduction in Two Speech Styles: A Comparison between English and Polish

*Małgorzata Kul and Paulina Zydorowicz*

## Overview

The study aims to compare vowel reduction in read and fully spontaneous speech in English and Polish. It hypothesises that (1) vowels exhibit stronger reduction in fully spontaneous speech in comparison with read speech in the two languages, (2) vowel reduction is more robust in English than it is in Polish, and (3) a high speech rate triggers vowel reduction. The aims were achieved by an acoustic analysis of interviews and wordlists from PAC (nine speakers) and the Corpus of Modern Spoken Polish in the area of Greater Poland (nine speakers). The study treats centralisation of formants and reduced vowel duration as vowel reduction (Lindblom 1963), which were normalised to compare the values across speakers. For Polish subjects, speakers' canonical schwa was operationalised as an average of peripheral vowels /i/, /a/ and /u/ due to the fact that Polish has no schwa (Jassem 2003). The comparison of two speech styles consisted in measuring spectral and temporal properties of vowel tokens from the wordlist and from the interviews. The rate-reduction hypothesis was tested by means of comparing vowel reduction for the three fastest and the three slowest speakers for each language and using Pearson correlation.

In light of the obtained results, the first two hypotheses were positively verified. The third one produced negative results. The study establishes a significant difference in vowel reduction across two speech styles – read and fully spontaneous – across two unrelated languages. It has been demonstrated that reduction in English is considerably stronger than in Polish. More specifically, in both languages duration followed the same pattern (towards shortening in spontaneous speech relative to read speech), whereas for formants, centralisation was established for English, but not for all Polish vowels. With respect to the third hypothesis, assuming a straightforward relationship between speech rate and reduction, the findings of the current study did not lend support to either language. As Zwicky notes, 'casual speech need not to be fast; some speakers [...] use a quite informal speech even at fairly slow rates of speech, while others [...] give the impression of great precision even in hurried speech' (Zwicky 1972: 607).

## Introduction

The chapter reports the results of a corpora-based study of vowel reduction in English and Polish across two speech styles, read and fully spontaneous. The study addresses the issue of vowel reduction which, following the centralisation theory (Koopmans-van Beinum 1980), consists in diminishing the vowel's distinctiveness, that is its quality and quantity. The process of vowel reduction modifies a vowel by pulling or dragging it to the most centralised point of the vowel space. The very term reduction deserves additional explanation in the context of vowels as its effect may be partial (reduction of a lax sound to a more centralised one) or complete (schwa elision). By the same token, a need arises to draw a distinction between phonetic and phonological reduction. The former stands for the obliteration of lexical distinctions that results from neutralisation of phonetic contrast between two or more vowels (Crosswhite 2003; Barnes 2006). It treats vowel reduction as a constituent of the phonological inventory of a language, irrespective of speaking style or tempo, and can be represented by schwas in the dictionary entries. As Carr (2008) notes,

> in many languages, unstressed vowels are often reduced to schwa, which involves no deviation from the neutral position of the tongue. A word such as 'personal' has reduced vowels in its unstressed syllables, both of them schwas: [ˈpʰɜːsənəl], but in the word 'personality', the syllable with primary stress has a non-reduced vowel: [ˌpʰɜːsəˈnælɪti]. (Carr 2008: 145–146)

Of course, the term 'schwa' is used in the above quote as a proxy for a mid-central vowel quality.

The latter, by contrast, is a universal, cross-linguistic and naturally occurring process (Farnetani and Busa 1999; Vayra et al. 1999; Nikolaidis 2003; Flemming 2005; Jaworski 2007). According to Lindblom (1963), phonetic reduction is 'an intrinsic propensity of vowels to degeneration to schwa when they occur in connected speech' (Lindblom 1963: 1781). Phonetic reduction may be then taken as any approximation of vowels towards schwa vowels that ensues from an increased speaking rate or decreased articulatory effort; for example, vowel reduction present in grammatical words. In fact, two main accounts of phonetic vowel reduction may be evoked (Lindblom 1963). One denotes centralisation of vowels, that is reduction shifts vowel quality towards a mid-central vowel. A competing account explains reduction as assimilation to following and preceding sounds by means of shifting the quality of the reduced vowel towards its neighbours. This is evident in certain environments such as palatalised consonants where vowel reduction might result in assimilation to the palatalised consonants, although not necessarily. In this study, phonetic reduction, as opposed to the phonological one is investigated. We treat phonetic reduction as a general tendency to centralise vowels and an approximation to schwa, rather than its full realisation.

In English, reduction of vowels is governed by various mechanisms: it can arise due to morphological alternations ('telephone'–'telephony'), contrast between stressed and unstressed syllables ('banana'), syllabicity ('kitten'), or topicality. Numerous proposals have been made to identify and explain the factors triggering reduction. Lindblom (1963), for instance, views vowel reduction as a natural property of contextual assimilation and, in fact, he first drew the distinction between phonological reduction (due to context) and phonetic reduction (due to degeneration resulting from casual speech). Others, following the phonological understanding of vowel reduction, claim that it is a function of stress (Crosswhite 2003; Barnes 2006), whereas Harris (2005) understands vowel reduction as information loss:

> [r]eduction follows two apparently contradictory routes in vowel space, yielding either centralised values (the 'centripetal' pattern) or the corner values a, i, u (the 'centrifugal' pattern). What unifies these vowels is the relative simplicity of their acoustic spectra compared to those of mid peripheral vowels. Spectral complexity can be taken as one measure of the amount of phonetic information present in a speech signal at a given time. On this basis, centripetal and centrifugal reduction can both be construed as resulting in a loss of phonetic information. (Harris 2005: 119)

Analysing vowel reduction in the setting of casual speech, Bybee (2009: 30) claims that 'vowels move closer to the neutral position and schwas grow shorter and shorter until they are simply skipped [...] as changes in the timing of the articulatory gestures'. In addition, a vowel undergoes reduction if it is in a second or subsequent token of a word (Fowler and Housum 1987; Baker and Bradlow 2009). Regardless of the theoretical stance, typically, lax vowels in prosodically weak positions are subject to reduction, at least according to certain theoretical analyses such as Chomsky and Halle (1968). In a similar vein, consonants also exhibit a parallel process of reduction, although on a smaller scale: lenition of voiceless stops in intervocalic position may serve as an example here (Watson 2006).

The study reported here takes into consideration vowel reduction across speech styles. Speech style, in turn, may be understood as 'the variation that occurs in the speech of a single speaker in different situational contexts' (Cheshire 1992: 324). The variation, evoked in the definition, is governed by a number of factors such as audience design (Bell 1984, 2001) or the amount of attention paid by the speaker (Labov 1994). Thus, a distinction can be made between formal vs. informal speech style, where the level of attention increases with the level of formality (Dziubalska-Kołaczyk 1990). Vowel reduction is highly pervasive in informal speech (Ernestus and Warner 2011); due to a specific design of one of the corpora used in the study (see section 'The methodology of the study' below), however, having recourse to formal speech for style comparison was not possible. Instead, the study compares a read to a fully spontaneous speech style, the former serving as a proxy for formal style. In fact, a number of languages have been reported to vary across the read/spontaneous distinction in the vowel space. Much of the published literature on vowel reduction has found that both duration and formants are reduced (shortened and centralised) to

Table 6.1 Comparison of speech styles across languages

|  | Study | Language | Types of speech material | Findings |
|---|---|---|---|---|
| **Vowel reduction (formants)** | Koopmans-van Beinum (1980) | Dutch | Isolated vowels, canonical word forms, read speech, retold story, conversational speech | Vowel quality contrast decreases in more spontaneous productions |
|  | Harmegnies and Poch-Olivé (1992) | Spanish | Spontaneous conversational speech versus laboratory speech (i.e. wordlist reading) | Vowel centralisation and greater within-category scatter in spontaneous versus laboratory speech |
|  | Laan (1997) | Dutch | Spontaneous speech on prepared topic, read speech (read version of the spontaneous speech transcript), isolated vowels | Smaller vowel space in both speaking styles as compared to vowels produced in isolation. More centralised vowel formant values in spontaneous speech (only for one speaker) |
|  | Bondarko et al. (2003) | Russian | Spontaneous speech (dialogues versus read speech (read version of the spontaneous speech transcript)) | Greater variability of formant values for peripheral vowels /a/, /i/ and /u/ in spontaneous speech |
|  | Moon and Lindblom (1994) | English | Citation forms (i.e. normal reading) versus clear speech | Less formant displacement due to context in clear speech |

*Source:* adapted from Spilkova (2014).

a greater degree in spontaneous speech than in read speech. Table 6.1 serves as an illustration of the recent findings regarding speech styles.

With regard to languages examined in the present study, two typologically unrelated languages were selected: English and Polish. Apart from different rhythmic properties, vowel inventories differ considerably between Polish and English, in both quality and quantity:

A comparison of Figures 6.1 and 6.2 reveals that all Polish vowels are of equal length and that Polish, unlike English, has no schwa and the mid-area of the vowel space is unpopulated, with the only exception the /ɨ/ sound. As Sobkowiak puts it, 'Polish vowels are never reduced so thoroughly to a mid-central quality of schwa' (Sobkowiak 2008: 132). He also observes that 'most English vowels come between Polish vowels located nearby' (Sobkowiak 2008: 130). On the other hand, Nowak (2006) has found that the 'soft' consonants have a very strong impact on Polish vowels in both the F1 domain and the F2 domain (although the impact of many other consonants is also non-negligible) and that this impact wanes as the duration of the vowel increases.

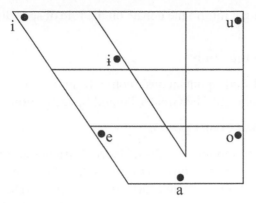

Figure 6.1 Vowels of Polish
*Source:* Jassem (2003: 105).

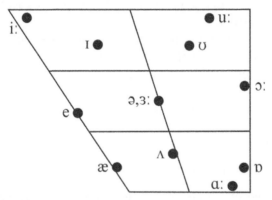

Figure 6.2 Vowels of British English
*Source:* Roach (2004: 242).

Thus, the present chapter attempts to verify the claim that phonetic vowel reduction is universal (Farnetani and Busa 1999; Vayra et al. 1999; Nikolaidis 2003; Flemming 2005) in two typologically unrelated languages and across two speech styles of various degrees of formality. In this chapter, two specific research questions are addressed. First, the study investigates the extent to which vowels are reduced in spontaneous speech in comparison with read speech in Polish and English. The second research question pertains to the role of speech rate in vowel reduction, as is assumed in previous scholarship (Jurafsky et al. 1998; Shockey 2003). It is then hypothesised that (1) vowels exhibit stronger reduction in fully spontaneous speech in comparison with read speech in the two languages, (2) vowel reduction in spontaneous speech is more robust in English and considerably less so in Polish due to typological differences, and (3) speakers with a high speech rate reduce vowels to a greater extent than slow speakers. Therefore, in addition to providing more data on differences between read and spontaneous styles for vowel reduction in Polish and

English, the results might inform the debate on the role of speech rate in the reduction of vowels.

## The Methodology of the Study

The data (both read and spontaneous) come from two corpora: Phonologie de l'Anglais Contemporain and The Greater Poland Speech Corpus.

### *Phonologie de l'Anglais Contemporain*

The Phonology of Contemporary English: Usage, Varieties and Structure is a project gathering a series of corpora whose purpose is 'to attain an effective and factual description and comparison of various accents of English' (Durand and Pukli 2004: 2). Based on a common protocol and following a uniform methodology, the project investigates contemporary English accents. In 2014, the corpus was composed of thirty-one surveys around the English-speaking world, 289 interviews and approximately 240 hours of validated recordings (https://www.pacprogramme.net (last accessed 6 November 2015)).

For the purpose of the present study, the Lancashire PAC corpus was used which comprises recordings of nine female speakers aged 23–83. The corpus contains four sets of data: formal interview, informal interview, a text passage and the wordlist. The wordlist includes 127 lexical items representing English vowels and sixty-five lexical items representing English consonants. The data selected for the present study come from the wordlist as well as the informal interview (for more details of data selection, see section 'The study').

### *The Greater Poland Speech Corpus*

The Greater Poland Speech Corpus is collected within the project Internetowy Korpus współczesnego, mówionego standardowego języka polskiego i gwary na obszarze Wielkopolski (The Internet Corpus of Contemporary Polish Standard and Vernacular Spoken in the area of Greater Poland). It must be stressed that the current project, though different from PAC in many respects, was inspired by the methodology applied to PAC.

The corpus is collected with the view to registering spontaneous speech data, as opposed to televised or radio performances (scripted or unscripted) of standard language users (eventually approximately seventy speakers) as well as vernacular users (eventually approximately twenty speakers) from the province of Greater Poland. The corpus collecting procedure consists of three stages: (1) subjects fill in a metadata questionnaire; (2) subjects participate in a spontaneous conversation; (3) subjects read a set of test words embedded in carrier phrases.

The high quality of the recording is ensured by using a professional Roland R-26 recorder and the lapel lavalier Rode microphones. The files are saved as a WAV format. The subjects are recorded in a quiet room during the spontaneous conversation session and in a soundproof room while reading the carrier phrases.

In order to ensure the highest degree of informality, the speakers are recorded in a 2+2 interview format, that is two interviewees who know each other hold a conversation with two interviewers. The interview lasts for about forty minutes and covers a range of topics such as studies and student life in Poznań, living, culture and entertainment in Poznań, as well as Internet use. The spontaneous speech session is followed by a reading task. In this task, subjects are asked to read a set of 182 carrier phrases containing the test words. The sentences are presented to the subjects in a randomised order.

Upon the completion of the project the electronic version of the corpus (transcripts and audio files) will be available on the website http://wa.amu.edu.pl/korpuswlkp/ (last accessed 12 February 2017).

## The Study

### The aim and hypotheses

The aim of the study was to analyse the process of vowel reduction in two typologically different languages, namely English and Polish, in two styles, reading versus spontaneous speech. Two criteria of vowel reduction were measured: vowel duration and the value of F1 and F2 (F3 marks information about lip rounding and hence was disregarded). Three hypotheses were tested:

• Hypothesis 1: Vowels exhibit stronger reduction in fully spontaneous speech in comparison with read speech in the two (typologically different) languages.
• Hypothesis 2: Vowel reduction in spontaneous speech is more robust in English and considerably less so in Polish due to typological differences.
• Hypothesis 3: Speakers with a high speech rate reduce vowels to a greater extent than slow speakers.

### The subjects

The subjects of the study were nine female speakers of Lancashire English and nine (four male and five female) speakers of Polish. The English subjects were aged 23–83. The speakers of Polish were aged 20–22 and came from the area of Greater Poland.

### The material and procedure

The hypotheses were tested on the basis of three vowels: English KIT, TRAP and FOOT and Polish /ɨ/, /a/ and /u/ as in byty 'entities', baty 'whips' and buty 'shoes'. The choice of these sets of vowels was motivated by the intention to make them comparable. The choice of the centralised /ɨ/ over a front /i/ results from the lack of high-frequency words fulfilling the conditions described below. For the study of English, the authors investigated one token of each vowel from the wordlist and five words per vowel extracted mostly from the informal interview. In Polish, three tokens of each vowel from the wordlist (that is carrier phrase) as well as three words per each vowel per speaker from the interview were examined. Altogether in English,

Table 6.2 Words selected for analysis

| Style | IPA | English | IPA | Polish |
|---|---|---|---|---|
| Scripted | /ɪ/ | pit/thick | i | *byty* 'entities' |
| | /æ/ | pat | a | *baty* 'whips' |
| | /ʊ/ | put | u | *buty* 'shoes' |
| Unscripted | /ɪ/ | this | i | *chyba* 'I guess' |
| | | big | | *szybko* 'fast' |
| | | bit | | *wszystko* 'everything' |
| | | fix | | *wszyscy* 'everybody' |
| | /æ/ | back | a | *czasy* 'times' |
| | | bad | | *czasem* 'sometimes' |
| | | dad | | *czasami* 'sometimes' |
| | | had | | *zasadzie* 'basically' |
| | | have (= possess) | | *zawsze* 'always' |
| | | haven't | | |
| | /ʊ/ | good | u | *dużo* 'a lot' |
| | | put | | *różne* 'various' |
| | | took | | *tutaj* 'here' |

the authors obtained twenty-seven tokens from scripted speech and 135 tokens from spontaneous speech. For Polish, eighty-one tokens from scripted speech and the same number from spontaneous speech were obtained. In total, 324 word tokens were analysed. The uneven number of tokens per language results from differences in the structure of the two corpora.

As regards the selection of words for analysis, the following criteria were considered: in English (relatively) high-frequency, (mostly) one-syllable words were selected (frequency is used in the sense of token frequency); reducible grammar words such as could were avoided; in Polish (relatively) high-frequency, (mostly) two-syllable words were selected where the focus vowel appeared in a stressed position (Polish due to rich morphology does not abound in monosyllabic words). Another important criterion in the word selection process was the phonetic environment of vowels. In order to facilitate the process of acoustic analysis, the selected vowels occurred in the direct neighbourhood of obstruents. Table 6.2 presents all lexical items whose vowels were analysed acoustically.

Upon extracting the words from the transcripts, the vowels underwent manual annotation in Praat (Boersma and Weenink 2014). The measurements of vowels were taken across the average duration of the vowel from onset to offset rather than the midpoint, as indicated in Figure 6.3. Vowel reduction was treated as distance (in terms of F1 and F2 as well as duration) from the least centralised vowel tokens to individually measured speaker's canonical schwa (for more detail see Kul 2010).

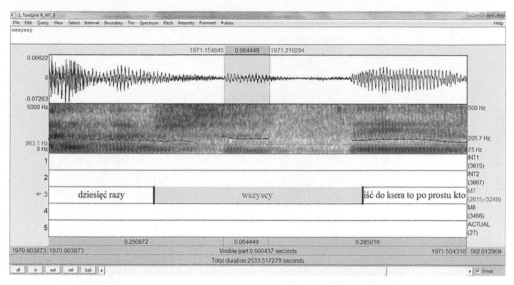

Figure 6.3  Exemplary annotation in Praat, illustrating vowel duration from onset to offset

Speech rate

Speech rate was operationalised as articulatory rate, that is without hesitation pauses and filled pauses and expressed as syllables per second. Local rate was not considered in this study on purpose, on the grounds that the study, among other things, seeks to verify whether the fastest speakers exhibit the highest reduction degree, rather than intending to perform an in-depth correlation of speech rate with a variety of factors where such a fine-grained method of calculating speech rate would be more appropriate (see section 'Discussion'). So as to assess the connection between vowel reduction and speech rate, Pearson correlation was used (hypothesis 3). Size effects for comparison of reduction across two languages (hypothesis 2) were given with the aid of a one-way ANOVA (between groups comparison).

## Results

In order to tease apart vowel reduction from speech style and cross-linguistic differences, the results are arranged according to the temporal and spectral domains of vowel production.

### Results for the First Hypothesis

It was hypothesised that vowels exhibit stronger reduction in fully spontaneous speech in comparison with read speech in the two languages. The comparison of the means obtained in the current study revealed that there were statistically significant differences for both Polish (read $M = 79.56$, $SD = 11.7$; spontaneous $M = 50.45$, $SD = 13.89$) and English (read $M = 131.68$, $SD = 13.17$; spontaneous $M = 76.54$, $SD = 18.52$)

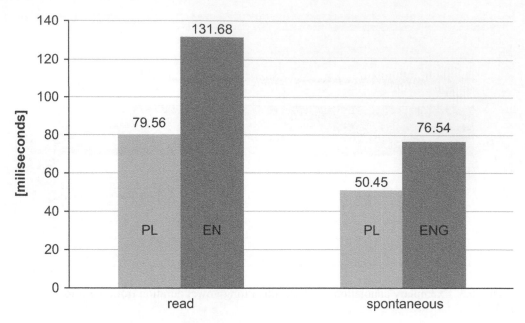

Figure 6.4 Means of duration for speech styles (females only)

between read and spontaneous speech with regard to duration of vowels. As for the student t-test, there were 162 vowel tokens per language, t (160)=1.975, and the p-value (one-tailed) of the obtained data is 0.04, indicating a satisfactory degree of statistical reliability.

According to Figure 6.4, the ratio of means of vowel duration in spontaneous speech was 58 per cent in English and 63 per cent in Polish, relative to read speech. This is a considerable difference across speech styles, pointing to a temporal under-shoot in spontaneous speech in comparison with the read speech style. For distribu-tion of reduction across the KIT, TRAP and FOOT vowels in English and /ɨ/, /a/ and /u/ in Polish, the analysis indicated that there was a certain variability among them and between the two languages considered:

As indicated in Figures 6.5 and 6.6, the three vowels considered in the study did not display similar patterns for temporal reduction. Thus, in Polish, the low central vowel /a/ was reduced to the lowest degree (as its realisation in spontaneous speech was 71 per cent of its realisation in read speech), whereas the FOOT vowel was the most reduction resistant in English (p<0.05). These differences stem from the dif-ferent arrangement of vowels and the density of population of the respective vowel spaces (Figures 6.1 and 6.2).

Turning to the spectral aspect of reduction, the outcomes for differences between read and spontaneous speech are presented below. Note that English female speakers were compared to Polish female speakers, whereas no English male speakers from the PAC corpus were available to compare with Polish male speakers (see section 'The methodology of the study').

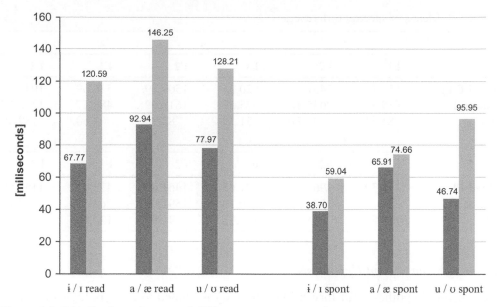

Figure 6.5 Distribution of temporal differences across vowels

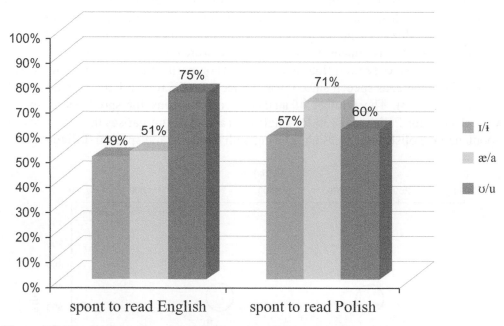

Figure 6.6 Distribution of temporal differences across vowels (per cent)

The analysis of differences between vowel space in read and spontaneous speech styles confirms the findings for duration and provides support for the first hypothesis, stipulating that vowels in spontaneous speech are reduced more in comparison with read speech, as evident in Table 6.3.

Table 6.3 Means of spectral differences

|            | ɪ       |         | æ       |         | ʊ       |         |
|------------|---------|---------|---------|---------|---------|---------|
|            | **F1**  | **F2**  | **F1**  | **F2**  | **F1**  | **F2**  |
| **Read Eng**   | 554.77  | 2451.19 | 820.21  | 1500.19 | 536.09  | 1044.22 |
| **Spont. Eng** | 439.31  | 2035.82 | 775.52  | 1618.92 | 488.57  | 1312.17 |
| **SD**         | 81.64   | 293.71  | 31.59   | 83.96   | 33.60   | 189.46  |
|            | **i**   |         | **a**   |         | **u**   |         |
|            | **F1**  | **F2**  | **F1**  | **F2**  | **F1**  | **F2**  |
| **Read Pl**    | 493.39  | 1967.50 | 771.65  | 1461.09 | 438.01  | 1157.88 |
| **Spont Pl**   | 333.76  | 1548.95 | 590.70  | 1591.08 | 262.55  | 989.15  |
| **SD**         | 112.87  | 295.96  | 127.95  | 91.92   | 124.06  | 119.30  |

### Results for the Second Hypothesis

The second hypothesis put forward in this study is related to the typologically-based assumption that, overall, vowel reduction is robust in English and considerably less so in Polish due to differences in the vowel inventories. In order to provide further insight into the relative differences between reduction in the two languages, between-group differences for duration and formants was calculated by means of a one-way ANOVA. For these calculations, means of the three vowels were considered, following the idea of centralisation (see section 'Introduction') and comparing the shrinking of the vowel space in spontaneous speech since it was subject to reduction, relative to read speech (Figures 6.5–6.8). The number of analysed vowel tokens for spontaneous speech was 216 (81 for Polish and 135 for English). Table 6.4 summarises the outcomes for spontaneous Polish and English, capturing both temporal and spectral differences

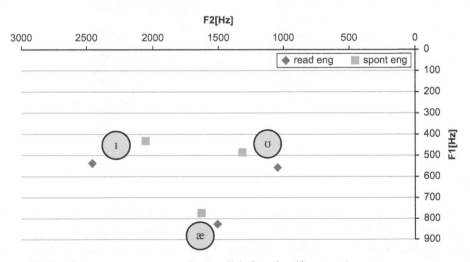

Figure 6.7 Read versus spontaneous for English females (formants)

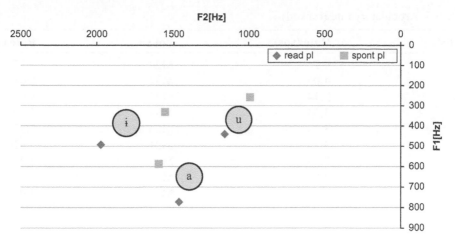

Figure 6.8 Read versus spontaneous for Polish females (formants)

Table 6.4 Means for speech styles

| | Spontaneous Polish | | Spontaneous English | |
|---|---|---|---|---|
| | **Means** | **SD** | **Means** | **SD** |
| **Duration (ms)** | 49.01 | 13.89 | 76.54 | 18.52 |
| **F1 (Hz)** | 400.73 | 133.95 | 567.8 | 181.56 |
| **F2 (Hz)** | 1361.04 | 217.32 | 1651.63 | 363.22 |

As far as duration of vowel is concerned, the difference between spontaneous Polish and English is significant F (1,216)=133.738, p=0.000. Turning to formants, a significant difference across languages for F1 was found: F1, F (1,216)=51.669, p=0.000. The comparison of F2 between spontaneous Polish and read English was also significant (F (1,216)=42.636, p=0.000).

To sum up, as hypothesised, a one-way ANOVA revealed no effect of reduction, both in its temporal and spectral aspects, suggesting that English vowels in spontaneous speech were reduced significantly more robustly than in Polish.

*Results for the Third Hypothesis*

The third hypothesis examined the role of speech rate in vowel reduction. In particular, it stipulated that speakers with a high speech rate reduce more than slow speakers. Below, articulatory rates for speakers from two corpora are presented in Table 6.5.

It must be observed that rates for Polish are significantly higher than for English. This can be accounted for in terms of age differences: the Polish speakers' ages ranged from 20–22, whereas the age of the English speakers ranged from 23–83. Indeed, previous scholarship has found that younger speakers tend to speak faster (for example, Verhoeven et al. 2004; Raymond et al. 2006; Jacewicz et al. 2009).

Table 6.5 Articulatory rate (ranked)

| English | Rate (sps) | Polish | Rate (sps) |
|---------|-----------|--------|-----------|
| ST | 4.26 | M24 | 6.17 |
| PK | 4.05 | M32 | 6.01 |
| MO | 3.74 | M35 | 5.63 |
| MC | 3.53 | M34 | 5.39 |
| JM | 3.43 | M23 | 5.33 |
| LB | 3.35 | M21 | 5.31 |
| SC | 2.98 | M33 | 5.2 |
| LC | 2.81 | M22 | 4.92 |
| MD | 2.65 | M25 | 4.9 |

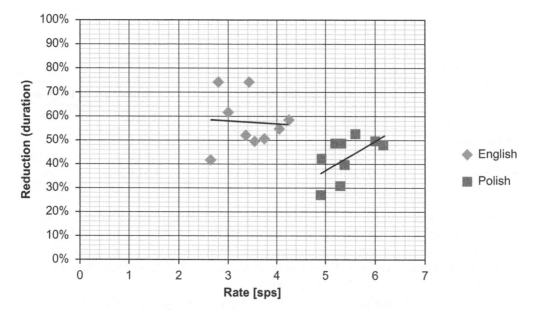

Figure 6.9  Correlation for articulatory rate and reduction of duration

As for correlation between reduction and articulatory rate, it was run separately for duration, F1 and F2.

Surprisingly, as it follows from Figure 6.9, for English the correlation was negative and non-existent (r=-0.06, N=9). This implies that the fastest speakers did not necessarily reduce their duration of vowels to the highest degree. In Polish, no correlation was found (r=0.58, N=9, p=0.102), denying the assumptions of hypothesis 3.

Figure 6.10 attested to the lack of correlation between articulatory rate and F1 which runs counter to the hypothesis (r=0.14 for English and r=0.02 for Polish). It appears that with respect to the tongue height, reduction is not a function of speech rate.

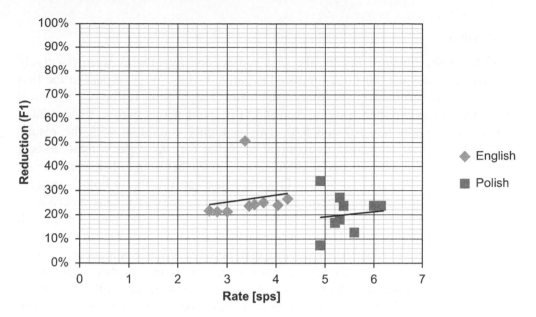

Figure 6.10 Correlation for articulatory rate and reduction of F1

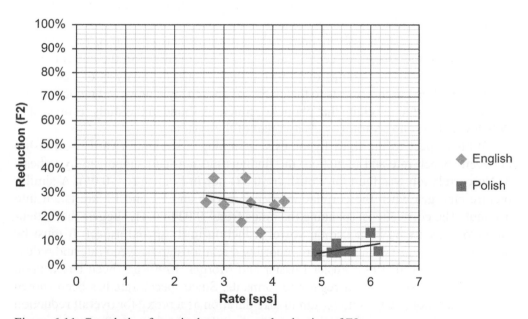

Figure 6.11 Correlation for articulatory rate and reduction of F2

Analysis of the link between F2 and articulatory rate reveals two opposing trends: a weak correlation was found in Polish (r=0.41), whereas in English no such correlation was established (r=-0.27). Furthermore, the correlation found for English was negative, which stands in stark contrast to the outcome obtained for Polish. This is visualised by Figure 6.11.

## Discussion

In light of the obtained results, the first and second hypotheses were positively verified, whereas the third one produced negative results. With respect to the first hypothesis, unsurprisingly the study establishes a significant difference in vowel reduction across two speech styles, read and fully spontaneous, across two unrelated languages (Figures 6.5, 6.7 and 6.8). This is highly consistent with the results obtained for other languages as reported in Table 6.1. As regards hypothesis 2 concerning the difference between vowel centralisation between Polish and English, vowel reduction was more robust in English. More specifically, in both languages duration followed the same pattern (towards shortening in spontaneous speech relative to read speech), whereas for formants, centralisation was established for English but not for all Polish vowels. Data presented in Figure 6.8 for Polish seem to indicate a general shift of the vowel triangle rather than pure reduction. Spontaneous vowels are characterised by lower F1 values. For the vowels /ɨ/ and /u/ this would mean more peripheral positions. Additionally, the /u/ vowel's F2 is shifted towards a lower value in spontaneous speech; that is, its position is also more peripheral in this respect.

In general, the major contribution of this chapter is to have shown that reduction in English is considerably stronger than in Polish (Table 6.4), which is in agreement with certain aspects of Polish phonology (lack of schwa; Jassem 2003). The very fact of undergoing the process of centralisation in Polish, observed in the current study, is compatible with the findings of Nowak (2006). Thus, the analysis of 324 vowel tokens from two corpora attests to the effects of speech style on vowel reduction and provides support to the claim that phonetic reduction, found in the study, is present in Polish which has no central vowels as a part of the system.

With respect to the third hypothesis, assuming a straightforward relationship between speech rate and reduction, the findings did not lend support to hypothesis 3. No correlation was found in Polish ($r=0.58$) nor in English ($r=-0.06$). A similar picture emerges when the correlations between rate and F1 and F2 are taken into account. The correlations, spanning the range from -0.02 to 0.41, suggest that articulatory rate exerts no influence on vowel reduction in its spatial aspect. It must be noted here that most of the literature reporting a relationship between rate and reduction (Jurafsky et al. 1998; Fosler-Lussier and Morgan 1999) has been based upon studies of duration alone, disregarding formants. Since speech rate has been shown to affect duration, there is no reason to take duration as a proxy for overall reduction of vowels, which, in addition to length, consists in formant changes. Perhaps it would be necessary to draw a line between spatial and temporal reduction in search of any link between rate and reduction of vowels. The chapter tentatively suggests that these two, the spatial and the temporal aspects, may be trending in different directions. Alternatively, the results obtained here may also lead to a suggestion that lexical items of high frequency (*dużo* 'a lot', *wszyscy* 'everybody', *tutaj* 'here', *czasu* 'time' (gen. sg.), 'this', 'have', 'good') may be undergoing the process of lexicalisation in the speaker's phonology and, as such, might be growing impervious to the effects of articulatory rate. Nevertheless, the issue of whether fast speech indeed fosters vowel reduction, as it is commonly assumed, remains an open question, well worthy of further investigation. Following Zwicky (1972), the current study seems to undermine the commonly assumed relation between fast speech and a high rate of speech which in turn contributes to an increased reduction rate.

## Limitations of the Study and Implications for Further Research

The aim of this chapter was to study the process of phonetic vowel reduction in two typologically different languages (English and Polish) in two speech styles (sentence reading and spontaneous speech). The preliminary results of the study provided evidence that the topic of vowel reduction, especially in Polish, is worth pursuing further and deserves a more exhaustive treatment. For a number of reasons the study as it currently stands needs to be treated as an introductory work-in-progress report rather than a final-study report. First, a small number of observations does not allow making generalisations from our pilot study. The speech material should be enlarged by analysing the speech samples from more speakers (which does not pose a problem for the Polish database, as the corpus includes recordings of seventy speakers; the Lancashire corpus is limited to nine speakers only). The second shortcoming consists in a lack of balance for fortis and lenis obstruents considered in the study, which might possibly have biased the preliminary results with the pre-fortis clipping affecting certain words in English, not Polish. Also, neither age nor gender were balanced (see Verhoeven et al. 2004; Raymond et al. 2006; Jacewicz et al. 2009).

In future research, other accents than Lancashire should be considered. Another possible research venue is to include phonetic context (preceding and following sounds) and prosody, with a special focus on rhythm, to extend the list of reduction variables studied in the present chapter, that is speech style and articulatory rate.

Finally, it is worth investigating the correlation between the vowel reduction and the reduction of consonants and consonant clusters. The question to be answered is: Do speakers who reduce vowels more preserve the consonants in their speech and vice versa? In other words, is there a compensation strategy (preserving vowels or consonants) which speakers apply to ensure that the message is intelligible and comprehensible to the listener? To answer these questions a parallel study on consonant reduction is needed.

## Acknowledgements

The first author gratefully acknowledges the financial support of the National Science Centre (grant number: 2012/05/D/HS2/03565) as well as the Ministry of Higher Education within the Narodowy Program Rozwoju Humanistyki Program (The National Program of Humanities Development) (grant number: 0113/NPRH2/H11/81/2013).

## References

Baker, R. E. and A. R. Bradlow (2009), 'Variability in word duration as a function of probability, speech style and prosody', *Language and Speech* 52, 391–413.

Barnes, J. (2006), *Strength and Weakness at the Interface: Positional Neutralisation in Phonetics and Phonology*, Berlin and NewYork: Mouton de Gruyter.

Bell, A. (1984), 'Language style as audience design', *Language in Society* 13, 145–201.

Bell, A. (2001), 'Back in style: reworking audience design', in P. Eckert and J. R. Rickford (eds), *Style and Sociolinguistic Variation*, Cambridge: Cambridge University Press, pp. 139–169.

Boersma, P. and D. Weenink (2014), Praat: doing phonetics by computer [computer program], Version 5.3.11, http://www.praat.org/ (last accessed 17 February 2017).

Bondarko, L. V., N. B. Volskaya, S. O. Tananaiko and L. A. Vasilieva (2003), 'Phonetic properties of Russian spontaneous speech', in *Proceedings of the 15th International Congress of Phonetic Sciences*, Barcelona, pp. 2973–2976.

Bybee, Joan (2009), 'Language universals and usage-based theory', in M. H. Christiansen, C. Collins and S. Edelman (eds), *Language Universals*, Oxford: Oxford University Press, pp. 17–40.

Carr, P. (2008), *A Glossary of Phonology*, Edinburgh: Edinburgh University Press.

Cheshire, J. (1992), 'Register and style', in W. Bright (ed.), *International Encyclopedia of Linguistics*, New York and Oxford: Oxford University Press, pp. 324–327.

Chomsky, N. and M. Halle (1968), *The Sound Pattern of English*, New York: Harper and Row.

Crosswhite, K. (2003), 'Vowel reduction', in B. Hayes, R. Kirchner and D. Steriade (eds), *Phonetically-based Phonology*, Cambridge: Cambridge University Press, pp. 191–231.

Cruttenden, A. (2014), *Gimson's Pronunciation of English*, 8th edn, London: Routledge.

Durand, J. and M. Pukli (2004), 'How to construct a phonological corpus: PRAAT and the PAC project', http://w3.erss.univ-tlse2.fr/membres/jdurand/DurandPukliPACtranscription.pdf (last accessed 20 December 2015).

Dziubalska-Kołaczyk, K. (1990), 'Phonostylistics and second language acquisition', *Papers and Studies in Contrastive Linguistics* 25, 71–83.

Ernestus, M. and N. Warner (2011), 'An introduction to reduced pronunciation variants' [editorial], *Journal of Phonetics* 39(SI), 253–260.

Farnetani, E. and M. G. Busa (1999), 'Quantifying the range of vowel reduction', *Proceedings of the 14th International Congress of Phonetic Sciences*, San Francisco, pp. 491–494.

Flemming, E. (2005), A phonetically-based model of vowel reduction, http://web.mit.edu/flemming/www/paper/vowelred.pdf (last accessed 13 January 2016).

Fosler-Lussier, E. and N. Morgan (1999), 'Effects of speaking rate and word frequency on pronunciations in conversational speech', *Speech Communication* 29, 137–158.

Fowler, C. and J. Housum (1987), 'Talkers signalling of new and old words in speech and listeners perception and use of the distinction', *Journal of Memory and Language* 26, 489–504.

Harmegnies, B. and D. Poch-Olivé (1992), 'A study of style-induced vowel variability: laboratory versus spontaneous speech in Spanish', *Speech Communication* 11, 429–437.

Harris, J. (2005), 'Vowel reduction as information loss', in P. Carr, J. Durand and C. J. Ewen (eds), *Headhood, Elements, Specification and Contrastivity*, Amsterdam: Benjamins, pp. 119–132.

Internetowy korpus współczesnego, mówionego standardowego języka polskiego i gwary na obszarze Wielkopolski (2015), http://wa.amu.edu.pl/korpuswlkp/ (last accessed 22 December 2015).

Jacewicz, E., R. A. Fox, C. O'Neill and J. Salmons (2009), 'Articulation rate across dialect, age, and gender', *Language Variation and Change* 21, 233–256.

Jassem, W. (2003), 'Illustrations of the IPA: Polish', *Journal of the International Phonetic Association* 33(1), 103–107.

Jaworski, S. (2007), Lenition processes in English and other languages: a hierarchy of susceptibility to inertia, unpublished PhD dissertation, Adam Mickiewicz University.

Jurafsky, D., A. Bell, E. Fosler-Lussier, C. Girana and W. Raymond (1998), 'Reduction of English Function words in SWITCHBOARD', *Proceedings of ICLSP98*, pp. 3111–3114.

Koopmans-van Beinum, F. J. (1980), *Vowel Contrast Reduction: An Acoustic and Perceptual Study of Dutch Vowels in Various Speech Conditions*, Amsterdam: Academische Pers B.V.

Kul, M. (2010), 'Towards a gradual scale of vowel reduction: a pilot study', *Poznań Studies in Contemporary Linguistics* 46(4), 429–456.

Laan, G. P. M. (1997), 'The contribution of intonation, segmental durations, and spectral features to the perception of a spontaneous and a read speaking style', *Speech Communication* 22, 43–65.

Labov, W. (1994), *Principles of Language Change: Internal Factors*, Oxford: Blackwell.

Lindblom, B. (1963), 'Spectrographic study of vowel reduction', *Journal of the Acoustical Society of America* 35, 1773–1781.

Moon, S. J. and B. Lindblom (1994), 'Interaction between duration, context, and speaking style in English stressed vowels', *Journal of the Acoustical Society of America* 96(1), 40–55.

Nicolaidis K. (2003), 'Acoustic variability of vowels in Greek spontaneous speech', *Proceedings of the 15th International Congress of Phonetic Sciences*, Barcelona, pp. 3221–3224.

Nowak, P. M. (2006), Vowel reduction in Polish, PhD dissertation, University of California, Berkeley.

Raymond, W. D., R. Dautricourt and E. Hume (2006), 'Word-medial /t,d/ deletion in spontaneous speech: modeling the effects of extra-linguistic, lexical, and phonological factors', *Language Variation and Change* 18(1), 55–97.

Roach, P. J. (2004), 'Illustrations of the IPA. British English: Received Pronunciation', *Journal of the IPA* 34(2), 239–245.

Shockey, L. (2003), *Sound Patterns of Spoken English*, Oxford: Blackwell Publishing.

Sobkowiak, W. (2008), *English Phonetics for Poles*, 3rd edn, Poznań: Wydawnictwo Poznańskie.

Spilkova, H. (2014), Phonetic reduction in spontaneous speech: an investigation of native and non-native production, PhD dissertation, Norwegian University of Science and Technology, Trondheim.

Statistics Calculator (2015), http://www.danielsoper.com/statcalc3/calc.aspx?id=43 (last accessed 12 December 2015).

The Phonology of Contemporary English (2015), https://www.pacprogramme.net (last accessed 6 November 2015).

Vayra, M., C. Avesani and C. Fowler. (1999), 'On the phonetic bases of vowel-consonant coordination in Italian: a study on stress and compensatory shortening', *Proceedings of the 14th International Congress of Phonetic Sciences*, San Francisco, pp. 495–498.

Verhoeven, J., G. de Pauw and H. Kloots (2004), 'Speech rate in a pluricentric language: a comparison between Dutch in Belgium and the Netherlands', *Language and Speech* 47(3), 297–30.

Watson, K. (2006), 'Phonological resistance and innovation in the North-West of England', *English Today* 22, 55–61.

Zwicky, A. M. (1972), 'On casual speech', *Papers from the Eighth Regional Meeting of the Chicago Linguistic Society*, Chicago: Chicago Linguistic Society, pp. 607–615.

# 7

# On 'Because': Phonological Variants and their Pragmatic Functions in a Corpus of Bolton (Lancashire) English

*Daniel Huber*

## Overview

This chapter intends to analyse patterns of full and reduced forms of 350 occurrences of 'because', collected from spoken Bolton (Lancashire) English. These patterns of full and reduced forms can be shown to be a function of the formality of context, the age of the speaker and the pragmatic function of 'because'. The chapter presents a number of pragmatic/discourse functions of 'because' in contemporary English in order to correlate the various forms with the different functions of 'because'. First, it will be demonstrated that many variants are available to native speakers, and that reduced forms are not consistently more frequent in informal contexts for all speakers: both disyllabic and monosyllabic variants occur in both formal and informal situations for virtually all speakers in the corpus, and it is only with the younger speakers in the corpus that monosyllabic variants predominate, in both contexts. Second, the chapter will demonstrate that younger speakers use 'because' in an extended range of pragmatic functions. Finally, it will be shown that both the incidence and the range of meanings of the monosyllabic variant 'cos' are related to the age of the speaker: except for the oldest speaker in the data, all speakers used monosyllabic forms of 'because', although their frequency increases in younger speakers.

## Introduction

This chapter intends to analyse patterns of full and reduced forms of 'because' in Bolton (Lancashire) English, as observed in 350 occurrences collected from five hours of semi-guided and free conversations in the corpus of spoken Lancashire English of the PAC programme (Durand and Pukli 2004, Durand and Przewozny 2012, 2015). These patterns of full and reduced forms will be shown to be a function of the formality of context, the age of the speaker and the pragmatic function of 'because'. While the data can be regarded as relatively small, they are varied enough to make sense of the observable patterns in terms of apparent time changes (Labov 1966, 1972), both

147

as far as the phonological variants of 'because' and its pragmatic uses are concerned. The chapter presents a number of pragmatic/discourse functions of 'because' in contemporary English in order to correlate the various forms with the different functions of 'because'. First, it will be demonstrated that there are many variants available to native speakers and that it is simplistic to expect reduced forms to be consistently more frequent in informal contexts for all speakers. As a matter of fact, both disyllabic and monosyllabic variants occur in both formal and informal situations for virtually all speakers in the corpus, and it is only with the younger speakers in the corpus that monosyllabic variants predominate (in both contexts). Second, the chapter will demonstrate that younger speakers use 'because' in an extended range of pragmatic functions. With respect to a specific discourse pattern, the data in the corpus provide important new insights as to their analysis. Finally, it will be shown that both the incidence and the range of meanings of the monosyllabic variant ''cos' are related to the age of the speaker. Except for the oldest speaker in the data, all speakers used monosyllabic forms of 'because', although their frequency increases in younger speakers.

## The Bolton (Lancashire) Corpus of the PAC Programme

Data for the following discussion derive from the Bolton (Lancashire) corpus of the PAC programme (see Durand and Przewozny 2012, 2015, and the Introduction to this volume). The recordings for the Bolton (Lancashire) PAC corpus were made by Emilie Noël in late 2002. The corpus comprises ten speakers, aged between twenty-three and eighty-three years at the time of recording. Speaker identifiers are ordered in function of their age at the time of recording (indicated in brackets): JM1 (23); MD1 (23); DK1 (29); ST1 (30); LB1 (38); SC1 (40); PK1 (58); MC1 (71); LC1 (77); MO1 (83). All except DK1 (29) are female speakers. All speakers are native speakers of the variety, given that they were born and bred in and around Bolton and had not spent extensive periods away from the location. Informants were recruited following the networking principle (Milroy and Milroy 1985): informants are family members, friends and acquaintances or friends of friends. Their relationships are shown in Figure 7.1.

All speakers had to complete the following five tasks in the PAC protocol: (1) reading out a wordlist aimed at revealing their formal vowel inventory and (2) another wordlist aimed at their formal consonant inventory; (3) reading out a text passage designed to contain various phonological features of formal spoken English (such as linking- and intrusive-r, tapping); (4) a formal, guided conversation (concerning education, childhood, pastime and professional life, among other subjects) as well as (5) an informal, non-guided conversation. While the formal conversation is conducted by the researcher (marked 'F' in the transcriptions below, for 'fieldworker'), the informal one is typically between two people who know each other well (family ties, friends). The protocol was thus designed to ensure a wide coverage of speech styles ranging from their most formal (wordlists) to fairly uncontrolled styles (informal conversation). Since the wordlists and the reading task did not contain instances of 'because', the following discussion is based on the occurrences of 'because' in the

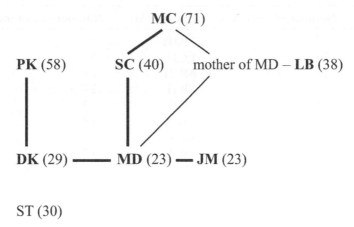

Figure 7.1 The network of informants in the Bolton (Lancashire) PAC corpus (informants are in bold; association lines mark a relationship)

formal and the informal conversations. One speaker, ST1 (30), was finally discarded from the present analysis because her files are incomplete: she only had the guided conversation so no comparison would have been possible between her more formal and informal styles with respect to the incidence of variant forms of 'because'.

The total length of the Bolton (Lancashire) corpus can be broken down as follows. The guided conversations of the nine interlocutors run to 8,386 seconds (nearly 140 minutes), with a mean length of 932 seconds (15.5 minutes) per conversation. The informal conversations run longer, to 9,568 seconds (nearly 160 minutes), with a mean length of 1,060 seconds (just short of 18 minutes). Table 7.1 summarises the length of the individual conversations.

Table 7.1 Length of conversations in the PAC Bolton (Lancashire) corpus

| SPEAKER ID | LENGTH | SPEAKER ID | LENGTH |
|---|---|---|---|
| MO1f | 14:49:00 (889s) | MO1i | 38:57:00 (2337s) |
| LC1f | 17:36:00 (1056s) | LC1i | 38:57:00 (2337s) |
| MC1f | 15:01:00 (901s) | MC1i | 25:40:00 (1540s) |
| PK1f | 14:21:00 (860s) | PK1i | 18:43:00 (1123s) |
| SC1f | 14:36:00 (876s) | SC1i | 21:03:00 (1263s) |
| LB1f | 16:44:00 (1004s) | LB1i | 12:31:00 (751s) |
| DK1f | 14:39:00 ( 879s) | DK1i | 25:12:00 (1512s) |
| MD1f | 18:39:00 (1119s) | MD1i | 25:12:00 (1512s) |
| JM1f | 13:22:00 (802s) | JM1i | 17:22:00 (1042s) |
| Total | 139:47:00 (8387s) | | 159:28:00 (9568s) |
| | **2h:19':47"** | | **2h:39'28"** |

Table 7.2 Tokens of 'because' by speaker, and by formal (f) and informal (i) conversation context

| Speaker ID | Number of instances | Speaker ID | Number of instances | Total |
|---|---|---|---|---|
| MO1f | 7 | MO1i | 6 | 13 |
| LC1f | 20 | LC1i | 17 | 37 |
| MC1f | 17 | MC1i | 29 | 46 |
| PK1f | 21 | PK1i | 28 | 49 |
| SC1f | 22 | SC1i | 27 | 49 |
| LB1f | 20 | LB1i | 18 | 38 |
| DK1f | 10 | DK1i | 21 | 31 |
| MD1f | 37 | MD1i | 17 | 54 |
| JM1f | 17 | JM1i | 17 | 34 |
| Total | 171 | | 180 | 351 |

The interviews thus total 17,954 seconds (nearly 300 minutes), which is nearly five hours of dialogue speech. Because of the format of the informal conversations, informants LC1 and MO1 share the informal conversation and MD1 led the conversation both with DK1 and JM1, and her conversation data come from her conversation with DK1. Since there was no a priori limit on the length of the recordings, the length of conversations shows considerable variation: the shortest being 751 seconds, the longest running to 2,337 seconds – both of these extremes are informal conversations. This explains why some informants yielded more tokens of 'because' than others.

The total number of occurrences of 'because' collected in PAC Lancashire equals 351 in interview speech. Curiously, they were divided between formal and informal virtually equally: 171 instances of 'because' could be identified in the formal conversations and 180 examples in the conversations (see Table 7.2). These data exclude six further occurrences of 'because' as part of the complex preposition 'because of', excluded from the present study both 'because' this complex preposition is rare in this corpus data and because it is syntactically different. The data also exclude occurrences of because by the fieldworker because she is not a speaker of the variety under study.

The frequency of occurrence of 'because' is one every 49.04 seconds in the guided conversations and one every 53.45 seconds in the informal conversations, which gives an average of one instance of 'because' every 51.30 seconds across the two styles of conversation. It is therefore pertinent to point out that there does not seem to be a significant difference in these data in the overall frequency of occurrence according to whether the interlocutor is talking to a stranger (the fieldworker) or with someone they know well.

Nevertheless, certain qualifications apply to the figures above. Since the interviews do not represent pure speaker time (because of the fieldworker's turns), the frequency data must be strictly taken as reflecting individual production during the length of conversational interaction. The overall figures do hide considerable variation between the speakers and much intra-speaker variation across the two styles, but given the small amount of data from individual speakers, no statistically relevant conclusions have been attempted to be drawn. Calculating the frequency of occurrence (the number of occurrences per conversation) for each speaker and each style gives a more detailed picture, revealing interesting differences among informants. As for the extremes, MD1 in her formal conversation uses 'because' every 30 seconds on average, while MO1 in her informal conversation uses 'because' every 390 seconds on average, that is nearly every 6.5 minutes. It cannot be determined what accounts for these differences in the frequency of use of 'because' in the informants: these variations are probably influenced by verbal dominance relations (who asks more than they argue their point), the conversation topic (recurrent questions in the formal conversations, uncontrolled topics in the informal conversations), although the relatively small amount of data do not allow conclusions other than hypothetical. The 350 instances of 'because' seem to be a dataset that is both sufficient and relevant for an analysis of patterns in a corpus of spoken contemporary English. I am not aware of studies of 'because' on such a scale.

A further observation to be discussed here is that the frequency data described above hide the fact that occurrences of 'because' are not evenly distributed during the interviews. As a matter of fact, there seems to be a 'clustering effect' in the frequency of own-speech occurrences of 'because' for virtually all the speakers: 'because' tends to cluster with further occurrences nearby and this seems to be related to a more general pragmatic/discursive strategy in spoken English. This effect is shown in the following excerpt, where 'because' occurs five times (in multiple discursive functions):

1. Clustering effect in a single turn
F: <Why Greece?>
PK1f_10-14: <Well because...people my husband worked with recommended Kefalonia because a lot of them had been, there and said it was really nice and they thought we might enjoy it.
because [X]'s been abroad
because he used to be in the TA ... the army thing ... and so he's been abroad but I'd never been abroad before ...
because we had a dog ... so we never went abroad and then

In this corpus, one can take spans of 20 seconds from an occurrence of 'because' and see if another occurrence follows in that lapse of time and, if so, take another span of 20 seconds from that occurrence and so on. While a 20-second span is admittedly arbitrary, it is slightly less than half of the average frequency of occurrence of 'because' presented above (51.3 seconds) and is, based on the data in the corpus, a convenient cut-off point in the distance between occurrences of 'because'. This span is long enough to include all closely hanging instances, quite possibly belonging to the same topic of discussion or very often even the same turn, while separating instances that clearly belong to separate topics/turns. Calculating in this manner, 'because' is found to occur no further than 20 seconds away from another occurrence of 'because' by the same speaker 64 per cent of the time in the formal conversations (110 occurrences out of 171) and 52 per cent of the time in the informal conversations (93 occurrences out of 179). This is an informal finding which possibly reflects the discourse strategy whereby speakers amass arguments and supporting points rather than just give one piece of argument relevant to the discussion, and it might have to do with the spiral patterns addressed in the section 'Discourse structure involving 'because': A – because B – so A'' below.

### Variant Pronunciations and Distribution of Forms of 'Because'

*Phonological Variants*

Being a disyllabic function word, 'because' occurs in a wide range of forms, from a disyllabic variant with a full vowel through various disyllabic forms with reduced vowels to monosyllabic variants with full or reduced vowels to forms which are vowel-less and are best transcribed as [pks] or [ks]. Variants in pronunciation diction-aries are listed in Table 7.3.

For RP, the *Longman Pronunciation Dictionary* (*LPD*) often cites widespread, educated, localised non-RP variants (Wells 2008: xiv); see Table 7.4.

Summarising the dictionary data, the pronunciation of 'because' shows variation along four axes in the standard accents registered in pronunciation dictionaries (see Table 7.5).
The cline of reduction can thus be given as follows:

2. Cline of reduction (for RP)
Disyllabic origin:
/biˈkɔːz/ – /bəˈkɔːz/ > /biˈkɒz/ – /bəˈkɒz/ > /biˈkəz/ – /bəˈkəz/ > /bikəz/ – /bəkəz/ > /pks/
Monosyllabic origin:
/ˈkɒz/ > /kəz/ > /ks/

The corpus data from Bolton (Lancashire) can be usefully compared to forms found in other accents, such as RP. The variant pronunciations in Bolton, Lancashire, accord-ing to the variants based on the *LPD* (Wells 2008: 75) and the *English Pronouncing*

Table 7.3 Variant pronunciations in *EPD* (2011)

| GA disyllabic monosyllabic | |
|---|---|
| | /bɪˈkɑːz/ ~ /bə-/ (/kɑːz/) |
| | /bɪˈkʌz/ ~ /bə-/ (/kʌz/) |
| | /bɪˈkəz/ ~ /bə-/ /kəz/ |
| RP disyllabic monosyllabic | |
| | /bɪˈkɒz/ ~ /bə-/ /kɒz/ |
| | /bɪˈkəz/ ~ /bə-/ /kəz/ |

Table 7.4 Variant pronunciations in *LPD* (2008)

| **GA disyllabic monosyllabic** | |
|---|---|
| | /bɪˈkʌz/ ~ /bə-/ (57%) |
| | /bɪˈkɔːz/ ~ /bə-/ (/kɔːz/) |
| | /bɪˈkɑːz/ ~ /bə-/ (41%) (/kɑːz/) |
| | /bɪˈkəz/ |
| | ~ /bə-/ |
| | /bəkəz/ |
| | (/kəz/) |
| | /-ˈkɔːs/ ~ /-ˈkɑːs/ (2%) (/kɔːs/ ~ /kɑːs/) |
| **BrE disyllabic monosyllabic** | |
| | §/bɪˈkɔːz/ ~ §/bə-/ ~ §/-s/ |
| | /bɪˈkɒz/ ~ /bə-/ ~ §/-s/ /ˈkɒz/ ~ §/ˈkɒs/ |
| | /bɪˈkəz/ |
| | ~ /bə-/ |
| | /bəkəz/ /ˈkəz/ ~ §/ˈkəs/ |

§ = widespread educated non-RP

Table 7.5 Four parameters of variation of 'because'

| Parameter | Values |
|---|---|
| Disyllabic or monosyllabic | /bəˈkɒz/ – /ˈkɒz/ |
| Phonemic voicing in final consonant | /z/ – /s/ |
| Vowel quality in the etymologically stressed syllable | 1 RP /ɔː/ – /ɒ/ – /ə/ |
| | 2 GA /ɔː/ – /ɑː/ – /ʌ/ – /ə/ |
| Reduction of unstressed vowel | /ɪ/ – /ə/ |

*Dictionary* (*EPD*) (Roach et al. 2011: 49), can also be thus grouped: that is, according to whether they are disyllabic or monosyllabic in origin and whether they have a full stressed vowel or some reduced vowel in the (etymologically stressed) second syllable. Another relevant axis of variation is whether they have final /z/ or /s/, the latter being non-RP or localised variants according to Wells (2008). Among such non-RP, localised variants *LPD* also lists /biˈkɔːz/, /biˈkɔːs/, with a long vowel, that is. Such variants with a long stressed vowel clearly exist in the corpus under study but they only occur in emphatic lengthening contexts. According to *LPD*, many speakers distinguish between strong /biˈkɒz/ (or /bəˈkɒz/) and weak /bikəz/ (or /bəkəz/). This behaviour is of course identical to the pattern of other grammatical words such as strong /ˈfɔː/ and weak /fə/. For these speakers the difference is then between a full versus a reduced vowel in the respective forms. However, *LPD* also mentions that some other speakers have 'an irregular strong' /biˈkəz/ (or /bəˈkəz/) variant where the 'strong form' has a reduced vowel. This pronunciation is similar to forms of 'very' with a reduced initial vowel /vəri/, also recorded in *LPD*. Disyllabic forms with /ə/

in the final syllable (/bɪˈkəz/ or /bəˈkəz/ or /bəkəz/) indeed occur some eighty times, although with different frequencies in the individual speakers, in all eight female speakers, while the only male informant, DK1, does not have this variant at all in his data. The Cambridge *EPD* (Roach et al. 2011: 49) adds a note to say that the forms with /ə/ are 'found only in a few phrases, most commonly in "because of the/a …" [in RP]'. This does not correspond to what is found in the Lancashire corpus since /(bə)ˈkəz/ forms are regularly found both in formal and informal conversations introducing clauses rather than in the complex preposition 'because of'. Incidentally, all six occurrences of 'because of' in the corpus are disyllabic, five of them have a full stressed vowel, only one has /ə/. This variety clearly has disyllabic /biˈkəz/ and /bəˈkəz/ used as a conjunction. Finally, all variants may co-occur with final /s/ instead of /z/ according to *LPD*. In the Lancashire PAC corpus, MC1 (71) is the only speaker who consistently has final /s/ in both formal and informal conversations, although another speaker, PK1 (58), also has a sporadic monosyllabic variant with final /s/ intervocalically as in PK1f_09 'X sometimes comes because he's [ˈkɒsiz] in as well'. With respect to the monosyllabic variant, Quirk et al. (1985: 899) point out that, as opposed to many other aphaeretic forms such as 'fraid' (for 'afraid'), 'deed' (for 'indeed'), 'cept' (for 'except'), the aphaeretic form ''cos'/'cause' (for 'because') does not necessarily occur in initial position. This is fully borne out in the corpus data from Bolton, Lancashire where no such positional restriction applies to ''cos'.

Table 7.6 gives a summary of the variant forms in the corpus. The table shows that all speakers have at least one disyllabic variant and all, except the oldest speaker, also have at least one type of monosyllabic variant. Furthermore, the table shows that

Table 7.6  Variant forms of 'because' in the Bolton, Lancashire PAC corpus

| Speaker ID (age) | Disyllabic (number of tokens) | | | Monosyllabic (number of tokens) | |
|---|---|---|---|---|---|
| | *Long vowel* | *Short vowel* | *Reduced vowel* | *Short vowel* | *Reduced vowel* |
| **MO1 (83)** | | bɪˈkɒz 9 | bɪˈkəz 4 | !! 0 | !! 0 |
| **LC1 (77)** | | bɪˈkɒz 17 / bʊˈkɒz 3 | bɪˈkəz 13 | ˈkɒz 4 | !! 0 |
| **MC1 (71)** | bɪˈkɒːs 3 | bɪˈkɒs 27 | bɪˈkəz 2 | ˈkɒz 12 | kəs 2 |
| **PK1 (58)** | | bɪˈkɒz 21 | bɪˈkəz 6 | ˈkɒz 11 / ˈkɒz 4 | kəz kz ks 6 / kəs 1 |
| **SC1 (40)** | bɪˈkɒːz 1 | bɪˈkɒz 24 / bɪˈkɒs 1 | bɪˈkəz 10 | ˈkɒz 6 | kəz 7 |
| **LB1 (38)** | bɪˈkɒːz 5 | bɪˈkɒz 9 | bɪˈkəz 22 | !! 0 | kəz 2 |
| **DK1 (29)** | | bɪˈkɒz 4 | !! 0 | ˈkɒz 25 | kəz 2 |
| **MD1 (29)** | | bɪˈkɒz 1 | bɪˈkəz 19 | ˈkɒz 2 | kəz 31 |
| **JM1 (23)** | bɪˈkɒːz 2 | bɪˈkɒz 11 | bɪˈkəz 2 | ˈkɒz 6 | kəz 13 |
| **Total** | 11 | 127 | 78 | 70 | 64  **350** |

there are further pronunciation variants of 'because' in the PAC Lancashire corpus that are not registered as variants in RP/GA in the *EPD* and *LPD* dictionaries.

Possibly the most trivial is the variant reduced to the extreme, [ks] ([kz]), which is used relatively frequently by MD1 (23) in the corpus.

3. [ks]~[kz] in both formal and informal contexts with MD1
MD1f_21: it's a bad idea because [kz] it's so hard travelling and the trains in England are terrible you can't rely on them
MD1f_36: whereas I'd feel terrible because [ks] I think you know if this was my grandma you know
MD1i_07: So I got there probably about half past, no maybe about six because [kz] then I had to come across
MD1i_08: And I had wine because [ks] I was so stressed out from the journey and that day and getting that parking <DK1: Naughty> ticket.

Another variant, however, deserves some attention. The form occurs with a single speaker, LC1 (77), on three occasions (out of her twenty-one occurrences) all in the formal conversation. It is best transcribed as [bʊˈkɒz] or [buˈkɒz], that is with a labial vowel in the unstressed syllable. This variant seems ultimately to be a derivative of /bəˈkɒz/ in the sense that a reduced [ə] can very easily be coloured phonetically by neighbouring consonants, in this case by the labial consonant [b] that directly precedes. Since there are no known regular alternations in English between unstressed /ɪ/ and /ʊ/, a form /bɪˈkɒz/ to be the origin of [bʊˈkɒz] is difficult to assume. In other words, it would seem that the prior existence of /bəˈkɒz/ was a necessary condition to the emergence of [bʊˈkɒz] in this variety of English. However, the speaker in question only has a single occurrence of [bəˈkɒz] in all her speech sample, which is therefore not a main variant for her. While the source of the lip rounding on the vowel is straightforward, it remains unclear why she replaces unstressed [ɪ] with [ʊ] when she does not produce examples with a reduced [ə] in this syllable.

4. Examples for [bʊˈkɒz]
LC1f_04: yes … [bʊˈkɒz] my brother was even brighter than I was
LC1f_15: while I was with Mother, it was a wonderful escape … [bʊˈkɒz] the people in theatre are very interesting
LC1f_07: but in a way I was lucky … because [bʊˈkɒz] I'd been completely free since I was 39 … so I'd been able to make the most of my freedom

As the orthographic transcriptions show, all three tokens occur after a pause and in her formal conversation. The form [bʊˈkɒz] is emphatic, but it is not exclusive in that context. LC1 also uses [bɪˈkɒz] in post-pause positions:

(5) LC1f_14: so … and I'd always been in plays at church … because [bɪˈkɒz] I could shout up

In conclusion, it can be said that the corpus data from Bolton, Lancashire, reveal the presence of a wide range of pronunciation variants of 'because'. This accent shows the full range of variation described for British accents in *LPD*, including non-RP variants. There is one speaker who uses a variant with final /s/ consistently – a variant which is non-RP. Moreover, the Bolton accent seems to offer a very rare variant, only three occurrences in the corpus, that is not listed in pronunciation dictionaries: /bʊˈkɒz/ with labial colouring of the unstressed vowel. What is interesting in these variants is that they are disyllabic variants that occurred in the relatively formal context of the guided conversations: they are produced in rather careful speech.

*Distribution of Forms across Speech Styles and Speakers: Signs of Change in Apparent Time*

Tables 7.7 and 7.8 present the distribution of all 350 occurrences of 'because' in formal versus informal conversation in the corpus. The tables are arranged according to the age of speakers in descending order from top to bottom, and the variants are listed according to the degree of reduction across the row.

One striking observation about the data in these tables is that there is no unique variant that would either cue a formal or an informal style: the variants overwhelmingly occur for all speakers in both formal and informal conversations. That said, three speakers out of nine do have variants that they used exclusively in the less formal context, and, in addition, these variants (or at least their distribution) are not identical for the five speakers: MC1 has /kəs/ (two times), and DK1 uses both a disyllabic, /bɪˈkɒz/ (four times), and a monosyllabic reduced form, /kəz/ (two times),

Table 7.7 Data from the formal conversations

| Speaker ID (age) | Disyllabic (number of tokens) | | | Monosyllabic (number of tokens) | |
| --- | --- | --- | --- | --- | --- |
| | Long vowel | Short vowel | Reduced vowel | Short vowel | Reduced vowel |
| MO1 (83) | 0 | bɪˈkɒz 4 | bɪˈkəz 3 | 0 | 0 |
| LC1 (77) | 0 | bɪˈkɒz 10 / bʊˈkɒz 3 | bɪˈkəz 3 | ˈkɒz 4 | 0 |
| MC1 (71) | bɪˈkɒːs 1 | bɪˈkɒs 11 | bɪˈkəs 1 | ˈkɒz 4 | 0 |
| PK1 (58) | 0 | bɪˈkɒz 8 | bɪˈkəz 3 | ˈkɒz 6 / ˈkɒz 3 | kəs 1 |
| SC1 (40) | bɪˈkɒːz 1 | bɪˈkɒz 9 | bɪˈkəz 6 | ˈkɒz 2 | kəz 4 |
| LB1 (38) | bɪˈkɒːz 2 | bɪˈkɒz 7 | bɪˈkəz 3 / bɪkəz 6 | 0 | kəz 2 |
| DK1 (29) | 0 | 0 | 0 | ˈkɒz 10 | 0 |
| MD1 (29) | 0 | 0 | bɪˈkəz bɪkəz # | ˈkɒz 1 | kəz kz ks 21 |
| JM1 (23) | bɪˈkɒːz 1 | bɪˈkɒz 7 | bɪˈkəz 1 | ˈkɒz 3 | kəz 5 |
| Total | 5 | 59 | # | 33 | 33  170 |

Table 7.8 Data from the informal conversations

| Speaker ID (age) | Disyllabic (number of tokens) | | | Monosyllabic (number of tokens) | |
|---|---|---|---|---|---|
| | Long vowel | Short vowel | Reduced vowel | Short vowel | Reduced vowel |
| MO1 (83) | 0 | bɪˈkɒz 5 | bɪˈkəz 1 | 0 | 0 |
| LC1 (77) | 0 | bɪˈkɒz 7 | bɪˈkəz 10 | 0 | 0 |
| MC1 (71) | bɪˈkɒːs 2 | bɪˈkɒs 16 | bɪˈkəs 1 | ˈkɒz 8 | kəs 2 |
| PK1 (58) | 0 | bɪˈkɒz 13 | bəˈkəz 3 | ˈkɒz 5 / ˈkɒz 1 | kəz kəs kz 6 |
| SC1 (40) | 0 | bɪˈkɒz 15 / bɪˈkɒs 1 | bɪˈkəz 4 | ˈkɒz 4 | kəz 3 |
| LB1 (38) | bɪˈkɒːz 3 | bɪˈkɒz 2 | bɪˈkəz 13 | 0 | 0 |
| DK1 (29) | 0 | bɪˈkɒz 4 | 0 | ˈkɒz 15 | kəz 2 |
| MD1 (29) | 0 | bɪˈkɒz 1 | bɪˈkəz bɪkəz 4 | ˈkɒz 1 | kəz kz ks 10 |
| JM1 (23) | bɪˈkɒːz 1 | bɪˈkɒz 4 | bɪˈkəz 1 | ˈkɒz 3 | kəz 8 |
| Total | 6 | 68 | 37 | 37 | 31 **179** |

exclusively in the informal conversation, while MD1 uses /bɪˈkɒz/ (once) in her informal conversation.

6.a Variants exclusively found in the informal conversation for the given speaker

|  | Disyllabic | Monosyllabic |
|---|---|---|
| MC1: | | /kəs/ (2) |
| DK1: | /bɪˈkɒz/ (4) | /kəz/ (2) |
| MD1: | /bɪˈkɒz/ (1) | |

In the cases of MC1 and DK1, it is true that they use their most reduced variants /kəs/, /kəz/, in the most informal context. DK1 and MD1 show yet another distribution: they use an emphatic /bɪˈkɒz/ in their informal conversation, and for DK1 this is his only use of a disyllabic variant.

On the other hand, there are three other speakers who used a particular variant exclusively in their formal conversation: SC1 used an emphatic /bɪˈkɒːz/ in her formal conversation, while LC1 and LB1 are even more intriguing because they used monosyllabic variants /ˈkɒz/ (four times) and /kəz/ (four times) respectively, in their formal conversation but not once in their informal conversation. Moreover, this variant is their only monosyllabic token in their whole material.

6.b Variants exclusively found in the formal conversation for the given speaker

|  | Disyllabic | Monosyllabic |
|---|---|---|
| SC1: | /bɪˈkɒːz/ (1) | |
| LC1: | | /ˈkɒz/ (4) |
| LB1: | | /kəz/ (4) |

While it is not surprising that there is no clear distributional difference between the variants in the semi-guided and the informal context, there are two points worth noting. One is that the variants used in the informal context are not necessarily the speaker's most reduced variants as shown by the use of /bɪˈkɒz/ by DK1 and MD1 exclusively in their informal conversation. The second is that for two of the speakers a monosyllabic variant occurs in the formal data but not in the informal data. Both these observations go against the expectation that if there is a form preferred in informal contexts, it should be monosyllabic ''cos' since its monosyllabicity implies reduction (from disyllabic 'because').

For three speakers out of nine there is a complete overlap between the types of variants they use in the two styles, meaning that for them informality is not encoded by the choice of the form per se. Moreover, given that the number of occurrences of variants used exclusively in formal or informal contexts, in the case of other speakers, is extremely low, the individual variant pronunciation of 'because' does not cue formal or informal context in the overwhelming majority of cases: in 323 out of 350 tokens (ca. 92 per cent), there is no way of knowing the degree of formality of the speech turn based on the particular variant used. The data above, however, do not mean that there are no differences in the frequency of use of each variant according to the formality of the situation. The oldest speaker, MO1, has relatively few tokens of 'because' to come up with a description of her pattern apart from the fact that she lacks monosyllabic variants. For LC1, informality seems to be cued by inversion of the ratio of /bɪˈkɒz/ to /bɪˈkəz/, in favour of /bɪˈkəz/ in the informal conversation. For MC1 and DK1, the reduced variant /kəs/ or /kəz/ makes its appearance as formality drops, and in PK1 /kəz/ or /kz/ becomes more frequent with respect to /ˈkɒz/ at the same level of formality. For LB1, disyllabic /bɪˈkəz/ clearly dominates over /bɪˈkɒz/ as formality loosens (and she virtually lacks monosyllabic variants, [kəz] only occurring twice in her formal (!) conversation as discussed above). DK1 and MD1 use a disyllabic form for emphasis in their more emotionally charged informal conversation. Finally, in the case of SC1 and JM1 (and MD1 apart from her use of an emphatic form informally), there is no obvious correspondence between their variants and their frequency and the formality of the conversation.

The most striking observation about these corpus data concerns the distribution and frequency of monosyllabic forms: 134 monosyllabic forms have been identified among the 350 in the corpus, which is over one third of all occurrences, ca. 38 per cent. Table 7.9 gives the forms and the proportion of the full and reduced forms (using the symbols >, <, and ≈ to mark these ratios).

On the one hand, there is again much individual variation. All speakers except MO1, the oldest speaker, use at least one monosyllabic variant at least occasionally. The frequency and the number of monosyllabic variants, however, vary considerably. LB1, for instance, uses only two instances of /kəz/ out of her thirty-eight occurrences, while she lacks, at least in her data, /ˈkɒz/. DK1, however, has only four disyllabic occurrences of his thirty-one tokens, twenty-seven thus being spread over twenty-five tokens of /ˈkɒz/ and two of /kəz/. Nevertheless, a very clear and consistent tendency

Table 7.9 Distribution of monosyllabic variants across speakers

| Speaker ID | Full vowel | Ratio | Reduced vowel |
|---|---|---|---|
| MO1 (83) | 0 | | 0 |
| LC1 (77) | 'kɒz | | 0 |
| MC1 (71) | 'kɒz | > | kəs |
| PK1 (58) | 'kɒz, 'kɒz | > | kəz |
| SC1 (40) | 'kɒz | ≈ | kəz |
| LB1 (38) | 0 | !!! | kəz |
| DK1 (29) | 'kɒz | > | kəz |
| MD1 (23) | 'kɒz | < | kəz, ks |
| JM1 (23) | 'kɒz | < | kəz |

emerges as far as the proportion of the full versus reduced variants is concerned. The oldest speaker, MO1 (83), does not use monosyllabic variants at all. Next oldest speakers, LC1 (77) and MC1 (71), do use a monosyllabic form but it nearly always has a full stressed vowel, /ɒ/. Also, MC1 uses the full variant more often than LC1, and it is perhaps not surprising to find her using /kəz/ twice to twelve tokens of /kɒz/. With PK1 (58) the incidence of a monosyllabic variant is close to 40 per cent of the time (across the two styles) and sporadically the variant /kəz/ makes its appearance. While SC1 (40) and LB1 (39) make use of a monosyllabic variant far less often than the other speakers in the corpus, they both have /kəz/. With the youngest speakers, DK1 (29), MD1 (23) and JM1 (23), the dominance of monosyllabic variants is clearly established even if all three do not show the same overall pattern. DK1, as already referred to, makes near-exclusive use of /'kɒz/ in his sample (87 per cent is monosyllabic), while MD1 and JM1 have a very clear preference for /kəz/, ca. 60 per cent and 38 per cent, respectively, among all the different forms they use. With at least one of the youngest speakers, MD1, the extremely reduced /ks/ variant is also very frequent. What these data demonstrate is that, on the one hand, monosyllabic variants gain ground through time and, on the other, the competition between a full-vowelled and a reduced-vowelled variant is increasingly in favour of the reduced variant. This pattern is compatible with an apparent time change analysis of these data.

## Semantics of 'Because' and Discourse

### The Grammatical Functions of 'Because'

The conjunction 'because' is a versatile and very frequent connector in English. The Longman Communication 3000, the word frequency appendix of the *Longman Dictionary of Contemporary English* (2009), lists it among the 1,000 words most frequently used both in speech and writing in English. As far as its grammatical functions are concerned, they range from subordinating conjunction, introducing adverbial clauses of cause or reason, to its use as 'style disjunct' and discourse marker. In *A Communicative Grammar of English* (Leech and Svartvik 2002: 107), 'because' is treated primarily as a connector indicating cause or reason in an adverbial 'because'-clause (along with prepositions like 'on account of', 'because of', 'from', 'out of', 'through'). In the *Cambridge Grammar of English* (Carter and McCarthy 2006: 57–58), 'because' 'is a subordinating conjunction which introduces clauses of cause and reason'. Quirk et al. (1985: 616, 1072) describe a function where 'because' is not an adjunct, but a 'style disjunct'. Carter and McCarthy (2006: 214, 218) explicitly enumerate ''cos' among 'common spoken discourse markers' and say specifically that '''cos'' marks the reason/justification/explanation for asking the question rather than acting as a causal subordinator'. The PAC corpus data provide ample illustration for all these functions of 'because'.

'Because' can be used to express cause. Leech and Svartvik (2002: 107) give the following example for this meaning (their data come from the Longman Corpus Network):

7.a 'because' expressing 'cause':
The accident occurred because the machine had been poorly maintained.

Carter and McCarthy (2006: 57–58) give this example to illustrate the causal meaning of 'because':

7.b The government will not act because economic factors influence their thinking.

In both cases, the subordinate clause introduced by 'because' expresses the state of affairs that is presented as logically leading to the situation described in the main clause. Passot (2007: 122) notes that such 'narrow scope' interpretations are rather rare in speech data. This is fully borne out in the corpus, since the closest we get to with a 'cause' reading is in the following utterance:

8. JM1f_01: I think … I got confused because [biˈkɒz] those loads of words are together

Another function of 'because', according to Leech and Svartvik (2002: 109), is indicating reason concerning the way a person interprets the events and acts upon this interpretation rather than concerning the events themselves. In these cases '[t]he main clause indicates the consequence of the reason clause' (Leech and Svartvik: 109). 'Because' cannot introduce participial and verbless clauses when functioning as a conjunction of reason (Quirk et al. 1985: 564; Leech and Svartvik 2002: 204). Leech and Svartvik (2002: 107, 109) give the following examples for reason meaning (their data come from the Longman Corpus Network):

9.a 'because' expressing 'reason':
The party opposed the aircraft because they were out of date.
We have to lunch early on Saturday because the girls are always in a hurry to go out.

In the *Cambridge Grammar of English* (Carter and McCarthy 2006: 57–58), because has a 'reason' interpretation in this example:

9.b Because the snow had set in, we decided to abandon the excursion to the mountain top.

Huddleston and Pullum (2002: 727) note that the subordinate situation, with reason, can be simultaneous with, or earlier, or later than the matrix clause:

9.c
He was angry because he couldn't find his keys.
He was late because he had overslept.
He didn't want to go with them because it would be dark soon.

The Lancashire corpus provides plenty of examples for the 'reason' reading:

10.
LB1i_13: Everybody knew Mandy because [bikəz] she's so loud
MO1f_04: they decided to form a club. So er, my husband was er, (laughter) appointed chairman … and er … because [b(ə)kəz] he always had the most to say
LC1f_16: And then in retirement, I joined the rambling club, and that was great because [bɪˈkəz] a lot of them are church people
LC1f_19: And they motored me up the coast, from Gibraltar to Barcelona so that was interesting because [kɒz] we stopped on the way
MC1f_10: So I've had, mini holidays I call them, and I usually I like to take them after Christmas because [bɪˈkɒs] … our winter is so … Burnley, in Burnley it's very depressing
PK1f_06: but yoga I really like because [bɪˈkəz] … it's stretching
SC1i_07: I mean I'm concerned as well because [bɪˈkɒz] it's the first time he's ever been on his own so … just like … you know I'm just like, you know
MD1f_12: and it was fascinating because [kəz] I'd never done anything about reading before
JM1f_05: it's quite hard to pinpoint exactly what I do because [kəz] it's it's quite varied really my role

As far as the particular phonological variants are concerned, many of the examples above carry a form that is the majority form for the given speaker, but this is not at all a regular correspondence.

Quirk et al. (1985: 616, 1072) note a function where 'because' is not an adjunct but functions as a style disjunct 'making more explicit the respect in which a comment is being "hedged"'. They distinguish between three types of 'because'-clauses (1985: 1077): restrictive adjunct, non-restrictive adjunct, and style disjunct. Their examples are presented below, where syllables in capital letters mark the tonic syllable of the utterance and the diacritics indicate the tone movement, rise (ÉA), fall (À) and fall-rise (Ǎ), on that tonic syllable:

11.
*Restrictive adjunct:*
Raven didn't leave the party early because CǍRol was there
*Non-restrictive adjunct:*
Raven didn't leave the party ÉARrly because CÀRol was there
*Style disjunct:*
Raven didn't leave the party ÉARrly because I CHÈCKED

Quirk et al. (1985: 1106) note that only adjunct 'because'-clauses, but not style disjunct 'because'-clauses, can correspond to a PP introduced by 'because of'. Style disjuncts are close equivalents of speech act-related adjuncts with Huddleston and Pullum (2002). The latter add that they can be found with questions as in their example:

12.
Are you nearly ready, because the bus is leaving in ten minutes?

In this function, the adverbial clause is final in the utterance, while, otherwise, reason clauses may either precede or follow their main clause (see also Carter and McCarthy 2006: 563). Quirk et al. (1985: 1073) note that such 'style disjuncts' 'realised by clauses are always separated from the matrix clause by intonation and punctuation'. It follows that in speech their identification should be relatively easy. According to Quirk et al. (1985: 615): 'Style disjuncts convey the speaker's comment on the style and form of what he is saying, defining in some way under what conditions he is speaking as the "authority" of the utterance.' These are their examples:

13.
He was drunk, because he had to support himself on a friend's arm.
I have nothing in my bank account, because I checked this morning.

This usage is indeed found in many examples in the corpus such as the following:

14.
MO1f_07: And er, but er, we've got quite a good, ... keen ... company ... because [bɪˈkɒz] er ... there, there's a, a sort of a national competition the er, the North West Federation,
LC1i_08: And after that he went to see him, and I think he probably put him in a better home because [bˈkɒz] he said after a while he was in a nicer home
LC1f_06: It wasn't that we were poor ... because [bɪˈkəz] ... printers got paid ... better than other tradesmen, they had one of the best unions

DK1i_07: make sure you ring him first because ['kɒz] it looks like a lot of garages are busy

MC1i_05: my neighbour next door kindly went up in my loft to take my case down because [bɪ'kɒs] the case that was down wasn't big enough

SC1f_15: when I came back home I was so homesick because [kəz] I just wanted my mum and dad

SC1i_13: I'll probably see her this weekend because ['kɒz] I'm off for four days

At the level of the whole corpus there is no direct correlation between the phonological variant and the discourse function of 'because'. This is not to say such correspondences do not exist, but it would be matter for a further study to establish such relationships in individual informants.

Carter and McCarthy (2006: 214, 218) explicitly enumerate ''cos' among 'common spoken discourse markers' linking segments where '''cos" marks the reason/justification/explanation for asking the question rather than acting as a causal subordinator'. In such cases, '[d]iscourse markers help speakers to negotiate their way through talk, checking whether they share a common view of the topic and of the nature of the unfolding discourse with their listener[.]'. Examples for this in the corpus include the following cases:

15.
JM1f_12: it makes you cope under pressure because [bɪ'kɒz] … people think it/ have you ever done that? People think it's a really easy job …

SC1i_19: well because [bɪ'kɒz] … I don't know if it's … because [bɪ'kɒz] … I don't know it would

One particular discourse marker function of 'because' is to delay turn alternation (Passot 2007: 130). In this case, there is a pause after 'because'. The form can be any variant that is available for the speaker, although, as the data clearly show, there is a tendency for a disyllabic variant to occur in this use precisely because it is before a pause signalling the wish for the speaker to continue. Below is a list of examples from the corpus:

16.a
LB1f_06: they are very good … to work for because [bɪ'kɒ:z] … they did let me leave

MD1f_13: whereas it was new to me because [kəz] … in Sheffield their speciality is … vision

MD1i_13: it might just be worth it because [bɪkəz] … then you can do your essay

MO1i_05: Well I won't be having any because [bɪ'kɒ:s] … er … my niece was on the phone this morning

JM1i_02: he's going to really dodgy places because [bɪkəz] … yeah, like … I was reading in the paper …

LC1f_07: I was very very lucky because [bɪˈkɒz] … erm … I don't think I would have been as happy if like a lot of girls they just went to these office jobs …

PK1f_06: but yoga I really liked because [bɪˈkɒz] … it's stretching it stretches your neck and you do it you see so I like that

PK1i_10: it's all new because [kɒz] … we haven't been f/…for a while 'cos /ks/ we used to go with/ when we had the dog

SC1f_03: so I think … just really where I live has had an influence on the way I speak because [bɪˈkɒz] … it's just … Lancashire accent

As a discourse marker, 'because' can also be used to introduce a clarification question as in the following example:

16.b
JM1i_14: is that what you? … because [ˈkəʒ] your Master's it was a Master's in …

This usage is very rare in the corpus and seems to be restricted to usage in younger speakers. Finally, while 'because' does not figure among the expressions 'used in everyday spoken language to downtone the assertiveness of a segment of discourse' in Carter and McCarthy (2006: 223), it is clear that this function is readily available for 'because' to take on.

17.
MD1i_05: it would have taken me half an hour … because [kəz] you know … 'cos everyone's going that way

LB1f_10: and it irritates me because [bɪˈkɒz] I think 'Get yourself a life'

Quirk et al. (1985: 1106) note that a 'because'-clause is sometimes used informally as equivalent to a 'that'-clause:

18.a
(Just) because I object to his promotion doesn't mean that I'm vindictive

This structure is strictly parallel to this example from Huddleston and Pullum (2002: 731) where they note that a 'that'-clause would be 'widely preferred in formal style':

18.b
Because some body parts have already been turned into commodities does not mean that an increasing trade in kidneys is desirable.

They also add finally that 'because' is often modified by 'just' and the matrix VP is 'more or less restricted to doesn't mean' (ibid.). No such examples could be identified in the corpus.

As far as the monosyllabic variant is concerned, Carter and McCarthy (2006: 57–58) remark that ''cos (which can also be spelt 'cause) is a reduced form of because. [...] It is widely used in spoken and more informal varieties of English. ['cos] is common in informal speech across the range of ages, social classes and educational background.' The form is available for any of the uses of 'because', apparently.

19.
We're not going to the club 'cos it's just too expensive.
She's probably on the first allowance 'cos she was probably earning about eighteen thousand.

Nevertheless, Carter and McCarthy (2006: 57–58) also add: 'In spoken English cos often functions more like a coordinating than a subordinating conjunction. In these instances cos invariably follows the main clause and functions to add to the information in the main clause.'

20.
She doesn't like animals 'cos she says we should keep the house clean. And she does, doesn't she?
What does he look like? 'Cos I've never actually met him.

Since all their examples correspond to what Quirk et al. (1985) call 'style disjunct', the data cited earlier clearly show that there is no necessary preference for a monosyllabic variant for the speakers in the Bolton (Lancashire) corpus.

*Discourse Structure Involving 'Because': A – Because B – so A'*

There is a special discourse structure involving 'because' in spoken English, which was studied by Passot (2007) in a spoken corpus of RP English. The pattern is also found in the Bolton (Lancashire) corpus and it shows aspects that have not been addressed in Passot's 2007 analysis. On certain other points, her fundamentally correct analysis can be nuanced and made more explicit.

The structure A – because B – so A' is a discourse progression device that consists of a number of distinct parts with specific functions. The following example is taken from Passot's work:

21.a
Passot (2007), BNC spoken, text=H49 n=968, PS1XG
A = [Erm <pause> they say they would not be willing to change their valuation,]
B = [because that was the valuation er come to by the District Value Office from <gap>,]
A' = so [they are not willing to, to come down in price]

Part A is submitted to the addressee as potentially consensual and B provides the elements that allow to reach such a consensus. A', headed by so, is a reformulation of A, which is now considered as part of the shared background. The difference in the formulation between A and A', in this example, shows a greater precision and a non-hypothetical stance in the latter: 'change their valuation' in A becomes the more specific 'come down in price' in A' and 'they would not be willing to' becomes 'they are not willing to'. Passot (2007: 126) calls this configuration modal shift because 'it betrays the symbolic stance taken by the speaker on the matter under discussion and the speaker's anticipation of the addressee's own posture'. At the level of grammatical devices, this modal shift can be expressed by modal auxiliaries, reporting verbs or intensive verbs and lexical choices, she observes. Discourse progresses in a 'spiral' because A' now represents the new consensus, having explicitly formulated the underlying argument(s) introduced by because B.

The following example illustrates what Passot (2007: 125) calls semantic or referential shift and that she describes as cases where 'the two ends of the pattern [A and A'] do not meet' and where 'there is enough difference between them to support the spiral hypothesis'. This scenario involves shifts in the precision of the terms used or the referencing of pronouns, for instance.

21.b
Passot (2007), BNC spoken, text=KP8 n=3457, PS52U
A =  [It's, what they've done is they've closed er, er, erm <pause> branch, an office
      <pause> massive office in London and they've moved them all over to Leeds]
B =  [because they can't get the people to <pause> take jobs in London <pause>]
A' =  so [they've transferred it all to Leeds]

In this example there is a loss of specificity of 'branch' > 'an office' > 'massive office' in A reprised by 'it all' in A', while there is a gain in finding the right term 'transferred' in A' for 'closed' > 'moved' in A. In this way, the consensus in A' is the fact of 'transfer (to Leeds)' rather than the precise term of what ('branch'/'offices') actually got transferred.

While Passot's analysis in terms of semantic content is correct, a different breakdown of the parts A and A' can be proposed, a division based on parallel syntactic features. The main reason for narrowing down the structure syntactically is that it brings out an important trait of the structure which has apparently changed through time as shown by the PAC recordings: the pattern A – because B – so A' is carried by syntactic parallels. Under this analysis, parts A and A' would be only constituted by the shortest stretch of utterance they share rather than the much longer stretches under Passot's analysis. Under this analysis, A and A' become shorter than under her analysis but still bring out the spiral character of the device. An additional piece of argument for the restricted analysis is that under this analysis so introducing A' really introduces the material that A' reprises. The following is a reanalysis of the modal shift example in (21a) above:

22.a
Reanalysis of BNC spoken, text=H49 n=968, PS1XG
Erm <pause> they say
A = [they would not be willing to change their valuation,]
B = [because that was the valuation er come to by the District Value Office from
<gap>,]
so
A' = [they are not willing to, to come down in price]

It has to be admitted that Passot uses this example to illustrate modal shift, and one grammatical device to bring this shift out is using reporting verbs, according to her. However, 'they say' is precisely absent from the restricted proposal because A' does not take it up. Such reporting verbs, unless reprised in A', will indeed likely be absent from the restricted analysis of A presented here. Essentially, it could indeed be argued that such a reporting verb can trigger the whole spiral pattern in the first place, in this sense being the trigger of the whole A – because B – so A' structure rather than being a part only of A. The difference in the breakdown between Passot's analysis and the present proposal is even more apparent in the reanalysis of the second example, (21b) above, the referential shift, since it excludes even more of the material included in Passot's analysis:

22.b
Reanalysis of BNC spoken, text=KP8 n=3457, PS52U
It's, what they've done is they've closed er, er, erm <pause> branch, an office <pause> massive office in London and
A = [they've moved them all over to Leeds]
B = [because they can't get the people to <pause> take jobs in London <pause>]
so
A' = [they've transferred it all to Leeds]

As was pointed out above, the main thrust of the consensus in A' concerns 'transfer (to Leeds)', and this restricted analysis brings this observation out neatly since while A has the general verb 'moved', A' has the specific verb 'transferred'. In this way, nothing is lost in the spiral discursive pattern.

What can also be seen in the proposed analyses above is that A' shows syntactic parallels with A that are not given particular importance under Passot's original analysis. The first example follows a simple structure of 'they + be willing to + VP' and both are negations, while the second is 'they + verb in present perfect + direct object + PP [to Leeds]' and both are assertions. The point is not the precise equivalence of the syntactic description here but the observation that A and A' show closely parallel syntactic structures (and further seem to agree in assertion/negation) while they are, crucially, not word-for-word repetitions. This is important because data from Bolton, Lancashire, show a certain number of occurrences of this discourse progression device but the patterns show considerable variation in the degree of syntactic parallels depending on the age of speakers: older speakers do not show such close parallels between A and A' whereas younger speakers do, which seems to reflect the emergence of this discourse structure. Moreover, word-for-word repetition will also have to be allowed for.

Let us now consider some examples from Bolton (Lancashire). The following are cases of modal shift.

23. Modal shift

23.a

SC1f_06

Yeah so, but I'm, yeah

A    [it would s/ I just wanted to do er … you know]

B    because [bɪˈkɒz] like … to show that I could do something else rather working and looking after children (laughter) you, you know. And er and I enjoyed doing it

so,

A'    [you know it wa/it was something for myself]

23.b

SC1i_25

A    … but [it's gonna feel strange] anyway not having him here <all day> even Christmas morning

B    because [bɪˈkɒz] like we used have him in here to open presents you know

so

A'    [it'll be strange]

23.c

MD1i_03

A    [Then I'll have to go back Sunday night]

B    because [ks] nine o'clock on Monday I'm at school, at Donnington er, doing those three assessments.

so

A'    [I've got to get back,] so I hope it's not foggy.

23.d

LB1f_15

A    [I'm set in .. ]

B    because [bɪkəz] … he takes the car

so

A'    [I can't go out]

The following are cases illustrating referential shift:

24.a

LC1f_15

In one way it satisfied me enormously, while I was with mother,

A [it was a wonderful escape]

B ... because [bʊˈkɒz] the people in theatre are very interesting, you get lots of laughs (?),

so

A' [it's a wonderful life]

and you do get addicted to it. It's a wonderful life and you do get addicted to it.

24.b

MC1f_04

A [I didn't want to go back in an office ...]

B because. [bɪˈkɒs] ... I,, wanted a job without stress

so,

A' [I had a part-time job at the local school, in the nursery kitchen, ]

24.c

MC1i_29

A and [they put me two coats of varnish on]

B because [bɪˈkəs] I/I can't ... I thought well I haven't time to paint it,

so

A' [he the carpenter varnishes it,] hundred and ninety seven pound!

24.d

PK1f_08

<F: So it's the breathing control?>

A Yes. So, [it's to do with brea/ and posture]

B because [ˈkəs] when you stand up straight and you're, and you breathe and do that, posture, you know you, stand right

so

A' [it's to do with your posture]

24.e

MD1f_04-05

A [that was strange]

B because [ˈkəz] I didn't know anybody because [kz] I'd gone to primary school in Bolton

so

A' [it was completely different] and er

24.f

DK1i_19

It's just rubbish anyway,

A [it's not ... ]

B because [kəz] it's just automatically generated code

so

A' [it's not what you would write normally.] <MD1: Right.>

Here are two examples from the corpus where one phrase is fronted, but they are still syntactically parallel.

25.a
PK1f_06
but
A   [yoga I really like]
B   because [bɪˈkəz] … it's stretching it just stretches you and I can do it you see,
so
A'  [I l-/I like that,]
    it's not fast or, it's just nice and, slow and, yes and I like it yeah.
25.b
SC1f_20
you know
A   [we had to go everywhere in car …]
B   because [bɪˈkəz] it's not safe for you just to walk about you know
so
A'  [everywhere we went, we were in car]

As can be seen, A and A' show the syntactic parallels as expected. The fronting of 'yoga' is justified by a contrast with another element preceding it. The fronting of 'everywhere we went' is internal to the turn. While Passot (2007) does not explicitly mention it, in the corpus under study here, there is no pause before 'so'.

To illustrate a more complex example with multiple occurrences of 'because' and the A – because B – so A' structure, consider the following turn:

26.
PK1f_10:
Well because [bɪˈkɒz] … people my husband worked with recommended Kefalonia because [ˈkɒz] a lot of them had been, there and said it was really nice and they thought we might enjoy it.
because [ˈkɒz]
A   [X's been abroad]
B   because [ˈkɒz] he used to be in the TA … the army thing … and
so
A'  [he's been abroad]
but
A   [I'd never been abroad before …]
B   because [bɪˈkɒz] we had a dog ...
so
A'  [we never went abroad]
and then

Here, 'because' has multiple functions. The first three introduce clauses of reason. While the fourth occurrence also gives a reason, the argumentation enters the spiral because 'so' picks up A, word for word practically, changing only the proper name to the pronoun. The final instance of 'because' is in a spiral again and gives the reason to A which allows a change of perspective in A' from 'I' to 'we'.

This example leads us to the consideration of cases where A and A' are virtually identical.

27.a

LC1i_13

A   [I do find it a lot better]

B   because [bɪˈkəz] … when you get into the car first of all you think 'and I must go to so and so and I must go to so and so and', your mind is half-taking/, taken up with what you're going to do.

so

A'   [I do find it a lot better to reverse] and/ <pause>

27.b

PK1f_08

<F: So it's the breathing control?> Yes. So,

A   it's to do with brea/ and posture

B   because [ˈkəs] when you stand up straight and you're, and you breathe and do that, posture, you know you, stand right

so

A'   it's to do with your posture.

Such examples can be regarded as the precursor of the later spiral structure in the sense that such repetition can fulfil the function of reprise in the narrative and give a summary of the reason that can lead to a consensus between the speakers. An interesting example in this context is the following turn:

28.

MC1i_02

A   [I've told people not to buy me presents.]

<F: Right.>

B   Because [bɪˈkɒːs] … I don't want all presents in my house at Christmas

so

A'   [I said please]

It is a form of repetition (with a change of aspect so A' is presented as more final and definite) but where 'people not to buy me presents' is transformed into 'please' rather than repeated. Obviously, in the past situation she could say something more like 'people, don't buy me presents'.

A variant of the pattern A – because B – so A' is when A' is not expressed (or reprised by a dummy 'yes') or is completed in a way by another speaker. This is illustrated in the following examples:

29.a

MD1i_05

as soon as I got out on to A64

A    [it was fine] ...

B    because [kəz] of course ... it's a dual carriage way

So ...

A'  [ _ ]

DK1    Yeah, I suppose you missed the M62 traffic ...

29.b

MC1i_09

A    but ... [I'm not bothering them]

B    because [bɪˈkɒs] I might ... decide to sell this house maybe,

so

<F: Oh right.>

A'  Yeah.

29.c

PK1i_27

A    he can't really get time of course [he's away for two days]

B    because [bɪˈkɒz] he's moving house

so

A'  [ _ ]

29.d

SC1f_13

<interviewer>

A    [yeah]

B    because [kəz] they only ... they only live right round the corner my sister lives
     round the corner and my dad xxx round the corner

so.

A'  [Yeah,] yeah, we're a close family yeah

29.e

SC1i_08

A    I mean it's probably, probably goo/ doing good to, to be away from us for like
     three days

B    because [bɪˈkəz] it's the first time he's e/ I mean he's been away with college to,
     you know, places for his, like assignments and things assignments and things but,
     you know, it's just that he's never been away with mates on his own before

so,

A'  [ _ ]

29.f

SC1i_12

A    [for the last few days]

B    because [kəz] like...she's busy all the time, isn't she?

so

A' [ _ ] But I'l/ I'll see/ I'll probably see her this weekend because I'm off
29.g
LB1i_12
A   we don't know how many children we're gonna be doing [hmm]
B   ... because [bɪkəz] they just won't bother coming in to school
so.
A' [ _ ]
29.h
DK1i_17
A   [it wasn't.]
B   because [kɒz] it was shut last night, the keys were in the xxx
so
A' [ _ ]
29.i
JM1f_04
A   I went to do that but obviously I've changed my mind again
B   because [bɪˈkəz] I'm not doing anything to do with geography now,
so.
A' [ _ ]
29.j
JM1i_05
A   Erm, my boss is forty but, she acts about twenty. (MD1 chuckles) Erm. and
    then ...
B   because [kəz] it's like a call-centre so all the/ everyone in/ most people who work
    there are sales agents and they're like, in their twenties.
So,
A' [yes.]
29.k
SC1i_07
A   I mean [I'm concerned as well]
B   because [bɪˈkɒz] it's the first time he's ever been on his own
so ...
A' just like ... you know [I'm just like], you know.

While in the first case, it could be argued that DK1's reply fills in A', the possibility
of having no overt A' at all, like in the rest of the examples in (29) above, shows that
there is no absolute necessity to express the A' part of the pattern. As to the phonological forms, the data reveal that there is no clearly predictable variant for this pattern:
both disyllabic and monosyllabic variants occur, either with a full or a reduced vowel.

There are signs in the corpus material that the pattern A – because B – so A' has
changed through time. While the pattern exists for all speakers, they do not all use
it in the same way. For instance, for MO1, the oldest speaker, 'so' seems to have its
value of true consecutive marker with a short pause after it:

30.a
MO1f_01
But
A  [I didn't go …]
B  because [bɪˈkɒz] my dad … thought … well it's not much higher than what you're doing anyway, you know
so,
A'  [there I stayed,] till I was fourteen.

Combined with 'because' there is an element of progression in the narrative but it does not contribute to building a consensus and it functions more like a reprise of the narrative. This reprise is even clearer in her other example, with a lot of narrative material between 'because' and 'so' and once again with a pause before 'so':

30.b
MO1f_07
A  [we've got quite a good, … keen company]
B  … because [bɪˈkɒz] er … there, there's a, a sort of a national competition the er, the North West Federation, and they've won the championship for years and years, and years, they've won the championship of that federation, for oh, I don't know about, over twenty years,
so,
A'  [they're really keen], there's about a dozen of them and er, they really are keen,

In this case, the word-for-word repetition seems to serve the purpose of picking up the narrative rather than signalling a consensus on the subject. This is a pattern that is found even in the youngest speakers.

30.c
MD1f_01
I went to school in Essex and er (silence) I always lo/ I had really good teachers,
A  [I was really lucky and]
B  because [pkəz] my sister had a few like dud teachers but mine were really nice and I used to like draw a picture and put: 'I love Mrs (X)' (laughter) and sit on her knee and stuff. Er,
so
A  [that was really lucky, and] er, (it was) er, quite a

In this example again, practically word-for-word repetition serves the purpose of picking up the narrative, while it does contain elements for the consensus on why she considers herself really lucky.

## Conclusions

Variants in the corpus data from Bolton (Lancashire) show an overall familiar range of phonological variants, from disyllabic to monosyllabic forms and from forms having a full stressed vowel to forms with a reduced vowel. Indeed, the full range of the reduction cline is found in the accent from /bɪˈkɒːz/ to /ks/. However, speakers do not necessarily use their most reduced variant exclusively in their informal conversation, and for two speakers in the corpus a monosyllabic variant occurs in the formal data but not in the informal data. Both these observations go against the expectation that the form preferred in informal style should be monosyllabic. It is to be noted that a number of speakers of this accent do use a long-vowel variant /bɪˈkɒːz/, a variant registered as non-RP in *LPD*, for purposes of emphasis both in the formal and informal conversations. A variant with a labial vowel in the first syllable has been identified sporadically with one female speaker: /bʊˈkɒz/. The variant /bɪˈkɒz/ does occur with all speakers; however, with younger speakers this is increasingly an emphatic rather than a neutral variant, the more frequent disyllabic form being /bəkəz/ for them. This is particularly clear in DK1 who only uses /bɪˈkɒz/ under emphasis in the corpus; therefore, this form counts as his solution for the long-vowelled /bɪˈkɒːz/ of other speakers. The oldest speaker, MO (83), only uses disyllabic forms such as /bɪˈkɒz/, /bɪˈkəz/. In the next age bracket, LC (77) and MC (71) do use monosyllabic forms but only with a full vowel, that is /kɒz/, /kɒs/. Speakers younger than sixty years of age use both full and various reduced forms. All these respective forms occur, for all speakers, in both the formal and informal conversations. Monosyllabic variants gain ground through time and the competition between a full-vowelled and a reduced-vowelled monosyllabic variant is increasingly in favour of the reduced variant. This pattern is compatible with an apparent time change analysis of these data. At the level of the whole corpus there is no direct correlation between the phonological variant and the discourse function of 'because'. The only such distribution is with cases where 'because' serves as a discourse marker to delay turn-taking and where it usually has a disyllabic form and is usually followed by a pause of suspense.

## References

Carter, R. and M. McCarthy (2006), *Cambridge Grammar of English*, Cambridge: Cambridge University Press.

Durand, J. and A. Przewozny (2012), 'La phonologie de l'anglais contemporain : usages, variétés et structure', *Revue Française de Linguistique Appliquée*, vol. XVII–1, Oral, norme et variation(s), pp. 25–37.

Durand, J. and A. Przewozny (2015), 'Le Programme PAC et la variation', in I. Brulard, J. Durand and P. Carr (eds), *La Prononciation de l'anglais : variation et structure*, Toulouse: Presses Universitaires du Mirail.

Durand, J. and M. Pukli (2004), 'How to construct a phonological corpus: PRAAT and the PAC project', *Tribune Internationale des Langues Vivantes (TILV)* 36, 36–46.

Huddleston, R. and G. K. Pullum (2002), *The Cambridge Grammar of the English Language*, Cambridge: Cambridge University Press.

Labov, W. (1972), *Sociolinguistic Patterns*, Philadelphia: University of Pennsylvania Press.

Labov, W. [1966] (2006), *The Social Stratification of English in New York City*, 2nd edn, Washington, DC: Center for Applied Linguistics and Cambridge: Cambridge University Press.

Leech, G. and J. Svartvik (2002), *A Communicative Grammar of English*, 3rd edn, London: Pearson Education Limited.

Milroy, J. and L. Milroy (1985), 'Linguistic change, social network and speaker innovation', *Journal of Linguistics* 21(2), 339–384.

Passot, F. (2007), 'A because B so A'. Circularity and discourse progression in conversational English', in A. Celle and R. Huart (eds), *Connectives as Discourse Landmarks*, Amsterdam/Philadelphia: John Benjamins, pp. 117–134.

Quirk, R., S. Greenbaum, G. Leech and J. Svartvik (1985), *A Comprehensive Grammar of the English Language*, London and New York: Longman.

Roach, P., J. Setter and J. Esling (2011), *Cambridge English Pronouncing Dictionary*, 18th edn, Cambridge: Cambridge University Press.

Wells, J. (2008), *Longman Pronunciation Dictionary*, 3rd edn, London: Pearson and Longman.

# 8

# On the New Zealand Short Front Vowel Shift

*Cécile Viollain and Jacques Durand*

## Overview

This chapter focuses on the New Zealand Short Front Vowel Shift by articulating the results of a phonetic-acoustic study conducted within the PAC programme, Trudgill's new-dialect formation model, and phonological theory. A push-chain shift hypothesis has been put forward in major publications on the basis of the ONZE recordings, and has mostly been modelled within the framework of Exemplar Theory. We do not share the rejection of phonological representations often advocated within such a framework and therefore provide an account of this phenomenon inspired by the framework of Dependency Phonology. On the basis of only four primes and the dependency relation, we attempt to represent this evolution through the historical competition between different systems that is characteristic of colonial environments.

## Introduction

Our starting point is New Zealand, which has a special place in the English-speaking world for two reasons. It is one of the last territories to have been colonised from the British Isles in the second half of the nineteenth century (Sinclair 1991; Hay et al. 2008), which is why the scientific community has at its disposal unique oral archives, the ONZE (Origins of New Zealand English) project's Mobile Unit and Intermediate Archive (Gordon et al. 2004; Maclagan and Gordon 2004; Langstrof 2006, 2009), which contain recordings from more than 400 informants born between 1851 and 1930; that is, the first speakers of this variety of English. In recent years, New Zealand has consequently become an exceptional laboratory for the study of linguistic evolution and change. These resources have allowed for in-depth accounts of the origins of New Zealand English (NZE hereafter), notably Trudgill's new-dialect formation model (2004), and they continue to fuel the debate on the phonological and phonetic characteristics of both early and modern NZE (Clark et al. 2015; Hay et al. 2015; Sóskuthy et al. 2017).

In particular, researchers have been able to reconstruct the scenario of change affecting eight vowels (KIT, DRESS, TRAP, FLEECE, START, STRUT, NEAR and SQUARE; Wells 1982) which have undergone progressive changes since the mid-nineteenth century. The first six have been described (Gordon et al. 2004; Watson et al. 2004) as being involved in what is called the Short Front Vowel Shift (SFVS hereafter), which is the main object of our study. As for KIT, DRESS and TRAP specifically, NZE has moved from an opposition historically based on three degrees of vowel height to two degrees since the modern vowels often have phonetic values of the following type: 'bid' [bəd] (or [bɐd]), 'bed' [bid] and 'bad' [bɛd] (or [bɐd]).

One major claim, which is virtually the general consensus, is that we are dealing with a push-chain shift (Martinet 1955) initiated by the TRAP vowel. This hypothesis is based on the observation, from the ONZE recordings, that hardly any early speakers born in the nineteenth century used a centralised KIT vowel (Langstrof 2006, 2009), which could have had a pulling effect or been part of a general realignment of values. On the other hand, we observe a relatively high TRAP vowel which rises as time goes on without the KIT vowel necessarily acquiring a clearly centralised value (Gordon et al. 2004; Trudgill 2004). This hypothesis can also be backed by socio-demographic arguments that support the idea that a relatively high quality of the TRAP vowel, used by immigrants from southern England, may have been favoured in the formation of the new dialect in New Zealand.

In this chapter, we discuss this well-documented phenomenon by replacing it in the yet unresolved sociophonological, historical and dialectological debate on the causes and mechanisms of linguistic change. Indeed, many questions arise as to the trajectory and dynamics of NZE in the last 175 years, as to the motivations for this change, and as to the comprehensive manner of capturing it and modelling it. Ultimately, studying the SFVS forces us to turn to the question of what generalisations should be captured by phonology. We take the view that fine-grained phonetic properties which are not explicable in terms of mechanical constraints (roughly, extrinsic versus intrinsic allophones) should ideally be part and parcel of phonological descriptions if we do not restrict the analysis to the lexical level. We remind the reader that even citation forms of words, which are the focus of many phonological analyses, are post-lexical entities in that they manifest the prosodic structure of a minimal isolated utterance. In our view, a phonological model which allows us to capture both contrastive and fine-grained properties (/l/-velarisation in many varieties of English for instance) is to be preferred to a model which is too spartan to do so.

In order to contribute to this debate, we build on empirical data and start (see the section 'The Short Front Vowel Shift in the light of the PAC New Zealand corpus data') by summarising our own detailed phonetic-acoustic study of a New Zealand corpus recorded in 2010 in Dunedin, Otago, following the methodology advocated within the PAC[1] research programme (Carr et al. 2004; Durand and Przewozny 2012). We compare our acoustic observations with other available descriptions of NZE and establish correlations between the subsystems observed and the speakers' profiles, which allows us to hypothesise the existence of two competing systems within our corpus.

We then turn to the debate on the phonology of the vocalic systems of English (see the section 'The debate on the phonology of the vocalic systems of English'). We explain that the changes that have affected and continue to affect the vocalic system of NZE have been accounted for within usage-based theories such as Exemplar Theory (Bybee 2001; Pierrehumbert 2001, 2006). By appealing to primitives defended within Dependency Phonology (Anderson and Jones 1974; Anderson and Ewen 1987; Anderson 2011 inter alia), we claim that a distinction between light and heavy vowels is central to the NZE system, which we interpret as an opposition between {V} and {VV} nuclei (tense/lax, long/short or monomoric/bimoric in other terminologies). This opposition is often blurred in sociophonetic work on NZE and we put forward a number of arguments to justify why we consider it central to understanding the NZE phonotactic patterns and various changes that have taken and are still taking place in this variety.

We also provide an analysis which looks at the NZE vocalic system from two different perspectives (see the section 'A Dependency Phonology interpretation'): underspecified lexical representations and more specified representations derived by non-destructive redundancy statements which capture some of the fine-grained properties that we assume have triggered the observable changes between our more conservative and our more advanced speakers. In doing so, we show broad support for Trudgill's new-dialect formation analysis (2004) which retraces the emergence of NZE in three successive stages corresponding to three generations of speakers, according to a neutral model of evolution which does not involve any other extra-linguistic factor, apart from the natural accommodation of speakers and demographic determinism.

Finally, we offer conclusions (see the section 'Conclusions') on what we have tried to tackle in this chapter, namely the demonstration that NZE, while it inherited deep-sea trends from southern British systems in the nineteenth century, has taken an autonomous route which is very different from Australian English notably, with which it is often too rapidly grouped as antipodean English (Przewozny and Viollain 2016).

## The Short Front Vowel Shift in the Light of the PAC New Zealand Corpus Data

Even though many specialists agree on a push-chain scenario for the TRAP, DRESS and KIT vowels, on the fact that START/STRUT and DRESS/FLEECE can function as light/heavy partners, as well as on the merger of NEAR/SQUARE in modern NZE, there are still many questions regarding the motivations and the underlying mechanisms that allow such a reconfiguration of the vocalic system to occur. In this chapter, we show how we can move on from the results of a phonetic-acoustic study based on fairly recent and authentic oral data to offer a theoretical interpretation of how these changes happened at the phonological level. We would like to point out that such work has not been done in the literature as many accounts of the New Zealand SFVS are either phonetic or phonemic (transcriptions and phonemic inventories, see Bauer and Warren 2008 for instance) but seldom include any degree of phonological abstraction.

*The PAC New Zealand Corpus*

The first step in our endeavour was to build a corpus which would prove relevant for our study of the New Zealand vowels. The methodology we used is that of the PAC programme, which is inspired by Labov's classical sociolinguistic work (1966, 1972, 1994, 2001 inter alia). It aims at building a large database of spoken English in its geographical, social and stylistic diversity, as well as testing contemporary phonological and sociolinguistic theoretical models on the basis of recent and authentic oral data. It builds and analyses corpora of recordings which are similar to those of the PFC programme on French phonology (Detey et al. 2016). Its protocol revolves around reading tasks and more spontaneous contexts such as informal dyadic conversations without the presence of the fieldworker (see the section 'Introduction').

The PAC New Zealand corpus was built in 2010 in Dunedin, the capital of the Otago region, in the southernmost part of the South Island. In its final version, it counts thirteen informants, that is eight women and five men from three distinct generations: the younger generation (three informants between the ages of 18 and 20), the intermediate generation (five informants between the ages of 43 and 51), and the older generation (five informants between the ages of 65 and 76). Despite its small scale, this corpus allows for an apparent time approach to the study of linguistic change. It is actually the most common approach to linguistic change used by researchers as it is significantly easier to put in place from a methodological point of view than the alternative real-time approach. Langstrof (2006: 25) defines its core principle as follows:

> If, at some specified point in time, two speakers of different age show different realisations of some linguistic variable X, this difference reflects change in X in that X changes from a realisation shown by the older speaker toward that of the younger speaker. **Ceteris Paribus**.

*Phonetic-acoustic Study of Eight Vowels*

For our phonetic-acoustic study, we selected tokens exclusively from the reading tasks, that is the two wordlists, the text and the short sentences that make up the protocol for the PAC New Zealand corpus (Viollain 2014). So as to avoid phonetic environments whose influence on the vocalic signal is too important, the following contexts were excluded:

- following /l, r, n, m, ŋ/
- preceding /w, j, t, d/
- preceding obstruent + liquid consonant cluster (for example /bl/)
- vowels adjacent to another vowel (as in the sequence 'the art')

In total, 2702 tokens were analysed, that is an average of 207 tokens per informant, which is small but enough to determine the characteristics of their vocalic systems, provided of course that these results be handled cautiously, as any scientific result should. The tokens included of course the eight vowels that are said to be involved in the SFVS in the literature on the subject, namely KIT (223 occurrences), DRESS (322 occurrences), TRAP (315 occurrences), FLEECE (246 occurrences), START (144 occurrences), STRUT (94 occurrences), NEAR (58 occurrences) and SQUARE (70 occurrences). Under Praat, we extracted the formant values for F1 and F2 for the monophthongs, and the formant values for F1 and F2 of the first element as well as the glide for the diphthongs, and compiled them in a spreadsheet for later statistical tests. The results were normalised following the Lobanov vowel-extrinsic procedure under the NORM software (Kendall and Thomas 2010), and R (2017) yielded a representation[2] of the distribution of the group means for all the vowels pronounced by all the PAC-NZ informants (see Figure 8.1).

We can easily gather from it that the high front area is overcrowded, so to speak, since DRESS, FLEECE, NEAR and SQUARE coexist in a small space compared with what is usually attested from a typological point of view (notably Maddieson 1984: 123–135; Gordon 2016: 49–51). We also note the centralised, but not fully central,

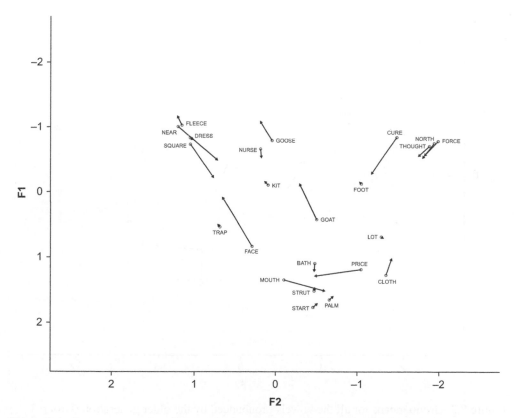

Figure 8.1 Group means for all the vowels pronounced by the PAC-NZ informants

value of KIT towards which the glide of both centring diphthongs, NEAR and SQUARE, converge. We notice that TRAP is rather high in the vocalic space, and no longer seems to be an open short front vowel but a mid-open one. Finally, we observe that STRUT and START have near-merged in terms of quality in the vocalic space. The difference between them is a quantitative one (light versus heavy in the terminology adopted here).

We statistically tested (using an ANOVA) the influence of age as a sociolinguistic variable on our formantic values so as to determine whether the eight vowels under study have changed between the older generation (Group 3) and the younger generations (Group 2 which corresponds to the intermediate generation and Group 1 which corresponds to the younger generation). Results show that age is relevant ($p<0.05$) for all the vowels under study, and notably for KIT, DRESS and TRAP, especially when comparing Group 3 and Group 2 (see Figure 8.2 and Figure 8.3). Indeed, Group 1 appears to be taking a somewhat different path, but as it only comprises three informants, we shall remain very cautious as to our conclusions.

As far as DRESS and TRAP are concerned, Groups 1 and 2 have closer and fronter realisations of these vowels than Group 3. In the same way, the former have closer

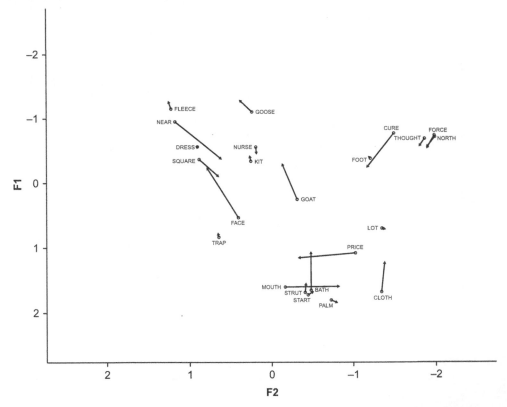

Figure 8.2 Group means for all the vowels pronounced by the older generation (Group 3, PAC-NZ corpus)

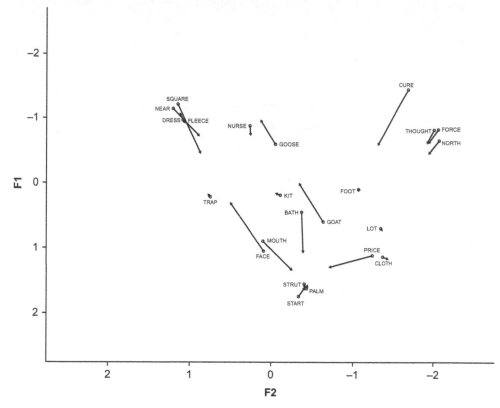

Figure 8.3 Group means for all the vowels pronounced by the intermediate generation (Group 2, PAC-NZ corpus)

and fronter realisations of the first element of SQUARE. As for KIT, the younger generations have more open realisations of this vowel than the older generation. Finally, Groups 1 and 2 have more central and more open realisations of STRUT and START than Group 3. Again, we would like to point out that we are presenting a small-scale phonetic-acoustic study, the results of which should be handled cautiously. We are using these results as a basis for subsequent phonological analyses.

*Two Competing Systems*

These statistical elements compel us to acknowledge that there are two different, and possibly competing, systems within our corpus, and by extension, within the New Zealand speaker community. More precisely, what we have chosen to call a 'conservative' system, in which the KIT, DRESS and TRAP vowels are still classically distinguished by three degrees of height, even though DRESS and TRAP are significantly higher than what can be found in other British varieties of English; and what we have chosen to call an 'advanced' system, in which there has been a redistribution of the short front vowels since KIT is centralised, TRAP is very high and DRESS has near-merged qualitatively with FLEECE, which is showing signs of diphthongisation.

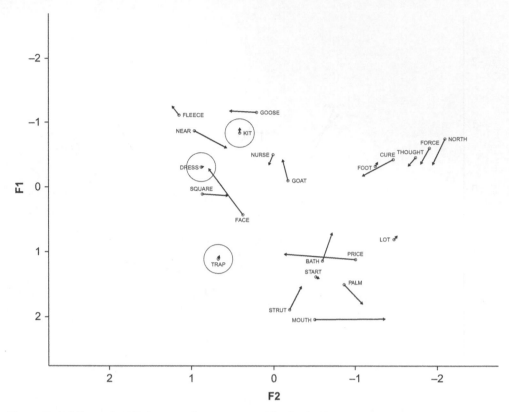

Figure 8.4 Means for all the vowels pronounced by RC3 (Group 3, PAC-NZ corpus)

In order to illustrate this coexistence within our corpus, we include the representations of the distribution in the vocalic space of the vowels pronounced by two of our informants: RC3 (Group 3) and SS1 (Group 2). The KIT, DRESS and TRAP vowels are circled in each representation in order to underline the opposite configurations of the short front vowels for an older, conservative informant (see Figure 8.4), and a younger, advanced informant (see Figure 8.5).

*Further Interrogations*

None of our older informants exhibits a centralised KIT vowel, whereas they all have, to different extents, a rather high TRAP vowel and a high DRESS vowel. On the other hand, none of our younger speakers exhibits a front KIT vowel, whereas they all have, to different extents, a very high TRAP vowel, and an even higher DRESS vowel. Consequently, in order to model what has been going on in NZE in between these two generations of speakers, we have to account for the first system (see Figure 8.4) mutating into the second system (see Figure 8.5). According to our data, we can postulate that this is what happened: from a system comprising three short front vowels (KIT, DRESS and TRAP), classically analysed in the literature as being distinguished by three degrees of height (open, mid-open and closed), we have moved on to a system

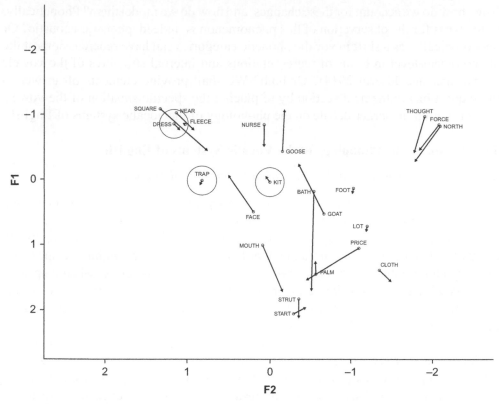

Figure 8.5 Means for all the vowels pronounced by SS1 (Group 2, PAC-NZ corpus)

comprising only two short front vowels (DRESS and TRAP) and a centralised vowel (KIT), following a push-chain shift.

We break down this process into three consecutive stages:

- First, the STRUT and START vowels become partners within the system. They are only distinguished in terms of quantity (phonetic duration). Simultaneously, or not, the TRAP vowel starts to rise, encroaching on the acoustic space of DRESS.
- Consequently, DRESS is pushed out of its initial acoustic space by TRAP, and therefore starts to rise in the vocalic space, encroaching on KIT. Simultaneously, the SQUARE vowel may have started rising, hence merging with NEAR in the vocalic space, which leads to the loss of opposition between these two vowels.
- Finally, the KIT vowel moves out of the way of DRESS, as it were, and therefore centralises. DRESS is consequently free to rise even more, as high as FLEECE, with which it becomes partner within the system. The two vowels are then only distinguished in terms of quantity (phonetic duration), with the frequent diphthongisation of FLEECE giving a clue as to its complex or heavy nature.

Now, how do we account for these changes, and how do we model them? Phonetically, as the basis for the observation of this phenomenon is, indeed, phonetic-acoustic? Or phonologically, as a shift in vocalic phonetic categories can have repercussions at the phonological level in terms of representations and internal structures of the vowels (Scharinger and Idsardi 2014)? Or both? We shall provide elements of answer to these questions in the next section by re-placing the specific situation of the vowels of NZE within the larger debate on the phonology of the vocalic systems of English.

## The Debate on the Phonology of the Vocalic Systems of English

### Accounts of the New Zealand SFVS within Usage-based Theories

The aforementioned changes, which have mostly been studied by phoneticians and sociolinguists in New Zealand, have been accounted for within usage-based theories such as Exemplar Theory (Bybee 2001; Pierrehumbert 2001, 2006). This approach postulates that all the occurrences of a word or sound are stored within the speaker's memory along with fine phonetic and contextual details. Therefore, when a speaker interacts with another speaker, they produce the most 'accurate', the 'fittest' occurrence of the word or sound from their cloud of exemplars. Langstrof (2006: 257) defines fitness in the following terms: 'the fitness of some variant is equivalent to it being an unambiguous instance of the phoneme it encodes'. This bio-linguistic model of change has been defended in a number of prominent works, such as De Boer (2000, 2001) or Blevins (2004) to name but a few. In such approaches, generalisations are not in fact absent, but are the result of the relation between the different representations of a single word or sound that are stored in the speaker's mind. In other words, whenever a speaker hears a word or sound, their cloud of exemplars is updated. Consequently, as far as vowels are concerned, vowel categories are updated on the basis of their surface realisations.

As far as the New Zealand SFVS is concerned, we would like to refer to Langstrof (2006: 250; see Figure 8.6) in order to schematise the initial state of distribution of the KIT, DRESS and TRAP vowels in the vocalic space, and how a bio-linguistic model of change can account for the phonetic changes affecting these vowels throughout the push-chain process. If we consider that A is TRAP, B is DRESS and C is KIT, we can visualise how A rising would cause the fittest variants of B, that is the most unambiguous variants of B compared to A, to be the closest variants. In a domino effect, this would cause the fittest variants of C to get out of the way, so to speak, either by centralising, which is what has happened in modern NZE, or by rising even more, which is what has happened in contemporary Australian English (Cox and Palethorpe 2001; Cox 2012; Przewozny 2016). In turn, this would cause the fittest variants of B to become even fronter, so as not to be confused with realisations of C, and to rise, as A also keeps on rising.

However, even though a model exclusively based on surface realisations is able to account for the permanent micro-processes of phonetic readjustment affecting part of the vocalic system of NZE, one question remains: how do these phonetic

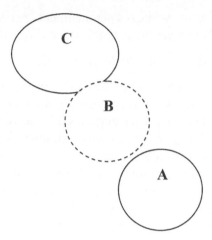

Figure 8.6 Initial state of distribution of the KIT, DRESS and TRAP vowels in the vocalic space in NZE
*Source:* Langstrof (2006: 250).

re-adjustments occur? In other words, is there real phonetic encroachment at some stage in the process or do vowels move 'together', in what's been called an 'equidistance' scenario?

*Generational Encroachment versus Encroachment 'Per Se': The Equidistance Scenario*

On the basis of the individual realisations of the KIT, DRESS, TRAP, FLEECE, START, STRUT, NEAR and SQUARE vowels (normalised values) by all our PAC New Zealand informants, we observe what we have called 'generational encroachment' which we clearly distinguish from actual encroachment. We observe encroachment 'per se' when the realisations of two different vowels clearly overlap in the vocalic space. That is what we witness with START and STRUT, NEAR and SQUARE and also with DRESS and FLEECE. That is not however what we witness with KIT, DRESS and TRAP which have their own rather separate spaces. What we do notice is 'generational' encroachment as the realisations of DRESS by our older generation of speakers (Group 3) overlap with the realisations of TRAP by our younger generations of speakers (Groups 1 and 2), or where the realisations of DRESS by our younger generations of speakers (Groups 1 and 2) overlap with the realisations of KIT by our older generation of speakers (Group 3).

Consequently, it appears that KIT, DRESS and TRAP have indeed changed and moved in the vocalic space. But, as all our informants' systems show that the KIT, DRESS and TRAP vowels possess their own separate phonetic spaces, it suggests that, at all times during the push-chain shift, KIT, DRESS and TRAP have kept their distances, so that the realisations of these three vowels have never merged in the vocalic space, and the realisations of one vowel have not 'de facto' invaded the realisations of another. Therefore, as far as the short front vowels are concerned, we speak in favour of the equidistance scenario for their diachronic change as it is what we witness on the basis of our data. Indeed, where we witness encroachment 'per se', we have mergers or near-mergers but not a chain reaction as in the KIT, DRESS and TRAP push-chain shift.

*The Relevance of Weight for the Vocalic System of NZE*

We would now like to re-place these observations in the debate on the phonology of the vowel systems of English. One of the central issues which has long faced scholars is the distinction between two categories of vowels, that have been variously described as short versus long, lax versus tense, simplex versus complex, monomoraic versus bimoraic, ATR versus RTR, or light versus heavy to select a few terms from the literature. The issue is complex and not all modern varieties of English should arguably receive the same type of analysis. The vowel system of Scottish English, for instance, has often been argued to be based on qualitative rather than quantitative oppositions (see Carr and Durand 2004 or Brulard and Durand 2015 for syntheses and further references).

In this chapter, we take the view that quantity, or weight as we shall call it, is paramount for NZE and that its vowels fall into two sets: light versus heavy in our terminology. First of all, there are a number of distributional arguments typical of non-rhotic varieties of English allowing us to separate the light vowels from the heavy ones. The crucial generalisation which is standardly mentioned is that only heavy vowels and diphthongs are allowed under stress in open final position: 'bee' [biː], 'car' [kɑː], 'fur' [fɜː], 'boy' [bɔɪ]. Note the absence of possible monomorphemes of the form *[lɪ], *[pʊ], *[tɛ], *[sæ] and so on (but 'lip' [lɪp], 'put' [pʊt], 'tell' [tɛl], 'sad' [sæd]). As there is no argument for postulating 'light' or monomoraic diphthongs in this variety, we conclude that the parallelism between a subset of vowels and diphthongs favours an analysis of the former as complex, long or heavy.

What is more, as we have seen, there are great movements occurring within the vocalic system of NZE, which reminds us of the Great Vowel Shift (GVS) (Jones 1989). That is why we, along with other researchers, have chosen to talk of a Modern GVS in this variety. It also reminds us of the Diphthong Shift which, according to Wells (1982), is characteristic of the Southern Hemisphere varieties of English, which include NZE. In order to illustrate these similar dynamics, we have selected the schematic representations of the GVS (Jones 1989: 222; see Figure 8.7), as well as the Diphthong Shift (Wells 1982: 256; see Figure 8.8) and the SFVS (Trudgill et al. 1998: 37; see Figure 8.9). The SFVS consequently appears as a phenomenon which makes NZE fit in the history of the evolution of English. However, the path that some of the vowels of NZE have chosen also definitely sets it apart from other varieties of English.

What we claim is that, if we have a chain-shift on the one hand (essentially affecting the KIT, DRESS and TRAP vowels) and mergers and near-mergers on the other (affecting the NEAR/SQUARE, DRESS/FLEECE and STRUT/START pairs), it is because KIT, DRESS and TRAP belong to the same subsystem, that is the light vowels, whereas DRESS and FLEECE, and STRUT and START, belong to two different subsystems (the first vowel

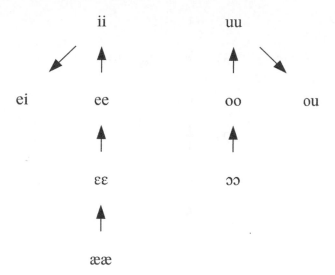

Figure 8.7 The Great Vowel Shift
*Source:* Jones (1989: 222).

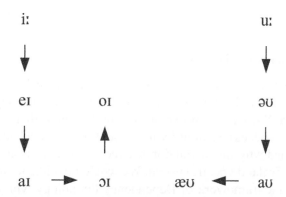

Figure 8.8 The Diphthong Shift
*Source:* Wells (1982: 256).

in each pair being a light vowel and the second one a heavy vowel). The loss of opposition between two or more vowels belonging to the same subsystem, and with high functional load (Wedel et al. 2013), which is not the case of the NEAR/SQUARE pair, would gravely endanger the intelligibility of the vocalic system as a whole.

We therefore speak in favour of the relevance of the notion of vocalic weight as far as the New Zealand vowels are concerned. Let us not forget that the New Zealand case forced Labov to reconsider his elementary principles of change, which initially posited that in chain shifts, long vowels rise whereas short vowels fall (1994: 116), and which he reformulated (1994: 176) in terms of lax versus tense nuclei of the vowels, and in terms of peripheral versus non-peripheral track in the vocalic space. We take it that his principles were an attempt to put at the centre of the model the

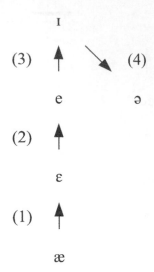

Figure 8.9 The Short Front Vowel Shift
*Source:* Trudgill et al. (1998: 37).

distinction between two subsets of vowels, which is crucial in the economy of the vocalic system of NZE.

**A Dependency Phonology Interpretation**

So far, we have put forward an equidistance scenario of push-chain shift affecting the short front vowels on the basis of the observation of a fairly recent New Zealand corpus of oral data. We have also explained why we think that a degree of phonological abstraction is necessary in order to account for the mechanisms that underlie this phenomenon and why the distinction between light vowels and heavy vowels is central to the New Zealand vocalic system. We would now like to offer a model of the SFVS inspired by the framework of Dependency Phonology which roughly follows the three stages postulated by Trudgill (2004) in his new-dialect formation theory.

*How does Dependency Phonology Deal with Vocalic Systems?*

Dependency Phonology (DP) is a phonological model which was initiated by Anderson and Jones's seminal work (1974) and was developed thereafter by various researchers (Anderson and Ewen 1987; Ewen and van der Hulst 2001; Anderson 2011, 2013 inter alia). DP assumes that phonological features are unary, and therefore always present the positive pole of a property. In particular, it is claimed that the vowel system is structured around three basic elements, labelled |A| (low/compact), |I| (palatal/acute) and |U| (grave). The |I|, |A|, |U| primitives are arguably not sufficient to handle all the phonological systems of the languages of the world, which is why an element of centrality (or energy reduction), symbolised by |@|, is also required (Anderson and Ewen 1987; Harris 1994; Harris and Lindsay 1995; Backley 2011). Therefore, if a language has only three vowels (/i/, /a/, /u/), this system can be represented on the basis of the |I|, |A|, |U| primitives alone as follows: the internal structure of /i/ can be represented as {I}, that of /a/ as {A} and that of /u/ as {U}.

One further crucial assumption made by DP is that the relation of government/ dependency is available within phonological systems and is, indeed, necessary as soon as phonological systems reach a certain degree of complexity. This relation can be expressed in three different ways: dependency/government of an element on/over another (symbolised as a semi-colon < ; >), co-presence of elements (symbolised as a comma < , >) and mutual government between elements (symbolised as a colon < : >).

Mutual government is rarely required for the characterisation of vowels at the contrastive level and will not be used here for lexical representations in NZE, but we invoke its use derivatively. On the other hand, government is central to our approach and, for example, many languages have oppositions with mid-vowels that require the use of the dependency operator < ; > (for example systems such as /i/, /e/, /ɛ/, /a/, /ɔ/, /o/, /u/ which will be typically represented as follows: /i/ = {I}, /e/ = {I ; A}, /ɛ/ = {A ; I}, /a/ = {A}, /ɔ/ = {A ; U}, /o/ = {U ; A}, /u/ = {U}). The use of dependency allows us to model the notion of a scale: as we go from {I} to {A}, we follow steps which decrease the presence of {I} and increase that of {A}. One basic consequence of this approach is that the structure of vowel systems is triangular, not quadrangular, as in the IPA tradition.

The other assumption that we make, following classical DP accounts, is that the phonological characterisation of segments involves two categorial elements (labelled C and V). This assumption is by no means universal within unary approaches and some specialists have argued for reducing all elements to a same type. For instance, within Government Phonology and its extensions (Kaye et al. 1985, 1990; Backley 2011), all primitives are of the I, U, A type, whereas in Radical CV Phonology, as developed by van der Hulst, all primitives are of the V, C type (see van der Hulst 2015 for discussion and further references).

Like all theoretical decisions, the reduction to only one set of primitives has associated costs. For instance, in current versions of Government Phonology, CV positions are postulated with conventions of lateral government whereas in DP, labellings with the C and V elements allow the projection of a metrical structure extending to the utterance as a whole.[3] As the core of our argumentation does not offer enough evidence for adopting one position rather than another, we will stick to a traditional account. Within DP, it has the advantage of illustrating the analogy with syntax which is based on categorial primary features (N and P) which are further specified by secondary features (animate, human, male, female and so on) analogous to elements such as I, A, U.

In our account, short monophthongs (light vowels) are associated with a simple categorial representation, that is {V}, whereas long monophthongs and diphthongs (our heavy vowels) are associated with a complex representation, that is {VV}. Note, however, that we treat schwa as part of the phonological system of English and treat it, lexically, as an unspecified vowel {V} that has no articulatory content. This is

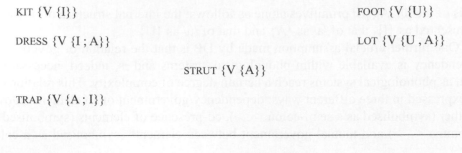

KIT {V {I}}                                      FOOT {V {U}}

DRESS {V {I ; A}}                               LOT {V {U , A}}

STRUT {V {A}}

TRAP {V {A ; I}}

LETTER / COMMA {V { }}

Figure 8.10 Redundancy-free representation of the conservative system of the light vowels of NZE

important as there is a long generative tradition stemming from Chomsky and Halle (1968) of treating schwas in varieties of English as always derived from full forms often attested in alternation (for example 'phot[ə]graph', 'ph[ə]tography', 'phot[ə] graphic'). But in many words, schwas do not alternate with anything (for example 'reck<u>o</u>n' or 'comm<u>a</u>') and in any case, in our view, most alternations central to SPE belong more to morphology or morphophonology (as argued in pre-generative accounts) than to phonology properly speaking. Derivatively, schwas are specified by the element |@|.

We start by positing a redundancy-free representation at the contrastive level of the 'conservative' system (see Figure 8.10) and of the 'advanced' system (see Figure 8.11) of the light vowels of NZE. Within the conservative system, we posit that the KIT, DRESS and TRAP vowels all have the {I} element. We consider that the STRUT vowel and the START vowel have merged qualitatively, but not quantitatively, and assign to both of them the primitive |A|. At a narrow phonetic level, they can both be represented as [ɐ], which we can specify as {A ; @}. The back vowels, on the other hand, do not require the use of dependency/government since there is only one mid-vowel, which we represent simply as {A , U}. Such a system, with more front vowels than back vowels, is by no means unusual but unbalanced. And, if we compare it with our characterisation of the advanced system in Figure 8.11, we can see that the system has 'mutated' into a more balanced system as far as front and back vowels are concerned, but differently organised in that KIT now occupies a place of its own in a 'marked' position at the centre of the phonological system. It no longer possesses the {I} element but has acquired the {@} element of centrality/reduction of energy.

Even though we have established this representation of the light vowels of NZE in DP, we are left to wonder how to account for the conservative system mutating into the advanced system. We are actually back to one of our initial interrogations, which was originally formulated on the basis of phonetic-acoustic data, and which is now formulated on the basis of the representation of the internal structure of part of the vocalic system of NZE. So, do we stop at this by perhaps assuming that one system transformed into another in one fell swoop? Or do we need more allophonic-

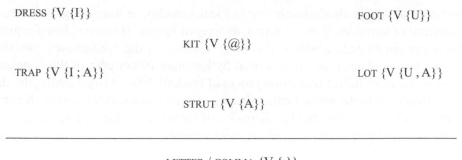

DRESS {V {I}}　　　　　　　　　　　　　　　FOOT {V {U}}

KIT {V {@}}

TRAP {V {I ; A}}　　　　　　　　　　　　　　LOT {V {U , A}}

STRUT {V {A}}

LETTER / COMMA {V { }}

Figure 8.11 Redundancy-free representation of the advanced system of the light vowels of NZE

like representations, more complex combinations of elements in order to account for the progressive mutations in these vowels? And how filled-in can these surface representations be?

We would like to assume here that phonology has to account for a substantial portion of the allophonic forms of underlying elements. The reason is not simply a desire to account for phonological change but also the observation that many so-called surface properties of phonological sequences (for example velarisation of /l/ in many varieties of English) interact in fundamental ways with morphosyntactic structure and cannot simply be assigned to an unspecified component (labelled 'phonetic') of linguistic representations. But, even if it is accepted that surface properties of phonological sequences somehow have to be integrated to phonology, what steps can be assumed to account for the transformation of the NZE conservative system into the advanced system? This is where Trudgill's new-dialect formation model proves useful.

*Trudgill's New-dialect Formation Model*

From a sociolinguistic perspective, New Zealand has been used as a laboratory for the study of the emergence and evolution of a variety of English in a colonial context and has led to a major publication, that is Trudgill's new-dialect formation model (2004), which retraces the emergence of NZE, on the basis of the observation of the ONZE data, in three successive stages. These stages correspond to three generations of speakers, according to a neutral model of evolution that does not involve any other extra-linguistic factor, apart from the natural accommodation of speakers and demographic determinism, which is why Trudgill speaks, in the subtitle to his work, of the 'inevitability' of colonial Englishes.

The first stage corresponds to the first immigrants who settle in the new colony. At that stage, there is rudimentary levelling and accommodation as the first immigrants essentially use the same dialect as in their region of origin. Only the very low-frequency and geographically restricted variants are eliminated. The second stage, which corresponds to the first native-born generation of speakers, is characterised by extreme variability as children learning to speak can choose from a highly inconsistent mixture of variables from different regions of origin. However, low-frequency variants are eliminated, which at that stage constitutes the well-known 'threshold rider' which postulates that variants used by less than 10 per cent of the population are lost in the new-dialect formation process (Trudgill 2004: 110). Finally, the third stage corresponds to the second native-born generation of speakers, and is characterised by levelling, focusing and the diffusion of the levelled, focused variants. There is wide and rapid propagation of the majority variants, which leads to the emergence of a new focused variety.

Trudgill's model has been criticised, notably for modelling an idealised 'tabula rasa' colonial context (Kerswill 2007: 657–659) in which the three stages are more likely to have coexisted rather than have neatly followed each other. It has also been criticised for being too socially neutral, so to speak, as studies have shown that some social factors, such as privileged interactions between speakers (Baxter et al. 2009) and community norms, have played a part in the focusing of the new dialect. We claim nonetheless that it offers a plausible interpretation of the likely stages in the formation of NZE and a solid basis for representing subsequent stages of the contemporary evolution of this variety.

*A Dependency Phonology Interpretation*

In DP, we can account for the competition between different systems that is characteristic of colonial contexts, and for the mechanisms that produce change as different lexical forms can be associated with distinct phonetic reflexes, which can be reanalysed at the contrastive level by the next generation of speakers. We look at the NZE vocalic system from two different perspectives: redundancy-free contrastive representations (see Figures 8.10 and 8.11) and more specified representations derived by redundancy statements. We stress that the relationship between the underspecified contrastive representations and the fuller representations is not derivational but the result of filling-in (non-destructive) mechanisms which are structure-building and not structure-changing (Kiparsky 1982).

Let's have a look at TRAP which, according to our data and data from other major works, is the trigger for the chain shift. We postulate that when New Zealand was colonised, what we call an 'Anglo-English' system, brought from the south of England by approximately half (51 per cent) of the settlers (McKinnon 1997, in Gordon et al. 2004: 444–445), started competing for prevalence with a more 'northern' or Scottish system, brought by 27.3 per cent of the settlers, especially in the southernmost part of the South Island. In the former system, we assume that the TRAP and START vowels had already started breaking with each other whereas, in the latter, both vowels were still partners within the system, namely they both had similar internal representations and similar phonetic expressions. We hypothesise that it is because the 'Anglo-English' system prevailed, as it was the system of a majority of the settlers, that it allowed for further changes in the internal structure of the TRAP vowel, and, in turn, to alterations in the internal structure of other vowels within the system.

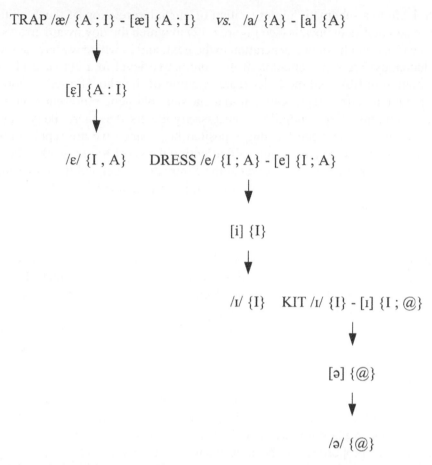

Figure 8.12 Schematic representation of the Dependency Phonology interpretation of the evolution of the KIT, DRESS and TRAP vowels in NZE

If we model this scenario in DP, we postulate that in the early days of the colony, the 'Anglo-English' TRAP vowel, whose internal structure can be symbolised as {A ; I} which is associated to an identical phonetic reflex {A ; I}, has won over the 'northern' TRAP vowel, whose internal structure can be symbolised as {A} which is associated to a phonetic reflex {A}. We postulate that, over time, closer realisations of TRAP, that is phonetic reflexes in which {I} has increased and {A} diminished, have led to a reanalysis at the contrastive level by the third generation of speakers. Therefore, the representations for the TRAP and DRESS vowels have become too similar, ambiguous: TRAP has started threatening DRESS, in which {I} has consequently also increased over time, which has also led to a reanalysis at the contrastive level. Here we have the domino effect that is typical of chain shifting. Therefore, DRESS has started threatening KIT, which from an initial representation {I ; @} progressively lost the {I} element in favour of the {@} element and ended up being reanalysed at the contrastive level as a central vowel.

We include a schematic representation of our interpretation of the evolution of the KIT, DRESS and TRAP vowels (see Figure 8.12) in which the downward arrows symbolise the transition from one generation to the next, and in which we have associated the redundancy-free representation at the contrastive level to a classical phonemic representation in IPA, and the fuller representation of the phonetic reflex associated to this redundancy-free representation to a classical phonetic representation in IPA. This representation, like Trudgill's, is necessarily idealised as there likely may have been some overlap between the stages posited here, since we are representing the equidistance scenario of push-chain shift affecting the short front vowels. The representation of the 'northern' TRAP vowel at the contrastive level and the representation of its phonetic reflex appear in light grey as this system was lost in the new-dialect formation process.

## Conclusions

To conclude, we turn to the major issues that we have tried to tackle in this chapter. First of all, we have briefly presented and defended an approach, that of the PAC programme. Like the PFC programme (Detey et al. 2016), it attempts to offer a model of corpus phonology which, on the basis of fieldwork, combines the insights of phonology, phonetics, dialectology and sociolinguistics. We have also provided a detailed description of the SFVS within the overall vocalic system of NZE and postulated a possible Dependency Phonology interpretation of the competing systems and the nature of the historical change. We have taken the view that fine-grained phonetic properties which are not explicable in terms of mechanical constraints (roughly, extrinsic versus intrinsic allophones) should ideally be part and parcel of phonological descriptions. A phonological model which allows us to capture both contrastive and fine-grained properties is to be preferred to a model which is too spartan to do so.

We have partly based our reconstruction on Trudgill's new-dialect formation model. Although this model has been legitimately criticised, we argue that it offers a plausible interpretation of likely stages in the formation of NZE and a solid basis for representing subsequent stages of the contemporary evolution of this variety. It seems to us that demographic determinism plays a prevalent part in the emergence of a new focused dialect, but such a process is probably not a fully neutral model as privileged interactions, identity and prestige have proved to be relevant in such situations.

Most importantly, we have demonstrated that NZE, while it inherited deep-sea trends from southern British systems in the nineteenth century, has taken an autonomous route, which is very different from Australian English with which it is often too rapidly grouped as antipodean English. It actually proves quite unique and autonomous in this system dynamics of the varieties of English as it has partly broken away from the motherland inasmuch as we witness reverse trends as far as the short front vowels are concerned. Indeed, in NZE the |I| element is increasing and the |A| element diminishing, whereas in England it is exactly the opposite, and in Australia as well, the initial push-chain shift is reversing in a pull-chain shift which is again reconfiguring a substantial portion of the vocalic system.

## Notes

1. PAC is an acronym for *Phonologie de l'Anglais Contemporain : usages, variétés et structure*. See www.pacprogramme.net
2. We would like to thank Hugo Chatellier for his invaluable help with our statistical calculations and analyses.
3. See the debate between Anderson (2013) and Scheer (2013).

## References

Anderson, J. M. (2011), *The Substance of Language: Volume III Phonology-syntax Analogies*, Oxford: Oxford University Press.

Anderson, J. M. (2013), 'Substance, structural analogy, and universals', *Language Sciences* 39, 15–30.

Anderson, J. M. and C. J. Ewen (1987), *Principles of Dependency Phonology*, Cambridge: Cambridge University Press.

Anderson, J. M. and C. Jones (1974), 'Three theses concerning phonological representations', *Journal of Linguistics* 10, 1–26.

Backley, P. (2011), *An Introduction to Element Theory*, Edinburgh: Edinburgh University Press.

Bauer, L. and P. Warren (2008), 'New Zealand English: phonology', in K. Burridge and B. Kortmann (eds), *Varieties of English: Volume 3 The Pacific and Australasia*, Berlin: Mouton de Gruyter, pp. 39–63.

Baxter, G., R. A. Blythe, W. Croft and A. J. McKane (2009), 'Modeling language change: an evaluation of Trudgill's theory of the emergence of New Zealand English', *Language Variation and Change* 21, 257–296.

Blevins, J. (2004), *Evolutionary Phonology: The Emergence of Sound Patterns*, Cambridge: Cambridge University Press.

Brulard, I. and J. Durand (2015), 'L'anglais écossais standard (SSE)', in I. Brulard, P. Carr and J. Durand (eds), *La prononciation de l'anglais contemporain dans le monde : variation et structure*, Toulouse: Presses Universitaires du Midi, pp. 151–166.

Bybee, J. (2001), *Phonology and Language Use*, Cambridge: Cambridge University Press.

Carr, P. and J. Durand (2004), 'English in early 21st century Scotland: a phonological perspective', *La tribune internationale des langues vivantes* 36, 87–105.

Carr, P., J. Durand and M. Pukli (2004), 'The PAC project: principles and methods', *La Tribune Internationale des Langues Vivantes* 36, 24–35.

Chomsky, N. and M. Halle (1968), *The Sound Pattern of English*, New York: Harper and Row.

Clark, L., J. Hay, T. Rathcke, J. Stuart-Smith and K. Watson (2015), 'How Scottish ancestry influenced early New Zealanders' vowel lengths', 2015 Conference of the Linguistic Society of New Zealand, University of Otago, Dunedin, New Zealand.

Cox, F. (2012), 'Variation and change in Australian English phonology', 8th Annual PAC Conference, 29 February–2 March 2012, Université Toulouse Jean Jaurès, Toulouse, France.

Cox, F. and S. Palethorpe (2001), 'The changing face of Australian English vowels', in D. Blair and P. Collins (eds), *English in Australia*, Amsterdam: John Benjamins, pp. 17–44.

De Boer, B. (2000), 'Self-organization in vowel systems', *Journal of Phonetics* 28, 441–465.

De Boer, B. (2001), *The Origins of Vowel Systems*, Oxford: Oxford University Press.

Detey, S., J. Durand, B. Laks and C. Lyche (2016), *Varieties of Spoken French*, Oxford: Oxford University Press.

Durand, J. and A. Przewozny (2012), 'La Phonologie de l'Anglais Contemporain : usages, variétés, structure', *Revue Française de Linguistique Appliquée* 17(1), 25–37.

Ewen, C. J. and H. van der Hulst (2001), *The Phonological Structure of Words: An Introduction* (Cambridge Textbooks in Linguistics), Cambridge: Cambridge University Press.

Gordon, E., L. Campbell, J. Hay, M. Maclagan, A. Sudbury and P. Trudgill (2004), *New Zealand English: Its Origins and Evolution*, Cambridge: Cambridge University Press.

Gordon, M. (2016), *Phonological Typology*, Oxford: Oxford University Press.

Harris, J. (1994), *English Sound Structure*, Oxford: Blackwell.

Harris, J. and G. Lindsey (1995), 'The elements of phonological representation', in J. Durand and F. Katamba (eds), *Frontiers of Phonology: Atoms, Structures, Derivations*, London: Longman, pp. 34–79.

Hay, J., M. Maclagan and E. Gordon (2008), *New Zealand English*, Edinburgh: Edinburgh University Press.

Hay, J., J. Pierrehumbert, A. Walker and P. LaShell (2015), 'Tracking word frequency effects through 130 years of sound change', *Cognition* 139, 83–91.

van der Hulst, H. (2015), 'The Opponent Principle in RcvP: binarity in a unary system', in E. Raimy and C. Cairns (eds), *The Segment in Phonetics and Phonology*, Chichester: Wiley-Blackwell, pp. 147–179.

Jones, C. (1989), *A History of English Phonology*, London: Longman.

Kaye, J., J. Lowenstamm and J.-R. Vergnaud (1985), 'The internal structure of phonological segments: a theory of charm and government', *Phonology Yearbook* 2, 305–328.

Kaye, J., J. Lowenstamm and J.-R. Vergnaud (1990), 'Constituent structure and government in phonology', *Phonology Yearbook* 7, 193–231.

Kendall, T. and E. R. Thomas (2010), 'Vowels: vowel manipulation, normalization, and plotting in R', *R package*, Version 1.1. [software resource: http://ncslaap.lib.ncsu.edu/tools/norm/].

Kerswill, P. (2007), 'Review of Trudgill, P. (2004), *Dialect contact and new-dialect formation: the inevitability of colonial Englishes*, Edinburgh: Edinburgh University Press', *Language* 83, 657–661.

Kiparsky, P. (1982), 'From cyclic phonology to lexical phonology', in H. van der Hulst and N. Smith (eds), *The Structure of Phonological Representations (I)*, Dordrecht: Foris, pp. 131–175.

Labov, W. (1966), *The Social Stratification of English in New York*, Washington, DC: Center for Applied Linguistics.

Labov, W. (1972), *Sociolinguistic Patterns*, Philadelphia: University of Pennsylvania Press.

Labov, W. (1994), *Principles of Linguistic Change: Vol. 1 Internal Factors*, Oxford: Blackwell.

Labov, W. (2001), *Principles of Linguistic Change: Vol. 2 Social Factors*, Oxford: Blackwell.

Langstrof, C. (2006), Vowel change in New Zealand English: patterns and implications, PhD dissertation, Christchurch, University of Canterbury, New Zealand.

Langstrof, C. (2009), 'On the role of vowel duration in the New Zealand English front vowel shift', *Language Variation and Change* 21, 437–453.

McKinnon, M. (1997), *New Zealand Historical Atlas*, Auckland: Bateman.

Maclagan, M. and E. Gordon (2004), 'The story of New Zealand English: what the ONZE project tells us', *Australian Journal of Linguistics* 24(1), 41–55.

Maddieson, I. (1984), *Patterns of Sounds*, Cambridge: Cambridge University Press.

Martinet, A. (1955), *Économie des changements phonétiques. Traité de phonologie diachronique*, Paris: Maisonneuve & Larose.

Pierrehumbert, J. (2001), 'Stochastic phonology', *GLOT* 5(6), 1–13.

Pierrehumbert, J. (2006), 'The statistical basis of an unnatural alternation', in L. Goldstein, D. H. Whalen and C. Best (eds), *Laboratory Phonology VIII Varieties of Phonological Competence*, Berlin: Mouton de Gruyter, pp. 81–107.

Przewozny, A. (2016), *La Langue des Australiens : Genèse et description de l'anglais australien contemporain*, Limoges: Lambert-Lucas.

Przewozny, A. and C. Viollain (2016), 'On the representation and evolution of Australian English and New Zealand English', in P. Fournier and H. Le Prieult (eds), *Approches pluridisciplinaires en phonologie anglaise, Anglophonia: French Journal of English Linguistics 21*, http://anglophonia.revues.org/727

R Core Team (2017), *R: A Language and Environment for Statistical Computing*, Vienna, Austria: R Foundation for Statistical Computing, http://www.Rproject.org/

Scharinger, M and W. J. Idsardi (2014), 'Sparseness of vowel category structure: evidence from English dialect comparison', *Lingua* 140, 35–51.

Scheer, T. (2013), 'Why phonology is flat: the role of concatenation and linearity', *Language Sciences* 39, 54–74.

Sinclair, K. (1991), *A History of New Zealand*, Auckland: Penguin.

Sóskuthy, M, J. Hay, M. Maclagan, K. Drager and P. Foulkes (2017), 'The closing diphthongs in early New Zealand English', in R. Hickey (ed.), *Listening to the Past: Audio Records of Accents of English*, Cambridge: Cambridge University Press, pp. 529–561.

Trudgill, P. (2004), *New-dialect Formation: The Inevitability of Colonial Englishes*, Edinburgh: Edinburgh University Press.

Trudgill, P., E. Gordon and G. Lewis (1998), 'New-dialect formation and southern hemisphere English: the New Zealand short front vowels', *Journal of Sociolinguistics* 2, 35–51.

Viollain, C. (2014), Sociophonologie de l'anglais contemporain en Nouvelle-Zélande : corpus et dynamique des systèmes, PhD dissertation, Toulouse, Université Toulouse Jean Jaurès, France.

Watson, C., S. Palethorpe and J. Harrington (2004), 'Capturing the vowel change in New Zealand English over a thirty-year period via a diachronic study', *Proceedings of the Tenth Australian International Conference on Speech Science & Technology*, pp. 201–206.

Wedel, A., S. Jackson and A. Kaplan (2013), 'Functional load and the lexicon: evidence that syntactic category and frequency relationships in minimal lemma pairs predict the loss of phoneme contrasts in language change', *Language and Speech* 56, 395–417.

Wells, J. C. (1982), *Accents of English*, Cambridge: Cambridge University Press.

any chance of spreading in a culture with an identity closer to another population which also has different linguistic features.

This chapter presents both studies, the methodology and the results they yielded. Although our second study is not completed yet, we present our preliminary results. The chapter is divided into several parts. The first part is an overview of previous research and it details the NCVS, its geography, its relation to other phenomena and a short sociolinguistic background. The second part focuses on the corpora and the methodology used in our first study, followed by our results and discussion. Then, the corpus and the methodology of our second study will be presented with the preliminary results and finally some general conclusions.

## The Northern Cities Vowel Shift

The Northern Cities Vowel shift is a change in the pronunciation of the lax vowels /ɪ/ (KIT), /ɛ/ (DRESS), /ʌ/ (STRUT), /ɔ/ (THOUGHT), /ɑ/ (LOT) and /æ/ (TRAP). These vowels are undergoing a chain shift within which the movement of one vowel in the phonetic scale sparks the movement of a neighboring one and so on (Gordon 2001: 7).

In Figure 9.1 the shades used for the different keywords correspond to the type of movement the vowels are subject to: /ɪ/, /ɛ/, /ʌ/ essentially move backwards; /ɔ/ and /ɑ/ move to the front, as well as the vowel /æ/ which also rises. The arrows correspond to the successive stages of the process. This indicates which phoneme was the first to trigger the chain shift (general raising of /æ/, all the way up to the front /ɪ/) and the subsequent movement of the others. Nevertheless, Labov excluded the raising of /æ/ in a pre-nasal environment because it is a phenomenon that occurs in every dialect of American English (Labov 1994: 197). What is important to mention is that the major raising of /æ/ is the starting point of the NCVS so that it helps to easily detect the first stage of the NCVS (Evans et al. 2000) even though there is no sign of the other stages.

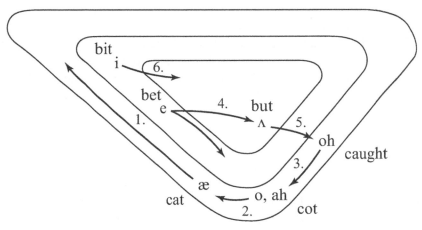

Figure 9.1 NCVS vowels
*Source*: Labov et al. (2006: 190).

Figure 9.2  The NCVS limits according to the ANAE
*Source:* Labov et al. (2006).

The NCVS was first noted and recorded in the major cities of Detroit, Chicago, Syracuse, Rochester and Buffalo. In these cities, five out of the six stages were ascertained in the speech of the population. These big cities are located in an area called the Inland North. In Figure 9.2, the Inland North and the limits of the NCVS are shown in a darker shade.

The Inland North is roughly an 88,000-square-mile area with a population of over 34 million people. Labov (2002: 15) defines it as the 'region of large cities bordering the Great Lakes'. As shown in Figure 9.2, it is indeed composed of Southern Michigan, Northern Ohio and Illinois. It extends to New York state and the cities of Rochester, Syracuse and Buffalo. The western limits are parts of Wisconsin with the city of Milwaukee, and eastern Iowa. The NCVS has also spread southwards with the emergence of shifted vowels found in a strip that extends from southern Illinois to St Louis through Springfield. This path follows the Interstate 55, which connects Chicago to St Louis (Labov et al. 2006: 122). Gordon (2001) confirms that some elements of the NCVS have spread southward to small towns along the way to St Louis. The NCVS is linked to big cities and the limits of the Inland North stop wherever there are much smaller towns. As Koffi (2014) explains, the ANAE (Labov et al. 2006) limited the study of the NCVS vowels to what he calls 'zones of influence' that refer to areas exerting some influence – e.g. economic, demographic and cultural – over other areas. For example, the NCVS is widespread in cities located in the state of Michigan such as Detroit, Flint, Grand Rapids; that is to say, cities that had a population of at least 100,000 in 2017 according to the

US Census Bureau. But the extreme north of Michigan and its Upper Peninsula are not areas where the shift is in place in the ANAE because there are no cities as big as those first associated with the NCVS (such as Chicago and Detroit) and no main highways either. These northern locations are therefore not considered as zones of influence.

The NCVS in the Inland North is also related to some other phonological processes. Had the COT (/ɑ/)–CAUGHT (/ɔ/) (or LOT–THOUGHT) merger been completed, the NCVS would never have been an option in this area. This merger is a process whereby the vowel /ɔ/ merges with the vowel /ɑ/ so that *cot* and *caught* are both pronounced /kɑt/. If these two phonemes merge, the NCVS is no longer a possibility. It was found that speakers whose pronunciation includes the COT–CAUGHT merger had no sign of shifted vowels because the fronting of /ɑ/ via the NCVS is an 'effective mechanism in relieving pressure towards the merger of /ɔ/ – /ɑ/'. In short, it means that if /ɑ/ is fronted then /ɔ/ cannot be merged with it. According to the pull-chain principle, /ɔ/ has to fill in the gap left by /ɑ/ as it does in the NCVS (Labov 2012: 31). According to the ANAE (Labov et al. 2006: 61), the Inland North vowels /ɔ/–/ɑ/ are mostly distinct from each other in perception and production. Nevertheless, the Upper Peninsula seems to be affected by the phenomenon, at least in the cities of Marquette and Sault Saint Marie, which are the biggest cities in the entire peninsula.

*The NCVS in the Upper Peninsula*

According to Thomas (2011: 274), 'linguistic factors are responsible for the origin of changes and social factors are responsible for their spread'. He also mentions how linguistic changes can be internally or externally motivated. On the one hand, internally motivated changes involve phonetic factors such as coarticulation, or a need for a new item or term in a language or dialect. On the other hand, externally motivated changes refer to language contact, that is to say that a specific innovation spreads to another language or dialect, or prestige-related changes, when a change occurs in a privileged group and spreads to groups with less power in society. It is believed that the NCVS has spread through language contact and mainly diffusion (Labov 2007: 26). When a linguistic variable is undergoing a certain change, it is not obviously present in every social class. The lower- middle class seems to be more affected than any other class. Usually, the new form has been used and implemented in a higher class of the society and is thus seen as a prestige variant that lower classes want to adhere to as 'the correct manner' of speaking. (Labov et al. 1972: 114).

However, each social group produces more prestige forms in formal speech and a lower proportion of prestige forms in informal speech. This prestige form is used consistently in the speech of the upper classes but is not used at all in the lower working class (Coates 1993: 2). The different types of speech style have an important impact on any spoken production; therefore it should not be neglected and taken into account in this study, which was not the case in our first study.

The sociolinguistic aspect of the NCVS is also important to take into account.

Language changes can be led by women, as they were found to use more innovative forms than men (Labov 1990), but also by young people as it can take up to three generations to use new forms (Herndobler 1977: 146), or even by ethnicity or a strong identity. Indeed, there is a certain relationship between a speaker's ethnic group and their use of language: ethnic groups can emerge using language. One of the most popular examples is the presence of African American Vernacular English (AAVE) (Labov 2012). Black communities living in Detroit are using their own dialect rather than following the NCVS, in which the city of Detroit is fully engaged. This resistance movement can be explained by their wish to preserve their own identity and to differentiate themselves from white communities. The Upper Peninsula is also caught up between two different identities: the Yoopers (inhabitants of the peninsula) and Canadians, due to the proximity of the border. When Rakerd and Plichta (2010) compared the vowel space of one speaker of lower Michigan and one speaker from the Upper Peninsula, they concluded that both informants had different phonological systems. Such a conclusion converges with Rankinen's (2014) hypothesis according to which there might be an influence of the Canadian Shift in the UP inhabitants' speech.

The Canadian Shift is a movement of the vowels DRESS and TRAP, triggered by the merger of CAUGHT and COT. This shift implies a backward shift of /æ/ followed by a downward and backward movement of /ɛ/ (see Figure 9.3). The movement of /æ/ was first discovered in Vancouver by Esling and Warkentyne (1993) and was named the Canadian Shift in 1995 after the research work of Clarke, Elms and Youssef (Clarke et al. 1995) who found the larger context of this development and also included the lowering of /ɛ/.

Boberg (2005) has observed the progress of the Canadian Shift in Montreal, though with a more retracted than lowered /e/. Older research included a shifted /ɪ/, but Labov et al. (2006) did not find any evidence of a shifted /ɪ/ in their data.

What is at stake here is the presence of two vowel shifts moving in opposite directions. The NCVS has a raising /æ/ which triggers the fronting of back vowels (i.e. Figure 9.1) when the Canadian Shift is completed with an opposite movement, the backing of /e/ triggers the backing of /æ/. The Upper Peninsula of Michigan has a common border with Canada and is thus caught up between two major vowel shifts, and the vowels involved in the movements are the same. With the Yoopers' identity being closer to the Canadians', we can thus wonder if the Yoopers would be more willing to follow the Canadian Shift instead of the NCVS.

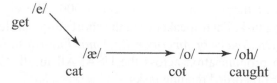

Figure 9.3 The Canadian Shift
*Source:* Labov et al. (2006: 220).

## First Study

*Corpora Used in the First Study*

Corpus 1: 1966–1970

The first set of speech data includes eight recordings from north Michigan that date back to 1966, 1967 and 1970 and whose vowel analyses should confirm previous results and conclusions regarding the absence of any shifted vowels in this area. Since our study aims at discovering any possible spread of the shift, it is necessary to compare the aforementioned recordings with more recent recordings that are included in Corpus 2 (see below). This first corpus and our results are used as a point of reference for any movement of the vowels affected by the NCVS.

The recordings selected in the first corpus were extracted from the University of Wisconsin–Madison Libraries Digital Collections,[1] which are free and available online. This collection includes millions of images, recordings and texts from the entire world. The collection has a total of ninety recordings carried out in Michigan. Out of these ninety recordings, twelve were initially selected from the collection since they were recorded in cities of Northern Michigan and its Upper Peninsula in the 1960s. The recordings were also chosen according to the informants' ages and genders so as to equally represent the population.

However, after starting to study these recordings, five of them had to be discarded because of their poor quality. The background noises made it impossible to closely study the vowels, or the speakers did not articulate enough when speaking, which made the spectrogram analyses difficult. Unfortunately, the five recordings that were discarded were all male voices, so we ended up with an unbalanced corpus composed of more female than male speech data. Yet, women are known to be those leading the use of innovative forms in a language (Callary 1975: 158), so there are slightly more chances to find evidence of shifted vowels in this corpus than in a corpus that predominantly includes male voices.

The seven recordings under study were recorded between 1966 and 1970. This first corpus is composed of two male speakers, aged 59 and 82, and five women aged between 19 and 64. Table 9.1 gathers information about the content of Corpus 1, especially data about locations (UP for Upper Peninsula and NM for Northern Michigan) and the speakers interviewed between 1966 and 1970.

In this corpus, only one of the speakers is not from the Upper Peninsula, and all of them are from rural areas. Indeed, none of the cities has a population of over 9,000 inhabitants, and two of them do not even exceed 2,000. The eight recordings are composed of a reading task. Each speaker read the short story entitled *Arthur the Rat*, a story used by *The Dictionary of American Regional English* in order to reference variations in English pronunciation across the USA. All in all, Corpus 1 contains twenty-five minutes of recorded reading tasks.

Table 9.1 Detailed information concerning Corpus 1

| Town/city of the recording | Upper Peninsula (UP)/ Northern Michigan (NM) | Population in 1960 | Gender | Age |
|---|---|---|---|---|
| Chassel | UP | 1,423 | Male | 59 |
| Gaylord | NM | 2,368 | Male | 82 |
| Gladstone | UP | 5,267 | Female | 64 |
| Ishpeming | UP | 8,857 | Female | 43 |
| Mohawk | UP | 1,918 | Female | 19 |
| Munising | UP | 4,228 | Female | 35 |
| Munising | UP | 4,228 | Female | 60 |

Corpus 2: 2005–2016

The first corpus is an interesting benchmark for our first study, but the aim of this study is to assess the extent of the spread of the NCVS in these rural areas today. Corpus 2 is the result of an extraction from the IDEA corpus (International Dialects of English Archive). IDEA was created in 1997 as the first 'online archive of primary-source recordings of English-language dialects and accents as heard around the world'.[2] It is a free online collection of recordings from all over the world which are more or less recent but are not older than 2000. The Michigan collection was not very large and contained only fifteen recordings in total. Out of the fifteen audio files, only three recordings matched the criteria for our research; that is to say that only three speakers were from the region under study. The others were from Southern Michigan where the shift has already been established by the ANAE (Labov et al. 2006). The three recordings date back to 2005–2008, which is a fairly recent period and thus useful for this research work. Table 9.2 gives details about the three speakers in this second corpus.

In this second corpus only male voices are recorded, and two of them are from the Upper Peninsula. Corpus 2 is also composed of recordings from towns whose populations do not exceed 10,000 inhabitants. The recording from Ishpeming is interesting because we also have a recording from this town in Corpus 1. A comparison will then be possible between the places of articulation of vowels pronounced fifty years ago and those pronounced today in the exact same town. In this corpus, the interviews are divided into two parts. The first part is a reading task in which the interviewee is asked to read a given text entitled *Comma Gets a Cure*, written by Jill McCullough and Barbara Somerville and edited by IDEA's Associate Editor

Table 9.2 Detailed information concerning Corpus 2

| Town/city | UP/NM | Population in 2010 | Gender | Age |
|---|---|---|---|---|
| Cheboygan | NM | 4,854 | Male | 40 |
| Ishpeming | UP | 6,472 | Male | 27 |
| L'Anse | UP | 2,004 | Male | 36 |

Table 9.3 Details concerning the last two recordings included in Corpus 2

| Town/city | UP/NM | Population in 2013 | Gender | Age |
|-----------|-------|--------------------|--------|-----|
| Alpena | NM | 10,295 | Male | 35 |
| Alpena | NM | 10,295 | Female | 23 |

Douglas N. Honorof. It has been written in compliance with Wells's lexical sets so that it is interesting when it comes to studying vowels. The second part of the recording is a spontaneous speech section. The speakers were asked to present themselves and to talk about their lives. The latter section is often about one minute long, but rarely more. It offers oral productions in which speakers are not focused on their pronunciations. It is a more natural way of speaking than reading tasks and can sometimes yield different results from reading sections. This spontaneous speech section is also useful because it gives us more information about the speakers, especially about where the interviewee lived during his/her early life so that we can filter out those who had just moved to Michigan, for example. Fortunately, the three selected speakers in this corpus had already been living in Michigan for a considerable amount of time.

These three recordings in the second corpus amount to only sixteen minutes in total, which is too short when considering Corpus 1. Through acquaintances and friends, we managed to add one more recording to Corpus 2. The speaker is a 23-year-old native speaker who has never left the town of Alpena, Michigan. Alpena is one of the biggest cities but is still a rather small community located in the northern part of the Lower Peninsula (i.e. not in the UP). Finally, through social networks, another person agreed to be recorded for the purpose of the study. The last speaker in this second corpus is from Alpena too. He has also been raised there and has lived there his entire life. He is about thirty-five years old and earns money by posting videos on the Internet. Every single video he posts is about events coming up in Alpena. Corpus 2 thus reaches a good twenty-four minutes of recorded voices in total. It is therefore equivalent to the first corpus as far as the amount of speech data is concerned. Table 9.3 presents details about the last two participants and the town of Alpena.

Alpena is the largest city in our second corpus and it is also the last large city before the Upper Peninsula. These two recordings contain two reading tasks. The speakers were asked to read the texts entitled *Arthur the Rat* and *Comma Gets a Cure*, both of which were also used for the recordings in the IDEA corpus. The aim was to make it easier to show a pattern if the same texts were studied. The two participants recorded their readings of the stories and were then asked to talk about themselves for a minute or two, but they refused to do this second task. This was one of the difficulties in compiling the corpus: asking people to record themselves for someone they do not know. Informants were usually glad to help us, read a passage or two and answer a couple of questions about their hometowns, but nothing more.

*Methodology for our First Study*

Praat

The two corpora described above allow us to obtain a set of vowel data to study. Vowels can be defined by their formant frequencies: on a spectrogram, the first two formants (F1 and F2) strongly contribute to the differentiation of vowels from one another. Therefore, we will use these values to study the possible movement of the NCVS vowels by trying to determine which vowel is used as compared to the standard one indicated in the *Longman Pronunciation Dictionary* (Wells 2008). Praat[3] was chosen to analyse the data collected in the two corpora previously described. It can be combined with scripts that allow extractions of different values such as the vowel formant values needed for this study.

SPPAS

The annotations made with Praat allowed us to use SPPAS to divide the words into phonemes, so that we could easily extract the formant values needed. The automatic transcription created by SPPAS inevitably contained errors that had to be corrected manually. Some phonemes were not correctly transcribed and, most of the time, the alignment was not precise enough. For example, phonemes surrounding the vowels were often included in the vowel selection. This problem mainly occurred when a fricative phoneme surrounded the vowel, so that it was a difficult task to clearly define where a phoneme starts and when it ends inside of a word, even when the marking was automatically processed. The new phonetically aligned tiers created by SPPAS, and corrected manually, allow us to run a script[4] with Praat that has been designed to extract the formant values of the vowel needed. The script only extracts the values of a given vowel and not the context in which it occurs: this type of information had to be manually added.

Plotting method

The next step was to create a vowel chart to plot the vowel measurements in order to clearly see where the NCVS vowels stand in terms of their place of articulation. We decided to use NORM,[5] a free web-based interface which is designed to manipulate, normalise and plot vowel formant data. We decided to use the Lobanov normalisation technique, created in 1971. Indeed, several studies such as Adank et al. (2004) compared different normalisation methods and concluded that the Lobanov technique was the most efficient. Once run through the normalisation and plotting suite, the plots show the formant values with F1 on the *x* axis and F2 on the *y* axis. This representation corresponds to the vowel trapezium. Several plots were created with individual vowels to see the precise movement of the vowels for a specific speaker, and several others were created with speaker and group means, mainly for data included in the first corpus, to have a point of reference for the second one.

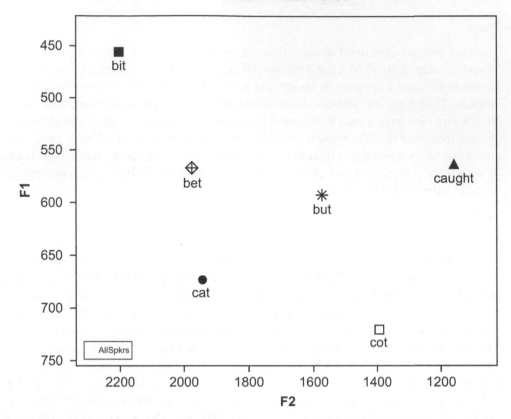

Figure 9.4 Mean values for the NCVS vowels of Corpus 1 from the 1960s

## Results of the First Study

For the sake of this chapter's length, we will only present the prominent and most interesting results. On the one hand, Figure 9.4 plots the mean values of the NCVS vowels extracted from Corpus 1. As expected, every vowel is in a non-shifted position and corresponds to the norms set by Peterson and Barney (Peterson and Barney 1952: 183) for the pronunciation of American vowels in 1960. On the other hand, Figure 9.5 plots the mean values of the NCVS vowels extracted from Corpus 2 and presents different results.

In the recordings made from 2005 to 2016, a clear fronting and raising of the vowel /æ/ means that we are observing what is to be interpreted as a completed first stage of the NCVS in our speakers' speeches. The vowel /æ/ is indeed fronter and higher than it was in the 1960s (see Figures 9.4 and 9.5). The second and third stages of the NCVS also appear clearly in Figure 9.5: /ɑ/ has moved to the front and /ɔ/ is lowered to the level of the vowel /ʌ/. In our second corpus in general, the lower elements are undoubtedly affected by the NCVS, whereas the

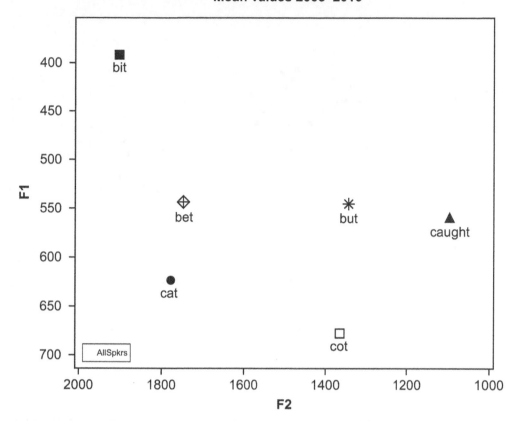

Figure 9.5  Mean values for the NCVS vowels from Corpus 2

upper elements do not show a clear shift. Indeed, the speakers' pronunciations of the vowels have not yet reached the last three stages of the shift, except for two of them, that is to say two inhabitants of the town of Alpena. Figure 9.6 is one example.

Figure 9.6 plots the NCVS tokens for one of the inhabitants of Alpena whose vowels present the most advanced stage of the shift. Besides, Alpena is the most affected town in our corpus. There are clear shifts of the vowels /æ/, /ɑ/, /ɔ/, /ʌ/, /e/ and /ɪ/ in a town where the NCVS has neither been recorded nor been listed yet. Alpena is far above the isogloss drawn by the ANAE (Labov et al. 2006) so that it confirms that the shift has undeniably started to spread up to Northern Michigan. The Upper Peninsula of Michigan has not been as affected as Alpena but shifted pronunciations of the vowels in this area have reached stage three of the NCVS, whereas that was not the case fifty years ago. When comparing vowel plots drawn from data of the 1960s to those of Corpus 2, we see clear movements of the lax vowels. Therefore there is no doubt that there is an evolution towards the NCVS pattern. We also ran into a specific and interesting case during our analyses. Figures 9.7 and 9.8 represent the /æ/, /ɑ/, /ɔ/

**Alpena F, 23**

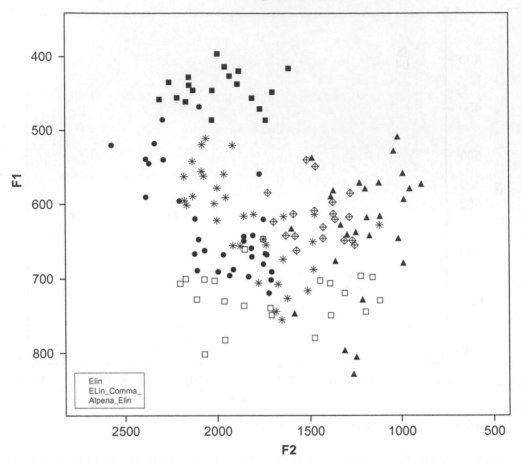

Figure 9.6 Tokens of the NCVS vowels of a female speaker of Alpena in 2016

tokens extracted from the speech of speakers living in Ishpeming, a small town in the Upper Peninsula of Michigan.

Figure 9.7 shows that the tokens of cot are clearly and expectedly differentiated from the tokens of trap in 1966. However, the cot–caught merger is very present because we can see that the cot and caught tokens overlap. Ishpeming is less than 25 kilometres away from Marquette, where the cot–caught merger is effective (Labov et al. 2006: 61). According to Labov (2012: 31), if the speakers' speech shows evidence of the cot–caught merger, it cannot be affected by the NCVS. While it is true that the shift is not present in Figure 9.7 where the merger is present, the 2008 recording in the exact same town provides us with different results, as shown in Figure 9.8. Indeed, Figure 9.8 depicts a clear fronting of /ɑ/, especially when compared to Figure 9.7 which represents the speech of somebody recorded more than forty years before. The tokens of /ɑ/ have moved closer to /æ/ in a lapse of forty years. There is no sign of

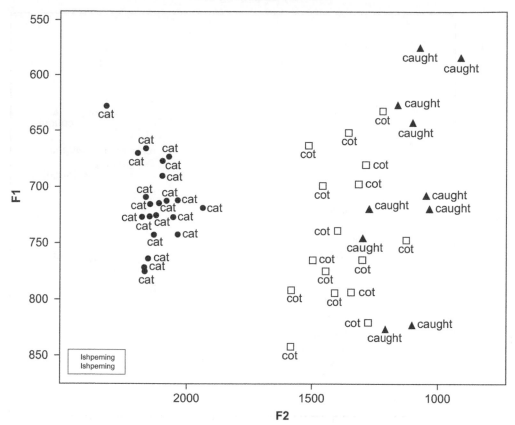

Figure 9.7 Tokens /æ/, /ɑ/, /ɔ/ from Ishpeming in 1966

the COT–CAUGHT merger in our male speaker of 2008 whereas the speaker is affected by the NCVS, at least up to its second stage.[6]

Caution must be taken when considering our 1966 speaker from Ishpeming because there is no personal data available, especially as to whether he has spent his entire life in Ishpeming or not. These results might also suggest that he had a strong Yooper identity, therefore being closer to the Canadians' and the Canadian Shift. However, we know that our 2008 participant was born and raised in Ishpeming but studied at Western Michigan University in Kalamazoo which is in the southern part of Michigan where the shift is effective. There is no information on whether he moved back to Ishpeming or stayed in Kalamazoo. The absence of the COT–CAUGHT merger in his speech may have several explanations: either our speaker moved to a place where the shift was already present, or it may be possible that the COT–CAUGHT merger has disappeared from Ishpeming over the past forty years.

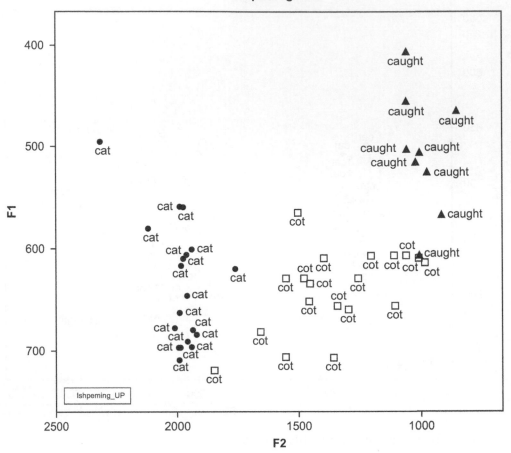

Figure 9.8 Tokens /æ/, /ɑ/, /ɔ/ from Ishpeming in 2008

Discussion

The first study allowed us to confirm that no shifted vowel was present in the speech of speakers from Northern Michigan in the 1960s. Even the first stage, the raising of /æ/, was not completed by our informants. Nevertheless, our informant from Ishpeming in 1966 raises the question of identity: was he closer to the Canadian Shift pattern because Ishpeming inhabitants used to have a stronger connection to Canadians? And has this sense of identity changed given that our 2008 informant doesn't have any sign of the Canadian Shift? Nonetheless, this first study offers evidence of a clear spread of the NCVS in the Upper Peninsula today. However, it could be improved in several respects. Indeed, we have little information about our speakers' backgrounds. This is problematic because the results obtained might not match those of speakers who where actually born and raised in the Upper Peninsula.

We tried to filter the types of speakers as much as possible, but for some of them no information was available about their early life or education. This was the risk of using recordings extracted from the Internet. The best solution would have been to collect the speech data ourselves, as well as personal data that inform any sociolinguistic study, which we did for our second study. A sociolinguistic approach would therefore be a welcome addition to our study. Indeed, this study offers evidence that the NCVS has been spreading to rural areas in Northern Michigan, but it does not indicate how. A sociolinguistic aspect would raise new research questions: Who is leading this change? Is the shift spreading through the media? What are the privileged channels of the expansion of the NCVS within Northern Michigan rural communities? Is it linked to the age or the social class of the speakers? What about ethnic groups and minorities in this area? These questions are at the heart of our second study.

## Second Study

### Corpus Used in our Second Study

One of the main drawbacks of our previous study was the lack of some important data in the corpora. In order to study the presence of the NCVS in the Upper Peninsula of Michigan, recent recordings from inhabitants of the region were needed. We thus decided to select and interview native speakers who had been living in the Upper Peninsula for their entire life. A total of six informants were interviewed in October 2016 in two parts of the Upper Peninsula. Some of them live near the biggest urban centre of the Peninsula, that is to say the city of Marquette, and the other informants are from rural areas in the extreme north of the Peninsula. The interviews were conducted on the basis of the PAC protocol since it includes material to collect sociolinguistic information and also comprises reading passages created for various acoustic studies.

### The PAC protocol

PAC (The Phonology of Contemporary English: Usage, Varieties and Structure) is an interdisciplinary linguistic research programme coordinated by Sophie Herment, Sylvain Navarro, Anne Przewozny-Desriaux and Cécile Viollain and launched by Professors Jacques Durand and Philip Carr in 2003. The programme's goal is to create a corpus of spoken English from various English-speaking locations, and speech data collection is based on the use of a common protocol. Such a corpus aims at

> giving a better picture of spoken English in its unity and diversity (geographical, social and stylistic); testing phonological and phonetic models from a synchronic and diachronic point of view, making room for the systematic study of variation; favoring communication between specialists in speech and in phonological theory; providing data and analyses which will help improve the teaching of English as a foreign language.[7]

The protocol is divided into three parts: reading tasks, a formal conversation, and an informal conversation. The formal conversation aims at providing information on the speaker, and at capturing a formal register of speech, which is important for our study. In order to guide these specific interviews, we used the LVTI (Langue, Ville, Travail, Identité) questionnaire, divided into the following themes: language, city, work, and identity.[8] In our interviews, we used the questions related to work as a way to initiate a formal conversation. Other questions revolving around language and the informants' relation to their own dialect were asked between two reading tasks, since the lengthiness of the reading tasks challenged some of our informants' goodwill. The informal conversation can be recorded between two or more informants with or without the presence of the fieldworker. During our interviews, we led the conversation between two of our informants by trying to remain as discreet as possible to get closer to a natural speech form. The recordings amount to about forty-five minutes per informant and twenty to thirty minutes per task, with the exception of the reading tasks.

We chose to use the PAC protocol as it fitted our goals and expectations. Even though the recordings were cumbersome tasks for both the informant and the fieldworker because of their lengthiness, the protocol allowed us to collect precious recordings and complete sets of information about our informants.

Informants

Our corpus is composed of six recordings. Yet one of the recordings that contained two informants' oral productions could not be analysed because of its poor quality. The informants were selected with the help of the 'snowball technique', which consists in using the social network of one or more participants to recruit other informants for the study (Milroy and Gordon 2003: 32). Through this technique we were able to find informants from different places, ages and genders. Table 9.4 presents detailed information about the six informants interviewed in October 2016.

Out of the six informants interviewed, three were men and three were women. Even though the small number of persons interviewed makes it difficult to reflect an

Table 9.4 Detailed information on our corpus

| Informant | Age | Gender | Town | Population in 2017 | Education |
|---|---|---|---|---|---|
| Informant 1 | 22 | Male | Marquette | 20,63 | Bachelor's degree |
| Informant 2 | 80 | Female | Munising | 2,21 | High school |
| Informant 3 | 46 | Female | Wetmore | 949 | Bachelor's degree |
| Informant 4 | 51 | Male | Wetmore | 949 | College |
| Informant 5 | 42 | Female | Tamarack City | 698 | Trade school |
| Informant 6 | 38 | Male | Tamarack City | 710 | College |

*Note:* The US Census Bureau does not have data for the city of Tamarack, MI. We used the population number of the town of Calumet, in which Tamarack is situated.

entire population, we tried to get as much diversity as possible. Our informants' ages vary from twenty-two for the youngest to eighty years old for the oldest. They were all born, raised and had spent their entire lives in the Upper Peninsula, which was the most important criterion for our research. The 2017 results from the US Census Bureau are used since they are the last official results posted since 2013. The six informants are from extremely rural areas, except for the first two who are from towns located next to the biggest urban centre of the peninsula.

*Methodology Used in our Second Study*

We decided to use Praat to annotate and extract our vowel formants, as we did in our first study. However, we did not use SPPAS because its results were not precise enough. We manually annotated each recording at the sentence level instead. Then, we added an extra tier to annotate at the phone level. Each recording and speech style is distinguished from the others because we needed to separate the results obtained with the wordlists from those obtained with the spontaneous productions. Our formant extraction method went through some changes too. We decided to use another script run with Praat, created by Emmanuel Ferragne.[9] That script was a semi-automatic extraction method. Once a tier has been created with the annotated vowels in Praat, that script makes it possible to stop and zoom in on the spectrogram for every vowel one by one in the tier. This technique allows us to visualise the formants in the spectrogram, and to adjust the points of extraction if they are not well placed. Therefore, that script helped us to extract more precise vowel formants, allowing us to adjust any error the machine might make at the exact moment of the values extraction.

The text files created by the script with the vowel values can be opened directly and processed with the software R,[10] to which we added the 'Vowels' packages for our vowel normalisation and 'PhonR' to plot our vowels. The Lobanov normalisation technique was also used in the second study, run with R instead of the NORM suite, which converted our Hz values to Bark values. We also decided to exclude any token of /æ/ in a nasal environment, as it already raises in General American English.

*First Results*

Our first results compare tokens of our NCVS vowels for the wordlist section of our interviews. Figure 9.9 presents the production of /ɪ/, /ɛ/, /ʌ/, /ɔ/, /ɑ/ and /æ/ in the wordlist section for our oldest informant and her grandson, our youngest informant aged twenty-two. Surprisingly, there are no evident differences between their vowel productions. The vowel /æ/ is not raised to the /ɪ/ level nor to the /ɛ/ level, and /ɑ/ still holds a back position since the first stage of the NCVS does not seem to be completed. The two informants live in the same area, next to Marquette, the biggest urban centre of the Peninsula. None of them is affected by the COT–CAUGHT merger, even though the /ɔ/ vowel seems to be moving front in our youngest informant.

We still need to compare these data with Peterson and Barney's values (Peterson and Barney 1952) in order to get a clear idea on the evolution of the shift. These results are from a reading passage, when informants pay the most attention to their

**Informants 1 and 2**

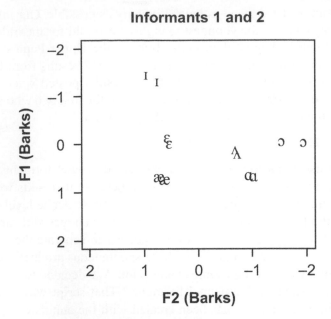

Figure 9.9 Tokens /ɪ/, /ɛ/, /ʌ/, /ɔ/, /ɑ/ and /æ/ from our first and second informants

pronunciation, which may explain the lack of differences in production between our youngest informant and his grandmother.

**Conclusion**

Our first study allowed us to demonstrate an evolution in the spread of the NCVS in Northern Michigan. We found evidence of shifted vowels in areas above the isogloss drawn by Labov. Yet our speakers are not all affected to the same degree: the speakers living closer to the isogloss were the most affected, and inhabitants of the Upper Peninsula, much further north, were the less affected as their speeches present only completed initial stages of the shift. The NCVS is thus no longer a phenomenon only occurring in big cities, a conclusion which Gordon (Gordon 2001) reached sixteen years ago. Today, more than ever, it also occurs in small towns outside the area first delimited in Labov's work (Labov et al. 1972). This evolution then questions the relevance of the name of the phenomenon. The Northern Cities Vowel Shift is not a phenomenon occurring solely in big urban centres anymore as its name would indicate. The NCVS is spreading to a broader area than the Inland North as previously delimited, so that it is necessary to question the extent of this phenomenon. Has it spread far up above Labov's isogloss? Are there any pockets of resistance to the shift to be found in areas of Northern Michigan that were not included in our study? Our second study aims at answering these questions. Our first results do not seem to indicate the presence of the NCVS in isolated towns of the Upper Peninsula of Michigan for now, but analyses of spontaneous speech might offer different results.

## Notes

1. See https://uwdc.library.wisc.edu/
2. See http://www.dialectsarchive.com/
3. Paul Boersma and David Weenink (2013), Praat: doing phonetics by computer [computer program], Version 5.3.51. Accessed in October 2015 from http://www.praat.org
4. The script was kindly offered by Professor Nicolas Ballier, University of Paris 7–Denis Diderot.
5. The NORM website http://lingtools.uoregon.edu/norm/ is part of the *LingTools* site, a service hosted by the Language Variation and Computation Lab http://blogs.uoregon.edu/lvclab/ in the University of Oregon's Linguistics Department, http://linguistics.uoregon.edu/
6. Stage 2 is the fronting of /ɑ/ after stage 1, the raising of /æ/.
7. Cited from http://www.pacprogramme.net/
8. See http://www.pacprogramme.net for more information on LVTI.
9. The script was kindly offered by Emmanuel Ferragne.
10. R Core Team (2013), *R: A language and environment for statistical computing*. R Foundation for Statistical Computing, Vienna, Austria, http://www.R-project.org/

## References

Adank, P., R. Smits and R. Van Hout (2004), 'A comparison of vowel normalisation procedures for language variation research', *The Journal of the Acoustical Society of America* 116(5), 3099–3107.

Boberg, C. (2005), 'The Canadian shift in Montreal', *Language Variation and Change* 17(02), 133–154.

Callary, R. E. (1975), Phonological change and the development of an urban dialect in Illinois', *Language in Society* 4(2), 155–169.

Clarke, S., F. Elms and A. Youssef, (1995), 'The third dialect of English: some Canadian evidence', *Language Variation and Change* 7(2), 209–228.

Coates, J. (1993), *Women, Men, and Language: A Sociolinguistic Account of Gender Differences in Language*, London: Longman.

Esling, J. H. and H. J. Warkentyne (1993), 'Retracting of /æ/ in Vancouver English', *Focus on Canada* 11, 229.

Evans, B. E., R. Ito, J. Jones and D. R. Preston (2000), 'Change on top of change: social and regional accommodation to the Northern Cities Chain Shift', *De Toekomst van de Variatielinguitiek*, 61–86.

Gordon, M. J. (2001), *Small-town Values and Big-city Vowels: A Study of the Northern Cities Shift in Michigan*, Durham, NC: Duke University Press.

Herndobler, R. (1977), *White Working-class Speech: The East Side of Chicago*, Doctoral dissertation, University of Chicago, Joseph Regenstein Library, Department of Photo duplication.

Koffi, Ettien N. Dr. (2014), 'The acoustic vowel space of Central Minnesota English in light of the Northern Cities Shift', *Linguistic Portfolios* 3, 2–20.

Labov, W. (1990), 'The intersection of sex and social class in the course of linguistic change', *Language Variation and Change* 2(2), 205–254.

Labov, W. (1994), *Principles of Linguistic Change, Volume 1, Internal factors*, Oxford: Blackwell.

Labov, W. (2002), 'Driving forces in linguistic change', in *2002 International Conference on Korean Linguistics* (2).

Labov, W. (2007), 'Transmission and diffusion', *Language* 83(2), 344–387.

Labov, W. (2012), *Dialect Diversity in America: The Politics of Language Change*, Charlottesville: University of Virginia Press.

Labov, W., S. Ash and C. Boberg (2006), *The Atlas of North American English: Phonetics, Phonology and Sound Change*, Berlin: Walter de Gruyter.

Labov, W., M. Yaeger and R. Steiner (1972), *A Quantitative Study of Sound Change in Progress* (1), Philadelphia: The US Regional Survey.

Milroy, L. and M. Gordon (2003), 'Style-shifting and code-switching', in *Sociolinguistics: Method and interpretation*, Oxford: Blackwell Publishing, pp. 188–222.

Peterson, G. E. and H. L. Barney (1952), 'Control methods used in a study of the vowels', *The Journal of the Acoustical Society of America* 23, 1.

Rakerd, B. and B. Plichta (2010), 'More on Michigan listeners' perceptions of /ɑ/–fronting', *American Speech* 85(4), 431–449.

Rankinen, W. (2014), 'The Michigan upper peninsula English vowel system in Finnish American communities in Marquette county', *American Speech* 89(3), 312–347.

Thomas, E. (2011), *Sociophonetics: An Introduction*, Basingstoke: Palgrave Macmillan.

Wells, J. C. (2008), *Longman Pronunciation Dictionary*, Harlow: Pearson Education Ltd.

# 10

## Levelling in a Northern English Variety:
## The Case of FACE and GOAT in Greater Manchester

*Hugo Chatellier*

### Overview

This chapter offers a description of the main phonological and phonetic features of the variety of English spoken in Manchester, England, on the basis of recent oral data from the PAC-LVTI project. Its starting point is a brief account of levelling in the north of England, a phenomenon that has attracted the attention of many sociolinguists recently. It has been argued that a supralocal northern variety is in expansion in the north of England, and Manchester, as a major urban centre of the north of England, is a prime candidate to test the diffusion of some of the supralocal variants. We then provide a synthetic description of Mancunian English according to previous studies, before presenting our own work, based on a corpus of thirty-one informants. Our results suggest that Mancunian English is not levelling towards a supralocal northern variety as far as FACE and GOAT are concerned, though other vowels appear to be subject to a more global case of levelling.

### Levelling in the North of England

Over the course of the twentieth century, linguists interested in the issues of variation and change have observed a progressive loss of localised features in England, leading to a greater homogeneity of different varieties at a regional, and sometimes national, level. One classic example of such homogeneity is the disappearance of Traditional Dialects, usually associated with rural areas. They have been progressively replaced by a smaller number of 'Modern Dialects', which are associated with much bigger areas (see Trudgill 2001: 11 inter alia). This phenomenon has been called 'regional dialect levelling' (Kerswill 2003: 223) and is defined as follows: 'a process whereby differences between regional varieties are reduced, features which make varieties distinctive disappear, and new features emerge and are adopted by speakers over a wide geographical area' (Williams and Kerswill 1999: 149).

It is linked to two mechanisms of linguistic change. The first is the 'geographical diffusion' of variants, often from a dominant centre to other areas. The second mechanism is called, somewhat awkwardly as Kerswill points out, 'levelling'. It is defined as 'the reduction or attrition of marked variants' (Trudgill 1986: 98) and is related to the phenomenon of accommodation: speakers who wish to communicate have been shown to tone down some of their own linguistic features and adopt some of their interlocutors'. These acts of 'short-term accommodation' (speakers usually revert to their typical features after the conversation) can lead, over a long period of time, to 'long-term accommodation' and levelling of some variants: 'If a speaker accommodates frequently enough to a particular accent or dialect, I would go on to argue, then the accommodation may in time become permanent, particularly if attitudinal factors are favourable' (Trudgill 1986: 39).

But why would regional dialect levelling be particularly prevalent now? Britain (2010: 197–199) puts forward a number of factors which have contributed to an increasing mobility of speakers in England, which has in turn led to more contact between speakers of different varieties:

- an increase in urbanisation, with a vast majority of the population living in urban areas;
- an increase in the number of people who go to university;
- an increase in mobility (for work- or leisure-related reasons for example);
- different family ties, with an increasing number of people living in single-person households.

Now, though regional dialect levelling should lead to a convergence of all varieties in a given area, studies have shown that the situation is not quite as straightforward. Trudgill (2001: 12) agrees that modern varieties are much closer to one another, at least from a morphological, syntactic and lexical point of view. However, it seems that these new varieties are currently diverging from a phonological point of view:

> The dialects and accents associated with these [Modern Dialect] areas are much less different from one another, and much less different from RP and Standard English, than the Traditional Dialects were. However, and this is crucial, in terms of phonology they are for the most part currently diverging, not converging.

One specific case of divergence from the standard that has attracted attention is the diffusion of supralocal variants for the vowels of FACE and GOAT (Wells 1982) in the north of England. While Standard Southern British English (SSBE) speakers have diphthongs in these lexical sets (respectively /eɪ/ and /əʊ/), Traditional Dialects in the north of England (with the exception of the far north and Merseyside) have /eː/ and /oː/ (Beal 2008: 133).

However, research on the realisations of FACE and GOAT in Tyneside (whose local variety does not traditionally have monophthongs for these lexical sets) has yielded interesting results (Watt 1998, 2002). Watt analyses the realisations of FACE and GOAT by thirty-two speakers. For each lexical set, three main realisations are used:

supralocal variants, found over a large area in the north of England ([eː] for FACE and [oː] for GOAT); local variants, which are centring diphthongs (respectively [ɪə] and [ʊə]); and national variants, similar to the diphthongs found in the south of England ([eɪ] and [əʊ]). Watt's results show that the most common variants are the supralocal variants [eː] and [oː], and that local variants are less frequently used by younger speakers (Watt 2002: 56). This indicates that the Tyneside variety of English is neither levelling towards the standard nor becoming more distinctive than surrounding varieties. An explanation put forward by Watt is that younger speakers consider local variants to be old-fashioned, and consequently disfavour them. At the same time, they wish to retain a northern identity, and adopting supralocal variants allows them to signal an attachment to the local community while sounding 'modern'.

Finally, one last argument supporting the claim that new dialect areas cover larger zones than those of Traditional Dialects comes from perceptual dialectology. As Beal reminds us (2010: 217), the 1970s saw huge administrative changes take place in England. The Local Government Act 1972 modified the boundaries of several counties and established metropolitan counties. These were usually created from several existing counties and centred around large urban areas (for example Greater Manchester). This administrative reform was not, however, without effects on dialects. People who were born in the same place, only a few years apart, could actually be born in different counties. Beal claims that one consequence of this reform was a shift in regional identities (2010: 221–222).

For instance, research on working-class speakers in Middlesbrough (Llamas 2007: 593–596) has shown that while many older speakers identify with Yorkshire, this is not the case for younger speakers who define their accent as 'Middlesbrough'. More generally, studies in perceptual dialectology (Montgomery 2006, 2012) have suggested that counties no longer serve as 'markers of linguistic identity' and have been replaced by major conurbations (Beal 2010: 220–221). The case of Manchester is particularly interesting, as Montgomery's work has revealed that Greater Manchester is now an emerging dialect area, while it was rarely recognised as a dialect area before (Montgomery 2012: 659–661).

## Manchester

Despite its importance as an urban centre in contemporary England (there were 2.7 million inhabitants in Greater Manchester in 2011, with more than 500,000 people in the city of Manchester alone[1]), the Mancunian variety (or 'Manc') has received relatively little attention compared to other varieties in the north of England (for example Newcastle), although a resurgence in studies focusing on Manchester has been observed recently (notably Baranowski and Turton 2015). As we mentioned earlier (Montgomery 2006: 214), until very recently Manchester was seldom recognised as a variety of its own. According to Montgomery, it is probably the media coverage which Manchester has received in the past few decades which has led to acknowledging the existence of a dialectal area centred around the city. The importance of Manchester's musical scene in the late 1980s and early 1990s led to an increasing

## Consonantal System

Traditionally, Lancashire accents are thought to be rhotic, but Wells stresses that most urban Lancashire varieties, and Manchester English, are non-rhotic nowadays: /r/ is not realised in coda position (see also Beal 2008: 139). Wells does mention, however, a patch of residual rhoticity in the north of Greater Manchester, near Accrington and Rochdale (1982: 367–368).

As with most urban accents in England, Manchester English is subject to the phenomenon known as H-dropping.[2] Baranowski and Turton show that H-dropping is stable in 'Manc' (age is not a significant variable), with working-class male speakers having the highest rate of H-dropping (2015: 298–302).

Two other consonantal features that are widely attested in many other varieties of English are also found in Manchester English, namely TH-fronting and T-glottalling. Baranowski and Turton's work on the first phenomenon, the realisation[3] of /θ/ and /ð/ as respectively [f] and [v], reveals that this is a change led by younger speakers, as age is the strongest predictor as in other urban English varieties. There is also evidence that supports the claim that TH-fronting is a male-led change (2015: 302–306).

As for T-glottalling, the authors note that glottal replacement ([ʔ] for /t/) is more frequent than pre-glottalised variants ([ʔt] for /t/), which are often found in the southern varieties. Glottalling in final position (for instance in 'cat'), for which age is a significant predictor, has now spread to all social groups, which leads Baranowski and Turton to conclude that this is a change which is now near completion (2015: 307–308). On the other hand, T-glottalling in intervocalic position is not quite as widespread yet. Age is still a significant predictor, but contrary to glottalling in final position, so are gender and social class. This suggests that T-glottalling in intervocalic position is a more recent change, led by males and working-class speakers (2015: 308). Baranowski and Turton claim that T-glottalling started in Manchester as a phonological process affecting only codas, before spreading to other 'non-stressed (t)s' (2015: 310).

One characteristic that Manchester English shares with the majority of the linguistic north, is the absence of a clear /l/ versus dark /l/ allophony: /l/ is realised as [ɫ] in all positions (Wells 1982: 370–371; Cruttenden 2014: 221; Baranowski and Turton 2015: 297), whereas SSBE speakers use a clear allophone [l] before vowels and /j/, and the dark allophone [ɫ] in all other positions (Cruttenden 2014: 217–221).

Finally, there are also more localised consonantal characteristics in Manchester English. One example is the non-coalescence of <ng>, attested in the west of England (Trudgill 1999: 59). Indeed, 'Manc' retains /ŋg/ in environments where most other English accents have /ŋ/, as in 'ring' and 'singer' (Wells 1982: 365–366; Baranowski and Turton 2015: 296–297). Baranowski and Turton note however that the (ing) variable (in the word 'jumping' for instance) is usually pronounced [ɪn], except in the most formal speech styles.

## PAC-LVTI

The LVTI[4] project follows in the footsteps of the PAC programme in that it aims at recording corpora of native speakers of contemporary English and shares the same goals as the original programme (Durand and Przewozny 2015: 63, Chatellier 2016: 168–191). A common protocol of Labovian inspiration is applied to all locations under study, allowing us to obtain comparable oral data with several degrees of formality, thanks to the following tasks (see the 'Introduction' to this book):

- the reading of two wordlists;
- the reading of a text;
- a semi-guided interview between the informant and the fieldworker, based on a sociolinguistic questionnaire;
- an informal conversation, ideally between two informants and without the fieldworker.

However, while LVTI shares a common protocol with PAC, a new set of questions, integrated into the formal interview, has been devised in order to investigate more closely the dynamics of urban varieties of English. Moreover, whereas traditional PAC studies include from ten to twenty speakers, the PAC-LVTI protocol is planned to be applied to larger groups of speakers (sixty informants per location on average).

Greater Manchester is the first location investigated by PAC-LVTI. The first recordings took place in 2012, and after four fieldwork trips between 2012 and 2015 the PAC-LVTI Manchester corpus now counts sixty-seven speakers, which makes it the largest corpus within the PAC programme database.

*Methodology*

Among the sixty-seven speakers from the PAC-LVTI corpus, thirty-one (fifteen male and sixteen female speakers aged 22 to 65 years old) were selected for a phonetic-acoustic analysis of the vocalic system of Manchester English (see Chatellier 2016). Informants were selected in order to constitute a representative sample of the different socio-economic groups within our corpus (unfortunately this was not always possible) and were divided into three groups, G1, G2 and G3, which we can respectively equate with working class (WC), upper working class/lower middle class (UWC/LMC) and middle class (MC).

Note that not all of our speakers come from within the M60, and some of our speakers originate from the area to the north of Manchester, which will be of interest when we discuss our results on FACE and GOAT.

The reading tasks were fully transcribed in standard orthographic transcription under Praat, as well as, for each speaker, five to ten minutes of both the semi-guided interview and the informal conversation.

In order to investigate the presence of monophthongal variants of FACE and GOAT in Mancunian speech, a formant analysis of the realisations of each speaker was conducted. So as to avoid phonetic environments whose influence on the vocalic signal is too important, the following contexts were excluded:

- following /l, r, n, m, ŋ/
- preceding /w, j, t, d/
- preceding obstruent + liquid consonant cluster (for example /bl/)
- vowels adjacent to another vowel (as in the sequence 'the art' for instance)

Vowels were manually segmented and the values of F1 and F2 were automatically measured at 1/3 and 2/3 of the duration of the vowel. Values were then manually checked and discarded when there was a clear mismatch between the formant measured and the auditory evaluation of the token. Finally, our results were normalised using the Lobanov procedure (Lobanov 1971). This left us with a total of 15,556 tokens (710 FACE tokens and 865 GOAT tokens) on which we based our analysis. The statistical significance of our results was also tested.

## Results

We shall provide here a summary of the main findings of our study, focusing mainly on the realisations of our WC and MC speakers, and what they involve at a phonological level, before discussing FACE and GOAT in the section 'FACE and GOAT' below. Where relevant, we shall also underline the effect of sociolinguistic factors such as age, socio-economic group or gender on our results.

Figure 10.1 shows the mean values of F1 and F2 for each standard lexical set (with the exception of COMMA, LETTER and HAPPY). It is hard to decide whether FOOT and STRUT are pronounced with the same vowel on the basis of Figure 10.1 alone. Previous studies on the subject have indicated that the presence of a FOOT–STRUT split is strongly correlated to social class, and so, average realisations for all speakers cannot really shed light on the absence of an underlying opposition for WC speakers. In the same way, the vowels of TRAP and BATH seem quite similar, but this tells us nothing of their duration.

Nonetheless, other vocalic features are already noticeable. There seems to be a contrast between FORCE and NORTH, with the former being a closer and backer vowel. The vowel of GOOSE is very fronted: it has now become a front vowel. Finally, the way FACE and GOAT are represented indicates that they are diphthongs in Manchester English. We shall get back to this and put forward an explanation for this situation (see the section 'FACE and GOAT') but we wish to focus on the realisations of the different socio-economic groups for the moment.

### FOOT and STRUT

A first look at the realisations of FOOT and STRUT reveals that their F1 and F2 values are similar among WC speakers (see Figure 10.2). On the other hand, there is a clear difference between these vowels for MC speakers (see Figure 10.3). These results are corroborated by a t-test (Baayen 2008: 75–77): the formants of FOOT and STRUT

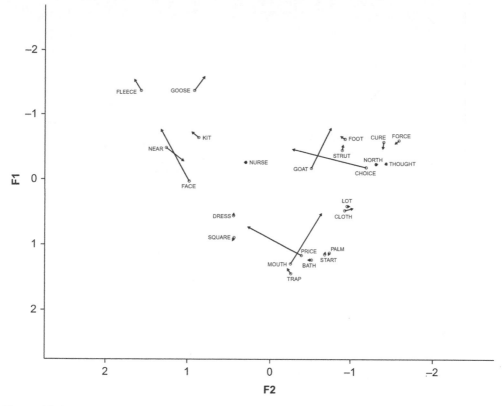

Figure 10.1 Average F1 and F2 values for the standard lexical sets (all speakers)

are not significantly different for WC speakers (this is also the case for UWC/LMC speakers), while there is a significant difference for MC speakers for both formants (respectively $p=2.813.10-14$ for F1 and $p=0.006378$ for F2[5]). We interpret these results as showing a lack of opposition between FOOT and STRUT for WC speakers, which is in accordance with previous studies. In other words, our data confirm that the presence of a FOOT–STRUT split is correlated with social class.

*TRAP and BATH*

MC speakers also show values for the vowel of BATH that suggest this vowel is backer than TRAP, though it is not located quite in the same area as START (or PALM, but the smaller number of tokens for this lexical set makes it difficult to draw definitive conclusions).

A closer examination of the reading tasks reveals that most MC speakers use the same short vowel in TRAP and BATH, with the exception of DS1, who clearly exhibits a vowel similar to that of START in BATH words. Besides, most WC speakers also use the short vowel of TRAP in BATH words. However, for these speakers, the opposition between TRAP/BATH and START relies solely on length, as both vowels have a similar quality. This is not the case for MC speakers, who usually display differences in

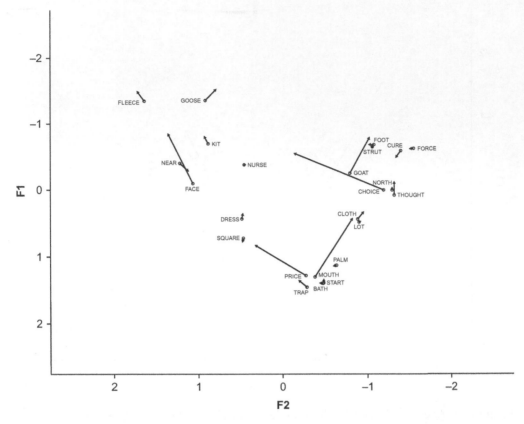

Figure 10.2 Average F1 and F2 values for the standard lexical sets (WC speakers)

quality as well as length between TRAP and START, even if they use a short vowel in BATH.

This has interesting consequences for the phonological status of length in the vocalic system of Manchester English, though we shall not discuss them here (see Chatellier 2016: 296–303). Again, our results are consistent with previous work on northern varieties: the fact that a short vowel for BATH is found in the speech of most MC speakers indicates that this feature does not seem to suffer from the same negative evaluations as the absence of a FOOT–STRUT split (see the section 'Vocalic system' above). Many informants were aware of this aspect of northern English, and pointed it out to us when justifying the description of their own speech as northern (for instance here is LN1's description of her own Manchester accent: 'I think it's northern in terms of the fact that I use flat As').

*FORCE and NORTH*

From a phonetic point of view, the vowel of FORCE is often closer and backer than that of NORTH. This is corroborated by a t-test, which shows that F1 and F2 values for FORCE and NORTH are significantly different, for all groups of speakers. However, the

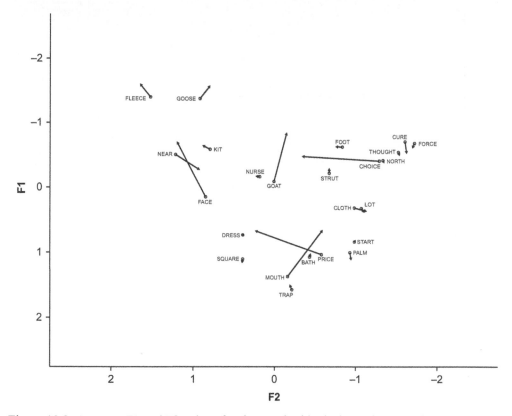

Figure 10.3  Average F1 and F2 values for the standard lexical sets (MC speakers)

inspection of the realisations of individual speakers reveals that many female speakers do not display this distinction, in particular among MC speakers. This implies that despite what our graphs suggest, a phonological opposition between FORCE and NORTH is not always present in the speech of Mancunians. Incidentally, nine informants (eight belong to the WC or UWC/LMC) exhibit a particularly clear distinction between FORCE and NORTH. Among these nine informants, six originate from the north of Manchester (within the boundaries of the M60), which supports Baranowski and Turton's hypothesis that the contrast between the two vowels may be stronger in the north of the city.

*GOOSE*

As Figure 10.1 indicates, GOOSE is very fronted in our corpus. Though GOOSE-fronting is mentioned in the literature, the extent of this phenomenon warrants further investigation. We initially suspected that the phonetic environment of the GOOSE tokens might have been responsible for the high F2 values. This is for example the case of coronal and palatal consonants. However, we excluded initial /t, d, j/ before proceeding with the extraction of formant values (see the section 'Methodology'). This leaves us with initial /k, g, tʃ, dʒ, ʃ, ʒ/, which make up close to 60 per cent of all GOOSE tokens (112 tokens). As is shown in Figure 10.4, these tokens are clearly fronted.

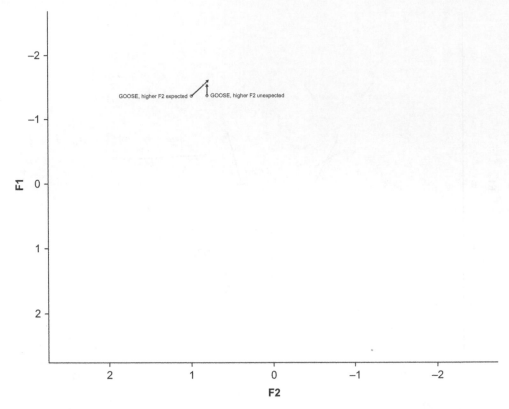

Figure 10.4  Average realisations for GOOSE

What is unexpected, however, is the fact that the tokens which do not start with one of the consonants mentioned above (that is /k, g, tʃ, dʒ, ʃ, ʒ/), which make up 40 per cent of all GOOSE tokens (77 tokens), are almost as fronted as the other tokens (see Figure 10.4). Once more, this supports Baranowski and Turton's claim that GOOSE is fronted in all environments in Manchester English (unfortunately, we cannot investigate GOOSE-fronting before /l/ as such contexts were excluded). There does not seem to be much difference between the typical GOOSE realisation of WC speakers and that of MC speakers. This is corroborated by an ANOVA, which reveals that social class is not a significant factor, contrary to gender and, above all, age: younger speakers exhibit significantly more fronting.

*FACE and GOAT*

The most common realisation of FACE in our corpus is a diphthong, not unlike the main variant found in SSBE. Monophthongs do exist in the speech of our informants but they are limited to a small number of contexts, for example 'make' in the text (Chatellier 2016: 265). Considering the high frequency of this item, and given that it is not found in final position in a rhythmic group in the task in question, the use of these monophthongs can probably be accounted for with usage-based frameworks (see Bybee 2001 and Pierrehumbert 2006 inter alia), and we do not think that they are the sign of a levelling process towards a supralocal northern variety.

However, other uses of monophthongs deserve a closer analysis. Indeed, one speaker in particular, VH2 (and, to a lesser extent, her husband IH1), makes a greater use of monophthongs in FACE compared with the rest of the informants. VH2 regularly uses monophthongs in all tasks, even in wordlists, which leads us to believe that her monophthongs do not have the same status as those sometimes encountered in the speech of other speakers. Unfortunately, due to the presence of background noise during the recording, formants could not be measured accurately for most of these tokens, and the measures were excluded during the verification process. Nevertheless, VH2 also makes use of diphthongs, notably in words such as 'weight' or 'eight', which used to have a final fricative in Middle English (Wells 1982: 357). Consequently, 'wait' and 'weight' constitute a minimal pair for her.

The sociolinguistic profiles of VH2 and IH1 are similar, and their study further supports the hypothesis that Manchester English is not levelling towards a supralocal northern variety as far as FACE is concerned. In fact, both belong to the oldest generation of speakers in our corpus; IH1 was born in Wigan and VH2 in Westhoughton, and they currently reside in Horwich, close to Bolton. All these locations are outside of the area demarcated by the M60. Furthermore, they do not define themselves as Mancunians, or even Greater Manchester speakers: VH2, for instance, describes her accent as 'Lancashire'.

At first sight, the case of GOAT looks similar to that of FACE, but further investigation of our speakers' realisations reveals two major differences. First, even though the majority of GOAT realisations are clear diphthongs, a greater number of WC and UWC/LMC speakers (six informants) show monophthongs with an [oː]-like quality in conversational context, whereas very few GOAT tokens are realised with a monophthong in the reading tasks. As could be expected, given the results for the vowel of FACE, we find VH2 and IH1 among these six speakers. Once more, VH2 exhibits the greater number of monophthongs for GOAT: she hardly uses diphthongs, even in the reading tasks.

It is worth noting that none of the speakers who regularly use monophthongs is under the age of thirty, which bodes ill for the diffusion of these variants in Manchester English. Second, there is fronting of both the nucleus and the glide of the GOAT diphthong among MC speakers, which appears clearly on Figure 10.3. We found social class to be highly significant (p<2.10-16 for both nucleus and glide), and these results echo again those of Baranowski and Turton. We also found gender to be highly significant, with women showing more advanced tokens, but the lack of MC female speakers over fifty-five in our corpus prevents us from concluding, at this stage, that there is a straightforward correlation between gender and GOAT-fronting in our corpus.

Given these results, we are inclined to conclude that there is no sign of levelling towards a supralocal northern variety as far as FACE and GOAT are concerned. Our speakers, especially among the youngest generations, exhibit few monophthongs and favour diphthongal realisations.

## Discussion

Our results regarding FACE and GOAT might be surprising in the light of studies showing a diffusion of supralocal variants in the north of England (see the section 'Levelling in the north of England' above). Nevertheless, we think that the investigation of sociolinguistic evaluations associated with these variants can shed light on the subject. The diffusion of monophthongs for FACE and GOAT is an example of change from above[6] (Labov 1999: 78): it operates above the level of consciousness. Watt's informants were aware of the existence of monophthongs for FACE and GOAT, and chose to adopt them to express their identity of Northerners. The same variants also seem to be prominent in York (Haddican et al. 2013: 382–384).

Our own informants are also aware of these variants, just as they recognise the presence of a FOOT–STRUT split or BATH-broadening in the south of England, even though they cannot name these phenomena in those terms. These characteristics were often mentioned when our speakers wished to describe a northern accent. However, if monophthongs for FACE and GOAT are mentioned in the PAC-LVTI corpus, they are not associated with a general northern accent, nor with a supralocal variety. Instead, they are associated with the area directly to the north of Manchester. For instance, during one conversation, JA1 talks about people in Greater Manchester who say 'No [oː], no [oː], I don't think so [oː].' Her father PA1 agrees and claims this is typical of people from the Bolton area. This leads us to suspect that these variants do not share the same sociolinguistic evaluations as those that they have in Newcastle: we suggest that monophthongal variants of FACE and GOAT in Manchester are not associated with a supralocal accent, but with the varieties located in the north of Greater Manchester.

It is particularly interesting to compare monophthongal variants of FACE and GOAT with other variants that show diffusion in Manchester English, namely fronted variants of GOAT and GOOSE. Not a single informant seems to be aware of the existence of these variants, and no mention of them is to be found in our recordings. This is hardly surprising for GOOSE: several studies on the subject have concluded that GOOSE-fronting is a change taking place below the level of consciousness (notably Haddican et al 2013: 393, in York). Fridland (2008: 449–450) stresses that groups of speakers who traditionally do not take part in the same linguistic changes as the rest of their community are also affected by GOOSE-fronting.

So why are speakers of different English varieties all over the world adopting these variants? Unfortunately, it is too early at this stage to give a definite answer. One avenue that could be explored brings us back to Labov's principles on linguistic change: GOOSE and GOAT would be involved in a chain shift. According to Labov's principle III, 'in chain shifts, back vowels move to the front' (Labov 1999: 116): this is consistent with what we have observed in Manchester English. Furthermore, while all groups of speakers now use fronted variants of GOOSE, the fronted variants of GOAT are, for the moment, only used by MC speakers. This echoes the patterns seen in other (seemingly unrelated) varieties of English, for instance Philadelphia. If GOAT is fronted in these varieties, it appears to lag behind the fronting of GOOSE: 'When /ow/

is fronted, it is always in parallel with /uw/ and considerably behind it' (Labov 1999: 208). In the light of the absence of clear social evaluations of fronted variants, this raises the question of the role of system-driven factors, namely balance and economy of the system, in what could potentially be a case of global levelling.

## Conclusion

Our work shows that the Mancunian variety is clearly a northern variety of British English. It lacks a FOOT–STRUT split and the lexical distribution of the 'short a' is more limited compared with southern varieties. These features appear to be quite stable in our data, which suggests that the Mancunian variety does not seem to be levelling towards the standard and retains its northern characteristics. Other vocalic features, which are more localised, are also found in Manchester English, particularly among WC speakers: there is an opposition between FORCE and NORTH, and realisations of happy, when in final position, are frequently more open.

The main goal of this chapter was the investigation of monophthongs in FACE and GOAT in Manchester English, which could have been linked to the diffusion of a supralocal variety in the north of England. Our results suggest that no levelling towards the supralocal variants of FACE and GOAT is taking place in Manchester. We believe that monophthongal variants of FACE and GOAT do not share the same sociolinguistic evaluations in Manchester as in other parts of the linguistic north. In Manchester, they are not associated with a 'general' northern accent, but with the varieties spoken in the northern areas of Greater Manchester, and so cannot be used to express local loyalty, contrary to the same variants in Tyneside English.

That is not to say that Manchester English is not currently levelling towards another variety. Our results, which are consistent with Baranowski and Turton's work on Manchester, indicate that GOOSE is now fully fronted, and that GOAT-fronting appears to be under way. This change has been observed in several other varieties of English. However, studies suggest that this is a change from below: no specific sociolinguistic evaluations are associated with the fronted variants, and speakers do not seem to be aware of their existence. If this change is indeed not sociolinguistically motivated, an investigation of the internal dynamics of the system of Mancunian English might be fruitful in explaining this change.

## Notes

1. Office for National Statistics 2012.
2. The term H-dropping implies that /h/ is present in the phonemic system but not realised. However, it is also possible, for speakers who consistently exhibit 'H-less' pronunciations, to consider that they lack a /h/ phoneme in their inventory.
3. One could also argue that /θ/ and /ð/ are gradually merging with /f/ and /v/ in certain positions, but Wells is adamant that this is only a neutralisation at the phonetic level: according to him, there are no examples of hypercorrection such as *[leθt] for 'left', which supports the existence of an opposition at the phonological level (1982: 328–329).
4. LVTI stands for *Langue, Ville, Travail, Identité* (French for 'Language, Urban life, Work, Identity').

5. We considered a probability value of less than 0.05 to be statistically significant (Baayen 2008: 68).
6. It is not, however, a classic example of change from above: change is not led by the dominant social class, namely the middle class here.

## References

Baayen, R. H. (2008), *Analyzing Linguistic Data. A Practical Introduction to Statistics Using R*, Cambridge: Cambridge University Press.

Baranowski, M. and D. Turton (2015), 'Manchester English', in R. Hickey (ed.), *Researching Northern English*, Amsterdam and Philadelphia: John Benjamins, pp. 293–316.

Beal, J. (2008), 'English dialects in the North of England: phonology', in B. Kortmann and C. Upton (eds), *Varieties of English. Volume 1: The British Isles*, Berlin: Mouton de Gruyter, pp. 122–144.

Beal, J. (2010), 'Shifting borders and shifting regional identities', in C. Llamas and D. Watt (eds), *Language and Identities*, Edinburgh: Edinburgh University Press, pp. 217–226.

Boersma, P. and D. Weenink (2017), Praat: doing phonetics by computer [computer program], Version 6.0.28, http://www.praat.org/ (retrieved 23 March 2017).

Britain, D. (2010), 'Supralocal regional dialect levelling', in C. Llamas and D. Watt (eds), *Language and Identities*, Edinburgh: Edinburgh University Press, pp. 193–204.

Bybee, J. (2001), *Phonology and Language Use*, Cambridge: Cambridge University Press.

Chatellier, H. (2016), Nivellement et contre-nivellement phonologique à Manchester : étude de corpus dans le cadre du projet PAC-LVTI, PhD dissertation, Toulouse, Université Toulouse Jean Jaurès, France.

Cruttenden, A. (2014), *Gimson's Pronunciation of English*, 8th edn, London and New York: Routledge.

Durand, J. and A. Przewozny (2015), 'La variation et le programme PAC : phonologie de l'anglais contemporain', in I. Brulard, P. Carr and J. Durand (eds), *La prononciation de l'anglais contemporain dans le monde : variation et structure*, Toulouse: Presses Universitaires du Midi, pp. 55–91.

Ferragne, E. and F. Pellegrino (2010), 'Formant frequencies of vowels in 13 accents of the British Isles', *Journal of the International Phonetic Association* 40(01), 1–34.

Fridland, V. (2008), 'Patterns of /uw/, /ʊ/ and /ow/ fronting in Reno, Nevada', *American Speech* 83(4), 432–454.

Haddican, B., P. Foulkes, V. Hughes and H. Richards (2013), 'Interaction of social and linguistic constraints on two vowel changes in northern England', *Language Variation and Change* 25(3), 371–403.

Kerswill, P. (2003), 'Dialect levelling and geographical diffusion in British English', in D. Britain and J. Cheshire (eds), *Social Dialectology: In Honour of Peter Trudgill*, Amsterdam: John Benjamins, pp. 223–243.

Labov, W. (1999), *Principles of Linguistic Change. Volume 1: Internal Factors*, Oxford: Blackwell.

Llamas, C. (2007), '"A place between places": Language and identities in a border town', *Language in Society*, 36(4), 579–604.

Lobanov, B. M. (1971), 'Classification of Russian vowels spoken by different speakers', *Journal of the Acoustical Society of America* 49(2B), 606–608.

Montgomery, C. (2006), Northern English dialects: a perceptual approach, PhD dissertation, University of Sheffield, England.

Montgomery, C. (2012), 'The effect of proximity in perceptual dialectology', *Journal of Sociolinguistics* 16(5), 638–668.

Office for National Statistics (2012), 2011 Census – population and household estimates for England and Wales, March 2011, retrieved 16 July 2012 from http://webarchive.nationalarchives.gov.uk/20160105160709/http://www.ons.gov.uk/ons/dcp171778_270487.pdf (accessed 3 February 2016).

Pierrehumbert, J. B. (2006), 'The next toolkit', *Journal of Phonetics* 34, 516–530.

R Core Team (2016), *R: A Language and Environment for Statistical Computing*, Vienna: R Foundation for Statistical Computing, http://www.Rproject.org/

Trudgill, P. (1986), *Dialects in Contact*, Oxford: Blackwell.

Trudgill, P. (1999), *The Dialects of England*, 2nd edn, Oxford: Blackwell.

Trudgill, P. (2001), 'Received pronunciation: sociolinguistic aspects', *Studia Anglica Posnaniensia* 36, 3–13.

Watt, D. (1998), *Variation and Change in the Vowel System of Tyneside English*, PhD dissertation, Newcastle: University of Newcastle, England.

Watt, D. (2002), '"I don't speak with a Geordie accent, I speak, like, the northern accent": contact-induced levelling in the Tyneside vowel system', *Journal of Sociolinguistics* 6(1), 44–64.

Wells, J. C. (1982), *Accents of English*, 3 vols, Cambridge: Cambridge University Press.

Williams, A. and P. Kerswill (1999), 'Dialect levelling: change and continuity in Milton Keynes, Reading and Hull', in P. Foulkes and G. Docherty (eds), *Urban Voices: Accent Studies in the British Isles*, London: Arnold, pp. 141–162.

# 11

# A Study of Rhoticity in Boston: Results from a PAC Survey

*Sylvain Navarro*

## Overview

The English spoken in Boston has long been characterised by non-rhoticity, but a gradual return to rhoticity has been observed over the last few decades (Wells 1982; Wolfram and Shiling-Estes 2006; Staun 2010). However, a renewal of the empirical data and discussions seems much needed as only few recent studies have offered systematic analyses of rhoticity in the region (Nagy and Roberts 2004; Irwin and Nagy 2007; Nagy and Irwin 2010).

In this chapter, we wish to discuss the results of a survey conducted in Boston within the PAC programme (Durand and Przewozny 2012; Brulard et al. 2015). We briefly describe our post-Labovian approach to data collection as well as our annotation and coding method using Praat and Dolmen for the extraction of the coding information. Our data have been analysed auditorily and an /r/ coding system has been implemented for ten speakers who showed variable rhoticity (the remaining three showing stable non-rhoticity) amounting to a total of 3,050 tokens. This coding system takes into account factors such as the position of /r/ within the syllable (onset or coda) and its phonological environment, as well as the stress level and quality of the pre-/r/ vowel for coda-/r/.

From a quantitative standpoint, our results show that rhoticity in Boston is highly variable, with individual rates of coda-/r/ realisation ranging from 23 per cent to 93 per cent, and it seems register-sensitive since wordlists yield higher rates of realisation than spontaneous speech tasks. Rhoticity is also more frequent in final position than in pre-consonantal position which echoes the classical findings of Labov (1966) in New York City. Stress proves to be a relevant factor since the frequency of realisation of coda-/r/ increases with the level of stress of the syllable. Our analyses of pre-/r/ vowels are in line with the results of Irwin and Nagy (2007) as we find words of the NURSE lexical set to favour /r/ realisation dramatically (99 per cent) while other vowels yield results around 65 per cent, with the exception of schwa whose unstressed status disfavours /r/ realisation.

Although we have not investigated r-intrusion systematically in variably rhotic Bostonian speakers, we have found a few cases of intrusive 'r' in the connected speech tasks of our protocol. Since r-intrusion usually does not appear in rhotic systems, we argue that these occurrences point to an underlyingly non-rhotic system. We thus hypothesise that the Bostonian variety is indeed undergoing a shift towards rhoticity as a prestige feature, with speakers who favour coda-/r/ in monitored registers and speakers for whom the change towards a rhotic system is complete.

## Introduction

Boston is a remarkable city in many regards. Historically, it is both one of the earliest British colonies in North America and the cradle of the American Revolution. Linguistically, it has long been influenced by the speech of southern England and continued to imitate some of its accent features even after the independence of the USA.

Boston was founded in 1630 by Puritan colonists from England who were hoping to establish a colony in which their moral and religious values would be strictly upheld. Boston was one of the first permanent British settlements in North America after Jamestown and Plymouth, respectively founded in 1607 and 1620. The city was named after the English town of Boston, Lincolnshire which was home to many of the first colonists. In 1692, Boston was unified with the neighbouring provinces of Plymouth, Maine, New Brunswick and Nova Scotia as well as the islands of Martha's Vineyard and Nantucket, forming the new province of Massachusetts Bay. Up until 1750, Boston was the largest, most populated and most prosperous city in North America, and exerted a great cultural influence over the other North American colonies. The economic and political links between Boston and England remained strong thanks to the constant arrival of new settlers from Great Britain, but in the second half of the eighteenth century, Boston started to assert its own identity and to confront the authority of the Crown of England. The Boston Tea Party in 1774 and the battles of Lexington and Concord in April 1775 marked the beginning of the American Revolution which drew to a close with the signing of the Treaty of Paris in 1783 and the official recognition of the independence of the colonies. Boston's heritage is thus American and British, and this duality is reflected in its speech.

The English spoken in Boston, although typically American in many respects, has indeed long been characterised by a number of features which are shared by southern British speakers. These features include the presence of a 'broad a' in BATH words (that is a more open and retracted vowel than the /æ/ of TRAP) and non-rhoticity. There is still no consensus on the origins of Boston's non-rhoticity. Some specialists (Wells 1982; Staun 2010: 290) argue that the de-rhoticisation of Southern British English started after 1750 and that Boston (as well as other areas of the Northeastern Seaboard) became non-rhotic through the imitation of the southern British practice. Others (Kurath 1928; Kytö 2004; McMahon 2000) support the hypothesis that the south-eastern counties of England (which were home to many of the early settlers) were already non-rhotic in the early seventeenth century and that the first settlers brought r-less forms to New England. A variationist explanation is provided by Downes (1998: 158) which reconciles the two hypotheses:

> [i]f we accept a late date r-lessness as a prestige feature in southern England, any r-variability of the earliest coastal colonial English would have been at least confirmed towards continuing r-loss by its status in England. It would have been mobile persons of the travelled upper strata of American urban and plantation society who would have been the force behind this diffusion.

A full description of /r/ variation in the USA is far beyond the goals of this contribution, but it is essential at this point to recall that the standard accent in the USA, namely General American, is a fully rhotic variety of English.

Consequently, descriptions of Boston English have traditionally mentioned non-rhoticity as one of the most striking features of this variety. For instance, Wolfram and Shiling-Estes (2006: 106–107) describe the region surrounding Boston as follows: 'To this day, Eastern New England survives as an r-less island in the midst of a sea of r-fullness.' According to Staun (2010: 290), 'Eastern New England is the only consistently non-rhotic dialect in North America.' While useful for pedagogical purposes, these descriptions seem to indicate that non-rhoticity is ubiquitous and consistent in the region, which is a bit misleading. Indeed, as early as 1967, Parslow, in his doctoral thesis, describes the return of coda-/r/ in Boston: '[O]f all present phonological developments in the Boston dialect the most apparent is the re-introduction of r-timbre in vocalic nuclei' (1967: 127). He notes that it is the central vowel of NURSE words which first favours the return of coda-/r/. Wells confirms this observation and underlines the fact that the Bostonian pronunciation has lost the prestige it once enjoyed: '[F]ar from continuing as a centre for the dissemination of non-rhotic pronunciation, [Boston] is itself becoming rhotic' (1982: 521). More recently, Irwin and Nagy (2007, 2010) have provided quantitative data which help determine the factors conditioning rhoticity in Boston. Their most recent work (2010) is based on the analysis of fifty-five speakers from eastern New England (Boston and New Hampshire). It shows that the reintroduction of rhoticity entails a progressive and uneven return of 'r' in various phonological environments. Besides, this reintroduction of coda-/r/ does not affect the population in a homogeneous way. They comment: 'No speaker was either categorically r-ful or categorically r-less, and thus no social group was categorically r-ful or r-less' (2010: 254). Individual frequencies of coda-/r/ realisation range from 5 per cent to 92 per cent with an average of 53 per cent. They identify the age of the speakers as a relevant factor since younger speakers produce more coda-/r/ than older generations, and they stress the importance of the speakers' socio-professional situations. They appeal to the notion of a linguistic marketplace (*marché linguistique*, Bourdieu 1982) which seeks to evaluate the importance of language use in the various broad socio-professional categories. Thus, speakers who hold a bureaucratic, managerial or executive position are pressured to exhibit a more controlled and normative use of the language, close to the General American standard, hence more rhotic. Conversely, speakers with a lower-skilled job tend to use a more 'local' pronunciation, which in the case of Boston involves non-rhoticity. Irwin and Nagy also point out the importance of a number of linguistic factors such as pre-/r/ vowel quality and phonological environment. They confirm Parslow's (1967) observation that the vowel which favours coda-/r/ realisation the most is that of NURSE, followed in that order by START, SQUARE, CURE, NEAR, FORCE/NORTH and finally letter whose unstressed status favours /r/ vocalisation. They also find coda-/r/ realisation to be more frequent in final pre-vocalic (linking-r context) and prepausal positions than in pre-consonantal position. Like most non-rhotic varieties (except those of the south of the USA, see Bailey 1969), typical Boston English is characterised by the presence of supposedly categorical r-sandhi in linking ('store[r] is') and intrusive ('law[r] is') contexts (McCarthy 1991, 1993; Uffman 2007). However, Irwin and Nagy's analysis shows that linking-r is in fact a variable process whose frequency of realisation is 74 per cent. Let us also acknowledge a phenomenon of hypercorrection known as hyper-rhoticity (Britton 2007) which leads certain speakers, notably those with variable rhoticity, to pronounce a non-etymological 'r' outside of intrusion contexts, as in 'cough' [kɒɹf] (by analogy with 'wharf'), 'dog' [dɒɹg] or 'pizza' [piːtsəɹ]. Parslow (1967) found that a third of the informants in his sample had occurrences of hyper-rhotic pronunciations but Irwin and Nagy (2007, 2010) do not mention any hyper-rhoticity. As far as our data are concerned, we can already mention that all the realised non-etymological 'r' cases appear in sandhi contexts (r-intrusion).

## Methodology

### PAC Boston Survey

The data we analyse in this chapter have been collected within the PAC programme (La Phonologie de l'Anglais Contemporain : usages, variétés et structure, see the introduction to this volume). The PAC protocol is based on the recording of five tasks, including the reading of two wordlists and a text as well as a formal conversation conducted by the fieldworker and an informal conversation between the informant and a friend or family member. This protocol is designed to observe potential stylistic variation on a continuum ranging from a highly monitored register (reading tasks) to a more natural and spontaneous register (informal conversation). We also go beyond standard sociolinguistic practice by filling out a detailed individual form which provides us with valuable sociolinguistic information about the informant's background (education, professional status, ethnicity, proficiency in other languages, and so forth).

Fieldwork for this corpus was carried out in two consecutive phases: eight speakers were recorded in February 2009 by Cécile Viollain (Viollain 2010) and seven more were recorded in October 2009 by Cécile Viollain and Sylvain Navarro. We kept thirteen out of the fifteen informants as two of them failed to complete the entirety of the PAC protocol. There were five women and eight men who could be split into three age groups: 19–26 years old (mostly students), 30–49 years old, and

53–67 years old. Various socio-professional categories are represented from working class to upper-middle class. It should be noted that some of the informal conversations had to be carried out with the fieldworker rather than a friend or relative. All our informants were born, grew up and lived most of their life in the Greater Boston area. We also want to mention that three of the speakers, who showed stable non-rhoticity, have been coded for r-sandhi (see Durand et al. 2014, 2015) and have not been included in the present analysis of variable rhoticity.

*Data Annotation Method*

As is required within the PAC programme we have created a baseline of standard orthographic transcription using Praat (Boersma 2014; Boersma and Weenink 2018) for all five tasks of the protocol. The reading tasks were transcribed in their entirety and five to ten minutes of each conversation were also transcribed.[1]

The tier of orthographic transcription was then duplicated onto a second tier to carry the auditory coding information. PAC is a large decentralised research programme and we are committed to a cumulative approach to research. That is why the basic coding system for rhoticity, which is common to all surveys exhibiting variable rhoticity, has been designed to provide a first scanning of the data and minimise theoretical preconceptions. Our system is largely inspired by those implemented within the PFC programme (Phonologie du Français Contemporain, see Durand et al. 2003, 2009). It must be readable and understandable by non-specialists of phonology and therefore it does not take too many details into account, such as vowel quality (which requires an analysis of the vowel system of the variety under study) and level of stress of the syllable (given the lack of universal agreement among specialists on the relative stress properties of words within the speech chain). However, each individual researcher is encouraged to integrate further parameters by enriching this basic coding system on yet another tier. It is this method that has been followed for the present work. We will thus present the basic coding system for rhoticity as well as the more detailed system we have implemented. The coding information was extracted using Dolmen (Eychenne and Paternostro 2016) which offers a specific PAC mode that takes into account the metadata (survey, speaker ID, task) contained in the file names. The table generated by Dolmen was then exploited in R studio.

The basic coding system for variable rhoticity in (1) aims at accounting for the presence vs. absence of /r/ (Field 1), its position within the syllable (Field 2), and its phonological and morphosyntactic environment (Fields 3 and 4). It consists of a series of digits inserted immediately after the <r> in the duplicated tier of orthographic transcription.

(1) PAC coding system for variable rhoticity
Field 1 (presence vs. absence of /r/)
0: /r/ non-realised
1: /r/ realised
2: /r/ uncertain realisation

Field 2 (position within the syllable)
1: /r/ in an onset
2: /r/ in a rhyme
Field 3 (for /r/ in rhyme position)
1: /r/ followed by word boundary # (/r/ is word-final)
2: /r/ followed by $C_{1-n}$ (e.g. 'part', 'stormed')
3: /r/ followed by $C_{1-n}$ V (e.g. 'party', 'stormy')
Field 4 (if 1 in field 3)
1: _#V (next word is vowel-initial, e.g. 'far out')
2: _#C (next word is consonant-initial, e.g. 'far from')
3: _## rhythmic boundary/pause

Although /r/ is systematically pronounced in onset position in most varieties of English, some southern accents in the USA or dialects such as African American Vernacular English (AAVE) may delete intervocalic /r/ (Wells 1982: 544) in non-foot-initial position and our coding system must be able to account for such deletion. Besides, as the location of non-pre-vocalic /r/ within the syllable is theory-dependent (some authors such as Harris (1994) place it in the nucleus rather than in the coda), we chose the term 'rhyme' rather than 'coda' in order to remain as neutral as possible.

Let us provide a few examples. The word 'r11ed' is coded <r11> since /r/ is realised in onset position, while the word 'par123ty', pronounced [pɑɹi] receives <r123> as /r/ is realised in a rhyme and is followed by a consonant and a vowel. In the sequence 'Wher1211e is my br11other0213?' pronounced [wɛɹizmaɪbɹʌðə], the /r/ of 'Where' is realised in final position before a vowel-initial word, the first /r/ of 'brother' is realised in an onset and the second /r/ is non-realised in final position before a rhythmic boundary.

It has been known since Parslow (1967) that words belonging to the NURSE lexical set have been at the forefront of the return to rhoticity in Boston (and other varieties, see Feagin (1990) for a similar analysis of southern USA accents) so it seemed essential for us to account for the quality of the pre-coda-/r/ vowels. In order to do so, we added an extra field to our coding scheme. The lexical set coding in (2) follows Irwin and Nagy (2007, 2010) in grouping NORTH and FORCE together.[2]

(2) Extra coding field: Pre-r vowel
1: [ə] lettER
2: [ɜ:] NURSE
3: [ɪə] NEAR
4: [ɛə] SQUARE
5: [aː~ ɑː] START
6: [ɒ~oə~ɔ:] NORTH/FORCE
7: [ʊə] CURE

We also wanted to account for the level of stress of the syllable as this factor has also been shown to influence coda-/r/ realisation (Irwin and Nagy 2007). We therefore added another coding field split into three large and consensual categories (3).

(3) Extra field of coding: level of stress
1: syllable is tonic (nuclear stress, e.g. 'Give this to **Ar**nold')
2: syllable is stressed (primary or secondary stress, e.g. '**More** people attend every year')
3: syllable is unstressed (e.g. 'He's very **ar**ticulate or She's my sis**ter**')

Such a coding scheme is necessarily subjective to some extent, but in the absence of absôlute consensus on the stress properties of connected speech, we believe that this approach will allow us to assess the influence of stress on the realisation of coda-/r/ in Boston. It should also be noted that the <3> index (for unstressed syllable) in the case of a pre-/r/ /ə/ is redundant. However, the semi-automatic extraction of the coding information requires that we keep a consistent number of digits in each coding expression.

## Results

### Rhoticity across the Reading and Conversational Tasks

The various tasks of the PAC protocol usually allow us to observe different stylistic registers of speech, from the most monitored in the wordlists to the most spontaneous in the informal conversation. We have thus measured the frequency of realisation of coda-/r/ in the various tasks. Figure 11.1 below shows the frequency of realised coda-/r/ for each speaker in each task.

The first conclusion to be drawn from Figure 11.1 is that rhoticity is variable across speakers, with individual rates of rhoticity (for all tasks) ranging from 23 per cent for PM1 to 93 per cent for ED1, with a mean of 62 per cent for the 3,050 coded tokens. These results suggest that the hypothesis of a return to rhoticity in Boston is valid. The speakers in Figure 11.1 have been ranked according to their ascending ages yet we are conscious that the limited size of our corpus does not allow for an apparent time analysis.

Wordlists clearly appear to be the most productive tasks with a mean 77 per cent of realised coda-/r/, and the difference between the two wordlists is not significant (p > 0.05). While performing this task, speakers pay extra attention to the individual items they are reading and tend to make an effort to pronounce every <r> which is present orthographically. This effort is particularly obvious in the production of several informants who vocalise /r/ when pronouncing the index numbers of the wordlists (as required by the PAC protocol) but realise /r/ in the item itself; for instance, FB1: '45 bard' [fɔːɾifaɪv baːɹd], '54 father' [fɪftifɔː faːðəɹ], or GA1: '74 fair' [sɛvəntifɔː fɛɹ], '94 start' [naɪnɾifɔː stɑːɹt]. Indeed, these informants seem to focus their attention on the pronunciation of the items only and provide us with a much more spontaneous

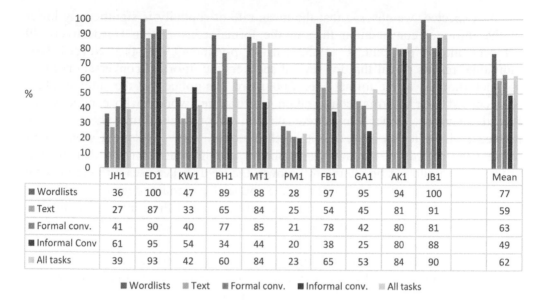

| | JH1 | ED1 | KW1 | BH1 | MT1 | PM1 | FB1 | GA1 | AK1 | JB1 | | Mean |
|---|---|---|---|---|---|---|---|---|---|---|---|---|
| ■ Wordlists | 36 | 100 | 47 | 89 | 88 | 28 | 97 | 95 | 94 | 100 | | 77 |
| ■ Text | 27 | 87 | 33 | 65 | 84 | 25 | 54 | 45 | 81 | 91 | | 59 |
| ■ Formal conv. | 41 | 90 | 40 | 77 | 85 | 21 | 78 | 42 | 80 | 81 | | 63 |
| ■ Informal Conv | 61 | 95 | 54 | 34 | 44 | 20 | 38 | 25 | 80 | 88 | | 49 |
| ■ All tasks | 39 | 93 | 42 | 60 | 84 | 23 | 65 | 53 | 84 | 90 | | 62 |

■ Wordlists  ■ Text  ■ Formal conv.  ■ Informal conv.  ■ All tasks

Figure 11.1 Individual frequencies (%) of realised coda-/r/ in each task

pronunciation of the index numbers. This behaviour suggests that Boston speakers are aware of the prestige of the rhotic norm and that they try to conform to it under circumstances in which they can monitor their linguistic production. The concerns shared by some of the informants that our work might contribute to tarnishing the image of the r-less Boston accent seem to indicate that non-rhoticity has become a stigmatising feature that receives negative evaluations.

As for the text, it yields a mean 59 per cent of realised coda-/r/, that is to say below the overall mean for all tasks combined. For six out of the ten speakers, the rate of rhoticity is lower in the text than in the formal conversation (as reflected in the mean values), which is rather unexpected insofar as the text provides the informants with orthographic cues that should help them realise coda-/r/. These lower frequencies can partially be explained by the fact that the frequency of realised coda-/r/ in sandhi contexts (linking-r) is lower in the text than in conversations (81 per cent vs. 90 per cent). In an effort to provide a more articulate rendering of the text, the speakers tend to isolate words and to adopt a slower delivery, yielding lower rates of realised linking-r. However, if we remove the linking-r contexts from our data, we still observe a lower mean rate of rhoticity in the text than in the formal conversation. This may be due to the fact that the informants focus more on overall fluency than on the pronunciation of individual segments. Another reason may be that some speakers are tempted to 'give the fieldworkers what they came for' and tend to produce a more stereotypical non-rhotic Boston accent. We will not retain the latter hypothesis as the most relevant, but we will see below (in the section 'Elements of sociolinguistic analysis') with the case of JT1, a non-rhotic speaker who produces no r-sandhi, that using a Boston accent can amount to an identity statement.

As expected, we observe that the mean rate of rhoticity is significantly lower in the informal conversation than in the formal conversation (respectively 49 per cent and 63 per cent, $\chi^2 = 19.521$, df = 1, p-value = 9.948e-06). Nevertheless, individual results reveal that for several speakers the informal conversation yields as much rhoticity as the formal one, if not more. We notice that the latter speakers all recorded their informal conversation with the fieldworker who conducted the formal interview. Under such circumstances, although the atmosphere is more relaxed and the topics more casual in the informal conversation, it seems logical that the register of the informants should remain consistent and that their /r/ production should not be altered. Moreover, the fieldworker uses a rhotic General American-like accent which might have induced a certain degree of phonetic convergence. On the other hand, speakers who recorded their informal conversations in optimal conditions (with one or two friends/relatives in the absence of the fieldworker) all exhibit a lower degree of rhoticity in the informal conversation. Thus FB1, GA1, BH1 and MT1 display a 35 per cent decrease in rhoticity, on average, between the two tasks. These results suggest that our informants adapt their coda-/r/ production to the formality of the situation more or less consciously and that they are aware of the prestige of the rhotic norm. Certain cues suggest that in spite of variable rhoticity, the individual grammar of some speakers is characterised by underlying non-rhoticity. FB1 is a convincing example since he produces 78 per cent of coda-/r/ in the formal conversation and 38 per cent in the informal conversation. More importantly, he produces a few occurrences of r-intrusion such as 'draw[ɹ]ing around', 'botega[ɹ] and'. There is general consensus among specialists (Giegerich 1999; Hay and Sudbury 2005; Sóskuthy 2009) that r-intrusion is a phenomenon that emerges by analogy with linking-r in systems that are losing rhoticity or are indeed non-rhotic (however, see Harris 1994 for an alternative modelling of the emergence of r-intrusion). Therefore, it seems reasonable to think that for some Boston speakers, rhoticity is a superposed feature (Becker 2014), and that the discrepancy we observe between formal and informal registers involves the insertion of coda-[ɹ] over a low-rhoticity underlying system rather than the deletion of underlying coda-/r/.

*Influence of pre-/r/ Vowel Quality*

The phonetic quality of the pre-/r/ vowel is often cited as the most influential factor in the conditioning of coda-/r/ pronunciation in Boston (and other varieties with variable rhoticity). As early as 1967, Parslow notices that /r/ is more frequently realised when preceded by a central vowel. More recent work by Irwin and Nagy (2007: 141–142) confirms the significance of this factor. Our data seem to conform to Irwin and Nagy's findings as can be seen in Figure 11.2, where the frequency of realised coda-/r/ for each lexical set is displayed. Figure 11.2 also displays the latter frequencies with the exception of sandhi environments as it can be argued that coda-/r/ is resyllabified in onset position in such cases (see section 'Phonological and morphosyntactic environment' below).

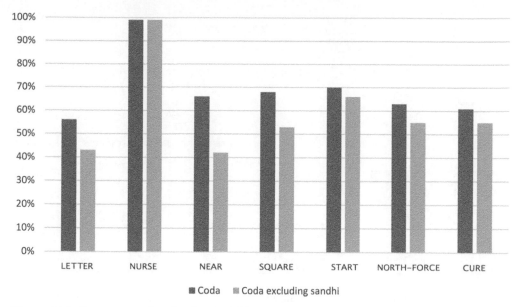

Figure 11.2 Frequency of realised coda-/r/ for each lexical set (for all speakers in all tasks)

Figure 11.2 clearly confirms that NURSE favours the realisation of coda-/r/. Out of 414 coded occurrences, only one is not realised in a spontaneous speech task (JH1: 'I know for sure that'). In other words, /r/ is categorically realised after the stressed central vowel /ɜː/. This tendency corroborates the claim that /ə/ and /r/ share a partially common featural content or, in a unary feature-based framework, that there is an element of centrality within the representation of English approximant /r/ (Harris 1994; Gick 1999, 2000). Irwin and Nagy (2007: 141) also comment on the impact of a following tautosyllabic consonant (they use the lexical set NURSE for closed syllables vs. FUR for open syllables). Since our coding scheme takes into account _/r/## vs. _/r/ $C_{1-n}$# vs. _/r/$C_{1-n}$V, we could theoretically establish this distinction as well. However, this calculation is not relevant for NURSE insofar as our data only provide us with a single occurrence of non- realised /r/ after final /ɜː/.

As can be seen in the conditional inference tree (hereafter CIT; Hothorn et al. 2006) in Figure 11.3, the trigger effect of NURSE on the realisation of coda-/r/ is statistically significant (p-value <0.001) whereas the letTER lexical set has a significantly disfavouring effect on coda-/r/ realisation (p-value <0.001). The latter result was expected due to the unstressed nature of the corresponding syllables. Nonetheless, it must be taken cautiously. As we will see (in section 'Phonological and morphosyntactic environment' below), in some environments the central quality of schwa (similar to that of /ɜː/) may in fact have more effect on coda-/r/ realisation than its lack of prominence.

The remaining lexical sets show relatively similar frequencies. Contrary to Irwin and Nagy (2007: 141), our data do not seem to involve a statistically higher frequency of coda-/r/ realisation after back vowels than after front vowels. If it were the case,

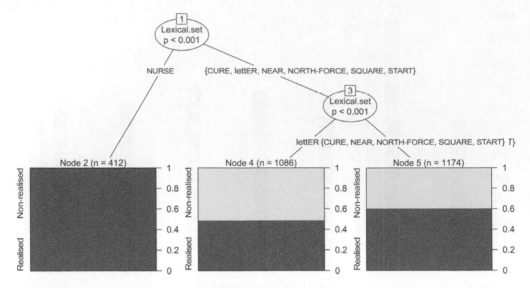

Figure 11.3 Conditional inference tree showing the influence of the lexical set on coda-/r/ realisation

we would see a further branching of our CIT separating NEAR and SQUARE, on the one hand, and START, NORTH-FORCE and CURE, on the other. We observe the same results whether we include or exclude linking-r cases.

*Influence of Stress*

The influence of the degree of stress on the realisation of coda-/r/ is not really taken into account in the work of Irwin and Nagy (2007, 2010). They do oppose full vowels and schwa in their coding but they do not offer a systematic analysis of stress. In comparing the frequencies of realisation of coda-/r/ after /ə/ and /ɜː/ ('stressed schwa'), they conclude that 'The clear effect of stressed syllables favouring (r-1) may be readily explained by the greater articulatory effort and duration in stressed syllables' (Nagy and Irwin 2010: 267). This conclusion is supported by Piercy's (2012: 82) study of partially rhotic speakers from Dorset in West Country England.

Figure 11.4 displays the frequencies of realisation of coda-/r/ (including and excluding linking-r contexts) for each of the three stress categories defined in (3), based on all environments, for all speakers in all tasks. It confirms that coda-/r/ realisation increases proportionally with the degree of stress of the syllable. Another CIT illustrates that the effect of stress is significant (p-value <0.001).

According to Nagy and Irwin (2010: 267), who compare the results of their Boston survey to those obtained in other American locations (New York, Philadelphia, Memphis, Davenport and Anniston), this effect is universal throughout rhotic and variably rhotic varieties. Our data are in line with those observations since the two speakers in our sample whose rhoticity is the most stable also conform to the overall pattern in Figure 11.4.

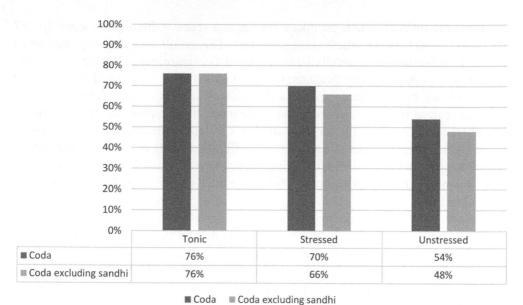

Figure 11.4 Frequency of realised coda-/r/ for each degree of stress (for all speakers in all tasks)

## Phonological and Morphosyntactic Environment

The coding scheme we have implemented (see section 'Data annotation method' above) provides us with information on the phonological and morphosyntactic environment of coda-/r/. Table 11.1 displays the mean frequencies of coda-/r/ realisation for all speakers in each of the environments described in (1). We have grouped together the wordlists and the connected speech tasks (text and conversations) for better readability.

Unsurprisingly, we first notice that, in all applicable contexts, rates of rhoticity are higher in wordlists than in all the connected speech tasks combined. As mentioned above (see section 'Rhoticity across the reading and conversational tasks'), wordlist reading is a highly monitored task in which speakers tend to exploit orthographic cues to pronounce every orthographic <r> and therefore target the prestige rhotic norm.

Table 11.1 Rate of coda-/r/ realisation in various phonological and morphosyntactic environments

|  | Word-medial | | Word-final | | | |
|---|---|---|---|---|---|---|
|  | $/r/C_{1-n}\#$ | $/r/C_{1-n}V$ | $/r/\#\_V$ | $/r/\#\_C$ | $/r/\#\#$ | Mean |
| Wordlists | 80% | 63% | NA | NA | 78% | 78% |
| Connected speech | 66% | 58% | 87% | 43% | 69% | 61% |

The environment which produces the highest score is final pre-vocalic /r/ (87 per cent), in other words, the linking-r context. This result was also expected since linking-r realisation has generally been described as categorical in Boston (McCarthy 1991, 1993). Note, however, that more recent studies such as Nagy and Irwin's (2010) reveal that linking-r is in fact variable, although it clearly constitutes the environment in which realisation of coda-/r/ is favoured the most. In such contexts, the pronunciation of [ɹ] is favoured by the fact that final /r/ can be resyllabified in onset position of the rightmost word. The surface syllabic affiliation of /r/ in linking-r contexts is subject to some debate, but its acoustic properties as well as its rhythmic conditioning point to ambisyllabicity (McCarthy 1993; Bermudez-Otero 2011; Viollain, Navarro and Durand, this volume).

Before a rhythmic boundary or pause (/r/##), /r/ is realised in 69 per cent of cases in connected speech, which is a higher rate than in all remaining contexts. Our initial hypothesis was that stress might have an influence in this particular environment insofar as the tone-unit final position, for which the LLI rule often applies, increases chances for the involved syllables to have tonic stress. A chi-square test confirms the effect of stress on the realisation of coda-/r/ in this environment ($\chi^2 = 16.673$, df=2, p-value=0.0002396) but, quite unexpectedly, the CIT (Figure 11.5) that we have built indicates that the 'unstressed' category actually favours coda-/r/ realisation.

The latter result seems rather counter-intuitive insofar as the 'unstressed' category clearly disfavours coda-/r/ in other environments. However, we notice that 140 of the 149 unstressed syllables in /r/## correspond to schwa (lettER), and in this particular context schwa massively favours the realisation of /r/ (112/140=80 per cent) compared with other vowels. Therefore, a potential explanation is that the final schwa of a word situated in a prosodically strong position may receive added

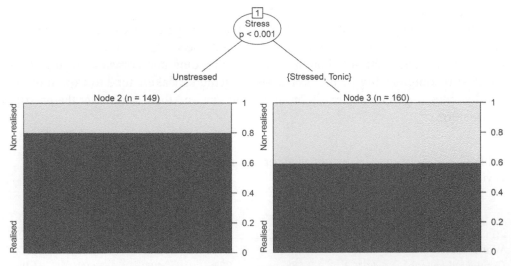

Figure 11.5 Conditional inference tree showing the influence of stress on coda-/r/ realisation

articulatory effort and length, which may in turn draw the vowel closer to NURSE and thus promote final /r/ realisation.

Rhoticity drops to 43 per cent when final /r/ is followed by a consonant-initial word (/r/#_C) which is the least productive environment in our corpus. Interestingly, this frequency of realisation of a pre-consonantal /r/ is significantly lower (p-value <.00001) across a word boundary than it is within words (63 per cent).

At the lexical level (i.e. in word-medial position), we observe a significant difference in coda-/r/ realisation between words in which /r/ is followed by one or more consonant(s) (e.g. 'park', 'stormed'; 80 per cent in wordlists and 66 per cent in connected speech) and words in which /r/ is followed by one or more consonant(s) and a vowel (e.g. 'party', 'Berklee'; 63 per cent in wordlists and 58 per cent in connected speech). This difference is significant both in wordlist reading ($\chi^2 = 6.8986$, df = 1, p-value = 0.008626) and in connected speech ($\chi^2 = 5.4538$, df = 1, p-value = 0.01953).

At this point we have to acknowledge a limitation in our coding system as the latter does not indicate the syllabic affiliation of post-rhotic consonants. However, this limitation is in accordance with the approach defended by the PAC programme which seeks to reduce pre-theoretical assumptions to a minimum in designing the annotation system. Accounting for the hetero- or tautosyllabicity of these consonants would indeed require the coder to adopt a specific theory of syllabification based on the Maximal Onset principle (MaxOnset, Pulgram 1970; Selkirk 1982) or Maximum Coda (Wells 2008), for instance.

Nevertheless, if we examine our data under the MaxOnset hypothesis, we find that in most cases, when word-medial coda-/r/ is followed by one or more consonants and a vowel (or syllabic consonant), the post-rhotic consonants can be assigned to the onset position (e.g. 'par.ty', 'ear.thy', 'Ber.klee', 'thir.sty', etc.). We do find a few occurrences of words in which a post-rhotic consonant cluster does not constitute a possible English onset, but they either involve morphologically complex words (e.g. 'apartment', 'department', 'partly', 'regardless') or compounds (e.g. 'force-feed', 'forthcoming', 'Thursday', 'Georgetown'). This amounts to saying that, considering the phonotactics of English, our coding strategy still accounts for hetero- vs. tautosyllabicity of post-rhotic consonants, at least in monomorphemic words. Therefore, we may say that tautosyllabic post-rhotic consonants favour coda-/r/ realisation.

**Elements of Sociolinguistic Analysis**

We would like to complement this phonological analysis of rhoticity in Boston by looking at some of the extra-linguistic factors that may affect coda-/r/ realisation. We have already established earlier that the various tasks of the PAC protocol give access to differently monitored language registers and we have argued that rhoticity generally increases with the formality of the situation.

The age and gender of the speakers have also been mentioned as essential conditioning factors (Irwin and Nagy 2007, 2010). As shown in Figure 11.1 above, ranking our speakers in ascending ages does not reflect any obvious age-based tendency. Our sample is most likely too limited to observe a significant age effect, even after reintroducing the three fully non-rhotic speakers. However, we do observe a significant difference between men and women (47 per cent and 52 per cent rhoticity respectively, p-value=0.02839) which, as often mentioned by sociolinguists, shows that women are more likely to lead linguistic change and use more prestige (here rhotic) forms (Labov 2001).

The information sheets which are standardly filled out for each of the PAC informants provide us with more fine-grained information on the individual sociolinguistic trajectories of the speakers. They notably reflect how educational and cultural factors may influence usage. For instance, among the four older speakers in our corpus, two have high individual rates of coda-/r/ realisation (AK1 84 per cent and JB1 90 per cent) and the other two are non-rhotic (DG1 and RK1, not represented in Figure 11.1). Upon inspection of their information sheets, we notice that AK1 describes her education at a Catholic institution as strict on linguistic uses and that JB1 was born in a very cultivated and highly educated family. On the other hand, the non-rhotic speakers both come from working-class families and grew up in blue-collar neighbourhoods. Such results should be expected as local forms are usually more common in lower socio-economic classes (Wells 1982: 14). The speakers' levels of education also usually correlate with their usages but our data do not reveal any correlation between high frequency of coda-/r/ realisation and advanced degrees. As a matter of fact, two of the least rhotic speakers in our survey (KW1 47 per cent and PM1 28 per cent) are PhD students. However, both admit to having a strong attachment to the Bostonian culture and identity, notably through a passion for local sports teams.

This discrepancy between a speaker's usage and their theoretical positioning on what Bourdieu (2001: 84–85) calls the linguistic market is particularly obvious in the case of one of our non-rhotic speakers. JT1 is a twenty-five-year-old (at the time of recording) middle-class man who attended a two-year college training programme to work for criminal justice and, given his occupation, would be expected to be a user of General American. Yet, JT1 is fully non-rhotic and takes great pride in this pronunciation through a company he co-owns which produces t-shirts sporting the slogan 'No R Lifestyle – Not Just an Accent'. As we briefly mentioned (in the section 'Rhoticity across the reading and conversational tasks'), we believe that this non-rhoticity is 'controlled' by JT1 to some extent. Contrary to genuinely non-rhotic speakers, who generally pronounce final /r/ in pre-vocalic contexts (linking-r), this speaker avoids virtually all potential linking-r occurrences (for instance, 'So kick in the door I mean like "what's up"', 'Too bad we couldn't get any color ink', 'The people there are just'). By deleting (more or less consciously) coda-/r/ to reach typical Bostonian non-rhoticity, JT1 also deletes linking-r which is present in genuinely non-rhotic speakers' speech. Thus, it seems that JT1 adopts a militant approach to non-rhoticity which pushes him towards a style where only onset /r/ can be pronounced.

## Conclusion

In this chapter we hope to have given an idea of the range of different results that the corpora of the PAC programme can yield on the quantitative and qualitative levels. While the systematic coding of rhoticity has allowed for a solid analysis of the phonological conditioning of coda-/r/ realisation, the various tasks of the protocol offered an insight into stylistic variation, and the individual information sheets of the informants have helped us bring out complementary sociolinguistic interpretation which was otherwise 'concealed' in our data. Even though our corpus is not extensive in terms of number of speakers, it can yield in-depth analyses that allow statistical work (Viollain and Chatellier 2018).

Notably, we have shown that rhoticity is extremely variable in Boston and that pre-/r/ vowel quality and level of stress are the most relevant factors in the realisation of coda-/r/. The central quality of the NURSE vowel indeed has a dramatic favouring effect on rhoticity, while the unstressed nature of letER hinders the realisation of coda-/r/. However, our data also reveal that in a strong prosodic position, letER in fact significantly favours rhoticity. We believe that the latter finding further supports the claim that /ə/ and (a fortiori) /ɜ:/ share at least some featural content with English approximant /r/, as argued by a number of authors (Harris 1994; McMahon et al. 1994; Gick 1999, 2002; Navarro 2018).

Thanks to the four tasks of the PAC survey protocol and in spite of the limited size of our corpus, we have been able to observe a great amount of stylistic variation. Our results show a clear tendency for Bostonians to increase their level of rhoticity when they have more control over their production and the presence of r-intrusion suggests that rhoticity is a superposed feature, at least for some speakers.

Finally, we have shown that a small but properly devised corpus like PAC Boston can give us some sociolinguistic insight and help us account for atypical linguistic behaviours. The guided interviews and the individual sociolinguistic portraits have revealed that beyond the educational and socio-professional levels of the informants, a strong attachment to the Boston identity and culture seems to correlate with low rhoticity. However, an expansion of this corpus seems necessary if we want to achieve a better social stratification of the data and provide statistically solid results on this aspect.

## Notes

1. For more information on the PAC transcription conventions, see Durand and Przewozny (2015: 79–83).
2. Irwin and Nagy (2007: 139) found no statistical difference in the rate of realisation of /r/ between the NORTH and FORCE lexical sets and combined them into a single category.

## References

Bailey, C. J. N. (1969), 'Introduction to southern states phonetics: chapters 5 and 6', *University of Hawaii Working Papers in Linguistics* 6, 105–203.
Becker, K. (2014), '(r) we there yet? The change to rhoticity in New York City English', *Language Variation and Change* 26(2), 141–168.

Bermúdez-Otero, R. (2011), 'Cyclicity', in M. Oostendorp, C. Ewen, E. Hume and K. Rice (eds), *The Blackwell Companion to Phonology*, vol. 4, 2019–2048, Malden: Wiley-Blackwell.

Boersma, P. (2014), 'The use of Praat in corpus research', in J. Durand, U. Gut and G. Kristoffersen (eds), *The Oxford Handbook of Corpus Phonology*, Oxford: Oxford University Press.

Boersma, P. and D. Weenink (2018), Praat: doing phonetics by computer (Version 6.0.37) [computer program] (retrieved 14 March 2018 from http://www.praat.org/).

Bourdieu, P. (1982), *Ce que parler veut dire : l'économie des échanges linguistiques*, Paris: Fayard.

Bourdieu, P. (2001), *Langage et pouvoir symbolique*, Paris: Seuil.

Britton, D. (2007), 'A history of hyper-rhoticity in English', *English Language and Linguistics* 11, 525–536.

Brulard, I., P. Carr and J. Durand (eds) (2015), *La Prononciation de l'anglais contemporain dans le monde : variation et structure*, Toulouse: Presses Universitaires du Midi.

Downes, W. (1998), *Language and Society*, Cambridge: Cambridge University Press.

Durand, J. and A. Przewozny (2012), 'La phonologie de l'anglais contemporain : usages, variétés et structure', *Revue française de linguistique appliquée* 2012/1, vol. XVII, 25–37.

Durand, J. and A. Przewozny (2015), 'La variation et le programme PAC', in I. Brulard, P. Carr and J. Durand (eds), *La prononciation de l'anglais contemporain dans le monde : variation et structure*, Toulouse: Presses Universitaires du Midi.

Durand, J., B. Laks and C. Lyche (2003), 'Linguistique et variation : quelques réflexions sur la variation phonologique', in E. Delais-Roussarie and J. Durand (eds), *Corpus et Variation en Phonologie du Français*, Toulouse: Presses Universitaires du Midi.

Durand, J., B. Laks and C. Lyche (2009), 'Le projet PFC : une source de données primaires structurées', in J. Durand, B. Laks and C. Lyche (eds), *Phonologie, variation et accents du français*, Paris: Hermès.

Durand, J., S. Navarro and C. Viollain (2014), 'Le "r" de sandhi en anglais : corpus et méthodologie', in C. Soum and A. Coquillon (eds), *La Liaison : Approches Contemporaines*, Berne: Peter Lang.

Durand, J., S. Navarro and C. Viollain (2015), 'R-sandhi in English: how to constrain theoretical approaches', *Global Communication Studies*, vol. 2, World Englishes, Makuhari, Japan: Global Communication Institute, Kanda University of International Studies, pp. 103–132.

Eychenne, J. and R. Paternostro (2016), 'Analyzing transcribed speech with Dolmen', in S. Detey, J. Durand, B. Laks and C. Lyche (eds), *Varieties of Spoken French*, Oxford: Oxford University Press.

Feagin, C. (1990), 'Dynamics of sound change in Southern States English: from r-less to r-ful in three generations', in J. Edmondson, C. Feagin and P. Mühlhäusler (eds), *Development and Diversity: Language Variation across Time and Space: A Festschrift for Charles-James N. Bailey*, Arlington: SIL/University of Texas, pp. 129–146.

Gick, B. (1999), 'A gesture-based account of intrusive consonants in English', *Phonology* 16, 29–54.

Gick, B. (2002), 'The American intrusive l', *American Speech* 77, 167–183.

Giegerich, H. J. (1999), *Lexical Strata in English: Morphological Causes, Phonological Effects*, Cambridge: Cambridge University Press.

Harris, J. (1994), *English Sound Structure*, Oxford: Blackwell.

Hay, J. and A. Sudbury (2005), 'How rhoticity became /r/-sandhi', *Language* 81, 799–823.

Hothorn T., K. Hornik and A. Zeileis (2006), 'Unbiased recursive partitioning: a conditional inference framework', *Journal of Computational and Graphical Statistics* 15(3), 651–674.

Irwin, P. and N. Nagy (2007), 'Bostonians /r/ speaking: a quantitative look at (R) in Boston', Penn Papers in Linguistics, *University of Pennsylvania Working Papers in Linguistics 13(2) Papers from NWAV 35*, 135–147.

Kurath, H. (1928), 'The origin of the dialectal differences in spoken American English', *Modern Philology* 25, 385–395.

Kytö, M. (2004), 'The emergence of American English: evidence from seventeenth-century records in New England', in R. Hickey (ed.), *Legacies of Colonial English*, Cambridge: Cambridge University Press.

Labov, W. (1966), *The Social Stratification of English in New York City*, Washington, DC: Center for Applied Linguistics.

Labov, W. (2001), *Principles of Linguistic Change. Vol. 2. Social Factors*, Oxford: Blackwell.

McCarthy, J. J. (1991), 'Synchronic rule inversion', in L. Sutton, C. Johnson and R. Shields (eds), *Proceedings of the Seventeenth Annual Meeting of the Berkeley Linguistics Society*, Berkeley, CA: Berkeley Linguistics Society, pp. 192–207.

McCarthy, J. J. (1993), 'A case of surface constraint violation', *Canadian Journal of Linguistics* 38, 169–195.

McMahon, A. (2000), *Lexical Phonology and the History of English*, Cambridge: Cambridge University Press.

McMahon, A., P. Foulkes and L. Tollfree (1994), 'Gestural representation and lexical phonology', *Phonology* 11, 277–316.

Nagy, N. and P. Irwin (2010), 'Boston (r): neighbo(r)s nea(r) and fa(r)', *Language Variation and Change* 22, 241–278.

Nagy, N. and J. Roberts (2004), 'New England: phonology', in E. W. Schneider, K. Burridge, B. Kortmann, R. Mesthrie & C. Upton (eds), *A Handbook of Varieties of English*, Berlin: Mouton de Gruyter.

Navarro, S. (2018), 'Rhotics and the derhoticization of English: a dependency phonology analysis', in H. van der Hulst and R. Böhm (eds), *Substance-based Grammar – The (Ongoing) Work of John Anderson*, Amsterdam: John Benjamins.

Parslow, R. (1967), The pronunciation of English in Boston, MA: vowels and consonants, PhD thesis, University of Michigan, Ann Arbor.

Piercy, C. (2012), 'A transatlantic cross-dialectal comparison of non-prevocalic /r/', *University of Pennsylvania Working Papers in Linguistics* 18(2), 77–86.

Pulgram, E. (1970), *Syllable, Word, Nexus, Cursus*, The Hague: Mouton.

Selkirk, E. (1982), 'The syllable', in H. Hulst and N. Smith (eds), *The Structure of Phonological Representations*, Dordrecht: Foris.

Sóskuthy, M. (2009), Why r? An analogical approach to intrusive-r, Master's thesis, University of Budapest.

Staun, J. (2010), *An Introduction to the Pronunciation of North American English*, Odense: University Press of Southern Denmark.

Uffman, C. (2007), 'Intrusive [r] and optimal epenthetic consonants', *Language Sciences* 29, 451–476.

Viollain, C. (2010), Sociophonologie de l'anglais à Boston : Une étude de la rhoticité et de la liaison, Master's thesis, Université de Toulouse 2 Le Mirail.

Viollain, C. and H. Chatellier (2018), 'De petits corpus pour une grande base de données sur l'anglais oral contemporain : quels enjeux à la lumière du programme PAC?' *Corpus* 18 – Les petits corpus.

Wells, J. C. (1982), *Accents of English*, 3 vols, Cambridge: Cambridge University Press.

Wells, J. C. (2008), *Longman Pronunciation Dictionary*, Harlow: Longman.

Wolfram, W. and N. Shiling-Estes (2006), *American English: Dialects and Variation*, Cambridge and Oxford: Basil Blackwell.

# 12

# A Corpus-based Study of /t/ Flapping in American English Broadcast Speech

*Bente Hannisdal*

## Introduction

### Background

Flapping, or tapping, of /t/ involves the realisation of /t/ as a voiced alveolar flap. It is a well-known feature of American English that has been widely discussed in the linguistic literature. Flapping is a highly complex phenomenon, which is potentially influenced by a number of linguistic and extra-linguistic factors (stress, syllabification, phonetic surroundings, morphology, lexical frequency, as well as social and stylistic factors). There is no consensus on the exact conditions for flapping, and there are often inconsistencies in pronunciation dictionaries and other sources with regard to flapping in individual lexical items. One reason for this lack of agreement is the extensive variation in the use of flapping in certain contexts. This chapter explores aspects of this variation and attempts to bring some clarity to the situation by supplying quantitative data on actual usage. The main goal of the study is to estimate the relative frequency of the flap versus the plosive in three variable environments and identify the characteristics of any variation patterns that emerge. A second aim is to suggest possible explanations for the variation or lack of flapping in certain items (many with accentually parallel forms that regularly display flapping) that have not been satisfactorily accounted for in previous works.

American English /t/ flapping has been extensively described and discussed in numerous sources. Many previous accounts are purely theoretical and focus mainly on establishing rules describing the exact phonological conditions under which flapping applies, often by proposing various abstract mechanisms (for example Kahn 1976; Kiparsky 1979; Selkirk 1982; Nespor and Vogel 1986; Jensen 1993; Harris 1994; Davis 2005). Variation in the use of flapping has received less attention. The studies which have an empirical basis typically make use of experimental data, where subjects read wordlists or sentences (for example Zue and Laferriere 1979; Egido and Cooper 1980; Turk 1992; de Jong 1998; Steriade 2000; Riehl 2003; Fukaya and Byrd 2005; Kaplan 2008; Herd et al. 2010; Warner and Tucker 2011). A few studies have used corpora: Patterson and Connine (2001) use the SWITCHBOARD speech database, which is a collection of 2,400 telephone conversations, while Eddington (2006, 2007) and Byrd (1994) collect their data from the TIMIT corpus, where 630 speakers read the same ten sentences. There is thus a certain shortage of large-scale empirical studies looking at naturally occurring speech.

In addition to identifying the linguistic conditions governing the flapping rule, previous work has focused on various aspects of flapping, such as the phonetic outcome of the flapping process (for example de Jong 1998; Fukaya and Byrd 2005), the potential neutralisation with /d/ (for example Malécot and Lloyd 1968; Zue and Laferriere 1979; Turk 1992; Herd et al. 2010), and measuring frequency of usage (for example Zue and Laferriere 1979; Byrd 1994; Patterson and Connine 2001). Most accounts focus on intervocalic /t/ between a stressed and an unstressed syllable, which is the prototypical flapping environment. The present study investigates flapping of /t/ in three environments that have been little investigated from a quantitative perspective: post-nasally (as in 'county'), post-laterally (as in 'guilty'), and between unstressed syllables, the second of which is closed by one or more consonants (as in 'negative', 'competent'). The basis for the analysis is large amounts of speech collected from American news broadcasts.

*The Phonetics of Flapping*

The phonetic result of the flapping process is normally a rapid voiced flick of the tongue tip against the alveolar ridge. The sound is most commonly symbolised as [ɾ] but has also been represented by other symbols (see Bauer et al. 1980; Wells 1982, 2008; Upton et al. 2001; Jones 2011). Most accounts refer to the phenomenon as 'flapping'; some prefer to call it tapping (notably Harris 1994; Jones 2011), while others use the term 't-voicing' (namely Wells 1982, 2008). The question of whether the resulting segment is best described as a tap or a flap has been subject to some discussion (see Picard 1997), and de Jong comments that 'much more work on tongue motion must be done before we can be certain that there is a useful distinction to be made between flaps and taps' (1998: 284). If we follow the definitions provided by Trask (1996) for instance, the typical articulation is a tap, where the tip of the tongue makes a very brief contact with the alveolar ridge before returning to its starting position, while a retroflex flap is used only before or after /r/, as in 'party', 'better' (see also Wells 1982: 251). In the present discussion I will use the term flap(ping) as a collective term for all the lenited voiced realisations of /t/, simply because that seems to be the most commonly used appellation.

A number of studies have investigated the acoustic or articulatory characteristics of flaps (for example Zue and Laferriere 1979; de Jong 1998; Fukaya and Byrd 2005; Warner and Tucker 2011), and they show that flapping is a gradient phonetic process of lenition. Compared to the non-flapped voiceless aspirated [t] the flap typically involves a reduction in duration, decreased articulatory contact, and voicing.

Reported realisations range from a voiced plosive to a vowel-like approximant, with considerable variation in articulatory duration.

*Factors Influencing Flapping*

One of the key issues in the literature on /t/ flapping has been identifying the factors conditioning the appearance of flap versus stop, and this remains one of the most challenging questions in American English phonology. Many accounts focus on establishing the exact linguistic conditions for flapping. However, several previous studies, as well as sheer observations of American English speech, show that there is a considerable amount of variation in the application of the flapping rule. In certain contexts flapping is optional, while in others it seems to be blocked. The following paragraphs give a brief presentation of some of the most important factors that potentially affect the occurrence and frequency of flapping.

Surrounding segments

When it comes to the phonetic contexts for flapping, the accounts vary in the segmental environment they consider relevant. There is general consensus that /t/ flaps intervocalically (including before syllabic /r, l/), as in 'nutty', 'shooting', 'later', 'bottle', and in the environment between /r/ and a vowel, as in 'party', 'hurting'. Some sources also include /n/ in the preceding environment, as in 'plenty' (for example Kenyon 1950; Bronstein 1960; Selkirk 1972; Egido and Cooper 1980), but it should be noted that the phonetic outcome in this context is typically deletion of /t/ and a flapped nasal. When it comes to the possibility of flapping after /l/, scholars are divided. Some descriptions include the post-lateral environment as one of the contexts for flapping of /t/ (notably Kenyon 1950: 127; Bronstein 1960: 74; Selkirk 1972: 197; Bauer et al. 1980: 38; Wells 1982: 251; Spencer 1996: 231; Staun 2010: 76). Others claim that flapping after /l/ is forbidden or restricted to non-standard speech (for instance Harris 1994: 218; Hammond 1997: 12; Vaux 2000: 3; Kreidler 2004: 118; Carr and Honeybone 2007: 134; Kaplan 2008: 5; Jones 2011: xi).

Stress

There is general consensus that flapping is prosodically governed, but there is some disagreement as to exactly how. The most common environment for American English flapping is between a stressed and an unstressed syllable, as in 'city', 'fighting', 'hotter', 'metal'. Zue and Laferriere (1979) refer to this as the 'flapping environment', and some scholars seem to limit the occurrence of flapping to this context (for example Trager 1942; Malécot and Lloyd 1968; Selkirk 1972). However, most researchers observe that flapping also takes place between unstressed syllables, as in 'sanity', 'reality', 'hospital', 'negative' (see Kahn 1976; Zue and Laferriere 1979). The critical part of the environment seems to be the following unstressed vowel, and according to Kahn (1976: 91) any level of stress on the vowel after /t/ will prevent flapping. Flapping is thus normally blocked in words where /t/ is between a weak and a long vowel, as in 'attitude', 'comatose', 'hesitate', 'territory', because the syllable following /t/ is heavier than the one preceding it. However, this stress constraint applies only to word-internal flapping, as pre-stress flaps are common across word boundaries, as in 'get out', 'at all', 'not even', and so on.

Some accounts do not distinguish between the unstressed environment and the post-stress environment when it comes to the frequency of flapping (for example Kahn 1976; Harris 1994: 196), while others note that flapping between unstressed syllables is less common (namely Zue and Laferriere 1979; Vaux 2000; Riehl 2003). There are, however, several different unstressed environments, and not all of them allow flapping to the same extent, or at all. Flapping seems to apply most readily in cases where /t/ occurs before a final syllable consisting of a single vowel or a syllabic /r/ or /l/, as in 'quality', 'community', 'monitor', 'capital'. It is less prevalent in words where /t/ precedes a vowel and one or more consonants, such as 'positive', 'conservative', 'heritage', 'competent', 'separatist', presumably because of the weight of the final syllable. Finally, there are some words where the prosodic and segmental environment would predict flapping of /t/, but where the process seems to be blocked, such as 'heretic' and 'Mediterranean'.

Syllabification

The choice of plosive versus flap is often seen as related to syllable structure. However, researchers do not agree on what part of the syllable the flap belongs to. Some hold the view that flaps are syllable-final (for example Selkirk 1982; Wells 1990, 2008), while Giegerich (1992) states that all flaps appear in syllable onsets. Scholars such as Kahn (1976) and Gussenhoven (1986) analyse flaps as ambisyllabic, while others refer to foot structure and claim that /t/ flaps when non-foot-initial (notably Kiparsky 1979; Turk 1992; Jensen 1993). Moreover, there is no universal agreement on how English words should be syllabified. For example, Jones (2011) generally follows the Maximal Onset principle, syllabifying any VCV string as V.CV, such that all the words relevant for this study have syllable-initial /t/. Wells (1990, 2008) adopts the principle that consonants are syllabified with whichever of the two adjacent vowels is more strongly stressed, and with the leftward syllable if the two vowels are equal. Eddington and Elzinga (2008) conducted an experiment where informants were asked to syllabify words with medial /t/, to test whether the stop and the flap are associated with a particular syllable position. The results showed that [t] was significantly favoured in onsets, while the flap was not consistently placed in either onsets or codas, nor was it analysed as ambisyllabic. They thus conclude that syllable position cannot be considered a crucial condition for flapping in American English and suggest stress and the quality of the following phone as the most important factors.

Flapping and paradigm uniformity

The general conditions for the flapping rule would predict flapping of /t/ word-medially between unstressed syllables. An interesting exception, first noted by Withgott (referenced in Steriade 2000), is found in the word 'militaristic'. The two accentually parallel forms 'capitalistic' and 'militaristic' behave differently when it comes to flapping: /t/ is flapped in the former but not in the latter. Steriade (2000) explains this contrast with reference to paradigm uniformity (PU). According to this principle, the difference between the two words can be attributed to the base forms 'capital' and 'military', which have flap and stop respectively (flapping is blocked in 'military' because of the secondary stress and full vowel following /t/). Generalising the non-flapped [t] from 'military' to the derived form ensures that the paradigm {'military', 'militar(istic')} becomes less variable phonologically. Steriade tested the PU theory by having twelve subjects read a list of ten base words ('positive', 'primitive', 'relative', 'rotary', 'fatal', and so on) and their derivatives ending in -istic ('positivistic', 'primitivistic', 'relativistic', 'rotaristic', 'fatalistic', and so on).[1] She found that, while the speakers differed in their use of flapping in the base form, eleven of the twelve pronounced the derived form with the same /t/ allophone as in the base, which she interprets as evidence supporting the PU hypothesis.

The PU explanation has been contested by several scholars (notably Riehl 2003; Davis 2005; Eddington 2006) on the grounds that it does not clarify the role of variation, and cannot account for other exceptions, such as 'Mediterranean'. Riehl (2003) replicated Steriade's experiment but had her six subjects repeat each word twelve times. Her study revealed considerable intra-speaker variation – with subjects varying between stop and flap in the same word – and showed that speakers do not maintain uniform paradigms with regard to flapping across multiple repetitions. Eddington (2006) also points out that variation in pronunciation poses a challenge for Steriade's PU model. He argues for thinking in terms of statistical tendencies rather than categorical interpretations, and proposes a linguistic analogy model, which predicts all instances of stop versus flap, not just the exceptional cases. The distribution of /t/ allophones is then based on analogy to stored memory tokens of past linguistic experience. In an American speaker's mental lexicon, most instances of 'capital' for instance presumably contain a flap, which explains the preference for flapping in the derivative, but some may contain [t], which explains the variability noted by Riehl.

In the present context the most interesting observation from the above studies is the substantial variation in the use of flapping in TIVE words, which supports the notion that this unstressed environment differs from the one where /t/ precedes a final open syllable (as in 'quality', 'affinity') when it comes to the likelihood of flapping.

Social factors

In terms of social evaluation, flapping seems to be a fairly neutral feature and is certainly not overtly stigmatised. A few of the older sources, however, describe /t/ flapping in negative terms. Thomas (1958) comments that flapping is among those allophones of /t/ that 'suggest substandard speech' and that intervocalic flapping is 'the principal shortcoming among native speakers' (1985: 48), and Bronstein (1960: 74) describes flapping of /t/ as characteristic of 'less cultivated American speech'. None of the newer accounts describes flapping in such terms, but some comment that there is a correlation with style, in that flaps are more likely to occur in informal casual speech than in formal registers (see Churma 1990; Riehl 2003; Staun 2010). By virtue of being a reduction feature, flapping may be expected to display style-shifting related to changes in attention to speech (Labov 1972). Attention-based differences are more likely to reflect differences in phonetic explicitness or degree of phonetic reduction (see Dressler and Wodak 1982; Lindblom 1990). By the same token, flapping can be hypothesised to correlate with speaker sex, as men have been found to reduce more than women (for example Trudgill 1974; Milroy 1976; Henton 1992; Bell et al. 2003). The fact that women tend to favour phonetically explicit pronunciations may be linked to the Sex/Prestige Pattern (Hudson 1996), as unreduced forms are often regarded as more 'correct' than reduced articulations.

There have been few studies into the sociolinguistic aspects of flapping, but the data from these seem to support the hypotheses presented above. Bell (1982) examined flapping in New Zealand English and found that radio newscasters increased their use of /t/ flaps on the commercial local stations compared to the more prestigious national network station. Warner and Tucker (2011) looked at the realisation of flaps in American English and found more extensive reduction in conversational style than in the more formal reading passage and wordlist styles. When it comes to gender, the studies by Zue and Laferriere (1979) and Byrd (1994) both reveal significant differences, with men producing more flaps than women.

Lexical frequency

High-frequency words typically exhibit a greater degree of phonological reduction, while low-frequency words tend to be articulated more carefully. This correspondence between reduction and frequency of occurrence has been attested in several sources (for example Scheibman 2000; Bybee 2001, 2007; Jurafsky et al. 2001; Gahl 2008) and is explained by reference to the fact that high-frequency words are accessed faster and elicit less effort, and that repetition leads to articulatory routinisation. Flapping has been claimed to be related to word frequency (notably Staun 2010: 76; Jones 2011: xi), and in their study of post-stress flapping Patterson and Connine (2001) found that words with high lexical frequency were significantly more likely to be pronounced with a flapped /t/ than lower-frequency items.

**The Study**

The present study investigates flapping of /t/ in three environments, which for the sake of convenience will be referred to as NT, LT and TIVE:

- NT between the alveolar nasal /n/ and an unstressed vowel or syllabic /r, l/, as in 'plenty', 'advantage', 'centre', 'mental'.
- LT between the alveolar lateral /l/ and an unstressed vowel or syllabic /r/, as in 'guilty', 'penalty', 'shelter'.
- TIVE between two unstressed vowels, the second of which is followed by one or more consonants, as in 'positive', 'conservative', 'competence'.

These variables represent areas where there is considerable variation in usage, often disagreement regarding the status of flapping, and little quantitative evidence.

The data consist of a corpus of broadcast speech collected from various American news channels. The analysis of the NT variable uses speech data from sixteen news presenters and programme hosts, while the analysis of LT and TIVE includes additional data from commentators, analysts and reporters. The total number of analysed tokens is 3,974. All the speakers have a General American accent, as defined by Wells (1982, 2008), Upton et al. (2001) and Kretzschmar (2008) for instance.

The data has been analysed with a focus on determining the distribution of the voiced flap versus the voiceless (aspirated) plosive. Flapping has thus been treated as a binary variable, and flaps have been identified auditorily, using voicing as the main criterion (see de Jong 1998; Fukaya and Byrd 2005). As mentioned above, the production of flaps involves a range of articulations, varying in duration and degree of closure. Voiceless realisations can also occur (see Laver 1994: 225; de Jong 1998). However, the present focus has been on the use/non-use of flapping, rather than the exact phonetic nature of the flap variant. All voiced realisations, which range from a firmly closed [d] to an alveolar approximant with no closure, have been counted as flaps. Only a handful of voiceless tokens were encountered, and these are excluded from the analysis.

In addition to examining the frequency of flapping in the NT, LT and TIVE environments, the study analyses flapping in relation to speaker sex, speech style and word frequency, to explore whether flapping follows the typical variation patterns of reduction features. With support from the quantified results, I will also attempt to account for the absence of flapping in certain contexts and words.

The stylistic range within news broadcasts is fairly limited. The format is relatively formal to begin with, considering the fact that the speech is publicly transmitted and often scripted. There is, however, a certain variation within the newscast genre. In the present analysis I have distinguished between reading style and interview style. In the former, the speaker presents the news stories, normally by reading a script and looking directly into the camera. In the latter, the presenter interviews one or more subjects, either in the studio or via satellite, or leads panel discussions. The speech is now often unscripted and improvised and is interactional rather than purely transactional.

The analysis of word frequency effects has also taken into consideration the distinctiveness of news discourse. Lexical frequency is typically measured by reference to general corpora such as the American National Corpus. Newscast language, however, covers a relatively narrow range of topics, typically involving politics and international affairs, which is reflected in the vocabulary used. Thus, there are many words that have a low frequency in general corpora but that occur very often in American newscasts, such as 'executive', 'interview', 'Pentagon', 'militant', 'conservative'. The frequency of a lexical item has therefore been measured locally, against the frequency of other words in the present corpus, which provides a more accurate representation of its usage level in the context investigated here.

## Results and Discussion

The analysis reveals that all the speakers produce flaps to varying degrees in the NT and TIVE environments, while only some have occasional flapping of post-lateral /t/. The three environments will be discussed separately. Flapping has been treated as a binary variable, with realisations classified as either flap or stop.

### NT

Flapping in /nt/ sequences typically involves deletion of /t/ and a nasalised flap. Other possible outcomes are a nasalised vowel followed by a flap, simply deletion of /t/, or voicing of /t/, giving [nd]. The last alternative is heard almost exclusively in the words 'seventy' and 'ninety'. The analysis of the NT variable includes all items where /nt/ occurs between vowels (as in 'plenty') or between a vowel and a syllabic /r/ or /l/ (as in 'winter', 'mental'). Typically, the preceding vowel is stressed, but there are also a few tokens where both surrounding syllables are stressless, as in 'seventy', 'carpenter'. I have excluded words such as 'sentence' and 'mountain', where glottalling or nasal release of /t/ is the typical pronunciation.

The results of the quantitative analysis reveal that flapping is very common post-nasally. As shown in Table 12.1, the flap variant has an overall score of 62.1 per cent.

Since NT tokens occur quite frequently the data has been collected only from sixteen news presenters. All the speakers have flapping in the post-nasal environment, but there is considerable inter-speaker variation, with individual scores ranging from 25 per cent to 96 per cent. There is also a considerable gender difference, with males flapping more than females. Only one of the male subjects has a flap score below 60 per cent, while the same applies to five of the females. The mean flap score for the women is 54.2 per cent, compared to 70.9 per cent for the men (see Table 12.2). An independent-samples t-test shows that the gender difference is significant at the 0.05 level.

The observation that men flap more frequently than women is in line with the typical behaviour of lenition features and is in accordance with previous studies. Men have been found to use more reduced forms than women, who tend to prefer more fully articulated forms and generally use more careful speech (see the section 'Social factors'). Previous work on American English flapping has also found a significant effect of speaker sex on either the frequency of flapping or the degree of lenition in the flap variant (Zue and Laferriere 1979; Byrd 1994; Bauer 2005).

Table 12.1 NT: total scores

|  | N | % |
| --- | --- | --- |
| flap | 1652 | 62.1 |
| stop | 1008 | 37.9 |
| Total | 2660 | 100.0 |

Table 12.2 NT: variant frequency by speaker sex

| | Women | | Men | |
|---|---|---|---|---|
| | N | % | N | % |
| flap | 756 | 54.2 | 897 | 70.9 |
| stop | 639 | 45.8 | 368 | 29.1 |
| Total | 1395 | 100.0 | 1265 | 100.0 |

*Note:* t(14) = 2.186, p = 0.046.

Table 12.3 NT: variant frequency according to style

| | Reading | | Interview | |
|---|---|---|---|---|
| | N | % | N | % |
| flap | 1213 | 60.6 | 439 | 66.7 |
| stop | 789 | 39.4 | 219 | 33.3 |
| Total | 2002 | 100.0 | 658 | 100.0 |

*Note:* $\chi^2$ = 2.99, p = 0.084.

Flapping was also expected to correlate with speech style, based on previous research on reduction features (see the section 'Social factors'), and this was tested by comparing the subjects' reading style and interview style. The shift from reading/ presenting to interviewing/discussing is hypothesised to involve a decrease in the level of attention paid to articulation, and consequently an increased use of flapping. The analysis revealed a certain rise in the usage level for the flap in interview style, as outlined in Table 12.3. However, the stylistic difference is not statistically significant, as confirmed by a chi-square test (p=0.084).

Part of the explanation for the modest difference between the two styles may lie in the small number of tokens in interview style. Some of the presenters hardly did any interviewing at all and are therefore underrepresented. Another factor is of course the somewhat artificial distinction between the two styles. The difference between reading and interviewing is perhaps not substantial enough to have a significant impact on linguistic behaviour in the same way as for instance the shift from conversational style to wordlist reading.

The final independent variable investigated is word frequency. The more common a lexical item is, the more likely it is to reduce, as attested in several studies (see the section 'Lexical frequency' above). In the analysis of post-nasal flapping, the most frequent NT words, occurring more than twenty times, were extracted from the corpus and compared with the rest. Among the most frequent items are 'international', 'interview', 'centre', 'twenty', 'ninety', 'identify' and 'Pentagon'. At the opposite end of the scale are words such as 'acquainted', 'amounted', 'phantom', 'quantity', 'romantic', 'tormented', 'vigilante' and 'warranted'. The total figures are given in

Table 12.4 NT: variant frequency according to lexical frequency

| | Words >20 | | Words <20 | |
| --- | --- | --- | --- | --- |
| | N | % | N | % |
| flap | 1328 | 70.3 | 443 | 57.5 |
| stop | 562 | 29.7 | 327 | 42.5 |
| Total | 1890 | 100.0 | 770 | 100.0 |

*Note:* $\chi^2 = 69.99$, p = 0.000.

Table 12.5 LT: total scores

| | N | % |
| --- | --- | --- |
| flap | 33 | 9.3 |
| stop | 321 | 90.7 |
| Total | 354 | 100.0 |

Table 12.4 and show a considerable difference between the two groups. The flap score is 70.3 per cent for the high-frequency words and 57.5 per cent for the less common items, which yields a p-value well below the 0.001 level.

The variant production patterns for post-nasal flapping are largely in line with previous findings for lenition variables, as well as previous observations of flapping, and they confirm the status of flapping as a typical reduction phenomenon.

## LT

The analysis of post-lateral flapping looks at words where the sequence /lt/ occurs between vowels (as in 'guilty', 'melting') or between a vowel and a syllabic /r/ (as in 'filter', 'alter'). LT items include words where the /l/ is non-syllabic as well as words with a syllabic lateral (such as 'penalty', 'faculty'). Relevant tokens are few and far between, and the analysis therefore includes data from reporters, commentators and analysts in addition to the sixteen main presenters. As shown in Table 12.5, a total of 354 words were collected, and thirty-three of these occur with a flap, giving a percentage score of 9.3.

Post-lateral flapping is thus rare, but not absent. In view of the many claims that flapping after /l/ is forbidden or restricted to non-standard varieties, a frequency of 9.3 per cent in newscast General American is surprisingly high.

Some sources state that flapping of /t/ in the LT environment is only possible if the preceding lateral is vocalised; that is, produced without tongue contact (Kahn 1976; Zue and Laferriere 1979). In the present study, however, all relevant tokens are pronounced with an audible lateral consonant, and no cases of vocalised /l/ were observed. The typical flap realisation with the present speakers is a voiced tap with a lateral approach (see Wells 1982: 251), but there are also cases where /t/ is nearly deleted, as well as realisations close to [d].

Table 12.6 LT: variant frequency by speaker sex

| | Women | | Men | |
|---|---|---|---|---|
| | **N** | **%** | **N** | **%** |
| flap | 5 | 3.6 | 28 | 12.9 |
| stop | 132 | 96.4 | 189 | 87.1 |
| Total | 137 | 100.0 | 217 | 100.0 |

*Note:* $\chi^2 = 7.71$, p = 0.005.

It is clear from the scores in Table 12.5 that the status of flapping after a lateral is very different from that of flapping after /r/ or /n/. In the post-nasal environment the outcome is typically deletion of /t/, while a flap (or tap) after /r/ is articulatorily unproblematic and extremely common. One possible explanation for the rareness of LT flapping may be that the sequence lateral + flap potentially violates the sonority sequencing principle (Clements 1990). This principle states that consonant sequences in syllable codas decrease in sonority from left to right, in accordance with the sonority hierarchy. Flaps are typically recognised as sonorants (for example Kahn 1976; Jensen 1993; Picard 1997; de Jong 1998) and are often ranked as higher in sonority than laterals (see Hogg and McCully 1987; Parker 2008). A coda [lɾ] sequence is thus disfavoured in English. An additional factor is that LT tokens themselves are relatively rare, at least compared to NT, which may contribute to rendering the /lt/ sequence less susceptible to reduction.

There are too few LT tokens to test for effects of speech style or lexical frequency. The only factor that could be tested quantitatively was speaker sex. The results of the gender comparison are presented in Table 12.6. They show that post-lateral flapping, while rare overall, is predominantly a male phenomenon. The men have an average flap score of 12.9 per cent, while the women flap in only 3.6 per cent of the cases.

The gender contrast is highly significant and matches the results for NT as well as previous findings for similar variables involving phonological reduction. It also lends supports to the view of post-lateral flapping as a lower standard feature, as it is almost completely absent from the female data.

*TIVE*

The TIVE environment comprises /t/ between two unstressed syllables, where the second is closed by one or more consonants (as in 'fugitive', 'hesitant'). The present analysis includes only those words where the vowel following /t/ is schwa or /ɪ/, excluding items such as 'comatose' and 'hesitate', which typically have secondary stress on the final syllable. In addition, words where the final syllable is an inflectional ending have been left out, such as 'elicited', 'eliciting', 'celebrities'. Since relevant tokens are relatively infrequent, data for TIVE are collected from reporters and commentators in addition to presenters.

Table 12.7 TIVE: total scores

|  | N | % |
| --- | --- | --- |
| flap | 612 | 63.7 |
| stop | 350 | 36.3 |
| Total | 962 | 100.0 |

Table 12.8 TIVE: variant frequency by speaker sex

|  | Women | | Men | |
| --- | --- | --- | --- | --- |
|  | N | % | N | % |
| flap | 286 | 65.6 | 326 | 62.0 |
| stop | 150 | 34.4 | 200 | 38.0 |
| Total | 436 | 100.0 | 526 | 100.0 |

Note: $\chi^2 = 0.49$, p = 0.484.

Table 12.9 TIVE: variant frequency according to style

|  | Reading | | Interview | |
| --- | --- | --- | --- | --- |
|  | N | % | N | % |
| flap | 314 | 59.4 | 298 | 68.8 |
| stop | 215 | 40.6 | 135 | 31.2 |
| Total | 529 | 100.0 | 433 | 100.0 |

Note: $\chi^2 = 3.35$, p = 0.067.

The overall results, given in Table 12.7, show that flapping is common but far from categorical in TIVE words. The flap variant has a frequency score of 63.7 per cent, which is lower than previous findings for intervocalic post-stress flapping (see for example Patterson and Connine 2001), and which confirms that flapping is highly variable in this environment.

The TIVE data was also tested for gender differences, with an expectation that the males would produce more flaps than the females. In contrast to the findings for NT and LT, there is no gender effect in TIVE. The average flap score is 65.6 per cent for women and 62.0 per cent for men (see Table 12.8). This result is surprising and may suggest that flapping in TIVE has a different status than post-nasal and post-lateral flapping. Alternatively, there may be other factors which have a stronger effect on /t/ realisation in this environment, and which override gender.

Reporters and commentators vary between producing scripted speech and participating in interviews or discussions, in much the same way as anchors and hosts do. The same stylistic analysis was therefore performed for TIVE as for NT. The results are shown in Table 12.9 and reveal an increase in flap production in interview style, but the difference is not statistically significant. Again, it may be that the two styles

Table 12.10 TIVE: variant frequency according to lexical frequency

| | Words >20 | | Words <20 | |
|---|---|---|---|---|
| | N | % | N | % |
| flap | 452 | 64.4 | 161 | 61.9 |
| stop | 250 | 35.6 | 99 | 38.1 |
| Total | 702 | 100.0 | 260 | 100.0 |

*Note:* $\chi^2 = 0.18$, p = 0.671.

are not different enough to reveal a potential stylistic effect, or that flapping is less influenced by attention to speech than other reduction features. It is also possible that a clearer pattern would emerge with a larger number of tokens.

The final independent variable investigated was lexical frequency. The flap score for TIVE items occurring more than twenty times was compared with that for the less frequent words. The results are outlined in Table 12.10 and show that there is very little difference between the two categories of words. The flap variant has a score of 64.4 per cent in the high-frequency words and 61.9 per cent in the low-frequency items.

None of the independent variables has had a significant effect on the use of flapping in TIVE, and at first glance TIVE flapping seems to be different from other reduction phenomena. If we look at the individual lexical items, however, some interesting patterns emerge. The relatively low flap score in the frequent words seems mainly to be due to a few items that deviate from the rest.

From Table 12.11 we can see that certain words stand out as having markedly lower flap scores than the others: 'militant', 'relative' and 'relatively' have an overwhelming preference for [t]. The lack of flapping in 'militant' can be a result of analogy, or paradigm uniformity, with 'military', as has been observed for 'militaristic' (see section 'Flapping and paradigm uniformity'). The case of 'relative(ly)' is more difficult to account for. All the other words ending in -tive have a clear preference for flapping, including accentually parallel items such as 'negative' and 'positive'. The other derivatives in -ly ('negatively', 'positively', 'definitively', 'consecutively') also have predominantly flapped /t/. The percentage score for flapping in 'relative(ly)' is 8.7, while it is 86.8 for the other -tive(ly) words. The contrast can also be found in derivatives ending in -ism, although the numbers are very low. The word 'relativism' occurs six times, each time with a plosive, while 'negativism' and 'positivism' occur three times altogether and are produced with a flap.

Riehl (2003) also notes a strong preference for [t] in 'relative'/'relativistic', though on a smaller scale. She suggests the obligatory contour principle (Leben 1973; Goldsmith 1976) as a possible explanation. This principle disallows adjacent identical features, and according to Riehl 'it is possible that the OCP constrains the sequence of two sonorants in these words for some speakers' (2003: 326). The two sonorants are then the /l/ and the flap, which is often described as a sonorant (for example Kahn 1976; Jensen 1993; Picard 1997; de Jong 1998). Such an analysis

Table 12.11 TIVE: variant distribution in the most frequent TIVE words (>20)

|  | flap | stop |
|---|---|---|
| separatist | 30 | 51 |
| conservative | 65 | 1 |
| militant | 6 | 60 |
| positive | 56 | 6 |
| relative | 8 | 51 |
| relatively | 1 | 43 |
| executive | 42 | 0 |
| representative | 40 | 1 |
| negative | 37 | 2 |
| sensitive | 31 | 4 |
| operative | 24 | 8 |
| alternative | 29 | 2 |
| initiative | 22 | 9 |
| heritage | 20 | 8 |
| narrative | 19 | 4 |
| competitive | 22 | 0 |

seems doubtful, however, as it would predict a [t] preference also in 'narrative' and 'heritage'. These words have the sonorant /r/ in the syllable preceding /t/, but this does not inhibit flapping (see Table 12.11). It appears, then, that it is the presence of the lateral /l/ which is the main factor determining the /t/ allophone in these words, as 'relative(ly)' is the only -tive word with /l/ in the immediately preceding syllable. I would suggest an explanation similar to that for LT items (see the section 'LT'), namely that the sonority sequencing principle plays a role. Since the flap is (at least potentially) more sonorous than /l/, flapping is disfavoured post-laterally. In 'relative(ly)' the /l/ does not immediately precede /t/, but they are only separated by a weak vowel. The low flap score may then be seen as related to the general avoidance of flapping immediately after /l/. It is worth noting that the flap scores for 'relative(ly)' and LT, as well as for 'militant', which also has a lateral preceding /t/, are strikingly similar, all falling around 9 per cent.

The word 'separatist' is the only other frequent item that also has a majority of [t] realisations. This word can be said to have a heavier final syllable compared to the -tive items, as it ends in a consonant cluster, which may lead to a preference for [t]. The other words in this category, which include 'competent', 'competence', 'hesitant' and 'pragmatist', are much less common and provide little basis for generalisations (the only exception is 'militant', which will be kept apart as it has other characteristics that may trigger a stop allophone (see above)). It can be noted, however, that the use of flapping in these words is lower than for the -tive items, but not rare. The overall frequency score for the group (excluding 'militant') is 44 per cent.

The TIVE words with the lowest score for flapping are words ending in -tism, such as 'nepotism', 'Semitism', 'magnetism' and 'patriotism'. The corpus contains very few of these items, but they are almost exclusively produced with a stop, except for two occurrences of flapping in '(anti-)Semitism'. The explanation for the avoidance of flaps in these words is presumably the potential stress on the syllable following /t/. Several pronunciation dictionaries have secondary stress on the -tis syllable, while Wells (1990) assigns tertiary stress to the syllable. This stress pattern will normally prevent flapping, based on the generalisation that the level of stress on the preceding syllable must be greater than or equal to that of the following syllable in order for flapping to apply. It can thus be argued that the -tism items are not really TIVE words as defined here, since only the syllable preceding /t/ is completely unstressed.

Another category of TIVE words are those ending in -tic(s) (as in 'heretic'). These are not included in the analysis, as flapping is forbidden in these items. The word 'politics' occurs regularly in the corpus, each time with an aspirated stop. A detailed discussion of the exceptional behaviour of these words is provided in the next section.

*-tic Words*

Why is flapping perfectly acceptable in 'heritage' but blocked in 'heretic'? The two words have the same number of syllables, the same accentual pattern, and the same vowels before and after /t/. One could even argue that the final syllable in 'heritage' is slightly heavier than the one in 'heretic', since the former ends in an affricate and the latter in a single plosive. In addition to 'heretic', there are a few other words ending in -tic which do not allow flapping of the /t/, notably 'lunatic' and 'politic(s)'. Wells (1990) comments briefly on the word 'politics' and argues that flapping is blocked here 'because the /ɪ/ of -ics counts as a full vowel, sufficient to outrank the weak vowel of the second syllable and thus capture the /t/' (1990: 81). However, he offers no reason for why this should be the case in 'politics' and not in 'heritage' or 'separatist' for instance. In the following, I will try to shed some light on the issue by looking at some characteristic of the -ic words.

The words 'heretic', 'lunatic' and 'politic(s)' belong to a small group of -ic items with exceptional stress placement. Words ending in the suffix -ic typically have stress on the syllable immediately preceding the suffix, while the exceptional words all have antepenultimate stress (see Fudge 1984: 41, 74). According to Hill (1974), who reviews a number of sources, the regular -ic words have their penult stress from Latin, while the exceptions are words taken directly from French, and originally had main stress on the final syllable and secondary stress on the antepenult. In addition, Hill points out, all the exceptional items have a middle syllable in which the pre-vocalic consonant, the post-vocalic consonant, or both, are sonorants ('heretic', 'lunatic' and 'politic(s)' have /r/, /n/ and /l/ respectively in the middle syllable). This leads to potential instability in the syllabicity, since the unstressed vowel in the middle syllable may be replaced by a syllabic consonant. This is clearly illustrated in 'Catholic', which can be pronounced with syllabic /l/ or compressed to two syllables. Hill gives examples of older spellings which reflect this suppression of the middle vowel, including 'pol'tic' for 'politic'.

If we relate these facts to the discussion of flapping, we may come closer to an explanation for the obligatory [t] in 'heretic', 'lunatic' and 'politic(s)'. First, the final syllable in these words may be felt as heavier than the one in 'heritage' for instance, because of the exceptional stress pattern, or it may be a remnant from the original final stress. In fact, some dictionaries assign secondary stress (though not always consistently) to the final syllable. Second, if the vowel in the middle syllable is prone to absorption into the preceding sonorant, this may affect the syllabification of the words, where the /t/ is no longer naturally syllabified with the preceding segment, and thus less prone to flapping. Lastly, I would add that, at least in 'lunatic' and 'heretic', the /t/ is arguably more loosely connected to the stem than in 'heritage', 'separatist' and 'competent' for instance. This morphological difference is evidenced by the existence of the forms 'luna', 'lunar', 'lunacy' and 'heresy', without /t/, versus 'inherit', 'inheritance', 'heritable', 'separate', 'separative', 'compete', 'competence', and so on, all with /t/. If the /t/ is felt as belonging more to the suffix than to the preceding syllable, this will have an inhibiting effect on flapping.

## Conclusion

The current analysis has provided an estimate of the frequency of flapping in the NT, LT and TIVE environments by supplying quantitative data on actual usage. The study has focused on broadcast speech, which to a large extent is scripted and produced in a rather formal setting. It is not inconceivable, therefore, that usage levels for flapping would be higher in spontaneous conversational speech. At the same time, it should be kept in mind that the language of modern news broadcasting is fairly informal. Newscasters typically aim for a conversational, personal style, with a focus on trans-mitting not just the message but also the emotion and credibility of the message (see Herbert 2000). Thus, while broadcast speech cannot be equated with the unmonitored 'vernacular', it is definitely closer to conversational speech than the experimental data typically used in previous studies of /t/ flapping.

The analysis has demonstrated that there is considerable variation in the use of /t/ flapping and that the factors conditioning its distribution are extremely complex. The three environments focused on here are particularly interesting, as there are disagree-ments in the literature on the status and frequency of flapping in these contexts. The results show that post-nasal flapping is quite common and varies in accordance with the typical behaviour of reduction features. Flapping after /l/ is rare, but a flap score of 9.3 per cent (33 tokens) shows that it is not blocked in American English and is not restricted to non-standard speech. The male dominance in both NT and LT flapping is in line with expectations and suggests that the stop and the flap have slightly different evaluative status, linked to the notion of phonetic explicitness as more 'correct'. The TIVE variable displayed somewhat different patterns, and the variation here seems to be related primarily to factors that only become visible when we look at the individual words.

The data presented here can contribute to shedding some light on the factors conditioning and influencing /t/ flapping in American English. It is obvious from the many accounts of flapping that stress and syllabification are considered important factors in the distribution of the flap variant. It is also evident, however, that the extensive variation in usage complicates matters, and makes it difficult to establish categorical rules for predicting flapping.

Perhaps the most important condition for flapping is that the stress level on the syllable preceding /t/ must be greater than or equal to that of the following syllable. However, there are a few cases where this condition does not apply. During the listening process for the present study, I observed several instances of post-nasal flapping before a primary stressed syllable, in 'Antarctica' and 'appointee'. There was also one occurrence of the word 'Socrates', with a flap.[2] These individual cases violate the stress condition – as the syllable following /t/ has a greater level of stress than the preceding syllable – and suggest that stress is not the only factor governing flapping, and that syllabification may be more important. Syllabification is not a straightforward concept, however, and there is no universal agreement on how English words should be syllabified.

One of the challenges of using stress or syllabification to predict flapping is the danger of circularity. Steriade (2000), for example, argues that if /t/ precedes a syllable with secondary stress it will be pronounced as a plosive. However, she defines a syllable as having secondary stress based on the presence of a plosive. The final syllable of 'primitive' for example is thus considered stressed when pronounced with a [t], and unstressed when produced with a flap.[3] A similar reasoning is presented by Iverson and Ahn (2007) and de Jong (1998). In my view it is problematic to use the presence of a plosive as a diagnostic for secondary stress. This would force us, based on the present findings, to consider -ive predominantly stressed in 'relative' but not in 'negative', which makes little sense. It would also complicate the explanation of the flapping in 'Socrates' and 'Antarctica' for example. In a similar manner, Wells (1990, 2008) uses syllabification to account for flapping. He states that /t/ only flaps if it is syllable-final. At the same time, a /t/ is defined as syllable-final if it can be realised as a flap. Syllabification does not work then as a 'predictor' for flapping, as it presupposes detailed knowledge of flap distribution. We also end up with syllable boundaries that do not always align with morpheme boundaries, as in 'magne.tism', or that differ between accents, as in RP 'monet.arism' and GA 'mone.tarism' (see Wells 2008).

Churma (1990) points out that all the phonological accounts of flapping are problematic and do not cover all cases. He argues in favour of using morphological structure as the main predictor for flapping and claims that 'this allows an explanation for why flapping is possible in "elitism"' (1990: 48). Churma's point is valid, but his example is not very good, as stress alone can explain the flapping in 'elitism'. However, morphological structure can account for the flaps in 'Antarctica' and 'appointee', and the absence of flapping in 'Mediterranean'. These words illustrate that morphology can override stress, as /t/ may be flapped before a primary stress if it precedes a morpheme boundary, and that flapping may be blocked before an unstressed syllable if the /t/ is morpheme-initial. Morphology can also explain the preference for [nd], rather than a nasal flap, in the words 'seventy' and 'ninety'. The decade suffix -ty is here preceded by a stem-final /n/, in contrast to 'twenty', where 'twen' is a bound morpheme (see Iverson and Ahn 2007: 262–263). Morphology thus seems to play an important role in the analysis of flapping and can explain some of the flap cases that defy the stress requirement. However, it is not sufficient to predict flapping, as there are cases where morpheme-final /t/ is predominantly realised as a plosive, such as 'separatist' and 'militant', and cases where a morpheme-initial /t/ can flap, such as 'twenty'.

The evidence presented here confirms the impression of flapping as a highly complex phenomenon, and further adds to that complexity. Word-medial flapping, with a few exceptions, is restricted to /t/ before an unstressed syllable. The analysis of TIVE further suggests that flapping of /t/ between unstressed syllables is less common than flapping of post-stress /t/. Morphological structure should also be taken into consideration, as it explains some of the exceptional cases. Stress and morphology combined seems to predict the 'possibility' of /t/ flapping fairly accurately. With regard to the 'probability' of flap occurrence, a range of other factors are also relevant. Syllable weight seems to play a role, as unstressed flapping is less frequent before a syllable closed by a consonant, as in 'sensitive', 'heritage', than before a final open syllable, as in 'sanity', 'obesity'. The likelihood of flapping decreases even further before a syllable ending in a consonant cluster, as in 'competence', 'separatist'. The quality of the preceding segment also exerts a significant influence. Flapping is less likely after an alveolar nasal than after a vowel, as evidenced by the present NT data. A lateral immediately before /t/, or in the preceding syllable, reduces the likelihood of flapping drastically, as seen from the analysis of LT and the exceptional behaviour of 'relative' and its derivatives. The sonority sequencing principle was suggested as a possible factor accounting for the low flap frequency after /l/. In addition, /t/ flapping is potentially influenced by extra-linguistic factors such as speaker gender, style and lexical frequency. The variant distribution patterns largely align with those observed for other reduction features, with higher flap scores for male speakers and high-frequency words. For TIVE, however, these factors seem to be overridden by the strong effect of the preceding segment and coda weight.

The findings discussed here highlight the variable nature of American English flapping and illustrate the importance of grounding the analysis in quantified data on actual usage. It is only when we have a large number of tokens that the patterns become visible, and large-scale corpus-based studies of flapping are still relatively scarce, particularly for the environments investigated here.

**Notes**

1. It could be argued that Steriade's test words are perhaps not ideal for investigating the potential PU effect at play in 'military'–'militaristic', as none of them is exact parallels (with regard to prosody and phonetic context), and, with the exception of 'voluntary', all of them permit flapping in the base. A better candidate would be 'monetary'–'monetaristic'.
2. Eddington and Elzinga (2008: 247) also mention 'Socrates' as an example of a word where flapping may occur before a secondary stress.

3. In her analysis of paradigm uniformity, Steriade argues that the presence of a stop in a base form indicates secondary stress in the following syllable, while a stop in the inflected form is an indicator of paradigm uniformity, not secondary stress, which undermines the whole stress argumentation (as pointed out by Riehl 2003: 280).

## References

Bauer, L., J. M. Dienhart, H. H. Hartvigson and L. K. Jakobsen (1980), *American English Pronunciation*, Copenhagen: Gyldendal.

Bauer, M. (2005), 'Lenition of the flap in American English', *University of Pennsylvania Working Papers in Linguistics* 10(2), 31–43.

Bell, A. (1982), 'Radio: the style of news language', *Journal of Communication* 32(1), 150–164.

Bell, A., D. Jurafsky, E. Fosler-Lussier, C. Girand, M. Gregory and D. Gildea (2003), 'Effects of disfluencies, predictability, and utterance position on word form variation in English conversation', *Journal of the Acoustical Society of America* 113(2), 1001–1024.

Bronstein, A. J. (1960), *The Pronunciation of American English: An Introduction to Phonetics*, New York: Appleton-Century-Crofts.

Bybee, J. (2001), *Phonology and Language Use*, Cambridge: Cambridge University Press.

Bybee, J. (2007), *Frequency of Use and the Organization of Language*, New York: Oxford University Press.

Byrd, D. (1994), 'Relations of sex and dialect to reduction', *Speech Communication* 15, 39–54.

Carr, P. and P. Honeybone (2007), 'English phonology and linguistic theory: an introduction to issues, and to "Issues in English Phonology"', *Language Sciences* 29, 117–153.

Churma, D. (1990), 'At the phonetics/phonology interface: (re)syllabification and English stop allophony', in Y. No and M. Libucha (eds), *ESCOL '90: Proceedings of the Seventh Eastern States Conference on Linguistics*, pp. 40–54.

Clements, G. N. (1990), 'The role of the sonority cycle in core syllabification', in J. Kingston and M. E. Beckman (eds), *Papers in Laboratory Phonology I*, Cambridge: Cambridge University Press, pp. 283–333.

Davis, S. (2005), 'Capitalistic v. militaristic: the paradigm uniformity effect reconsidered', in L. J. Downing, T. A. Hall and R. Raffelsiefen (eds), *Paradigms in Phonological Theory*, Oxford: Oxford University Press, pp. 107–121.

de Jong, K. (1998), 'Stress-related variation in the articulation of coda alveolar stops: flapping revisited', *Journal of Phonetics* 26, 283–310.

Dressler, W. and R. Wodak (1982), 'Sociophonological methods in the study of sociolinguistic variation in Viennese German', *Language in Society* 11(3), 339–370.

Eddington, D. (2006), 'Paradigm uniformity and analogy: the capitalistic versus militaristic debate', *International Journal of English Studies* 6(2), 1–18.

Eddington, D. (2007), 'Flaps and other variants of /t/ in American English: allophonic distribution without constraints, rules, or abstractions', *Cognitive Linguistics* 18(1), 23–46.

Eddington, D. and D. Elzinga (2008), 'The phonetic context of American English flapping: quantitative evidence', *Language and Speech* 51(3), 245–266.

Egido, C. and W. E. Cooper (1980), 'Blocking of alveolar flapping in speech production: the role of syntactic boundaries and deletion sites', *Journal of Phonetics* 8, 175–84.

Fudge, E. (1984), *English Word Stress*, London: Allen & Unwin.

Fukaya, T. and D. Byrd (2005), 'An articulatory examination of word-final flapping at phrase edges and interiors', *Journal of the International Phonetic Association* 35(1), 45–58.

Gahl, S. (2008), '*Time* and *thyme* are not homophones: the effect of lemma frequency on word durations in spontaneous speech', *Language* 84(3), 474–496.

Giegerich, H. J. (1992), *English Phonology: An Introduction*, Cambridge: Cambridge University Press.

Goldsmith, J. (1976), Autosegmental Phonology, Doctoral dissertation, MIT, Cambridge, MA.

Gussenhoven, C. (1986), 'English plosive allophones and ambisyllabicity', *Gramma* 10, 119–141.

Hammond, M. (1997), 'Vowel quantity and syllabification in English', *Language* 73(1), 1–17.

Harris, J. (1994), *English Sound Structure*, Oxford: Blackwell.

Henton, C. (1992), 'The abnormality of male speech', in G. Wolf (ed.), *New Departures in Linguistics*, New York: Garland Publishing, pp. 27–59.

Herbert, J. (2000), *Journalism in the Digital Age*, Oxford: Focal Press.

Herd, W., A. Jongman and J. Sereno (2010), 'An acoustic and perceptual analysis of /t/ and /d/ flaps in American English', *Journal of Phonetics* 38, 504–516.

Hill, A. (1974), 'Word stress and the suffix -ic', *Journal of English Linguistics* 8(1), 6–18.

Hogg, R. and C. B. McCully (1987), *Metrical Phonology: A Coursebook*, Cambridge: Cambridge University Press.

Hudson, R. A. (1996), *Sociolinguistics*, 2nd edn, Cambridge: Cambridge University Press.

Iverson, G. K. and S.-C. Ahn (2007), 'English voicing in dimensional theory', *Language Sciences* 29, 247–269.

Jensen, J. T. (1993), *English Phonology*, Amsterdam: John Benjamins.

Jones, D. (2011), *Cambridge English Pronouncing Dictionary*, 18th edn, ed. P. Roach, J. Setter and J. Esling, Cambridge: Cambridge University Press.

Jurafsky, D., A. Bell, M. Gregory and W. D. Raymond (2001), 'Probabilistic relations between words: evidence from reduction in lexical production', in J. Bybee and P. Hopper (eds), *Frequency and the Emergence of Linguistic Structure*, Amsterdam: John Benjamins, pp. 229–254.

Kahn, D. (1976), Syllable-based generalizations in English phonology, Doctoral dissertation, MIT, Cambridge, MA.

Kaplan, A. (2008), 'Markedness and phonetic grounding in nasal-stop clusters', qualifying paper, Department of Linguistics, University of California, Santa Cruz.

Kenyon, J. S. (1950), *American Pronunciation*, 10th edn, Ann Arbor, MI: G. Wahr.

Kiparsky, P. (1979), 'Metrical structure assignment is cyclic', *Linguistic Inquiry* 10, 421–441.

Kreidler, C. W. (2004), *The Pronunciation of English*, 2nd edn, Oxford: Blackwell.

Kretzschmar, W. A. Jr. (2008), 'Standard American English pronunciation', in E. W. Schneider (ed.), *Varieties of English 2: The Americas and the Caribbean*, New York: Mouton de Gruyter, pp. 37–51.

Labov, W. (1972), *Sociolinguistic Patterns*, Philadelphia: University of Pennsylvania Press.

Laver, J. (1994), *Principles of Phonetics*, Cambridge: Cambridge University Press.

Leben, W. (1973), Suprasegmental phonology, Doctoral dissertation, MIT, Cambridge, MA.

Lindblom, B. (1990), 'Explaining phonetic variation: a sketch of the H&H theory', in W. J. Hardcastle and A. Marchal (eds), *Speech Production and Speech Modelling*, Dordrecht: Kluwer, pp. 403–439.

Malécot, A. and P. Lloyd (1968), 'The /t/: /d/ distinction in American alveolar flaps', *Lingua* 19, 164–272.

Milroy, L. (1976), 'Phonological correlates to community structure in Belfast', *Belfast Working Papers on Language and Linguistics* 1(1), 1–44.

Nespor, M. and I. Vogel (1986), *Prosodic Phonology*, Dordrecht: Foris.

Parker, S. (2008), 'Sound level protrusions as physical correlates of sonority', *Journal of Phonetics*, 36, 55–90.

Patterson, D. and C. M. Connine (2001), 'Variant frequency in flap production', *Phonetica* 58(4), 254–275.

Picard, M. (1997), 'English flapping and the feature [vibrant]', *English Language and Linguistics* 1(2), 285–294.

Riehl, A. (2003), 'American English flapping: perceptual and acoustic evidence against paradigm uniformity with phonetic features', *Working Papers of the Cornell Phonetic Laboratory* 15, 271–337.

Scheibman, J. (2000), '*I dunno*: a usage-based account of the phonological reduction of *don't* in American English conversation', *Journal of Pragmatics* 32, 105–124.

Selkirk, E. (1972), The phrase phonology of English and French, PhD dissertation, Massachusetts Institute of Technology.

Selkirk, E. (1982), 'The syllable', in H. van der Hulst and N. Smith (eds), *The Structure of Phonological Representations Part II*, Dordrecht: Foris, pp. 337–384.

Spencer, A. (1996), *Phonology*, Oxford: Blackwell.

Staun, J. (2010), *An Introduction to the Pronunciation of North American English*, Odense: University Press of Southern Denmark.

Steriade, D. (2000), 'Paradigm uniformity and the phonetics-phonology boundary', in M. B. Broe and J. B. Pierrehumbert (eds), *Acquisition and the Lexicon. Papers in Laboratory Phonology V*, Cambridge: Cambridge University Press, pp. 313–334.

Thomas, C. K. (1958), *An Introduction to the Phonetics of American English*, 2nd edn, New York: Ronald Press Company.

Trager, G. (1942), 'The phoneme "t": a study in theory and method', *American Speech*, 17(3), 144–148.

Trask, R. L. (1996), *A Dictionary of Phonetics and Phonology*, London: Routledge.

Trudgill, P. (1974), *The Social Differentiation of English in Norwich*, Cambridge: Cambridge University Press.

Turk, A. (1992), 'The American English flapping rule and the effect of stress on stop consonant durations', *Working Papers of the Cornell Phonetics Laboratory* 7, 103–133.

Upton, C., W. A. Kretzschmar and R. Konopka (2001), *Oxford Dictionary of Pronunciation for Current English*, Oxford: Oxford University Press.

Vaux, B. (2000), 'Flapping in English', paper presented at the Linguistic Society of America Annual Meeting, Chicago, IL.

Warner, N. and B. Tucker (2011), 'Phonetic variability of stops and flaps in spontaneous and careful speech', *Journal of the Acoustical Society of America* 130(3), 1606–1617.

Wells, J. C. (1982), *Accents of English*, Cambridge: Cambridge University Press.

Wells, J. C. (1990), 'Syllabification and allophony', in S. Ramsaran (ed.), *Studies in the Pronunciation of English*, London: Routledge, pp. 76–86.

Wells, J. C. (2008), *Longman Pronunciation Dictionary*, 3rd edn, Harlow: Pearson/Longman.

Zue, V. W. and M. Laferriere (1979), 'Acoustic study of medial /t, d/ in American English', *Journal of the Acoustical Society of America* 66(4), 1039–1050.

# Index